MODERN IRISH LITERATURE

Sources and Founders

Modern Irish Literature

Sources and Founders

VIVIAN MERCIER

EDITED AND PRESENTED BY
EILÍS DILLON

CLARENDON PRESS · OXFORD
1994

Oxford University Press, Walton Street, Oxford OX2 6DP
Oxford New York Toronto
Delhi Bombay Calcutta Madras Karachi
Kuala Lumpur Singapore Hong Kong Tokyo
Nairobi Dar es Salaam Cape Town
Melbourne Auckland Madrid
and associated companies in
Berlin Ibadan

Oxford is a trade mark of Oxford University Press

Published in the United States
by Oxford University Press Inc., New York

British Library Cataloguing in Publication Data
Data available

Library of Congress Cataloging in Publication Data
Mercier, Vivian, 1919–1989
Modern Irish literature: sources and founders / Vivian Mercier;
edited and presented by Eilís Dillon.
Includes bibliographical references and index.
1. English literature—Irish authors—History and criticism.
2. Ireland—Intellectual life—20th century. 3. Ireland-
Intellectual life—19th century. 4. Ireland in literature.
I. Dillon, Eilís, 1920-   . II. title.
PR8753.M47   1994   820.9'9415—dc20   93–24542
ISBN 0–19–812074–5

1 3 5 7 9 10 8 6 4 2

Typeset by Seton Music Graphics Ltd., Bantry, Co. Cork, Ireland
Printed in Great Britain
on acid-free paper by
Bookcraft Ltd,
Midsomer Norton, Bath

Contents

Editor's Preface

When my husband Vivian Mercier died in November 1989, he left what he considered his most important work unfinished. It was to have been in two volumes, the culmination of a life of affectionate scholarship in relation to Irish literature in English. He was particularly pleased to observe the large part played in the Irish revival by graduates of his beloved University, Trinity College, Dublin.

The task of editing this volume was made easier by the existence of a first draft and many relevant footnotes. Vivian's scholarly standards were of the highest and the breadth of his knowledge of world literature was everywhere in evidence. Errors and oversights were extremely rare. There was also a complete table of contents for the first volume, and copious notes for the second, though unfortunately very little of this had been written.

In presenting the work in one volume, I was well aware that the material on Beckett and Joyce belonged properly to the second volume, where it would have been seen as a powerful influence on modern Irish writers. I also took the liberty of rearranging some of the chapters, placing the short chapter on European-Irish Literary Connections at the end. I was greatly helped by the fact that I was very familiar with all of Vivian's work, and especially with this project which we discussed in its various stages. It gives me great pleasure to be associated with it and to see a part, at least, of his larger plan come into existence.

Eilís Dillon

Introduction

DECLAN KIBERD

Through his later years, Vivian Mercier planned a two-volume study of Anglo-Irish literature. This would have offered a very personal view of those chosen texts which he had spent half a century explicating, but it would also have been a cogent account of the workings of the Protestant imagination as a force in the shaping of modern Ireland. All the best criticism, he contended, was but disguised autobiography, a man's interest in a work being simply the overflow of his interest in himself. The text, in the fullest Protestant sense, was a summons to self-interrogation. For Mercier literary criticism was never a discourse to be couched in an idiom of impersonal authority, but an active engagement with himself, his family, his national tradition. He never sought to separate the man who suffered from the mind which created, either in his comments on others or in his accounting for himself. In an era when teachers and students alike were told to avoid excessive use of the first person singular in presentations and essays, Vivian Mercier disarmed them all by insisting that the critic's personality must be a declared part of every equation which he construed. There was no lofty, external, objective court of appeal to be found anywhere, only a chamber filled with contending voices and ringing with the excitement of great ideas in perpetual struggle.

Readers of his books were sometimes amazed at the innocence with which he launched into another autobiographical preface before proceeding to the practice of criticism, but there was nothing self-important or self-congratulatory about such gestures: he simply wanted people to know where he was coming from. If Synge had said that the work of art is possible only to one man, at one time and in one place, then Mercier believed as much about the act of criticism. He knew that a man makes his own history well enough, but not necessarily in conditions of his own choosing; and he wanted his students to be fully aware of all the forces that spoke through him. In this, as in so much else, he was well ahead of his time and even today, when the pose of neutral authority has been abandoned by most honest analysts, we are all still learning how to be his contemporaries. Like many thinkers who seem to have a whiff of the future about them, Mercier was snatched from us before his work was fully done, and so instead of two volumes there is only this one. It contains, nevertheless, most of the material which would have gone into the first, and the major statements on Joyce and Beckett which would have been central elements in the second. Though it is hard to know precisely what shape Mercier's final work might have taken, there is in the essays which follow a consistency of approach and coherence of purpose which bespeak the man who wrote them.

*   *   *

He was born in Clara, County Offaly, in April 1919, a well-balanced individual with—as he liked to joke—a chip on each shoulder, one labelled 'Irish' and the other 'French'. From his maternal Irish ancestors he may have taken his warmth, his deep kindness, and his imaginative daring, while from his father's Huguenot stock may have come the intellectual rigour, the love of learning, and a certain sense of style. These two forces contended in his personality, but it was a conflict conducive to genius. After the mandatory schooling of a day boy at Clara, he found himself sent to Portora Royal School, Enniskillen, in 1928, where even today in the assembly hall a wooden chair is named for V. H. S. Mercier.

As its name proudly indicates, Portora was a 'loyal' institution and, while there, Mercier would have been given a thorough grounding in the tenets of the Protestant faith, which he put to such telling use in many of his essays. As a southerner in a school devoted to educating the sons of northern Unionists in a recently partitioned Ireland, he must have felt himself something of a rebel. Even then, his independence of mind was such that he confidently entered into correspondence with George Bernard Shaw on the subject of his *Intelligent Woman's Guide to Socialism* (1928). Mercier had been preceded to Portora, over half a century earlier, by Oscar Wilde, who was still in disgrace in 1928 and excised from the school's roll of honour. (His name has since been restored.) And just five years before Mercier's arrival, Portora had said farewell to a brave but short-sighted scrum-half named Samuel Beckett, who would soon be known in wider circles as a promising young scholar and writer. In 1934 the *Old Portora Union* reported the publication of *More Pricks Than Kicks*, a book whose punning title (at once biblical and obscene) tickled the young Mercier's fancy. He was amused to note, with his usual sardonic vigilance, that it never did find its way into the college library.

Like both Wilde and Beckett, Mercier went on to an arts degree at Trinity College Dublin. While there, he was elected a Foundation Scholar in English and French, was tutored by many of its charismatic teachers including the philosopher A. A. Luce and the French professor T. B. Rudmose-Brown, and took a first-class degree with gold medal.

Still only in his mid-twenties, he was awarded a doctorate for a thesis, as yet unpublished, on 'Realism in Irish Fiction 1916–1940', a notably contemporary subject in a Trinity which usually preferred students to treat of dead persons and remote times. Most heretical of all, however, was the choice of Irish rather than English writing as a topic. His room-mate at Trinity was Conor Cruise O'Brien, another figure with a reputation for intrepidity of action and sturdy independence of mind. 'Others read the books about the books: we just read the books themselves' was their youthfully arrogant motto. They were soon familiar to an audience beyond the Front Gate of Trinity. Anyone who reads a Dublin journal of the 1940s such as *The Bell* will find the evidence: in it they wrote (for good money, of course) a series of critiques of each of the national newspapers and magazines. Mercier's analysis of *The Irish Times* perfectly predicted its progress from ascendancy mouthpiece to in-house journal of the post-colonial managerial élites.

Trinity had no post for either of these immensely gifted men, and so O'Brien joined the Irish civil service and Mercier soon fetched up in City College, New York, as a professor of English with a growing family to support. In the midst of teaching, reviewing and the publication of scholarly monographs, he came to know many of that city's leading intellectuals, among them Jacques Barzun, Lionel Trilling, and the stars of the faculty at Columbia. Soon his name was featured in leading newspapers and magazines on both sides of the Atlantic. It would not be an exaggeration to say that in a number of early essays, he helped to create the climate in which the achievement of Samuel Beckett was finally understood. In brilliant exegeses, he assisted the more venturesome readers of the day through the difficult texts. Many would much later forget that it was Mercier who described *Waiting for Godot* as 'the play in which nothing happens—twice', a quip which rapidly took on the impersonality of folk tradition. In most of his articles on Beckett, he insisted on the writer's invincible Irishness. Even when fashionable existentialist interpretations sought to decontextualize Beckett's plays and landscapes, he patiently but persistently linked them back to the Ireland they had both known.

In his mid-thirties, Mercier suddenly decided to study and master the Irish language. His old tutor in Trinity, A. A. Luce, had warned Irish Protestants back in the 1920s that the compulsory study of Irish might turn their offspring into Catholics; and for an Irish Protestant gentleman, exiled in New York, its voluntary study must have seemed to many a doubly strange choice. For Mercier himself, it was an act of 'impatriation' (a term he borrowed from Leslie Fiedler), signifying that henceforth he would achieve a two-dimensional perspective on Irish realities. So, on sabbatical leave in Dublin, he studied Old and Middle Irish with experts at both Trinity and University College, receiving particular help with the lore of Early Irish from that prince among Celtic scholars, Professor David Greene. The book which grew out of this experience, Mercier's *The Irish Comic Tradition* (1962), was a portent in more ways than one. It posited a fundamental unity in the Irish literary tradition, a unity which somehow survived the transition from the Irish to the English language: and Mercier's new training permitted him to make breath-taking links between Swift and the Gaelic satirists, or between the techniques of early Irish story-telling and the narrative devices of the later Joyce. Up until its publication, Gaelic scholarship had—with very few exceptions other than Daniel Corkery and Thomas MacDonagh—been the preserve of linguists and grammarians rather than of literary critics. After it, things were never quite the same, and the following decade saw the emergence of Seán Ó Tuama, Breandán Ó Doibhlin, and entire squads of younger scholar-critics, all suddenly finding their voices and audiences.

In *The Irish Comic Tradition* Mercier treated of two strands, Gaelic and Anglo-Irish, which the post-independence generation had been taught to regard as contradictory rather than complementary. He was reaching back, beyond these divisions, to the possibilities opened up by Thomas MacDonagh in his *Literature in Ireland* (1916), a collection of lectures which had adopted a similar, holistic approach. Those possibilities had been aborted by the British firing-squad which executed the rebel leader, but almost half a century later Mercier reopened that agenda. His example inspired many others to take each literature out of its self-imposed quarantine. Just a few years later came the publication of *The Backward Look* (1967), Frank O'Connor's wonderful (if at times wondrously unscholarly) attempt to bring the entire literary history of the island under a single, beneficent, gaze; and Brendan Kennelly's *Penguin Book of Irish Verse* (1970) gave further encouragement to those committed to the essential continuity of the tradition. By then, it was becoming harder and harder for experts in Anglo-Irish literature to present themselves to the world with no knowledge of Irish, and patently absurd for Gaelic scholars to deny or discount the massive English influence on the more recent centuries of writing in the Irish language. Without ever quite announcing it as such, Mercier had launched the movement that now goes by the name of 'Irish Studies'.

This was an interdisciplinary activity in more than the literary sense, as any closer reader of *The Irish Comic Tradition* will see, for in it pioneering use is made of Freud and Frazer, as well as of Meyer and Murphy. If today it is almost *de rigueur* for the promising young scholar to cite Marx's *Eighteenth Brumaire of Louis Bonaparte*, this was not so lightly done back in the dark year of the Cuban Missile Crisis or the Cold War. All that Mercier had learned from his days at Trinity, his time in New York, his sessions with David Greene, was being brought to bear in a powerful and penetrating synthesis.

The book was an immediate success. It went into paperback form and was admired by an entire generation of undergraduates and rising scholars. It had, of course, its detractors: in a partition-minded Ireland, such begrudgers were inevitably to be found. Some scholars, painfully anxious to patrol the rigid borders separating Gaelic and Anglo-Irish studies, saw in Mercier's free-ranging mind a threat to their entrenched territorial interests. Others made predictable jibes about how a jack of all trades risks being a final master of none. Even among the literary intelligentsia, which might have been expected to offer unreserved applause, one or two cavils were entered by the sort of Irish person for whom it was still a point of honour to have no sense of humour at all. The national revival, they felt, had exploded the stage Irishman with his rollicking note and his wild ways—so who was Mercier to take up such abject tomfoolery?

In a trenchant essay called 'Our Wits About Us', written for the *New Statesman* in February 1963, Conor Cruise O' Brien defended his former room-mate's study. He endorsed its thesis that 'the ribald, the dangerously satirical, the grotesque and the obscene' were major elements of the national literary heritage, but he wickedly observed that for a certain kind of purist '*The Irish Comic Tradition* is a veritable *danse macabre* of the skeletons in the family cupboard'. This Irish person he christened Paddy Solemn:

Paddy Solemn shudders at the thought, and cringes at the sight or sound, of Brendan Behan; Paddy Solemn likes to use precise-sounding terminology in a vague way, and derives from this a bracing sense of intellectual rigour; Paddy Solemn likes to be thought of as a Thomist, and knows—for he is no fool, despite appearances—that this will do him no harm at all in an academic career bounded on all sides by bishops. . . . Paddy Solemn has, however, a secret fear. It is that Ireland Will Let Him Down. Of what avail his personal respectability if he is dragged down by a national entity which refuses to be respectable?

The Irish Comic Tradition was indeed a subversive book. It celebrated the same combination of learning and vulgarity, of wit and obscenity, in Joyce and Swift as in the ancient Gaelic lore; and it openly regretted the long-standing separation of those elements in much Anglo-Saxon writing. It savoured the carnivalesque world: the laughter of underlings it proclaimed as redeeming the upper orders from the straitjacket of official sobriety. Far from seeing Irish comedy as 'low', it redefined it as Rabelaisian—gay, healthy, philosophical. Coded into this analysis was a more complex view of the Irish Revival which held that its under-standable denial of 'buffoonery' need not entail a rejection of festive comedy or of carnivalesque vitality. For Mercier, laughter was not something to negate seriousness, but rather something which completed it. Wilde's 'trivial comedy for serious people', his jokes about eating and self-indulgence, his inversion of master-servant hierarchies, all these features of carnival found ready echoes in the Nighttown sections of *Ulysses*, in Synge's *Playboy*, even in Yeats's poetry and drama. Mercier's revival was one which relished not just robust dialect but witty oaths, curses, flytings; he heard in their energies a real alternative to single-minded, po-faced authority. In its basic contours, his book remarkably overlaps the sketch made by the Russian formalist Mikhail Bakhtin in his book *Rabelais and His World* (written in the 1930s at the height of the Stalinist terror, but published only in 1965.) In particular, Bakhtin's definition and exploration of the terms 'grotesque' and 'macabre' was astonishingly close to Mercier's. The latter, of course, knew nothing of the Russian's book when he constructed his own, but the publication of the Rabelais study in English in 1984 delighted him. It confirmed the rightness of his approach—especially his celebration of the human body as an image of the restored community to be found in medieval texts and also in *Ulysses*—and, although he was far too modest to say this, it must have demonstrated once again the prophetic instinct at work in all his finest criticism. Conor Cruise O'Brien had been correct in deducing from his friend's masterpiece that the Irish writers were, in some of their most forceful moments, the very reverse of 'respectable'.

O'Brien's essay was no pal's puff, however. Having defended Mercier's central literary argument, he went on in 'Our Wits About Us' to question the book's underlying political assumption of an unbroken, unprob-lematic Irish tradition. In his judgement, such a tradition was notable only by its absence: what he found was not continuity but a gapped and broken narrative. Opposing Mercier's essentialist model of an all-Ireland identity, he proposed a behaviourist alternative: there was really no 'Irish mind' as such, only a plurality of Irish minds, each one caught up in an Irish predicament, 'which has produced common characteristics in a number of those who have been involved in it'. Chief among these were wit and irony. Words were the only weapons available to a disarmed people who had sought over centuries to expose the difference between official pretence and actual reality.

These alternative models of Irish identity have dominated cultural debate in Ireland in the three decades since they were so outlined. Whatever view a critic takes of either model, he or she has inevitably ended up grappling with the arguments adumbrated in this energetic exchange. It was Mercier and O'Brien—rather than Paddy Solemn—who set the questions which would be addressed by the young in a debate which shows no signs of coming to an easy or an imminent conclusion.

*   *   *

Mercier was favoured by Richard Ellmann as the natural successor to his chair at Northwestern University, Evanston, but, even in those golden years of high acclaim, he knew that fate had other things in store. It would be a long time before there would be a book to set alongside *The Irish Comic Tradition*. His wife Gina was suffering from multiple sclerosis and the family therefore moved to the more suitable climate of Boulder, Colorado, at whose university he was Professor of English Literature from 1965 to 1974. There he nursed his wife until her death in 1971. Throughout this period he remained understandably quiet, apart from publishing *A Reader's Guide to the New Novel: From Queneau to Pinget* (1971). The essays in this volume deal with the authors named in the title and with the equally-fashionable Sarraute, Robbe-Grillet, Butor, Mauriac, and, most notably, Claude Simon (who would many years later receive the Nobel Prize). Avowedly introductory, they helped to make this unusual phase of French culture comprehensible to an English-speaking audience and they encouraged Mercier to give voice to the honorary Frenchman who had always been hidden just below the surface of his personality, a truth hinted in the dedication 'To the memory of my father William Cochrane Mercier (1885–1954), and all of our Huguenot ancestors in Ireland as well as France'.

It was, however, in the much-postponed, long-awaited study of Beckett that the real possibilities of the Franco-Irish connection were to be explored. After Gina's death, her husband was able to throw himself into the task, reworking many of his early essays into his second master-piece of critical placement and evaluation, *Beckett/Beckett*. Out of their shared background, he produced a study at once relaxed and rigorous, congenial and exacting, funny and learned, which argued that Beckett was another well-balanced Irishman with a chip on each shoulder and a penchant for dualism—one who set the eye against the ear, mind against body, woman against man, artist against philosopher, and so on. Nobody was much surprised when this book gave rise to a sequence of analyses by gifted scholars of the 'double vision' in Irish writing.

*   *   *

In 1974 Vivian Mercier married the novelist and translator Eilís Dillon, herself recently widowed but a long-standing friend since their years as students. The couple settled happily at Santa Barbara and he took up his last professorship, at the University of California. There he taught his favourite subjects and Eilís Dillon gave classes in the Irish language and in creative writing. It was, for both of them, a tranquil and happy period after a time of difficulty and pain. In those fruitful years, Mercier prepared many of the essays reproduced in this volume, some of them for books and festschrifts, others for oral delivery at conferences, others still as extended notes in learned journals. He retired from Santa Barbara in 1987 in order to settle with Eilís Dillon in Dublin and work further on this project, and his return led to a host of invitations to lecture at this or that literary festival. Inevitably, he obliged and won deserved fame as a fine platform speaker: few who heard his hilarious paper on Yeats's humour at the Sligo Summer School in 1986 will be able to read it here without recalling the dry little chuckle which punctuated its wholly unexpected themes. Mercier threw himself into these activities because he loved being in Ireland and because he felt reanimated by the company of younger people who shared his enthusiasms. His health was known to be fragile, but he was invariably spry, even jaunty, and often to be found in a crowd of children. He drew most of his force in these years from the loving support of his wife, whose work he supported and championed in turn: together they were a formidable, but utterly approachable, couple, and the contrast in their personal styles added greatly to the gaiety of their many dinner-parties in Rathgar at which two rising generations of Irishmen and women were made welcome. When it was announced that he had died on 3 November 1989 with his work unfinished, it was hardly credible. To his former student Anthony Roche, even the final illness had seemed but the most recent of a long series of Beckettian afflictions from which his supervisor would somehow recover and 'go on'. But it was not to be. His funeral service was held at St Patrick's Cathedral in a wholly ecumenical but none the less deeply Protestant mode. He would have enjoyed the hymns, the beautiful, austere words, but most of all, perhaps, the prospect of his former room-mate, by then the country's best-known agnostic, ascending the pulpit to give a brief, stoical address in which he remembered the complete kindness and spiritual rigour of his friend. As an instance of the latter, O'Brien cited Mercier's unusual ability to peer into the 'chilly depths' opened by Beckett, an ability which none of his Irish contemporaries could claim. Mercier was laid to rest in Clara, beside his father and mother.

*   *   *

It was fitting that he should have been buried after a service in the great cathedral of Swift and Irish Anglicanism, for he had been at all times a faithful servant of that tradition. Perhaps the most influential of all the essays reproduced here is the one which directly confronts the 'evangelical' element in the national literary renaissance. 'It would be outrageous to suggest that the true purpose of the Irish Literary Revival was to provide alternative employment for the sons of clergymen after disestablishment had reduced the number of livings provided by the Church of Ireland.' With these twinkling words he had opened his seminal 1979 lecture given at a conference in—of all places—Maynooth College. The thesis was clarity itself: that a generation of men and women from evangelical backgrounds, no longer able to accept the faith of their forefathers, attempted to aestheticize elements of Protestant thought. The argument ran parallel to that which sees Joyce as annexing for his own secular purposes the idea of 'epiphany' or the notion of art as transubstantiation.

In any good library can be found many books with titles like *Joyce Among the Jesuits* or *Joyce's Pauline Vision*, all based on the demonstrable conviction that Joyce remained obsessed by the Roman Catholicism he professed to reject. But it is not possible to find a full-length book on the Protestant element in Shaw. And the same might be said of each of the following: O'Casey, Beckett, Synge, and Yeats. It is too easily assumed that each moved from belief to apostasy without the kind of trauma which attended Joyce's loss of faith; and yet a book could easily be written, for example, on the way in which Yeats's view of poetry as a quarrel with the self may be a secularized version of the Protestant confession which is made on the understanding that 'every man is his own priest'. Ferguson's famous dialogue between the head and heart of an Irish Protestant became, in the Yeatsian modulation, a debate between Hic and Ille (or, as Ezra Pound liked to joke, Hic and Willie.) Yeats's acute sense in poem after poem of the dangers of image-worship may also be the outcome of his training in a Protestantism which remained for-ever sceptical about idols and images. The same suspicion is to be found in the writings of Beckett, whose motto is 'no symbols where none intended'. Indeed, Beckett's compulsive habit of stopping a play to remind the audience that it is only a play could be traceable to a low-church distrust of mimesis and is, viewed in a certain light, a sort of slow-motion re-enactment of the Puritan closure of the theatres. His stage is certainly as stripped of symbol and artifice as any low-church altar.

Seán O'Casey in his plays insists on the Protestant virtue of self-responsibility. In *The Plough and the Stars* it is drunken loyalist Bessie Burgess who actually sacrifices her life for another, while all around her idealists speechify about Christian self-sacrifice. And Shaw's *Saint Joan*, written in the same decade, asserts that the maid recently canonized by the Pope of Rome was in fact one of the first Protestant mystics, who listened to her own inner voices and needed no priest to mediate between her and God.

In all of these writings, Protestant ethical values are seen to emerge in sharp focus against a Roman Catholic backdrop, as if to suggest that an underlying imperative of the Irish revival was the production of a new kind of Catholicized Protestant or Protestantized Catholic—a wonderful theological hybrid more recently nicknamed by Brendan Kennelly a 'Protholic' or a 'Cathestant'. Mercier, in his happy marriage to a leading Catholic writer, was just such a hybrid, but he never repudiated his childhood faith; and in the 1979 lecture he offered a graphic sketch of the deposit which it left on Irish revivalism: its obsession with the Bible, its fascination with the transforming power of the 'word', its concern to establish links back to a Celtic church of St Patrick, and thus to predicate a spiritual unity at a time of post-Parnellite fragmentation. He might justly have added to that list a fixation on the connotations of the word 'revival'. His thesis was taken up and usefully extended by Terence Brown's collection *Irish Literature* (1988), which discovers Evangelical and calamitarian echoes in Yeats's apocalypse at the end of a poem like 'The Valley of the Black Pig'.

Why has it taken so long for these self-evident truths to be asserted by critics? Why has the intellectual history of Protestant culture in Ireland been neglected? At a time when murder-gangs prowl the streets of the north, it is perhaps understandable that intellectuals would shy away from any debate that savours of the sectarian. Another reason for this reticence lies in the fact that Protestantism, in its non-Anglican forms at any rate, has always placed a premium on private judgement and has been correspondingly wary of any grandiose, general statements. Mercier understood all this better than most, but he also agreed with Dean Victor Griffin's contention that southern Protestants had been too self-effacing. The problem was that as a consequence of such politeness— not to mention the notorious *Ne Temere* decree (which led the Catholic Church to insist that offspring of mixed marriages be brought up in the Catholic faith) and the usual emigration from rural parishes—they have been in certain places all but effaced. Back in 1912, Shaw had expressed his fear that the spiritual leadership of Irish Protestantism would pass to northern extremists, while 'the organisation of false gentility which so often takes its name in vain' in Dublin continued to peter out. That emptying-out of the more radical potentials of full-blooded Protestantism was attributed by Shaw to a shrewd awareness among sections of the ascendancy that an articulated version of 'self-election' could have its political issue only in the Republican ideal. Mercier at all times spoke with eloquent pride as a southern Protestant and a united Irelander, but he was very proud of his northern ancestors and educational experiences. In urging southern critics from Protestant backgrounds to be more forceful and more audible, he repeatedly held up such younger northern scholars as John Wilson Foster and Tom Paulin as models of the kind of forthrightness he desired. He was greatly encouraged, too, by the resurgence of interest in the later 1980s in the essays and ideas of Hubert Butler, believing that in the collective projects of such intellectuals the true history of literary Protestantism might be traced.

In the following essays may be found his own contribution to that enterprise, ranging in subject-matter from Evangelical revivalism, through the rediscovery of a usable Celtic past, the remarkable self-assertion of Shaw and the flirtations with continental decadence in Synge, down to the reworkings of the Portoran Bible by Samuel Beckett. Mercier's study shows that Shaw was not completely right when he claimed that Ireland's obsession with its own wretched condition had kept it out of the great stream of European Protestantism. This was certainly not true of Mercier, nor of the artists whose work he most admired; but it must be added that, as an ecumenist, he was equally happy to celebrate the workings of a Catholic imagination in the pages of Joyce.

The reader will find in these essays an unusual blend of old-world protocol and thoroughly contemporary method. In his immense learning, his addiction to the personal digression, his pedantic worry and scrupulous citation of sources, Mercier was a gentleman-scholar of a kind no longer produced, but he put these estimable qualities at the service of an unremittingly modern sensibility. Unlike many other gentlemen-scholars who shared his knowledge but perhaps lacked his energy, he wrote extensively, travelled widely, published enthusiastically, and crusaded mightily for new writers, new playwrights, new critics. These essays, devotedly saved, assembled, and annotated by Eilís Dillon, are his testament. Like his children and grandchildren, they are also the signals that he sent hopefully into the future.

1 The Rediscovery of the Gaelic Past

The Three Ages of Gaelic Studies

There are three ages or stages of Gaelic studies that can be differentiated before or during the Literary Revival. The first of these may be described, without much injustice, as the Age of the Charlatan, 1760–1830. It begins with the first publication by that arch-charlatan James Macpherson, whose alleged translations from Scots Gaelic are collectively known as *Ossian*. Many of the Irish writers who came forward to refute him and/or to take advantage of the interest he aroused all over Europe in Gaelic studies were themselves charlatans. I do not plan to waste my reader's time by recording their misdemeanours: only those few writers who possessed a genuine knowledge of Irish and used it to produce valuable texts and translations during this era will be discussed.

The next period, a happier one, may be called the Age of the Native (or Traditional) Scholar, beginning with the publication of James Hardiman's *Irish Minstrelsy* in 1831, and continuing into the 1870s. Even after that time, Standish Hayes O'Grady and Douglas Hyde showed some of the traditional spirit in their work. Although the scientific study of the older Irish language became possible in 1853 with the publication by Johann Kaspar Zeuss (1806–56) of *Grammatica Celtica*, the result of ten years' study of the Celtic languages by this highly trained German philologist, a pair of Irish traditional scholars, John O'Donovan and Eugene O'Curry, employing pre-scientific methods, edited and translated a surprising number of old manuscripts. They annotated these in great detail, using their knowledge of traditional genealogical and topographical lore. Other Irishmen, who had picked up a mixture of the old and the new learning, enlarged the territory cleared by these two pioneers. Presiding over the whole period by means of a number of institutions which he had helped to found or to consolidate was the many-sided George Petrie, Ireland's great nineteenth-century exemplar of the Renaissance Man—painter, typographer, archaeologist, architectural historian, museum curator, and collector of folk music—who dominated the age by his gift for friendship. His friends used to speak of him as 'Dear Petrie'.

The third period, the Age of the Foreign Scholar, which had in one sense begun with Zeuss, runs from the establishment of the *Revue Celtique* by Henri Gaidoz in 1870 to about 1922, the year in which the Irish Free State was founded. During this half-century, the foreign scholars doing productive work in Old and Middle Irish, the phases of the language which contained most of the sagas and myths so highly valued by the Revival writers, outnumbered the native scholars. Paradoxically, however, the most productive scholar of all, Whitley Stokes, was an Anglo-Irishman who had learned the new methods during his Trinity College years from a young German, Rudolf Siegfried. Foreign Celtic scholars with a particular interest in Gaelic literature as well as linguistics included Henry d'Arbois de Jubainville, Gaidoz, Carl Marstrander, the Scotsman John Strachan, Rudolf Thurneysen, Ernst Windisch, and, above all, Kuno Meyer, editor and translator extraordinary.[1]

CHARLATANS AND ANTI-CHARLATANS

It was the international success of Macpherson's imposture that made the English-speaking upper and middle classes in Ireland aware of the value of a cultural heritage that they had previously despised—and that many of them could only claim as theirs by right of conquest. An important function of the Royal Irish Academy (founded 1785) was to explore and preserve that heritage for the 'Protestant Nation' which had established Grattan's Parliament in 1782. Peers with Irish titles, Protestants who bore ancient Irish names, landlords whose ancestors had intermarried with famous Gaelic families, all took a new interest in their genealogies and in the history and literature of Ireland. The number of works in English published on Irish history, antiquities, literature, and music increased sharply after 1782, and did not noticeably diminish after the passing of the Act of Union in 1800. One need only consult the lists of subscribers—including persons raised to the peerage at the Union, no doubt for services rendered—printed in books of historical or antiquarian interest to confirm the existence of this trend.

In all fairness to the Royal Irish Academy, I should point out that one of the first papers read before it denied the authenticity of Macpherson's *Ossian*. The Revd Matthew Young, FTCD, later Bishop of Clonfert, had toured the Scottish Highlands in 1784, collecting Gaelic poems: 'he maintained that any poems that existed were Irish, and that

[1] J. S. Smart, *James Macpherson: An Episode in Literature* (London: David Nutt, 1905), gives a readable, fair-minded account of the Ossian controversy. For a survey of Celtic scholarship from its beginnings, see chapter 1, 'History in Ireland', in James F. Kenney, *Sources for the Early History of Ireland*, Ecclesiastical [all pub.] (New York: Columbia Univ. Press, 1929), i. 1–90. Though the focus is historical, there is much information on literary scholarship also.

Macpherson had founded his Ossian on some of these.'² The first comment of substance on Macpherson by an identifiable Irish author dates, however, from twenty years earlier: it appeared in the 1766 edition of an historical work by Charles O'Conor of Belanagare, a Catholic landowner who had been educated in the old Gaelic tradition and did everything in his power to foster it.³ Unfortunately, his own historical writing was vitiated by his uncritical acceptance of Roderic O'Flaherty's theories about the Phoenician origin of the Irish. General Charles Vallancey was equally credulous and moreover knew no Irish, but he did employ native scholars to edit and translate early Irish literary and historical sources, published in his six-volume *Collectanea* (1770–1804). Sir William Betham, like Vallancey an English official, is described by James F. Kenney as 'a kind of second Vallancey whose pet theory was the identity of the Irish language with Etruscan and of both with Phoenician'.⁴ Since the great scholarly achievements of 1830–70 were mainly the work of Catholic Irishmen, perhaps many of the absurdities of the period 1760–1830 might have been avoidable had the Protestant or English dilettante been humble enough to learn from the Catholic native scholar—especially when the latter deferred too humbly to his patron's allegedly superior culture.

Only one Anglo-Irish editor and translator of Gaelic texts in the eighteenth century was never guilty of such cultural arrogance: it is perhaps hardly surprising that this paragon was a woman, Charlotte Brooke. Her translations in *Reliques of Irish Poetry* (1789) are reasonably faithful verse renderings of verse originals; the Irish texts, printed in Irish characters, are placed by themselves towards the end of the volume, but they can easily be consulted and compared. Not only is she familiar with these, usually in more than one manuscript version, but she has an absolute conviction of their literary worth. Having decided which Irish text of a poem to use, she presents it as exactly as she can. She calls the narrative poems 'heroic', and instead of patronizing the love-songs from oral tradition, she confesses her inability to do them justice:

two or three little artless words, or perhaps only a single epithet, will sometimes convey such an image of sentiment, or of suffering, to the mind, that one lays down the book, to look at the *picture*. But the beauty of many of these passages is considerably impaired by translation; indeed, so sensible was I of this, that it influenced me to give up, in despair, many a sweet stanza.⁵

---

2 William F. Skene, 'Introduction', in *The Dean of Lismore's Book*, ed. & transl. Thomas McLauchlan (Edinburgh: Edmonston & Douglas, 1862), lviii.

3 Kenney, *Sources*, 57n.

4 Ibid. 61. For Vallancey, see Kenney *Sources*, 58–9.

5 Charlotte Brooke, *Reliques of Irish Poetry* (Dublin: George Bonham, 1789), 230.

After this introduction, one is distressed to find that a writer of such sensitivity lacked the originality to break through the neo-classical conventions of her time: so much so, that one has to translate her versions into modern colloquial English in order to appreciate how faithful they are.

Although her volume implicitly refutes Macpherson on every page, Charlotte Brooke never once deigns to mention him. She may have chosen 'Conloch' (a version of *Aided Conlaich/Aided Oenfir Aifi*) for its intrinsic pathos rather than to show up the absurdities of his 'Carthon', but she does not hint that the subject was ever treated before. In a long footnote to the same poem, she accurately summarizes the traditions about Deirdre without any allusion to Macpherson's anomalous 'Darthula'.[6] One is grateful for her tact in this respect, and even more grateful for the brevity of her preface, in which she apologizes for not being learned enough to supply a dissertation on ancient Irish poetry, referring her readers instead, with unconscious irony, to the works of O'Conor, Vallancey, and Sylvester O'Halloran. How wise she is to concentrate on what she knows and loves!

Theophilus O'Flanagan, who gave us the first full presentation in English of two sharply contrasting versions of the Deirdre story, took a more frankly polemical approach. His 'Proëme' or preface to *Deirdri* (1808) begins:

The following Story, from the Irish, is the foundation of Mr James Mac Pherson's *Darthula*. It is properly denominated with us, 'The tragical Fate of the Sons of Usnach.' Upon a comparison, the reader will be enabled to judge of the vast liberties taken with the original by Mr Mac Pherson, and also to observe his anachronisms and interpolations.[7]

O'Flanagan set the precedent—followed by O'Donovan, O'Curry, and many others—of printing the Irish text and a *literal* English translation on facing pages; he does not indicate his sources, but O'Curry cites the two TCD manuscripts that he probably used. O'Flanagan describes the longer version of the tale as 'a poetic composition, founded upon historic truth, for the purpose of amusement'.[8] The shorter, older version, from the Book of Leinster, he regards as the historical source of the other: for another fifty years or more, native scholars (O'Curry especially) were unable or unwilling to separate history from myth.

---

[6] Ibid. 13n.

[7] Theophilus O'Flanagan, *Deirdri, or, the Lamentable Fate of the Sons of Usnach*, in *Transactions of the Gaelic Society of Dublin*, i [all pub.] (Dublin: John Barlow, 1808), i. 1. Three separately paged pamphlets precede *Deirdri* in the bound volume of *Transactions*, which itself has a separate title-page and pagination.

[8] O'Flanagan, *Deirdri*, 12.

O'Flanagan's literal translations of the two texts, especially that of the longer, which is in classical Modern Irish, probably encouraged Lady Gregory and her acknowledged model, Douglas Hyde, in their use of the English spoken in Ireland. In the notes to *Cuchulain of Muirthemne* (1902) she lists O'Flanagan among the sources for her chapter 'The Fate of the Sons of Usnach'. Some of the verbal similarities between her version and O'Flanagan's seem too close to be explained merely as literal renderings of the same Irish text. They are closest at the moments when, translating verse literally into prose, they dare to reproduce the Irish syntax in English. O'Flanagan's 'Alas! heard she this night,/Naisi to be under cover in the earth' corresponds to Lady Gregory's 'Och! if she knew to-night, Naoise to be under a covering of clay.'[9] This construction based on Irish is of particular interest because Lady Gregory employs it far too often: so much that it always occurs in parodies of her 'Kiltartanese'. We know that Lady Gregory used Irish-English deliberately, imitating Douglas Hyde's example in his *Love Songs of Connacht* (1893). He in his turn may have been imitating O'Flanagan; indeed, he seems to have borrowed many phrases, and sometimes whole sentences, from O'Flanagan for his chapter on Deirdre in *A Literary History of Ireland* (1899).

Given O'Flanagan's uneasy vacillation between poetic diction and prose literalness, one might assume that he stumbled into Irish-English without premeditation, or even that he had an unsure command of standard English, but his commentary and notes, while often stilted, contain no solecisms. He possessed, at least intermittently, the ear of a poet. If he had not rendered '*air druim domhain*' as 'on the ridge of the world', would Lady Gregory have hit on the phrase by herself? Furthermore, the entire passage in which this phrase occurs reproduces quite faithfully the rhythm and structure of its original:

'Therefore,' said Conor, 'go thy way to know if her own countenance live upon Deirdri? for if her own visage live upon her, there is not on the ridge of the world, or on the extent of the earth, a woman that is more handsome than she.'[10]

A twentieth-century reader is likely to admire most the integrity with which O'Flanagan treats his older text. As we shall see, the Revival dramatists, including even Synge, lacked the courage to follow this plain-spoken version, in which Deirdre boldly forces Naisi to elope with her and spends a year after his death 'in the bed of Conor'. When the year is up, Conor hands her over to Eogan, who killed Naisi:

---

[9] O'Flanagan, *Deirdri*, 111. Lady Gregory, *Cuchulain of Muirthemne* (London: Murray, 1902), 134.

[10] O'Flanagan, *Deirdri*, 85. Gregory, *Cuchulain*, 127.

They drove the next day to the assembly of Murthemny. She was behind Eogan in a chariot. She looked, that she might not see both her gallants, towards the earth. 'Well, Deirdre,' says Conor, 'it is the glance of a ewe between two rams, you cast between me and Eogan.' There was a large rock near; she hurled her head at the stone, so that she broke her skull, and killed herself.[11]

Powerful though this is by twentieth-century reckoning, one is forced to acknowledge that if Macpherson had written with equal authenticity, *Ossian* might never have found a publisher. Nearly fifty years after Macpherson, the Gaelic Society of Dublin may have felt uneasy about O'Flanagan's translating verse into literal prose; at any rate, we often find in the notes to *Deirdri* something described as '*The English Versification, from the literal Translation, by Mr. WILLIAM LEAHY*'. This is always an exercise in neo-classicism, written as though Wordsworth and Coleridge's *Lyrical Ballads* (1798) had never been published. The first lines of Leahy's rendering of 'The Blackbird of Derrycarn', a beautiful nature-lyric from the Finn Cycle, offer a compendium of the poetic diction abhorred by Wordsworth:

> Hail tuneful bird of sable wing,
> Thou warbler sweet of Carna's grove!
> Not lays more charming will I hear
> Tho' round th' expansive earth I rove.[12]

Note particularly the periphrastic 'bird of sable wing' for 'blackbird' and the perverse inversion of normal syntax in line three.

Nevertheless, if one compares William Halliday's translation of Geoffrey Keating's *History of Ireland* with that of Dermod O'Connor (1723), it becomes clear that the standards for translation from Irish prose have changed radically, even if those for verse translation have not. O'Connor apparently must be credited with the first printed English version of the tale of Deirdre, because Keating thought it historical and therefore included it in his history. Halliday published one volume of Keating, with text and translation on facing pages, in 1811; he intended to produce a complete edition, but died the following year aged only 24. Where Halliday translates simply and literally, O'Connor paraphrases, adopts a patronizing tone and mingles some vapid commentary with the text. O'Flanagan and Halliday made a brave attempt to replace Macpherson with something more authentic. Unfortunately, by 1814 they were both dead, and the Gaelic Society of Dublin, which had intended, 'as soon as may be, to publish every Fragment existing in the Gaelic Language', perished with them.

Between the demise of the Gaelic Society and the foundation in 1840 by the Revd James Henthorn Todd, FTCD, of the longer-lived Irish

---

[11] O'Flanagan, *Deirdri*, 177.   [12] Ibid. 196.

Archaeological Society, one similar organization had a brief career. This was the Iberno-Celtic Society, founded in 1818 with the Lord Lieutenant as Patron and the Duke of Leinster as President; the membership included a score of peers and baronets and two Catholic bishops. In that brief era of good feeling, the commoners were divided almost equally between Catholics and Protestants; significantly, the Evangelicals were well represented among the latter. The Catholic members included James Hardiman and Revd Paul O'Brien, Professor of Irish at Maynooth. Betham was the secretary and treasurer; his future nemesis, George Petrie, was also a member, but the assistant secretary, Edward O'Reilly, was the driving force of the society and sole author of its only publication, vol. i, part 1, of its *Transactions* for 1820. This work, usually referred to as 'O'Reilly's *Irish Writers*', contains 'a chronological account of nearly four hundred Irish writers . . . carried down to . . . 1750; with a descriptive catalogue of such of their works as are still extant in verse or prose, consisting of upwards of one thousand separate tracts'.[13] Despite its antiquarian bias, it was the fullest survey of Irish literature, especially poetry, available for nearly eighty years. Douglas Hyde refers to it frequently in his *Literary History of Ireland* (1899). Though it contained only the briefest, frequently inaccurate, translated excerpts, some of the Revival writers must have felt reassured by it that they formed part of a great tradition.

The preface to *Irish Writers* offers a melancholy record of earlier literary societies that failed to produce even a single addition to the body of Irish scholarship; nevertheless, it expresses bright hopes for the future, promising 'another catalogue of works whose authors are not now known'.[14] These would have been mostly works in prose, which are not usually attributed to an author, unlike Irish poems. This catalogue in turn was to have been followed by the publication of a variety of texts in Irish, with or without English translations. The failure of the Iberno-Celtic Society may have been due to the growth of sectarian feeling among its members as the struggle for—and against—Catholic Emancipation intensified. In April 1830, according to Captain Thomas Larcom's records, O'Reilly was the first person appointed to the Topographical Department of the Irish Ordnance Survey, but he 'died almost immediately afterward'.[15] His successor, appointed in October of

---

[13] See the original title-page in the modern reprint: Edward O'Reilly, *A Chronological Account of nearly Four Hundred Irish Writers*, intro. Gearoid S. MacEoin (Shannon: Irish Univ. Press, 1970).

[14] O'Reilly, *A Chronological Account*, ix.

[15] 'Larcom Letters (Private): Memoir vol. 4', NLI MS. 7753, n. pag. This disagrees with the *DNB*, which gives August 1829 as the date of O'Reilly's death but assigns the sale of his 'many manuscripts in the Irish language' to 1830. For Larcom's amusing account of his first acquaintance with O'Donovan, see Lady Ferguson, *Sir Samuel Ferguson in the Ireland of His Day*, 2 vols. (Edinburgh: Blackwood, 1896), i. 62–3.

the same year, was John O'Donovan, whom Larcom, wishing to learn Irish, had discovered by chance drudging for the Irish Society. O'Donovan's accession marked the beginning of a new era of native Irish scholarship just as surely as O'Reilly's death marked the end of an older one.

THE AGE OF THE NATIVE SCHOLAR

Hardiman and Ferguson, 1831–34

Although the years immediately preceding Catholic Emancipation were full of literary as well as political activity, the rediscovery of the Gaelic past made no significant progress between 1820 and 1831. It is true that Thomas Crofton Croker began publishing folk-tales in 1825, but neither he nor anyone else at the time drew a firm line between recording folklore and writing fiction based on it. The most notable literary event in the years 1825–9 was the birth of a new kind of Anglo-Irish fiction, written by the Banims, Griffin, and Carleton, discussed in Chapter 2.

The editor of the first great work of Irish scholarship after Emancipation, James Hardiman, felt obliged to apologize for the Catholic partisanship of some of his notes, 'which were mostly written before the late conciliatory acts'.[16] No doubt they had already been set up by the printer before the great change occurred. Hardiman's *Irish Minstrelsy, or Bardic Remains of Ireland; with English Poetical Translations* (two vols., 1831) prints Irish texts of over a hundred lyrics and folksongs: in Donal O'Sullivan's words, it is 'the most important of our primary sources for Irish *song*'.[17] The older the original, the less reliable Hardiman's text of it is likely to be, but the love-songs and patriotic ballads from living oral tradition are peerless. These soon inspired Samuel Ferguson (1810–86) to produce English versions of which Máire Mhac an tSaoi has said, 'Almost, we have forgotten that they are translations.'[18]

Unhappily, the volunteer translators used by Hardiman were not similarly inspired. It is not excuse enough to say that they knew little or no Irish and were therefore dependent on Hardiman's 'literal essayings' for knowledge of the originals. Like O'Flanagan's William Leahy, they produced verse translations that are 'poetical' without being poetry, bad examples of a style already a generation out of date. The contribution of Hardiman's volumes to the Literary Revival was made largely at second hand. As the appendix of his four-part review of Hardiman in the *Dublin University Magazine* for 1834, Ferguson gave his own

[16] James Hardiman, *Irish Minstrelsy, or Bardic Remains of Ireland; with English Poetical Translations . . .*, 2 vols. (London: Joseph Robins, 1831), i. xl.

[17] Quoted by Máire Mhac an tSaoi in her introduction to the reprint (Shannon: Irish Univ. Press, 1971),

[18] Mhac an tSaoi, vi.

'surprisingly faithful and simple renderings' of twenty poems. Of this handful of translations, as Máire Mhac an tSaoi so justly says, 'our own present-day concept of our native cultural heritage is in great measure the outcome'.[19] Ferguson later made versions of a few more Hardiman songs, of which the best-known are 'Cean Dubh Deelish' and 'Youghall Harbour'. He also published, in the first article of his Hardiman review, the classic version of 'The County of Mayo' by his school friend George Fox. It is greatly to be regretted that Hardiman, unlike O'Flanagan, did not publish his own literal translations, except for a few buried in the notes. Ferguson, though, crammed his review with literal versions, the fruit of a private class for the study of Irish in Belfast which included himself, Fox, and Thomas O'Hagan, who in 1868 became the first Catholic Lord Chancellor of Ireland.

Ferguson's lyrical gift was a limited one at best, and it deserted him quite early. The last—and without doubt the best—of his original lyrics, the famous 'Lament for Thomas Davis', dates from 1847, when he was still under 40; all his poetry thereafter is narrative, satirical, or didactic. To the last group belong a few late poems which show genuine religious feeling. Apart from his translations of Irish songs, in fact, Ferguson's true lyrics could be counted on the fingers of one hand: except for the 'Lament', they date from the seminal year 1834, and include that haunting poem, 'The Fairy Thorn', a true lyrical ballad, if ever there was one. Perhaps it was Ferguson's knowledge of some of the Irish music to which the songs were sung that made his lyric touch more assured in his translations than in his original work. There is space to quote only one poem, so let it be his version of *Ceann Dubh Dilis*, a poem which made Charlotte Brooke retire in defeat:

CEANN DUBH DEELISH

Put your head, darling, darling, darling,
    Your darling head my heart above;
Oh, mouth of honey, with the thyme for fragrance,
    Who, with heart in breast, could deny you love?
Oh, many and many a young girl for me is pining,
    Letting her locks of gold to the cold wind free,
For me, the foremost of our gay young fellows;
    But I'd leave a hundred, pure love, for thee!
Then put your head, darling, darling, darling,
    Your darling black head my heart above;
Oh, mouth of honey, with the thyme for fragrance,
    Who, with heart in breast, could deny you love?[20]

[19] Mhac an tSaoi, vi.
[20] Samuel Ferguson, *Lays of the Western Gael, and Other Poems* (London: Bell & Daldy, 1865), 216.

John O'Donovan (1806–61)

The next publication of significance in illuminating the Gaelic past was, oddly enough, the modestly titled *Dublin Penny Journal*, a weekly launched on 30 June 1832. George Petrie became a regular contributor of both articles and drawings with the eighth number, and his friend John O'Donovan began contributing in September. Petrie's work is mainly concerned with archaeology and architecture, while O'Donovan's deals with history: for example, six excerpts from the Annals of the Four Masters relating to Dublin are translated and annotated. The first contribution signed in full by O'Donovan, a literal version of a poem in Irish attributed to 'Aldfred, king of the Northumbrian Saxons, during his exile in Ireland about . . . 685', exemplifies the skill in translation that he displayed for the rest of his life. Verse and prose alike are rendered in the same limpid, direct English prose:

> I found in the fair Inisfail
> In Ireland while in exile,
> Many women, no silly crowd,
> Many laics, many clerics . . .
>
> I found gold and silver,
> I found honey and wheat,
> I found affection with the people of God,
> I found banquets, and cities.[21]

His notes to the poem, like those in his vast later works, are full of information and, where possible, entertainment, but it is a little startling to find that he feels obliged to put forward 'historic evidence that we had *wheat* in Ireland in the ninth century'. Generations of ill-informed boastfulness and equally ill-informed disparagement regarding Gaelic civilization had imparted an almost paranoid concern for accuracy to genuine scholars.

Despite his vivid command of English, O'Donovan had little direct influence on the Revival except through his edition and translation of *The Banquet of Dun na n-Gedh and the Battle of Magh Rath*, published by the Irish Archaeological Society, 1842. Ferguson records that this work at once 'made a strong and lasting impression' on his imagination: so much so, that a generation later he published an epic poem in five books, *Congal* (1872) based on O'Donovan.[22] W. B. Yeats in turn said of his own late play *The Herne's Egg* (1938), 'the plot echoes that of Samuel Ferguson's "Congal", and in one form or another

---

[21] 'King Aldfred's Poem', *Dublin Penny Journal* (1832–3), i. 94.
[22] Samuel Ferguson, *Congal: A Poem, in Five Books* (Dublin: Edward Ponsonby; London: Bell & Daldy, 1872), v.

had been in my head since my early twenties'.[23] The word 'echoes'
seems carefully chosen, for he strays far indeed from Ferguson's poem.
It is the insult to Congal at the banquet that gives Yeats's play its focus
and title, rather than the battle provoked by this insult, which took
place at the modern Moira (County Down), in the part of Ulster that
Ferguson felt was peculiarly his own. The fantasy in Yeats's play rivals
that of the original *Banquet*: I feel sure that he must at one time or
another have read O'Donovan's translation and delighted in its
avoidance of archaic diction. At the time when he was writing *The
Herne's Egg*, Yeats was also helping Shri Purohit Swami to translate the
Upanishads and encouraging him to 'call a goddess "this handsome
girl", or even "a pretty girl", instead of "a maiden of surpassing loveliness"'.[24] If he did read O'Donovan, he must have appreciated such
renderings as 'fair-skinned yellow-haired women', a description that
even Browning might not have dared in 1842. One is reminded of
Yeats's own striking use of 'yellow' instead of the conventional 'golden'
to describe a woman's hair in 'September 1913' and especially in 'For
Anne Gregory'. It is possible, even, that O'Donovan was Yeats's source
for his choice of adjective, although the passage had long dropped from
his conscious mind. As O'Donovan grew older and more self-assured,
he became a yet more uncompromising translator: O'Curry and others
often bowdlerized, O'Donovan never. Striking examples of his plain
speaking will be found in one of his last works, *Annals of Ireland:
Three Fragments* (1860). In one anecdote, a pious king *insists* on drinking
from a certain stream after being warned that the local saint, Mura, uses
it as a latrine. In a different vein, later in the same book, the sombre
account of King Cormac Mac Cuileanáin's death during the rout of his
army, as faithfully rendered by O'Donovan, reminds one of Stendhal.

O'Donovan's supreme achievement was his seven-volume edition and
translation of the *Annals of the Four Masters*, *Annála Ríoghachta
Eireann* (1848–51), published in handsome format at the 'sole risk and
expense' of George Smith of Hodges and Smith, booksellers and publishers. After listing a number of nineteenth-century scholarly editions
that could never have been attempted but for O'Donovan's pioneering
work, the late Paul Walsh sums up: 'O'Donovan's edition . . . is the
fount and origin from which most of our subsequent historical com-
mentaries have been derived.'[25] He then drily adds that 'since his time,
numerous lists of place-names have been provided by editors of texts of

[23] *The Variorum Edition of the Plays of W. B. Yeats*, ed. Russell K. Alspach (New York:
Macmillan, 1966), 1311.
[24] *The Letters of W. B. Yeats*, ed. Allan Wade (New York: Macmillan, 1955), 846.
[25] Paul Walsh, *Irish Men of Learning*, ed. Colm O Lochlainn (Dublin: Three Candles, 1947),
269, 270. For the correct year of O'Donovan's birth, often wrongly given as 1809, see 263–4.

a non-historical character . . . the vast majority of their identifications are "pillaged from the printed works of John O'Donovan".' Among the pillagers one would include Standish James O'Grady and Lady Gregory—and Yeats, who borrowed from her.

Trinity College made O'Donovan an honorary Doctor of Laws, and his chair of Celtic Languages at Queen's College, Belfast, with an annual salary of £100 and no lectures, was essentially an honorary position too. His chief source of income for 1852 until his death was the Commission for the Publication of the Ancient Laws of Ireland, for which he transcribed nearly 2,500 pages of legal manuscripts in Irish and attempted a translation of these extremely difficult texts: given his imperfect knowledge of Old and Middle Irish, this was a sad waste of time that might more profitably have been bestowed on literature. He was the sole author of, or a leading contributor to, some ten volumes published by the Irish Archaeological Society and its peers; not only are his texts and annotations still of value to Celtic scholars, but a striking anthology could be made from his translations of prose and verse. It is a pity that the Revival made so little use of his great legacy.

George Petrie (1789–1866)

On the first of August 1835,[26] George Petrie—already with an established reputation as a painter and illustrator, and beginning to be known as an archaeologist—joined the Topographical Department of the Ordnance Survey of Ireland at the invitation of Captain Larcom of the Royal Engineers (later Major-General Sir Thomas Larcom). He was assigned the general superintendence of the department, but the natural sciences and economic and social statistics were in the hands of engineer officers; his own expertise was applied to the antiquarian and orthographical investigations: local history, the identification and description of ancient monuments, the correct spelling and derivation of place-names. O'Donovan had already been employed there for nearly five years. He was a tireless investigator, writing almost daily letters crammed with information from his field-trips throughout Ireland. Eugene O'Curry meanwhile transcribed passages of place-name lore, history and legend from manuscripts in the Dublin libraries. Petrie himself made meticulous descriptive notes and drawings, which he described as 'quotations from our ancient monuments', during his summer

---

[26] The date usually given is 1833, but NLI MS. 7753, already cited, includes a detailed list for the Topographical Dept. of appointments, daily pay rates and discharges, 1830–42. The standard work is J. H. Andrews, *A Paper Landscape: The Ordnance Survey in Nineteenth-Century Ireland* (Oxford: Clarendon Press, 1975). William Stokes, *The Life and Labours in Art and Archaeology of George Petrie* (London: Longmans, Green, 1868), is full of direct quotations from Petrie and his contemporaries, but its chronology is confusing and sometimes inaccurate.

field-trips.[27] The terms of his appointment made him responsible for producing a publishable 'memoir' to accompany the map of each county, drawing on all the information collected by the various branches of the Topographical Department—one of the Larcom's imaginative and far-sighted ideas. Petrie's paper 'On the History of Antiquities of Tara Hill', for which he was awarded a gold medal by the Royal Irish Academy in 1837, was to have formed part of the memoir for County Meath.

In the event only one memoir, that for part of the City of Londonderry (1837), ever saw the light. It was acclaimed by scientific bodies and the general public, but the British Government objected to the publication of further memoirs as too costly, and Petrie and his staff were gradually discharged in 1841–2. It was widely believed in Ireland that the authorities feared Irish national feeling would be heightened by such reminders of a turbulent history and an ancient culture, especially during the agitation for repeal of the Union. That Petrie's leading collaborators—and his wife, it was alleged—were Catholics did not pass without notice.[28] Fortunately much of the work done for the Ordnance Survey appeared under other auspices: the publication of the RIA and the Irish Archaeological and Celtic Societies, the Annals of the Four Masters, the *Dublin Penny Journal*, and the *Irish Penny Journal* (1840–1)—edited by Petrie during its one year of existence. Other less direct consequences of Ordnance Survey collaboration included Edward Bunting's last and largest compilation, *The Ancient Music of Ireland* (1840); Petrie's own masterpiece, *The Ecclesiastical Architecture of Ireland* (1845); O'Curry's professional lectures at the Catholic University (see below); and the earliest published versions from the Irish by the poet Mangan, whom Petrie had employed as a copyist in the Department.

In a work primarily concerned with literature, it is hard to do full justice to Petrie without being accused of irrelevance. Although he wrote much, he did not write very well, even in his closely reasoned *Ecclesiastical Architecture*. His only contribution to literature is one song, 'The Snowy-Breasted Pearl', translated from Irish. Nevertheless, one can't adequately present the sources of the Literary Revival without acknowledging the pivotal role of George Petrie. Although he lacked their charisma, he is more important in the long run than Thomas Davis, Douglas Hyde, and perhaps even Yeats. The educated Irishman

---

[27] George Petrie, *The Ecclesiastical Architecture of Ireland, Anterior to the Anglo-Norman Invasion; Comprising an Essay on the Origin and Uses of the Round Towers of Ireland*, 2nd edn. (Dublin: Hodges & Smith, 1845), x.

[28] NLI MS. 7753 contains a copy of a letter signed 'A Protestant Conservative' and dated 2 May 1842 alleging *inter alia* that 'Mr Petrie is a R.C. in disguise, his wife & family profess that faith publicly'. This letter from a disgruntled former employee hardly justifies Andrews' description of Petrie as 'a catholic'. 160.

of the 1880s inherited a perception of his country's past that was influenced at every turn by Petrie, often in ways that the perceiver could never have suspected. In every book about Ireland that he opened, there were likely to be illustrations of landscapes and monuments based on, but without acknowledgement of, Petrie's drawings; if it contained texts in Irish, these were likely to be printed in one of the three noble founts designed by Petrie. If he had the slightest interest in traditional music, he must have heard tunes collected by Petrie: some had been given to Moore, some to Bunting; others were published posthumously or in the only book on the subject Petrie found time to complete—*Ancient Music of Ireland* (1855), consisting of 147 airs, carefully annotated. Donal O'Sullivan writes: 'It would be difficult to speak too highly of this monumental work. . . . [Petrie] should be rated as great a nation-builder in the cultural sphere as was O'Connell in the sphere of politics.'[29]

Late Victorian Dublin contained three great cultural institutions that bore Petrie's stamp. His work had been shown in the very first exhibition of the Royal Hibernian Academy (1826): he continued to share its activities as artist, teacher, and officer until 1859, when he resigned from both the Academy and its presidency in protest against acceptance of what he felt was excessive government control. The Royal Irish Academy, which in the year of Petrie's death was finally preparing to elect him its next president, owed many items in its fine library of Irish manuscripts to his efforts. The National Museum of Ireland, on its foundation in 1877, took over the RIA Museum of Antiquities, first set in order by Petrie in 1829 and enlarged through his talents as a collector and fund-raiser from 1837 onwards. His last few months of life were spent in trying to complete the catalogue of what was already, and has remained, an unrivalled collection of pre-Christian and early Christian Irish Art.

In travelling about the Irish countryside, our hypothetical Late Victorian could use the Ordnance Survey maps to find a great number of prehistoric and early Christian sites and monuments: furthermore, he could learn to distinguish between pagan and Christian, Irish Romanesque and Anglo-Norman remains. Ever since Petrie's prize-winning 'Essay on the Origin and Uses of the Round Towers of Ireland' (1833), it has become more and more difficult for educated Irishmen—however full of Romantic sympathies—to believe that the famous towers were of Danish or Phoenician origin, or that they had been used for Druidic or Buddhist rites.

---

[29] Donal O'Sullivan, *Irish Folk Music and Song*, Irish Life and Culture iii (Dublin: Three Candles, 1952), 17–18.

Had his father not been a painter, George Petrie might have become one of the great Victorian scientists: as it was, his powers of observation, analysis, classification, and inductive reasoning were fully displayed in the essay on round towers and in its sequel, the *Ecclesiastical Architecture*, which may be regarded as giving the death-blow to the Age of the Charlatan. In 1837 Sir William Betham had resigned from the RIA Council and written a venomous letter to the President, the great mathematician and astronomer Sir William Rowan Hamilton, protesting against the award given to Petrie's Tara Hill essay. In 1845, however, Betham and his clique did not dare to protest, despite the explicit refutation of Betham's views in various passages of the *Ecclesiastical Architecture*. Petrie wrote to Lord Adare the day after this work was submitted to the RIA, 'The battle is over and won!' His account of the day of battle shows clearly how diverse was his involvement with the cultural life of Dublin: after midday dinner he sat down to read the *Nation*, but was interrupted by the need to compose a letter to the Secretary of the RIA; after tea, he went out 'to attend to my duties as visitor at the living model school of the [Royal Hibernian] Academy—a duty that I take great pleasure in, for the students like me, and attend more when I am there'.[30] He did not get home until 9:30, but had to wait another half-hour for news of his triumph at the RIA meeting.

One must insist that Petrie's knowledge of archaeology as well as architecture grew naturally out of his artistic vocation. As he wrote in 1821, he at first believed that 'the history and antiquities of Ireland, previous to the English invasion, [were] wholly unworthy of notice', or if not, they were impenetrably hidden 'in obscurity and darkness'. However, his profession as painter and illustrator gave him 'an opportunity of examining some of our ancient architectural remains'. His innate scientific curiosity was aroused, and he made up his mind 'to endeavour by extensive observation, in conjunction with historical research', to determine the date to which each should be assigned.[31] This combination of observation with historical research was the secret of his success in dating the round towers, the building of several of them having been recorded in the Irish annals. If his identifications at Tara are now considered unreliable, this is in part because the remains there are so much older than the documents with which he and his colleagues compared them. Nevertheless, he pointed the way to a more scientific history as well as to a more scientific archaeology. He was also the first scientific collector of Irish folk music, for 'he never failed, where it was possible, to note, not the air alone, but the words and

---

[30] Stokes, *The Life and Labours*, 208.   [31] Stokes, *The Life and Labours*, 24.

metre of the . . . song, . . . together with all the circumstances as to the locality, history, and source of the air'.[32] Thanks to his unique blend of imagination with observation, of the artistic with the scientific, Petrie not merely recorded the physical landscape of Ireland but transformed her mental landscape.

Eugene O'Curry (1796–1862)

The frankest tribute to the achievement of Eugene O'Curry was paid by the Breton Celtic scholar Henri Gaidoz:

O'Curry has passed his long life among the numerous manuscripts of the Irish middle ages, reading, collating, copying, translating; he had so saturated himself in them that this old language had become familiar to him before modern linguistics with Zeuss had reconstructed its grammar: no one knew this manuscript literature better than he. . . . Unfortunately, he lacked . . . that breadth of general knowledge which marks the learned man, the *scholar* . . .; above all, he lacked the critical faculty. For him, everything he found in his beloved Irish manuscripts had happened; and we know there is no shortage of the fabulous in the Irish annals, . . . which relate the history of Ireland from before the Flood![33]

Elsewhere in his review Gaidoz refers to O'Curry's 'precious work on the manuscript materials of [Irish] literature' (the title actually used by O'Curry was *Lectures on the Manuscript Materials of Ancient Irish History* (1861)). This stout volume of over seven hundred pages—458 of which contain the twenty-one lectures he delivered at the Catholic University, Dublin, in 1855–6—can be described without exaggeration as the prime source-book of the Literary Revival. Standish James O'Grady's *History of Ireland* (two vols., 1878–80) has sometimes been mistakenly assigned this role, but O'Grady, knowing no Irish, seems to have begun his work intending to synthesize the *MS Materials* with O'Curry's second series of lectures, *On the Manners and Customs of the Ancient Irish* (three vols., 1873). Among other writers familiar with O'Curry's great works we may cite Ferguson, Aubrey de Vere, Lady Gregory, and A. E.: Yeats included the *MS Materials* in 'a list of some forty best Irish books' (1895) under the heading 'Folklore and Legend'. Synge's 1902 article '*La vieille littérature irlandaise*' shows how carefully he had read the first lecture in *MS Materials*. The same work appears in a list of his own library made by Douglas Hyde, aged 20, alongside O'Curry's edition and translation of *The Battle of Magh*

---

[32] Stokes, *The Life and Labours*, 313.
[33] See the review by Henri Gaidoz of *Manners and Customs* in *Revue Celtique* (translated by V. M.), ii. 260–1.

Leana (1855) and 'A beautiful [MS] volume of poetry' transcribed by O'Curry and O'Donovan.[34]

The uninitiated might wonder what attraction poets and playwrights could possibly find in such forbiddingly titled works as O'Curry's, but in fact they are treasure-houses for the creative writer—especially at those points where they become the despair of the historian or the archaeologist. The only trace of misgiving shown by O'Curry himself occurs at the start of one lecture 'I almost begin to fear you will set me down as a story-teller myself, and not a lecturer upon the grave subject of the Materials of our Ancient History, before I shall have completed my intended notices of the pieces called Historic Tales.'[35] (273) The *MS Materials* offers to the careful reader of the appendices as well as the main text summaries of almost every prose tale and many important poems from the whole range of early Irish literature.

It is to the *Manners and Customs*, however, that one must turn for long quotations: for example, the *Táin Bó Cuailnge* is summarized in a half-dozen pages of the earlier work, but in the later one we find dozens of pages of almost continuous quotation from the *Táin* to illustrate such topics as weapons, military training, dress and ornaments. O'Curry's discussion of the magical practices of the Druids in *Manners and Customs* must have fascinated A. E., whose bibliographer lists it among 'Books known to A. E. in youth'.[36] I am not sure how familiar Yeats was with this work: although it contains the earliest retelling in English known to me of *Tochmarc Etáine*, it may not be the source of his narrative poem 'The Two Kings', written in 1912. Lady Gregory, however, cites O'Curry as her first source for the chapter 'Midhir and Etain' in *Gods and Fighting Men* (1904). What I *am* sure of is that O'Grady inspired the following crucial passage in *The Land of Heart's Desire* (1894):

> a Princess Edain,
> A daughter of a King of Ireland, heard
> A voice singing on a May Eve like this,
> And followed, half awake and half asleep,
> Until she came into the Land of Faery,
> Where nobody gets old and godly and grave,
> Where nobody gets old and crafty and wise,
> Where nobody gets old and bitter of tongue.

34 'Appendix 1', in Dominic Daly, *The Young Douglas Hyde* (Dublin: Irish Univ. Press, 1974), 174–80. J. M. Synge, *Collected Works*. Prose ed. Alan Price (London: Oxford Univ. Press, 1966), ii. 353. W. B. Yeats, *Uncollected Prose*, ed. John P. Frayne (New York: Columbia Univ. Press, 1970), i. 386.
35 Eugene O'Curry, *Lectures on the Manuscript Materials of Irish History*, re-issue (Dublin: William A. Hinch, Patrick Traynor, 1878), 273.
36 Alan Denson, *Printed Writings of George W. Russell (A.E.): A Bibliography* (Evanston, Illinois: Northwestern Univ. Press, 1961), 178.

Mary Bruin, the speaker, is herself soon lured away to the Land of Heart's Desire by a fairy child whose singing echoes these last three lines. In his summary of the tale O'Curry cannot resist translating in full the poem of seven stanzas with which Midir invites Edain

> To a wonderful country which is mine,
> Where the people's hair is of golden hue,
> And their bodies the colour of virgin snow . . .
>
> Where no one ever dies of decrepit age . . .[37]

Yeats's haunting three lines are surely a gloss on the last line quoted above. O'Curry recounts this love story in the first of his two lectures 'Of Druids and Druidism in ancient Erin'—those most likely to attract Yeats's attention. Two further points: Yeats adopts O'Curry's unusual spelling 'Edain'; also, he seems to have stored away the phrase 'virgin snow' for retrieval decades later in *The Herne's Egg*.

One must resist the temptation to multiply examples: an entire book might be written on the Revival's debt to O'Curry. Take for instance the tragic story of Baile and Aillinn: we might have waited another century for its discovery had he not decided to give the full Irish text and a literal translation as 'evidence' that literacy existed in second-century Ireland.[38] Yeats's narrative poem 'Baile and Aillinn' was written in 1901 and first published in 1902; the footnote to the first printing refers readers to Lady Gregory's *Cuchulain of Muirthemne*, which may have been his only source because, like her, he omits the charming motif of the two writing tablets—made from the trees that grew out of the lovers' respective graves—which sprang together and could never again be separated. Lady Gregory knew this motif from O'Curry and from Kuno Meyer's edition of a variant text: her omission of it suggests a failure of her imagination. Lacking this wholly satisfying conclusion to the story, Yeats invented an even more remarkable one in 'Ribh at the Tomb of Baile and Aillinn', written in 1934. Were it not for O'Curry, this tale of star-crossed lovers might have appeared in English too late to haunt Yeats's imagination in his prime as well as in old age.[39]

O'Curry was almost 60 when Newman appointed him a professor at the Catholic University: until then, his career was that of a traditional Irish scribe. For example, he copied for the press the whole of his brother-in-law John O'Donovan's Annals of the Four Masters, yet his own name did not appear on a title-page until 1855. O'Curry's four

---

[37] Eugene O'Curry, *On the Manners and Customs of the Ancient Irish*, ed. W. K. Sullivan, 3 vols. (London: Williams & Norgate, 1873), ii. 192–3.

[38] O'Curry, *MS Materials*, 463–7, 472–5.

[39] Gregory, *Cuchulain*, 305–6; see also 'Note by W. B. Yeats on the conversation of Cuchulain and Emer', 23, quoting O'Curry, *MS Materials*, 446.

contributions to the learned journal of the new university, *The Atlantis: A Register of Literature and Science*, were destined to put the Revival further in his debt. The first was his edition and translation of 'The Sick-bed of Cuchulainn and the Only Jealousy of Eimer', which became, via Lady Gregory, the source of one of the best of Yeats's later verse plays, *The Only Jealousy of Emer*. His other contributions were texts and translations of the 'Three Most Sorrowful Tales'—also known as the 'Three Sorrows of Story-Telling'. 'The Exile of the Children of Uisnech' was already well-known thanks to O'Flanagan and others; 'The Fate of the Children of Lir', as O'Curry notes, has been translated by Griffin, though Gregory refers only to *Atlantis* in *Gods and Fighting Men*; the true novelty was the *editio princeps* of 'The Fate of the Children of Tuireann', again with a full translation. The two latter stories, though never as popular as the tale of Deirdre, soon became widely known, partly as textbooks published by the Society for the Preservation of the Irish Language; though often retold and occasionally dramatized, neither found classic expression in a work comparable to Yeats's *Deirdre* or Synge's *Deirdre of the Sorrows*. Nevertheless, no discussion of the omnipresent image of the swan in Yeats's work can afford to overlook the Children of Lir, who were forced to haunt the lakes and seas of Ireland for years in the form of swans.

Manner and Customs did not appear until eleven years after O'Curry's death; this long delay must not be attributed to the laziness of the editor, W. K. Sullivan, but to his excessive industry: the entire first volume of nearly 700 pages is taken up by his preface and introduction. His main object in writing the latter was 'to bring . . . Irish Archaeology and History, as treated of by O'Curry, into connection with those of the other countries of Northern and Western Europe'.[40] Sullivan, Professor of Chemistry at the Catholic University and editor of *Atlantis*, was somewhat of a polymath: having studied under Liebig at Giessen, he knew German well and was thus able to keep abreast of the latest developments in Celtic philology, but he had set himself an impossible task. Gaidoz, in the review already quoted, said, 'Mr. Sullivan would have better served the memory of his friend . . . by publishing his lectures without this indigestible commentary.'

Happily, fine literature can be made out of poor history, as Aristotle was among the first to recognize. Gaidoz admits that *Manners and Customs* is 'an encyclopaedia of ancient Ireland drawn from the Irish manuscripts themselves'; it is the reader's business 'to disentangle mythology from legend, to distinguish reality from fiction'. The Revival

---

40 O'Curry, *Manners and Customs*, i. 13.

writers felt little need for such distinctions, provided that their reading stimulated the imagination. Doubtless they ignored Sullivan's introduction as pedantic while feeling grateful to him for including in vol. iii the first edition and translation of a long and moving episode from the *Táin Bó Cuailnge*, 'The Fight of Ferdiad and Cuchulain'. Whitley Stokes, in a characteristically savage review of 'this fantastic book', demolished whatever reputation Sullivan had as a Celticist and even questioned O'Curry's command of Middle Irish.[41] Nevertheless, *MS Materials* stands unassailable today, regardless of its successor. Sullivan's best work is forgotten now, but for its time his long article 'Celtic Literature' in the ninth edition of the *Encyclopaedia Britannica*, with its copious bibliography, served as a landmark.

John O'Daly and the Ossianic Society

In their anxiety to recover the ancient history of Ireland, O'Curry especially and O'Donovan to a lesser degree tended to ignore the living Irish language, with its treasures of folklore and folksong. It would be hard to discover from their published works that original poetry was still being written in Irish within their lifetimes, a fact that the editor and publisher John O'Daly (1800?–78) almost never allows us to forget. Born in the parish of Modeligo in the Decies (Déise Mumhan), County Waterford, he loved to recall his own and his father's friendships with the Munster poets. The religious poet Tadhg Gaelach O'Suilleabháin (d. 1799) was often a guest of Eamonn, the father, before John was born; another religious poet, Patrick Denn, was born in Modeligo in 1781. John remembered meeting a less reputable figure, the famous Donncha Rua Mac Conmara, then blind and over 90, 'about 1808', at the parish school of Modeligo, which he visited to impose an '*Income tax*' (his dues as a poet) on both master and scholars.[42]

A brief obituary in the *Irish Builder* described O'Daly as 'a much-neglected man' despite his friendship with Petrie, O'Curry, and O'Donovan, and so he has remained. There is no entry for him in the *DNB*, nor is his name mentioned in James F. Kenney's otherwise all-inclusive chapter 'History in Ireland'—doubtless because his interests were exclusively literary. At least one later edition of *The Poets and Poetry of Munster*, his most popular if not his most important work, manages to omit his name altogether! Is this because he 'renounced the Catholic creed' for a time and 'became a pious Biblical', teaching Irish to the

[41] Whitley Stokes in *Revue Celtique*, iii. 90–101; Gaidoz' quotations from *Revue Celtique*, ii. 262 (tr. V. M.).
[42] *The Irish Language Miscellany: A Selection of Poems by the Munster Bards of the Last Century*, collected and ed. John O'Daly (Dublin: John O'Daly, 1876), iii–iv.

Wesleyans of Kilkenny?[43] He had returned to his ancestral faith by 1845, the year he left Kilkenny for Dublin, opened a bookshop in Anglesey Street, and started organizing what became the Celtic Society. O'Daly intended this to be a more democratic version of the Irish Archaeological Society, with an annual membership charge one-third that of the older society: this 'will enable any man of the middle classes to join'. He was encouraged by the *Nation*, and Thomas Davis and other Young Irelanders lent their names; more tangible assistance was given by William Elliott Hudson (1796–1853), a generous patron of Irish culture, who paid the editors of all the Celtic Society publications and settled the debts of the Society just before its merger with the IAS in 1853. In the same year, that of his death, he helped O'Daly to found the Ossianic Society. In 1845 Hudson had advanced £300 to James Duffy to help start the 'Library of Ireland', whose importance will be indicated in Chapter 3.[44]

O'Daly's first publication, *Reliques of Irish Jacobite Poetry* (1844), was unmistakably in the Hardiman tradition: he supplied the text and commentary—and, unlike Hardiman, a literal translation—but Edward Walsh provided the metrical English versions: these are better than those by Hardiman's fumblers but not in the same class as Ferguson's. The Dublin publisher abandoned the project after fifteen eight-page weekly numbers had appeared; O'Daly prefaced the second edition, issued in 1866 over his own imprint, with a brief, affectionate memoir of Walsh (1805–50). O'Daly's next venture in the same genre was much more successful: not only did he himself publish a complete volume but he profited by his new translator's high reputation as a poet. James Clarence Mangan always appears in library catalogues as the author of *The Poets and Poetry of Munster* (1849). On the title-page, O'Daly represents his own share in the book as the provision of biographical sketches for the Gaelic poets: in fact, he must also have chosen most of the poems, persuaded Mangan to Anglicize them in the original metres, and edited the music and the Irish texts. This is the moment to insist that O'Daly borrowed only three or four texts from Hardiman during his entire life, while making available in print for the first time more than 150 poems and songs.[45]

43 John Keegan, in a letter quoted in D. J. O'Donoghue, *The Life and Writings of James Clarence Mangan* (Edinburgh: Patrick Geddes; Dublin: M. H. Gill, 1897), 168.

44 O'Daly issued a single-sheet 'Prospectus' for 'The Irish [sic] Celtic Society' in September 1845 that includes the remark about the middle classes and lists Davis and Charles Gavan Duffy as members of the Provisional Committee. For W. E. Hudson, see the unsigned memoir, almost certainly by O'Daly, in *Transactions of the Ossianic Society*, iv. pp. xv–xx.

45 See 'Introduction', xi–xii, and 'James Clarence Mangan', xiii–xvi, in *The Poets and Poetry of Munster: A selection of Irish songs by the poets of the last century, with poetical translations by the late James Clarence Mangan, now for the first time published. With the original music, and biographical sketches of the authors* by John O'Daly (Dublin: John O'Daly, 1849). To verify the comparison between Hardiman and O'Daly, consult Risteard de Hae and Brighid ni Dhonnchadha, (eds.), *Clár Litridheacht na Nua-Ghaedhilge 1850–1936*, 3 vols. (Dublin: Oifig Dhíolta Foilseacháin Rialtais, 1938), i. 161–5, and compare with the contents of *Irish Minstrelsy*.

In his life of Mangan, D. J. O'Donoghue complains that the translations made for O'Daly 'are rarely of high poetical merit. . . . Of the
fifty-six poems in the book, not much more than a dozen are worthy of
Mangan's gifts.' There is truth in this criticism: the poet seems to have
felt hampered when writing in the metre of the original poem, usually
to fit the traditional music transcribed by O'Daly. Freer versions by
Mangan of several of these poems may be found elsewhere: they are, in
O'Donoghue's words, 'rather voluntaries on Irish themes than translations';[46] this is also a fair assessment of the versions published serially
in the *Dublin University Magazine* under the title *Anthologia Hibernica*.
One must add that Mangan was gravely ill during the preparation of
the O'Daly book and died before its publication: the possibility that
some of the weaker translations are not even by a debilitated Mangan
but by O'Daly himself cannot be totally ruled out.

In 1860 O'Daly published a second series of *The Poets and Poetry
of Munster*: besides new Irish texts it included forty-six verse translations
by the young George Sigerson (1836–1925) under the pseudonym
'Erionnach'. Sigerson, who became deservedly famous in medical research
and prominent in other fields, did not possess great artistic gifts, but he
had studied Irish. In a memorial preface to the third edition of Sigerson's
Bards of the Gael and Gall (1925), Douglas Hyde, who himself belonged
to the O'Daly tradition, paid this tribute to Sigerson's collaborator:

O'Daly was a fine Irish scholar of the old traditional type, and had acquired as
a result of ceaseless searching a great number of Irish MSS. He had made an
excellent collection of poetry out of these for Mangan.[47]

The Ossianic Society made the unprecedented rule that each officer
and council member 'must necessarily be an Irish scholar'; this and the
small annual subscription of five shillings guaranteed that it would be
the most democratic body yet organized for Irish studies, foreshadowing
the even greater democracy of the Gaelic League forty years later. John
O'Daly was the Honorary Secretary throughout the brief life of the
society, 1853–61, and printed all of its six volumes of *Transactions* as
well as editing vols. iv and v. The object of the Society was to publish
Irish manuscripts 'relating to the Fenian period of our history, and
other historical documents, with literal translations and notes'.[48] As one
might expect, none of the works published would now be classed as
historical, but some of them enchanted the writers of the Revival. The
first two volumes contained two rather tedious narratives from the Finn

---

[46] O'Donoghue, *The Life and Writings*, 167, 168.

[47] Douglas Hyde, 'A Memorial Preface', in George Sigerson, *Bards of the Gael and Gall*, 3rd
edn. (Dublin: Talbot Press; London: T. Fisher Unwin, 1925), x.

[48] 'General Rules', prefixed to each volume of the *Transactions*.

cycle: Lady Gregory abridged them in *Gods and Fighting Men*, but they did not inspire any creative work. Nicholas O'Kearney's English versions were pedestrian, and his commentary in vol. ii was longer than the text and translation together.

The next two volumes were the best of the series by far, inspiring Yeats's *The Wanderings of Oisin* as well as some interesting work by other writers. It was perhaps unlucky for O'Daly's reputation that he entrusted the edition of *Laoidh Oisín ar Thir na n-Og* ('The Land of Youth') in vol. iv to Brian O'Looney rather than undertaking it himself, but since the original (*c.*1749) was by a known poet, Michael Comyn, it is to him rather than to the editor that credit is given. Another outstanding—though incomplete—text in vol. iv is *Macgnímartha Finn* ('The Boyhood Exploits of Finn Mac Cumhail'), edited and translated by O'Donovan. This lively narrative included a fragment of early Irish nature poetry, O'Donovan's translation of which Standish James O'Grady hailed as worthy of the Greek lyric poet Alcman; it begins, 'Spring, delightful time!' Kuno Meyer, Kenneth Jackson, and Gerard Murphy, all of whom had studied the complete text of the poem, agree on its beauty but on very little else: their translations differ widely. To quote Jackson's last printed comment after more than thirty-five years' study, 'There are several obscurities in this difficult poem, and some words whose meaning is unknown.'[49] One thing is certain, however: John O'Donovan lacked the scholarship to translate this ninth/tenth-century text.[50] The rest of the Ossianic Society's manuscripts were in classical Modern Irish—as was the Annals of the Four Masters, for example— and presented their editors with relatively few difficulties.

Yeats amplified Comyn's poem and enriched its meaning by having his Oisin visit two other islands besides the Land of Youth, characterizing the three as 'Vain gaiety, vain battle, vain repose' in a late poem, 'The Circus Animals' Desertion'. The idea of the third island, in which everyone is lulled asleep by the shaking of 'a branch soft-shining with bells', surely came to Yeats from a Modern Irish version of *Echtra Chormaic* in vol. iii, translated by Standish Hayes O'Grady under the title 'How Cormac Mac Airt Got His Branch'. This magic object is described in the first paragraph of the tale as 'a glittering fairy branch with nine apples of red gold upon it . . . when any one shook it wounded men and women with child would be lulled to sleep by the

49 Kenneth Hurlstone Jackson, *A Celtic Miscellany*, rev. edn. (Harmondsworth: Penguin Books, 1971), 307. For his transl., 'May-time', 63–4. Kuno Meyer, 'Song of Summer', *Selections from Ancient Irish Poetry*, new edn. (London: Constable, 1959), 54–5, and note, 113. Gerard Murphy, 'May-day', *Early Irish Lyrics* (Oxford: Clarendon Press, 1956), 156–9, and note, 233–4.

50 O'Donovan, however, instantly recognized Zeuss's achievement. See his review of *Grammatica Celtica* in *Ulster Journal of Archaeology* (1859), vii. 11–32, 79–92.

sound'. Another property of the branch made it even more appropriate as a symbol to Yeats: it induced forgetfulness—'and whatever evil might have befallen any one he would not remember it at the shaking of the branch'.[51] The bell-branch forms the central image of another early Yeats poem, 'The Dedication to a Book of Stories' (first publ. 1890).

The third volume of the *Transactions* has much else to recommend it. O'Grady's introduction is full of succinct information and criticism indispensable to the understanding of the Finn cycle and medieval Irish notions about prose style. His translation of the romantic tale *Toruigheacht Dhiarmuda agus Ghráinne* ('The Pursuit of Diarmuid and Gráinne') has become classic: as early as 1865 Ferguson acknowledged his debt to 'the spirited version of Mr O'Grady' in an introductory note to his own poem 'The Death of Dermid'.[52] It was probably a source for Joyce's *Finnegans Wake* and certainly one for that unhappy dramatic collaboration between Yeats and George Moore, *Diarmuid and Grania* (1901). Lady Gregory essentially follows O'Grady, sometimes word for word, in *Gods and Fighting Men*, except that she avoids his archaisms. She also wrote a three-act, three-character tragedy, *Grania*, in 1912; it attempts to make sense for a modern audience of Gráinne's return to Finn, her elderly husband, after he has caused the death of her young lover, Diarmuid. O'Grady edited and translated one further item in vol. iii, a long poem whose English title is 'The Lamentation of Oisin after the Fenians'. This must be one of the sources for the passages of dialogue in *The Wanderings of Oisin*: Yeats himself supplied a note saying, 'The poem is founded upon the Middle Irish dialogues of Saint Patrick and Oisin and a certain Gaelic poem of the last century.'[53] He was mistaken in thinking that the language of the poems was older than early Modern Irish, but the hostility between saint and hero at the end of *The Wanderings of Oisin* suggests that he also knew the first poem in vol. iv of the *Transactions*, 'The Dialogue of Oisin and Patrick'. The most notorious of its quatrains, much appreciated by Frank O'Connor, runs as follows in O'Daly's literal translation:

> Were my son Oscur and God
> Hand to hand on Cnoc-na-bh-Fionn,
> If I saw my son down,
> I would say that God was a strong man.[54]

[51] *Toruigheacht Dhiarmuda agus Ghrainne; or, The Pursuit after Diarmuid O'Duibhne, and Grainne the Daughter of Cormac Mac Airt, King of Ireland in the Third Century*, ed. Standish Hayes O'Grady, Transactions of the Ossianic Society (Dublin: Printed for the Ossianic Society, by John O'Daly, 1857), iii. 213.

[52] Ferguson, *Lays*, 154.

[53] *The Variorum Edition of the Poems of W. B. Yeats*, ed. Peter Allt and Russell K. Alspach (New York: Macmillan, 1957), 793.

[See opposite for n. 54]

The whole poem is worth reading, if only as an extreme example of outrageous humour. Pious though he was in his later years, O'Daly sees the joke and does not flinch from the blasphemy, which shows, after all, only a pagan's invincible ignorance.

O'Daly's other volume of the *Transactions*, the sixth and final one, containing the Second Series of *Laoithe Fiannuigheachta* or Fenian poems, offers nothing so amusing or enchanting as the First Series. As for vol. v, its editor, Owen Connellan (1800–69), would seem to have emptied the contents of his desk drawers into it. Nevertheless, it was the source of *The King's Threshold*, an early play by Yeats. The work that supplies the volume with its title is *Imtheacht na Tromdháimhe* ('The Proceedings of the Great Bardic Institution' in Connellan's cumbrous and imprecise translation). This is a prose satire on the rivalry between bards and saints at the court of the generous King Guaire: it has some very funny moments even in the too-literal translation. Yeats confessed that he 'twisted it about and revised its moral' so much that the play became a tragedy in which the poet Seanchan fasted to death in protest against Guaire's limitation of bardic privileges. In the earliest version (1903) of *The King's Threshold* Guaire gave his crown to Seanchan rather than incur the odium of having caused his death. Yeats concludes the note already cited with these words: 'One of my fellow-playwrights is going, I have hope, to take the other side and make a play that can be played after it, as in Greece the farce followed the tragedy'.[55] The play referred to, Lady Gregory's *The Shoelace*, was never performed at the Abbey and was published only posthumously.

DECLINE AND RENEWAL: THE 1870S

The Ossianic Society published no further volumes after 1861 because its membership was declining: 195 members who were so far in arrears that they had not subscribed for vol. v. had their names dropped from the membership list published in vol. vi. The Irish Archaeological and Celtic Society struggled on until the death of its founder, J. H. Todd, in 1869, after which it published only one more book before its official demise in 1880. It seems strange that the original IAS published its lavish volumes in the 'hungry Forties', and that these were matched by Petrie's *Ecclesiastical Architecture* and the early volumes of O'Donovan's edition of the Four Masters in the same famine decade. Why should the

---

54 *Laoithe Fiannuigheachta; or, Fenian Poems*, ed. John O'Daly, Transactions of the Ossianic Society (Dublin: Printed for the Society, by John O'Daly, 1859), iv. 47. See also Frank O'Connor, *Kings, Lords, & Commons* (New York: Knopf, 1959), 28.

55 Yeats, *Variorum Plays*, 315.

1860s and the early 1870s show a relative decline in Celtic studies in Ireland? We must partly blame the calendar: the deaths of O'Donovan, O'Curry, Petrie, and Todd followed each other in rapid succession during the sixties. Apart from this, Irish society was being polarized in new ways. We shall see in Chapter 3 how the Catholic Church reacted to Evangelical Protestantism after the famine; Protestants reacted in their turn to the threat and then the actuality of Disestablishment, which was legislated in 1869. The Fenian movement, however, suggests an even deeper fissure: whereas Young Ireland, its predecessor, attracted some young Protestants like Davis and Mitchel, all the Fenian leaders belonged to the Catholic community.

Despite the failure of the Fenian rising in 1867, a feeling began to spread abroad, for the first time since the famine, that Ireland might have a future as well as a past. Disestablishment, the new legislation for the redistribution of land, the foundation of the Irish Party at Westminster, all drew the attention of the educated away from antiquarian studies. The new emphasis on learning spoken Irish had a progressive as well as a regressive aspect: Pearse and many others of his generation would come to regard the language as an indispensable feature of a new, independent Ireland. The Society for the Preservation of the Irish Language was founded in 1876 and the more democratic and dynamic Gaelic Union in 1878. Douglas Hyde was an active member of the latter from its foundation; when it merged with the Gaelic League in 1893, its periodical Irisleabhair na Gaeilge, *The Gaelic Journal* (1882–1909) was continued by the League. As already stated at the beginning of this chapter, studies in Old and Middle Irish became the preserve of Continental and British scholars.

O'Daly died in 1878, just as his ideas about the importance of the living language were beginning to prevail. In one respect, however, he remained in advance of his time: his use of the Roman alphabet for texts in Irish. In the introduction to an important collection of religious poetry edited by himself, *Timothy O'Sullivan's (commonly called Tadhg Gaelach) Pious Miscellany* (1858), he justified the practice by explaining that the readers for whom he has collected the poems of his father's friend and other writers, including original poems in both Irish and English by Patrick Denn, are illiterate in Irish: although native Gaelic speakers, they have learnt to read only English in school and do not know the Gaelic alphabet. This book was not for 'the middle classes' and contained no translations; except for one version by Mangan, the same is true of *The Irish Language Miscellany* (1876), O'Daly's final selection from his beloved Munster bards. He was, by the way, earlier responsible for the first printing, without translation, of that most notorious of Munster poems, Brian Merriman's *The Midnight Court*. Despite its ribaldry, John Eglinton called it 'the best Irish poem', and Yeats wrote an introduction for Arland Ussher's translation (1926).[56] By coincidence, Ussher's little volume also included his version of *Eachtra Ghiolla an Amaráin*, a longish humorous poem by Donncha Rua Mac Conmara that O'Daly had been the first to publish in both Irish and English. John O'Daly might have said more truly than most men, 'In my end is my beginning': the introduction of the *Irish Language Miscellany* shows him still reminiscing about the poets he had met in his youth and declaring his readiness to buy good Irish manuscripts 'at a fair value'.

Standish Hayes O'Grady (1832–1915)

The traditional Irish scholar did not become extinct with O'Daly: he had left behind him a friend and collaborator whose birth and education were the antithesis of his own. Whereas O'Daly was once described as 'vulgar in appearance and manners' and had only a parish-school education, Standish Hayes O'Grady was the son of an admiral, the nephew of a peer, and educated at Rugby School and TCD. When he went to Rugby, aged 14, he was already 'deeply versed in the language and traditions of the countryside' near Castleconnell, County Limerick, where Irish was still being spoken. His first book, which he edited under the pseudonym 'S. Hayes', was *Adventures of Donnchadh Ruadh Mac Con-mara* (1853), already mentioned as having been published by O'Daly. After the issue of his Ossianic Society volume in 1857, he disappeared from Celtic scholarship during a quarter of a century. For some ten years he led an adventurous life as a sailor, gold-miner, and civil engineer; after inheriting property from his father, he made use of some of his leisure to study Arabic.

In 1882, however, he stood for the chair of Celtic at Edinburgh; unsuccessful there, four years later he undertook to compile a catalogue of the Irish manuscripts in the British Museum which was left unfinished at his death. The printed sheets of his contribution, however, were available to scholars for many years before being published in 1926 as the first volume of the completed work. I wonder if any other library catalogue has ever been quite so idiosyncratic; bibliographical information varies from the cursory to the minute, but O'Grady is rarely content with this: he comments, annotates, engages in literary criticism

56 *Mediae Noctis Consilium Auctore Mac-Gilla-Meidhre . . . (Curtha a g-lodh le Tomas Mhic Lopuis, ag Loch an Chonblaig Oghair*, MDCCC [i.e., Dublin: John O'Daly, 1850?]). John Eglinton, 'The Best Irish Poem', *Anglo-Irish Essays* (Dublin: Talbot Press; London: Unwin, 1917), 47–56. W. B. Yeats, 'Introduction', *The Midnight Court and The Adventures of a Luckless Fellow*, transl. Percy Arland Ussher (London: Cape, 1926), 5–12.

and supplies lively translations of his favourite passages. No wonder Robin Flower described it as 'a book for the general reader to be read often and again for pleasure'. Having read widely in the work myself, I can testify to the pleasure, even where the manuscripts deal with law or medicine, though of course the poetry is the most attractive. No Revival writer appears to have sought access to the unpublished work: fortunately, O'Grady poured many of the fruits of his labours into a cornucopia entitled *Silva Gadelica* (two vols. 1892), a collection of thirty-one Irish tales varying widely in length and subject matter; the second volume contains the English translations, which equal or surpass those he made for the Ossianic Society. Lady Gregory pillaged the *Silva* for *Gods and Fighting Men*, and James Stephens found there some of the best stories in his *Irish Fairy Tales* (1920). Among the works chosen by O'Grady, many of which appeared in print for the first time, were four saints' lives, a number of legends from the cycles of the traditional kings (including the 'Death of Fergus Mac Leide', a possible source for *Gulliver's Travels*), four humorous stories that he classes simply as fiction, and several items from the Finn cycle. One of these last, *Agallamh na Senórach*, is by far the longest selection in the book: it recounts conversations between St Patrick and two survivors of the Fianna, Oisin and Cáilte, who tell him everything they can remember of pagan lore about places and deeds precious to Finn and his fellows. Unlike the poems published by the Ossianic Society, this works shows saint and heroes treating each other with great courtesy: some awareness of it underlies the nostalgia for paganism felt, in greater or lesser degree, by every writer of the Revival.

Also important to the Revival were O'Grady's two contributions to Eleanor Hull's *The Cuchullin Saga in Irish Literature* (1898): a translation entitled 'The Great Defeat on the Plain of Muirthemne' (*Bríslech Mor Maige Murthemne*) and an analysis with extracts in translation from a modern manuscript of *Táin Bó Cuailnge*. O'Grady's last major work to be published, an edition and translation of *Caithréim Thoirdhealbhaigh* or *The Triumphs of Turlough* (two vols., 1929), appeared when the Revival proper was already over. Robin Flower's introduction to this work includes a four-page biography of O'Grady and pays tribute to his 'extraordinary command of the resources of the English language, which makes his versions at once a brilliant interpretation and a lively commentary on their originals'. Flower also refers to 'the ever-present humour, often in so right a harmony with his subject.'[57] At times, though, his fellow scholars must have thought his humour rather out of place. He showed a cavalier attitude to the new Celtic scholarship in the preface to the second volume of *Silva Gadelica*:

here is raw material for 'keltologue' and 'philologue', for folklorist, comparative mythologist, and others. Personally, I cannot boast of being anything that ends in either '-logue' or '-ist': that is to say in these countries; were I back in the United States, I should of course profess at least the arts of 'breathist', 'eatist', 'sleepist', and 'walkist'.[58]

O'Grady was neither a charlatan nor a dilettante, but he refused to submerge the gentleman in the scholar. For better or worse, we may never see his like again.

Whitley Stokes (1830–1909)

Whitley Stokes, the eldest son of Petrie's biographer, had an attitude to scholarship very different from O'Grady's: his father, William Stokes, FRS, Regius Professor of Physic in TCD, was one of a brilliant generation of Dublin physicians who strove to make medicine a science. It is hardly surprising that scientific philology rather than history or literature attracted the younger Stokes to Irish studies, although he was friendly with O'Curry and O'Donovan. He graduated from TCD before Rudolf T. Siegfried was appointed the first Professor of Sanskrit and Comparative Philology in 1862 (having been a lecturer in the same subjects since 1858, but in fact Siegfried had been visiting Dublin for a number of years before achieving this recognition, and it was from him that Stokes learned German rigour. Stokes chose as his first Herculean labour the editing of all the Old and Middle Irish glosses and glossaries not yet published. Only when he had finished this task did he turn to literature; here too, in the words of James F. Kenney, 'His achievement was prodigious: of the Old and Middle Irish literature now available in scholarly editions and translations a much larger portion is due to him than to any one other man.'[59] In a sense, this is as true today as it was in 1929, but Stokes's works are 'available' only in highly specialized libraries. Even in his lifetime, his impact on the Revival was far smaller than it should have been because most of his work that was of literary interest appeared in learned journals or from specialist presses in France, Germany or even India: incredible as it may seem, his official employment from 1862 to 1882 was devoted to the study and codification of the native laws of India!

---

57 All quotations and biographical data about O'Grady are from Robin Flower, 'Introduction: 1. Standish Hayes O'Grady', in Seán (Mac Ruaidhrí) Mac Craith, *Caithreim Thoirdhealbhaigh*, ed. Standish Hayes O'Grady, 2 vols., Irish Texts Society XXVI & XXVII (London: Simpkin, Marshall, 1929), i. pp. ix–xiii.

58 *Silva Gadelica: A Collection of Tales in Irish*, ed. & transl. Standish H. O'Grady, 2 vols. (London: Williams & Norgate, 1892), ii. p. xxv. Kuno Meyer in a review regretfully concludes that whereas 'it was hoped that the *Silva Gadelica* would leave far behind the work of earlier native scholars', in fact 'Such hopes were destined to be disappointed'. For example, 'Dr O'Grady's spelling is a mixture of the usages of ten centuries. 'See *Revue Celtique* (1893) xiv. 321–37.

59 Kenney, *Sources*, 74.

I do not entirely agree with Kenney's judgement that Stokes's translations show 'an accuracy, felicity and conciseness that have never been surpassed': he was more accurate than both O'Donovan and O'Grady—and certainly more concise than the latter—but he could not match their felicity. The late David Greene, himself a master of English prose as well as a great Celtic scholar, preferred O'Grady. Still, we must forever regret that Stokes did not produce the edition and translation of the *Táin Bó Cuailnge* which, Kuno Meyer says, he was already meditating in the late 1850s. He was better fitted to edit the text—more correctly speaking, texts—than any other scholar of his time. No doubt it was the translation that raised insoluble problems: on the one hand, the passages of archaic verse in the earliest text still cause difficulty for translators; on the other hand, it would have been hard in those days to find a printer or publisher in the English-speaking world willing to undertake an unexpurgated translation. Furthermore, if one were found, Stokes would still have been subject to attack by Irish nationalists for exposing his country to ridicule, as Synge was attacked in 1907. Publication on the Continent could not have averted this last risk. In a penetrating article on the political aspects of the translations actually made of the work, Maria Tymoczko sums up the problem as follows:

The fact is that *Táin Bó Cúailnge* . . . was an embarrassment. It could not be translated fully and accurately if the political aims to establish the Irish as dignified and to display their ancient and noble culture were to be achieved.[60]

As she points out, not until Thomas Kinsella's *The Táin* (1969) did a translator 'undertake a transposition of the sexual and grotesque elements of the tale, as well as the bizarre cultural and tonal background'.[61]

If Stokes's sister Margaret, herself a scholarly popularizer of early Christian Irish art, had thought of persuading him to publish a volume of his translations without the original texts, its effect on the Revival might have been powerful indeed, but again the problem of whether to expurgate would have arisen. As things are, *Lives of Saints from the Book of Lismore* (1890) is probably his most immediately attractive book for those who know no Irish. He was the first editor and translator of some of the most interesting early religious texts, including the apocalyptic *Fís Adamnáin*; this he first published privately at Simla in 1870; a translation, 'Adamnain's Vision', appeared in *Fraser's Magazine* (1871). As recently as 1984, the Dublin Institute for Advanced Studies reprinted his edition and translation of *The Martyrology of Angus the*

---

[60] Maria Tymoczko, 'Translating the Old Irish Epic Tain Bo Cuailnge: Political Aspects', in *Nimrod's Sin*, ed. Norman Simms (Hamilton, N.Z.: Outrigger Publishers, 1983), 8.

[61] Tymoczko, 15.

Culdee, but many of his most important translations are available only in the files of the *Revue Celtique*; a few are also in Cross and Slover's *Ancient Irish Tales*, which is not always in print. My own choices are 'The Second Battle of Moytura', 'The Destruction of Da Derga's Hostel', 'The Death of Muirchertach mac Erca', and especially, 'The Voyage of Mael Duin'—the imaginative pinnacle of early Irish literature.

It was Lady Gregory who made most use of Stokes, but we find Yeats rebuking Douglas Hyde for overlooking 'The Death of Cuchullin' in *The Story of Early Gaelic Literature* (1895). Yeats's review of Hyde describes that story as 'among the greatest things of all legendary literature'. Just before this assertion there is a passage which vividly illuminates the uneasy relationship between Irish scholarship and the Literary Revival:

Hyde is so anxious to convince his little groups of enthusiasts of the historical importance of the early Irish writings . . . that he occasionally seems to forget the noble phantasy and passionate drama which is their crowning glory.[62]

The unscientific—indeed anti-scientific—poet is better fitted to distinguish history from myth than the would-be-scientific scholar.

One cannot be absolutely sure that in 1895 Yeats already knew Stokes's 'Cuchulainn's Death', abridged from the Book of Leinster, which was published in the *Revue Celtique*, vol. iii (1877), and republished in Eleanor Hull's *The Cuchullin Saga* in 1898; the fact remains that priority in print belongs to Stokes and not to Standish James O'Grady, who gave a later version of the story in the final chapter of *History of Ireland*, vol. ii (1880). It is to Stokes in the first instance that we owe the archetypal image of the hero defying his enemies which inspired Oliver Sheppard's famous statue commemorating the 1916 Rising. In his last play, *The Death of Cuchulain* (1939), Yeats refers to the statue, but he also seems to echo Stokes when he makes Cuchulain say:

> I have put my belt
> About this stone and want to fasten it
> And die upon my feet . . .

After the hero has received his fatal wound and asked his enemies' permission to drink from a nearby lake, Stokes's translation runs as follows:

'We give thee leave,' said they, 'provided that thou come to us again.'
   'I will bid you come for me,' said Cu Chulainn, 'if I cannot come myself.'
   Then he gathered his bowels into his breast, and went forth to the loch.
   And there he drank his drink and washed himself, and came forth to die, calling on his foes to come to meet him.

---

[62] Yeats, *Uncollected Prose*, i. 359.

Now a great mearing went westwards from the loch and his eye lit upon it, and he went to a pillar-stone which is in the plain, and he put his breast-girdle round it that he might not die seated nor lying down, but that he might die standing up. Then came the men all around him but they durst not go to him, for they thought he was alive.[63]

Kuno Meyer (1858–1919)

With the entry of so gifted a foreigner as Kuno Meyer upon the Irish literary scene, the Age of the Native Scholar had clearly come to an end. As Kenney says, 'In the extent and quality of his work as editor and translator he rivalled Whitley Stokes.'[64] Meyer translated much early Irish prose and poetry into German, but he also made use of a remarkable command of his second language to produce English versions that can hardly be improved on. Many of these are prose translations of poems whose beauty he was the first to see and to rescue from fading manuscripts. The best examples will be found in *Selections from Ancient Irish Poetry* (1911); almost every poem in the book is a treasure, yet we would possess very few of them but for the research of Meyer. 'The Monk and his Pet Cat', simultaneously witty and affectionate, charms almost every reader. 'On the Flightiness of Thought' is a profound religious meditation which seems very modern because of its introspection. In the sections of the anthology devoted to nature poetry, love poetry, and impressionistic or satirical quatrains, those unfamiliar with literature in Irish will find much to surprise them. The most enigmatic poem is 'The Lament of the Old Woman of Beare', which Meyer pieced together from two somewhat garbled manuscripts.[65] Thanks to him, everyone agrees that this contains the scattered limbs of a great poem, but textual critics are still disputing about how the body should be put back together. There is even dispute about whether the poem is pagan or Christian. Since 1911, many poets have tried to give us a more satisfying English version than Meyer's without total success.

We have to thank Meyer too for making available a number of longer works, in prose or a mixture of prose and verse. Among these is the only Gaelic tale that challenges comparison with Rabelais, *The Vision of Mac Conglinne* (1892). Meyer based his lively translation on one made by a native scholar, William Maunsell Hennessy (1829–89), published in *Fraser's Magazine* (1873). This wild mixture of fantasy,

---

[63] Quoted in his obituary, *Celtic Review* (1909), vi. 72. The translation is quoted from *Ancient Irish Tales*, ed. Tom Peete Cross and Clark Harris Slover (New York: Henry Holt, 1936), 337–8.

[64] Kenney, *Sources*, 78.

[65] For Meyer's translation, based on an edition he published in 1899, see *Selections from Ancient Irish Poetry*, new edn., 90–3, and the note on it, 114. Murphy, *Early Irish Lyrics* (1956), gives a new edition and translation, based on five MSS, 'which are clearly corrupt in many places', 207.

satire, and parody inspired Austin Clarke's play *The Son of Learning*, first performed in 1930 as *The Hunger Demon* at the Dublin Gate Theatre. Another poet, Padraic Fallon, wrote a version for radio, first broadcast in 1953. Long before, Yeats had adopted the strategy he was also to use in *The King's Threshold*, purging the tale of almost all its humour to produce 'The Crucifixion of the Outcast', a story in *The Secret Rose* (1897). Whereas Aniér Mac Conglinne, the poet hero of the Irish tale, triumphs over Church and State, Yeats's Cumhal actually suffers the crucifixion that Aniér adroitly escapes. Cumhal thus enacts the supposed role of the *fin de siècle* artist in bourgeois society.

The Voyage of Bran son of Febel (two vols, 1895–7) included an essay by Alfred Nutt, 'The Celtic Doctrine of Re-birth', with illustrative material translated by Meyer, as well as Meyer's editions and translations of the haunting title poem and a series of imaginative and humorous tales about Mongan Mac Fiachna. James Stephens's 'Mongan's Frenzy' draws on these, as does Austin Clarke's play *The Plot Succeeds* (1950). Two other items in Stephens's *Irish Fairy Tales*, 'The Story of Tuan Mac Cairill' and 'The Boyhood of Fionn', are also indebted to Meyer, while part 1 of *In the Land of Youth* (1924) is based on 'The Adventures of Nera' (*Echtra Nerai*), a text which Meyer was the first to edit and translate.

It seems pointless to continue this list of works great and small that are indebted to Meyer: his influence on George Moore is of much greater interest and significance. Several pages of *Salve*, the second volume of *Hail and Farewell*, offer an affectionate character sketch of 'Kuno Meyer, the great scholar-artist'.[66] Despite Moore's chronic egotism, we can see that he respects Meyer for his brave, uncomplaining struggle against arthritis. Moore also reveals in this passage some of the Irish poems that have most stirred his imagination. 'Have you discovered another Marban—another Liadain and Curithir?' he asks Meyer, Marban being the hermit in the dialogue poem 'King and Hermit' and the others a pair of unlucky lovers from a poem named after them; Meyer first published these poems in 1901 and 1902, respectively. On an earlier page of *Salve*, *à propos* of a blackbird singing in Moore's garden in Ely Place, we find the following tribute to Meyer:

A blackbird delighted the hermits of old time, those that were poets, and we are grateful to one for having recorded his pleasure in the bird's song, . . . and to Kuno Meyer, who discovered the old Irish poem and translated it.[67]

---

[66] George Moore, *Hail and Farewell: Ave, Salve, Vale*, ed. Richard Allen Cave (Gerrards Cross, Bucks: Colin Smythe, 1976), 378; but see the whole passage, 377–83.

[67] Moore, *Hail and Farewell*, 555.

This probably refers to 'The Blackbird' in *Selections*, although other poems also praise the bird's song.

The poem that most influenced Moore, however, was 'To Crinog': Meyer's note to this poem in *Selections* says, in part, 'Crinog was evidently what is known in the literature of early Christianity as . . . *virgo subintroducta . . .* a nun who lived with a priest, monk, or hermit like a sister or "spiritual wife"'.[68] From this little seed, perhaps passed on by Meyer in conversation, sprang a great tree, the two-volume work entitled *A Story-Teller's Holiday*, which achieved its final shape in 1928. The theme of this collection of fictions grave and gay is thus stated in the preface:

in the third and fourth centuries the pious were encouraged by the Church to go into temptation, and by resisting it to win for themselves higher places in heaven . . . a practice early forbidden by Rome, but which continued in Ireland into the twelfth and thirteenth centuries. I had it from Kuno Meyer.[69]

The first story in the book is that of Liadin and Curithir, two poets whose tragedy came about because Liadin had taken a vow of chastity and broke it when St Cummin put them to the ordeal of sleeping together. A happier, highly humorous story is that of Father Scothine, from the notes to *The Martyrology of Oengus the Culdee*, translated by Whitley Stokes.[70] No doubt Meyer drew Moore's attention to the passage, which was later made use of also by Austin Clarke, who may be regarded as a disciple of both Meyer and Moore. Those interested will find much else to enjoy in Moore's busman's holiday. It is time now to turn to the history of the new literary movement in English. We shall find that, while it drew great power from the rediscovery of the Gaelic past, it was also deeply involved, like the Gaelic League, in the discovery of the Gaelic present—its folk life and folklore.

---

[68] Meyer, *Selections*, 112; but see James Carney, 'A Chrinoc, cubaid do cheol', *Éigse: A Journal of Irish Studies*, iv. 280–3, which interprets the poem as addressed to a psalter that the poet had used as a student and has found again many years later.

[69] George Moore, *A Story-Teller's Holiday*, 2 vols., Issued for subscribers only (New York: Horace Liveright, 1928), i. pp. vii–viii.

[70] For Moore's source and his treatment of it, see Vivian Mercier, *The Irish Comic Tradition* (Oxford: Clarendon Press, 1962), 43–4.

2 Irish Writers and English Readers: Literature and Politics, 1798–1845

'remember by being as Irish as you can you will be the more orig[i]nal and true to your self and in the long run more interesting even to English readers.'

W. B. Yeats to Katharine Tynan,
13 August 1887[1]

'Mad Ireland hurt you into poetry,' wrote Auden in his elegy for W. B. Yeats.[2] That was in 1939, but fifty years later it seems to be taken even more for granted that to be born Irish is a fortunate fate for a writer. Auden has been dead for some years, but, as he prophesied, 'Now Ireland has her madness and her weather still'; for 'madness' of course read 'politics', which, madder all the time, presumably hurts more and more Irish people into poetry, drama, or fiction. Furthermore, since the six north-eastern counties are the most politicized part of Ireland, the poets of the rest of the country may be excused for thinking, with mild paranoia, that it is harder for them to win recognition in the outside world than for those born 'up there'.

Even so severe a critic of Anglo-Irish literature as Daniel Corkery partly agrees with this view:

For very many years past [he wrote in 1931], Anglo-Irish literature has been sitting between two stools: when the land is under stress of a national movement the literature makes an effort to seat itself on the truly Anglo-Irish stool,— the writers make an effort to express their own land; but when it is again at peace, the literature returns to the colonial stool—an attitude that pays better—with less work besides, for to 'explore' your own land for the foreigner . . . is far lighter work than to express it to itself.[3]

Malcolm Brown, unlike the sceptical Corkery, goes the whole hog. Having suggested that Shaw, Yeats, and Joyce were three of the four 'most distinguished writers in the British Isles during the first half of the

[1] W. B. Yeats, *Collected Letters*, ed. John Kelly (Oxford: Clarendon Press, 1986), i. 35.
[2] W. H. Auden, *Collected Shorter Poems 1927–1952* (New York: Random House, 1967), 142.
[3] Daniel Corkery, *Synge and Anglo-Irish Literature: A Study* (Cork: Cork University Press; London: Longmans, Green 1931), 10.

twentieth century'—the fourth being D. H. Lawrence—he goes on to ask why all three happened to be natives of Dublin.

A tentative answer that insinuates itself into our thought is that culture must breed where most is going on, where the most profound and excruciating issues drive towards resolution. For, if Dublin in the last hundred years was the least opulent city in the British Isles, it was at the same time the most exciting.

Out of what is civic excitement generated, if not out of history?[4]

When one reads Brown's admirable book *The Politics of Irish Literature: From Thomas Davis to W. B. Yeats* right through, it becomes evident that Irish politics and Anglo-Irish literature are not as closely integrated as the above quotation would lead one to suppose. Someone familiar with that literature but ignorant of Irish history will find on every page of Brown a piece of information or a flash of insight to illuminate previously obscure passages in Joyce and Yeats, but why this particular kind of history produced this particular kind of literature may remain as obscure as ever. Shaw, Yeats, and, especially, Joyce were detested, ridiculed, or misunderstood by the majority of their fellow Irishmen—and vice versa. Though Ireland underwent a revolution in their lifetimes, these writers all felt it was the wrong revolution: provincial and regressive, rather than international and progressive, in the opinion of Shaw and Joyce; too plebeian and democratic to satisfy Yeats.

To improve our perspective of the relationship between literature and politics, let us distance ourselves from the objects of scrutiny further than Brown chose to do. Anglo-Irish literature began to separate itself decisively from English literature with the publication of *Castle Rackrent* in 1800—I offer no apology for so hackneyed a view. Perhaps a study of its first half-century will throw into high relief some of the uncertainties and ambiguities in its relationship with politics that may have escaped notice at a later, less tentative period of its development.

In the 1980s as in the 1800s, the blessing and the curse of Irish writing in English lie in its ready access to a world-wide audience. Corkery says with some justice, though he overstates his case as usual, that all the Anglo-Irish writers he disapproves of 'would have written quite differently if extra-mural influences, such as the proximity of the English literary market and the tradition of expatriation, had not misled them from the start. Whether these extramural forces can be withstood as long as England and Ireland speak the same language is another question'.[5] In the first half of the nineteenth century, Irish writers were

---

[4] Malcolm Brown, *The Politics of Irish Literature: From Thomas Davis to W. B. Yeats* (London: George Allen & Unwin, 1971), 3.

[5] Corkery, 26.

far more dependent upon London publishers than they are now. America offered readers but no royalties, while the reading public in the British possessions was still negligible. Translation into other European languages—unlikely in any case to earn money for the original author—rarely occurred until a writer had won a London reputation. Despite his many contributions to the widely circulated *Dublin University Magazine*, James Clarence Mangan remained unknown in France because he did not write for London periodicals: otherwise, he might have been acclaimed as the Irish rival of the much-admired Edgar Allan Poe. William Carleton was unique in that he supported himself for a dozen years (1829–42) without an English publisher.

With the exception of Carleton in prose fiction and Mangan—and, of course, Davis and Ferguson—in poetry, the shape of Anglo-Irish literature up to 1848, and indeed for most of the century, is dictated by readers in Great Britain: when these are interested in Ireland, our literature proliferates; when they are not, it begins to wither. There are really only three historical 'moments' in the five decades which arouse the fears and curiosity of those readers: first, the 1798 Rising and the consequent legislative union of Great Britain and Ireland in 1801; then the peak years in Daniel O'Connell's campaign for Catholic civil rights, from 1823 to the passing of the not entirely satisfactory Emancipation Act in 1829; and finally, the great famine of 1845–7, with its aftermath of lethal epidemics, eviction, and emigration. The movement in the 1840s for repeal of the Union does not seem to have been regarded in Britain as a serious threat, while the abortive rising of 1848 was overshadowed by more dangerous revolutions on the Continent. The sheer enormity of the famine could not be ignored, however.

The ambitious Belfast publishing firms of Simms and M'Intyre, which had opened a London office in 1844, chose to inaugurate its new fiction series of monthly volumes, at the precedent-shattering price of one shilling each, with Carleton's *The Black Prophet: A Tale of the Irish Famine*. The date was April 1847, and Carleton's grimly powerful novel seems an incongruous choice for first place in a popular series primly named 'The Parlour Library'; it had, however, already been serialised in the *Dublin University Magazine* the year before. The two shrewd Belfast men appear to have gauged their British and Irish audiences correctly, for they published Carleton's equally topical *The Emigrants of Aghadarra* in January 1848 and reprinted his 1839 novel, *Fardorougha the Miser*, the following November. In February 1849 they became for the third time the first publishers of a Carleton novel, *The Tithe Proctor*.[6]

---

[6] J. R. R. Adams, 'Simms and M'Intyre: Creators of the Parlour Library', *Linen Hall Review*, 4:2 (Summer 1987), 12–14.

Fearing to Speak of Ninety-eight: Maria Edgeworth, Moore, and Others

The Rising in 1798 and the years of foreign war and domestic polarization that led up to it proved difficult for the new Anglo-Irish literature to transmute into art. This was hardly surprising, given the traumas that Anglo-Irish society as a whole had suffered. Irish Protestants had many reasons to fear the future. No doubt the risk of a French invasion was uppermost in their minds: the incursion at Killala by a small force in 1798 had not been defeated very easily; what would happen if a much larger force, like the one that was prevented only by bad weather from landing at Bantry Bay in 1796, should secure a beach-head? Almost equally frightening was the awareness of political division within the Protestant communities. Open hostility to the Established Church among Presbyterians had disappeared, but they still resented their exclusion from public office by the Test Act of 1704. A substantial minority of Presbyterians and a significant number of members of the Church of Ireland had made common cause with the common enemy by joining the United Irishmen (1791–8). The common enemy was, in one sense, France rather than the Catholic Irish: the hostility of the French Revolution to Catholicism had made the British Government aware that the Irish priesthood at least were their potential allies. This explains the paradox that Maynooth College and the Orange Order were both founded in 1795. The usefulness of the Protestant Ascendancy to the British Government was seen to be diminishing: perhaps this is sufficient explanation for the failure of nerve that made the Irish Parliament vote itself out of existence in 1800.

The savagery of the fighting in Wexford and neighbouring counties, which were normally seen as among the most tranquil in Ireland, was without parallel since the seventeenth century; the reprisals that followed were equally savage. As a result, many Protestants in the South of Ireland had uneasy memories born of atrocities suffered by their own community and of others which they had inflicted on members of the majority. It is worth noting that, besides the many thousands of rebels who perished more or less anonymously, a surprising number of Irish peers and high-ranking military officers died on the battlefields opposing them.

It was the British reaction to these accumulated shocks and perils—together with the hope that better times would follow the Union—which supplied an audience for the first generation of Irish novelists: Maria Edgeworth, Sydney Owenson (later Lady Morgan), and the Revd Charles Robert Maturin. At first, none of these dared focus directly on 1798, though Miss Edgeworth and Maturin had firsthand knowledge of some of the year's events. *Castle Rackrent* was in print early in 1798, but the Edgeworths and their London publisher wisely postponed publication until 1800. The four last paragraphs of the novel are attributed to the 'Editor' of Thady Quirk's manuscript and seem to have been written by Richard Lovell Edgeworth. They include this sentence: 'It is a problem of difficult solution to determine whether a union will hasten or retard the amelioration of this country.' This shows that the novel was published before the Act of Union was finally passed and that Edgeworth was in two minds about its passage, so much so, in fact, that he *spoke* twice in its favour but *voted* twice against it because of the bribery systematically employed to secure its passage.[7]

The original title-page insisted that *Castle Rackrent* portrayed the manners of the Irish Gentry only before 1792, the first year of Grattan's Parliament. It was no accident that R. L. Edgeworth took up permanent residence in Ireland that year: a sort of postscript to his unfinished *Memoirs* states, 'In the year 1782, I returned to Ireland . . . with the sincere hope of contributing to the melioration of the inhabitants of the country, from which I drew my subsistence.'[8]

In 1782–3, he played an important part in the unsuccessful movement to reform parliamentary representation in Ireland; as he prophetically warned, 'A venal Parliament may, by degrees, yield everything but the name of Freedom.'[9]

Maria Edgeworth made no fictional use of her 1798 experience save in the brief ninth chapter of *Ennui* (1809). Although he is 'conscious of having acted in a manly and generous manner', Glenthorn, the hero, says:

I was hooted, and pelted, and narrowly escaped with my life . . . but the alarms of the rebels, and of the French, and of the loyalists; and the parading, and the galloping, and the quarrelling, and the continual agitation in which I was kept, whilst my character and life were at stake, relieved me effectually from the intolerable burden of ennui.

The key to this passage will be found in Maria Edgeworth's continuation of her father's memoirs, where she gives an eye-witness account of Richard Lovell Edgeworth's farcical yet nearly fatal experiences with the loyalists of Longford, who mistrusted his liberal views to the ludicrous extent of suspecting that he was a spy for the French.[10]

---

7 Marilyn Butler, *Maria Edgeworth: A Literary Biography* (Oxford: Clarendon Press, 1972), 182.
8 Butler, *Maria Edgeworth*, 77.
9 See his 'Address to the Electors of Longford', in *Memoirs of Richard Lovell Edgeworth, Esq.*, 2 vols. (London: R. Hunter, 1820).
10 Butler, *Maria Edgeworth*, 138.

Maturin's *The Milesian Chief* (1812) seems to have been the first Irish novel that could be described as 'about' 1798: the heroine jilts her English fiancé in favour of the title-character, a rebel leader; all ends in tragedy. It was Lady Morgan who, in *The Wild Irish Girl* (1806), had evolved the formula borrowed by Maturin and others: whatever the surrounding circumstances, a pair of passionate lovers must occupy the centre of the plot—one representing the old Gaelic, Catholic culture, the other the newer English or Anglo-Irish ethos. As the title suggests, Lady Morgan's novel has a Gaelic heroine, Glorvina, who is 'wild' only in being unsophisticated; by birth and instinct she is an aristocrat. Maturin shows Romantic sympathies by making his hero of Gaelic descent in *The Wild Irish Boy* (1808) as well as in *The Milesian Chief*. It may seem surprising that his published sermons are decidedly Tory and Evangelical, but the example of Sir Walter Scott, whose Romanticism grew naturally out of his Tory love for old times and old customs, demolishes the seeming paradox.[11]

Passion was alien to Maria Edgeworth's experience and incompatible with her comic gift, but in *Ormond* (1817) she contrasts the two cultures by creating two male cousins to represent them. Sir Ulick has abandoned Catholicism and exemplifies the Irish Parliament at its most corrupt, while Corny keeps the Gaelic system alive in his isolated little 'kingdom'. Harry Ormond, the hero, is the ward first of Ulick and then of Corny, but in his maturity he imitates neither, determined to be a modern, enlightened landlord. In this he resembles Lord Colambre, the title-character of *The Absentee* (1812), who pays his first visit to Ireland to inspect the estate of which his father is the absentee landlord. Like R. L. Edgeworth, Colambre finally makes his home on that estate, but he has already begun the process of 'melioration' during his first visit. He dismisses Garraghty, his father's unjust agent, and replaces him with an honest one, Mr Burke. This theme of the good landlord as *deus ex machina* is repeated over and over again by later Irish novelists, including even Carleton, who knew better than most how rare a phenomenon was a landlord of R. L. Edgeworth's calibre.

As the century progressed, Maria Edgeworth's humour and optimism seemed more and more at odds with the realities of Irish life: the age of reason was over. In a letter of the 1830s she explained precisely why she gave up writing about Ireland after *Ormond*:

[11] Maturin's *Sermons* (Edinburgh: Constable; London: Hurst, Robinson, 1819) are less polemical than his home-grown *Five Sermons on the Errors of the Roman Catholic Church* (Dublin: William Folds, 1824). See Claude Fierobe, *Charles Robert Maturin (1780–1824): L'homme et l'oeuvre* (Paris: Editions universitaires, 1974), 432–53.

It is impossible to draw Ireland as she now is in a book of fiction—realities are too strong, party passions too violent to bear to see, or care to look at, their faces in the looking-glass. The people would only break the glass, and curse the fool who held the mirror up to nature—distorted nature, in a fever. We are in too perilous a case to laugh, humour would be out of season, worse than bad taste.[12]

Lady Morgan, on the contrary, profited by the increasing tension: she found the courage to publish a novel about 1798 a whole generation after that catastrophic year. Robert Lee Wolff describes *The O'Briens and the O'Flahertys* (1827) as her 'finest and most complex novel', while at the same time stressing its 'pessimistic outlook' and 'elaborate Gothic effects'.[13]

Both Maturin and Lady Morgan perpetuated the 'Gothick' tradition of Ann Radcliffe and 'Monk' Lewis—so brilliantly ridiculed in Jane Austen's *Northanger Abbey*—whereas Maria Edgeworth was an acknowledged forerunner of Miss Austen and Scott.[14] This retrogressive tendency was somewhat excusable, since Ireland shared a number of characteristics with Italy, the chosen territory of the Gothick Novel. Her scenery was wild and unfamiliar and many of her people, besides being very poor and sometimes romantically lawless, still spoke a foreign language. Best of all, perhaps, from the standpoint of the Protestant British reader, Ireland and Italy had in common the picturesque, sinister, superstitious, and yet prestigiously ancient Roman Catholic Church. The reader of popular fiction finds something infinitely seductive in what he or she most disapproves of.

In all fairness, it must be acknowledged that both Maturin and Lady Morgan, after their fashion, showed much awareness of the politics and economics of contemporary Ireland as did Maria Edgeworth. Private passions, vices, and even crimes, are portrayed against a background of British usurpation and oppression which makes them almost excusable; Lady Morgan is especially indignant about the penal laws against Catholics. Perhaps her pessimism, like Maturin's, was more realistic than the two generations of Edgeworthian optimism.

Thomas Moore's *Irish Melodies* also show a reluctance to confront 1798 and its brief sequel, Robert Emmet's rising in 1803. Moore was a personal friend of Emmet, though not privy to his political and military

---

[12] Butler, *Maria Edgeworth*, 452.

[13] Quoted from the catalogue compiled by the late Robert Lee Wolff to introduce Series Two of his editions of 19th-cent. fiction, *Ireland: From the Act of Union to the Death of Parnell* (New York: Garland, 1978), 13. This is a wonderfully concise summary of the 77-vol. edition. Even where I am quite familiar with the authors covered—notably Maria Edgeworth and Carleton—I find Wolff an invaluable aid to memory.

[14] Scott in his 'postscript' to *Waverley* (1814) described his object in that novel as 'in some distant degree to emulate the admirable Irish portraits drawn by Miss Edgeworth.' Butler, 394.

activities, and his parents too were in sympathy with the United Irishmen. Nevertheless, the *Melodies* were not Moore's own idea. A shrewd Dublin music publisher named William Power commissioned him to write English words to Irish airs, including those in Edward Bunting's first collection (1797); Power had already engaged Sir John Stevenson to arrange the tunes for the piano. Sir Walter Scott had fostered Scots cultural nationalism by collecting the words of many ballads in *Minstrelsy of the Scottish Border* (1802): their language was fairly easily understood by English readers possessed of good will and a brief glossary. No comparable body of popular verse was available to Moore because he knew no Irish. Translation was therefore out of the question, but he had a natural gift for music and was well-trained in it besides; as a result, he succeeded in preserving many native folk tunes by skilfully fitting his own English words to them—an endeavour which he described as 'truly National'. He very reluctantly allowed 'an edition of the Poetry of the Irish Melodies, separate from the Music', after refusing one for a number of years, being 'well aware' how much his verses 'must lose . . . in being detached from the beautiful airs to which it was their good fortune to be associated'.[15]

In the first series of the *Melodies*, published in 1808, there is a striking contrast between two songs printed not far apart: while the first line of one urges the hearer to 'Remember the glories of Brien the brave [Brian Boru]', the other warns, 'Oh! breathe not his name'. Moore is very explicit in his notes about which eleventh-century glories his readers are to remember, but neither verse nor footnote reveals that Robert Emmet is the hero of the second lyric. We are assured, nevertheless, that 'the tear that we shed, though in secret it rolls, / Shall long keep his memory green in our souls.'

Memory, then, is the main, if not the only, theme of the *Melodies*. It is as if Irish history had ended on 1 January 1801, or at the latest on the day of Emmet's execution. Only the vaguest aspirations towards a better future are entertained, in a very few poems: otherwise we hear of nothing but 'a nation's eclipse'—to quote the song Moore wrote on the death of Henry Grattan in 1820. Those who know only the *Melodies* might never suspect that Moore campaigned manfully for Catholic Emancipation in prose and verse: his prose satire *Memoirs of Captain Rock . . .—Written by Himself* (1824) was his weightiest contribution to that cause, but the verse satires in *Twopenny Postbag* (1813), 'by Thomas Brown, the Younger', were extraordinarily popular, reaching

---

[15] Thomas Moore, *The Poetical Works*, ed. A. D. Godley (London: Henry Frowde, Oxford Univ. Press, 1910), 180.

their fourteenth printing in less than fourteen months.[16] Paradoxically, the most Swiftian lines Moore ever wrote (see 'Letter IV') refer to the Roman Catholic Church:

> With all its theologic olio
> Of Bulls, half Irish and half Roman—
> Of Doctrine, now believ'd by no man—
> Of Councils, held for men's salvation,
> Yet always ending in damnation—[17]

They are attributed, however, to the pen of a Protestant bigot, Patrick Duigenan: he and others like him receive many sharp digs in this little volume of 'Intercepted Letters'. After the Emancipation Act, Moore vindicated the measure ironically in a prose work, *Travels of an Irish Gentleman in Search of a Religion* (1833), whose protagonist feels free to turn Protestant if he wishes, now that he has nothing material to gain by doing so. After this book appeared, Moore received invitations to run for Parliament in the O'Connellite interest from three Irish constituencies. Never having admired O'Connell and being now opposed to repeal of the Union, he found little difficulty in declining the honour.[18]

Moore's career began so early that it covers more than two generations of Anglo-Irish literature. In 1795, aged 14, he was contributing verse to *Antologia Hiberniea*, a monthly magazine edited by Richard Edward Mercier. The *Irish Melodies* were published in ten numbers and a supplement at irregular intervals from 1808 to 1834: although their genesis occurred in Dublin, it must be stressed that they were published in London, by the firm of J. Power. L. A. G. Strong remarks, 'Written for the English drawing-room, the *Melodies* took a long time to reach the people of Ireland'—those outside Dublin at any rate—but 'after 1860 they spread everywhere'.[19] It was not until 1831 that Moore came to terms with 1798 by publishing *The Life and Death of Lord Edward Fitzgerald*. Strong suggests that his decision to write on the 1798 hero was in a sense a political gesture:

Moore did not know Fitzgerald, had only seen him in the street, yet on this subject, selected by himself, at his own cost, in preference to a life of Canning [the late British Prime Minister] which would have had an assured financial success, he did his best work as a biographer. The name of Fitzgerald rekindled all the patriotic enthusiasm of his boyhood. . . . He recaptured the spirit that had inspired the Melodies, but with the benefits of a lifetime of experience. The

---

[16] Moore, *The Poetical Works*, 147–8.
[17] Moore, *The Poetical Works*, 153.
[18] L. A. G. Strong, *The Minstrel Boy: A Portrait of Tom Moore* (London: Hodder and Stoughton, 1937), 206–12.
[19] Strong, *The Minstrel Boy*, 138, 140.

memory of Emmet gleamed once more, and he paid tribute to the idols of his youth.[20]

One has to agree that the United Irishmen and their movement inspired the *Melodies*, but if we separate the songs from their tunes, is there one perfect lyric or elegiac poem among them? Even 'She is Far from the Land' disintegrates in the ninth line, with its smug yet illogical antithesis: 'He had lived for his love, for his country he died'. In truth, 1798 failed to inspire a single great work of imaginative literature, whether poem, drama, or novel. Its classic works are biographical: Wolfe Tone's *Autobiography* (Washington, 1826); the first volume of Miles Byrne's *Memoirs* (Paris 1863); Moore's life of Lord Edward; and perhaps that huge labour of love, Richard Robert Madden's *The United Irishmen, Their Lives and Times* (7 vols., 1843–6). The most intimate memoir—racked by guilt, fear, and sorrow—is the autobiography of William Farrell (*Carlow in '98* (1949)), edited by Roger McHugh; unfortunately, it came on the scene too late ever to become widely known.

Catholic Novelists and Catholic Emancipation: The Banims; Griffin

1825 is the conveniently memorable date that marks a new beginning in the Anglo-Irish novel: up to that year, the leading novelists were all at least nominally Protestant. But the most important literary event of the year was the publication of *Tales of the O'Hara Family*, whose authors, John and Michael Banim—alias Barnes and Abel O'Hara—are correctly described by Wolff as the 'first novelists to stem not from the Protestant Ascendancy but wholly from native Irish Catholic stock'. Two years later Gerald Griffin published his first work of prose fiction, and in 1828 William Carleton, a recent convert to the Church of Ireland from Catholicism, began contributing stories to the monthly *Christian Examiner*.

One might well say that the time was ripe for these novelists and story-tellers, now that their Protestant counterparts had been writing for almost a generation. Furthermore, Scott's publication of *Waverley* in 1814 and the series of novels which followed it became a challenge to ambitious young Irishmen like John Banim and Griffin: who would become 'the Irish Scott'? If and when such a writer appeared, he would find a ready-made audience awaiting him. To quote the words of a reviewer of John Banim's anonymously published work, *The Anglo-Irish of the Nineteenth Century* (1828), 'This novel will be much read. Its great topic—the policy of England toward Ireland—the question,

[20] Strong, *The Minstrel Boy*, 238.

What ought now to be done with the Irish Catholics? is uppermost at present in the public mind.'[21]

As we know, Moore had been addressing this question a dozen years before the new generation came on the scene. In the 1820s, however, the tension between Protestants—especially the growing number of Evangelicals in the Church of Ireland—and Catholics began to mount rapidly. In 1822 William Magee, the newly appointed Protestant Archbishop of Dublin, virtually declared war on the Roman Catholic Church in the charge he delivered at his primary visitation of the Archdiocese. By 1825 he was assuring a House of Lords committee on the state of Ireland: 'In truth, with respect to Ireland, the Reformation may, strictly speaking, be truly said only now to have begun.'[22] Catholic bishops were all the more disturbed because Magee was not an extremist Evangelical but, on the contrary, a conservative High Churchman. Also in 1825, there appeared the first monthly issues of *The Christian Examiner and Church of Ireland Magazine*, generally regarded as the mouthpiece of the Evangelical wing of the Church. Under the editorship of the Revd Caesar Otway it aimed at 'an union of Christian charity and Christian firmness': its pursuit of the latter made it appear more bigoted in Catholic eyes than Otway really intended it to be.[23] The early 1820s also saw the beginning of the fashion for public religious debates, in which members of the local Bible societies argued the Protestant case against a more or less equal number of Catholic priests.[24] These debates can hardly be said to have advanced the cause of Christian charity.

On the political front, Daniel O'Connell had founded the Catholic Association in 1823. Under his guidance it developed a programme much broader than the annual presentation of a petition for Catholic emancipation: by identifying itself as 'a Catholic protection organization' it appealed to a much larger constituency whose immediate grievances would not be solved by Emancipation. In the following year the bishops and parish clergy agreed to the collection of the 'Catholic Rent', one penny per month from each Catholic family. The committees set up to collect the Rent in more than half of the parishes of Ireland often formed the nuclei of political clubs. In any case, the contributors of the Rent 'may have eventually reached half a million': O'Connell found himself at the head of a mass movement.[25]

[21] Patrick Joseph Murray, *The Life of John Banim*, intro. Robert Lee Wolff (New York & London: Garland, 1978), xxviii.

[22] Desmond Bowen, *The Protestant Crusade in Ireland, 1800–70* (Dublin: Gill & Macmillan, 1978), 92. Magee is the focus of 83–96.

[23] Page 11 of a 12-page catalogue of 'Works Published by W. Curry, Jun. and Co.' bound in with a Curry publication, 1832, and doubtless with many others.

[24] Bowen, *The Protestant Crusade*, 96–108.

[25] Oliver MacDonagh, *The Hereditary Bondsman: Daniel O'Connell 1775–1829* (London: Weidenfeld & Nicolson, 1988), 212.

Undoubtedly a demand existed on the London literary market: what is surprising is that it was readily supplied by writers so close to the Gaelic tradition, which provided no model for realistic prose fiction except the brief oral narratives known collectively as *seanchas*. Longer prose narratives were known as *seanscéalta*, what the unscholarly reader of English would call 'fairy-tales'. There were also, of course, long and short narratives in verse, roughly corresponding to the Scots ballads and known as *laoithe* (lays). Novels, however, simply did not exist in the Irish language until the twentieth century. Carleton, a native speaker of Irish and the child of both a traditional story-teller and a traditional singer, may have been slow to win British readers precisely because he never quite mastered that quintessentially English and bourgeois genre, the novel. More surprisingly, though his hedge-school training made him literate in English and Latin, he remained illiterate in Irish: all the Irish words and phrases in his writings are spelt according to English phonetics. The same is true of the Banims' works; I assume that their grandparents were native Irish speakers, and perhaps their father was too, though as well as owning a farm he ran a gun and tackle shop in Kilkenny. By the beginning of the nineteenth century, however, only a small fraction of the still Irish-speaking population could read and write their own language: these were honoured as Gaelic scholars.

By coincidence, Gerald Griffin's first teacher was one of these rare figures: P. McElligott of Limerick, an honorary member of the Gaelic Society of Dublin, which published his learned but not very useful *Observations on the Gaelic Language*.[26] Gerald was only 7 when his family moved to the country from Limerick, so it is unlikely that he learned much Irish from McElligott: he may, however, be the only one of this group of novelists to have become literate in Irish. His biographer, Daniel Griffin, never condescends to mention the subject, perhaps thinking that it would lower himself and his brother in the eyes of the reader. Nevertheless, Gerald's posthumous collection, *Talis Qualis: or Tales of the Jury Room* (1842), includes what appears to be the first English translation of *Aided Chlainne Lir* ('The Fate of the Children of Lir') ever printed. Eugene O'Curry praised it and assumed that it was based on an Irish text closely related to that used for his own edition (*Atlantis* iv, 1863). He took it for granted that the translation of this famous mythological tale from early Modern Irish was by Griffin himself.[27]

---

[26] Daniel Griffin, *The Life of Gerald Griffin by His Brother*, 2nd edn. (1857; Dublin: James Duffy, 1874), 22. Griffin gives his name as 'Richard MacEligot', but see *Transactions of the Gaelic Society of Dublin* (1808), i. pp. xxvii and 1–40.

[27] Eugene O'Curry, 'The "Tri Truaighe na Scealaigheachta" (*i.e.* the "Three Most Sorrowful Tales"), of Erinn—II. "The Fate of the Children of Lir"' in *Atlantis* (1863) iv. 154–7.

John Banim (1798–1842) was only 23 when the verse tragedy, *Damon and Pythias*, was performed at Covent Garden; in preparing it for the stage he had the assistance of Richard Lalor Sheil, already a successful dramatist and later one of O'Connell's associates. Two other Irishmen, Maturin and James Sheridan Knowles, had had similar good fortune a little earlier. It seemed logical for Banim to move to London with his bride in 1822, but further theatrical success eluded him. Fortunately, even before he left Ireland, he had planned with his elder brother, Michael (1796–1874), that they should write a series of stories, long and short, about Ireland—obviously with Scott in mind. Patrick Joseph Murray, John's biographer, writing in 1857 with the generous help of the still-vigorous Michael, described John's intentions in undertaking the *O'Hara Tales* as follows:

to raise the national character in the estimation of other lands, by a portrayal of the people as they really were; but at the same time to vindicate them from the charges of violence and bloodthirstiness, by showing, in the course of the fiction, the various causes which he supposed concurred to draw forth and foster these evil qualities.[28]

In other words, the Irish weren't violent and bloodthirsty, but if they were they had good reason to be. Similar contradictions—or at best ambiguities—are found in John's own documented statements. When, incapacitated by his progressive illness—possibly multiple sclerosis—he appealed for help in England, he not unfairly described the 'uniform political tendency' of his work as 'the formation of a good and affectionate feeling between England and Ireland'; to an Irish audience gathered to honour him, he expressed himself somewhat differently, saying that his work was inspired 'by a devoted love of our country, and by an indignant wish to convince her slanderers, and in some slight degree at least to soften the hearts of her oppressors'.[29]

What this meant in practice can be illustrated by a passage in the first O'Hara tale, *Crohoore of the Bill-Hook*, by Michael Banim:

His attention was here riveted by the miserable man opposite to him, who at once . . . poured out a speech in his native tongue, adopting it instinctively as the most ready and powerful medium of expressing his feelings; for one who boggles, and stammers, and is ridiculous in English, becomes eloquent in Irish . . . 'Who talks of the good we can do?—we look not to do good; we are not able nor fit to do good; we only want our revenge! And that, while we are men, and have strong hands, and broken hearts, and brains on fire, with the memory of our sufferings—that we can take. Your father, young man, never writhed in the proctor's [tithe-collector's] gripe; he has riches . . . so that the robber's visit was

[28] Murray, *Life of John Banim*, 93.   [29] Murray. *Life of John Banim*, xlvi–vii.

not felt or heeded: but look at me! . . . I have nothing to eat, no house to sleep in; my starved body is without covering; and those I loved, and that loved me, the pulses of my heart, are gone.'[30]

The destitute man then goes on to give further details of his oppression by the corrupt tithe-proctor and his eviction by his landlord. He naturally arouses the sympathy of Pierce Shea, the hero, who, in 'this moment of frenzy and inebriation' takes the Whiteboys' oath.

The reference to Irish in this passage illuminates the great stylistic problem confronting the truly native writer of English: how can he render the speech of the Irish countryman without falling into the 'bull-and-blunder' convention associated with Irish characters on the English stage, from Shakespeare and Ben Jonson onwards. Once Scott had exploited broad Scots in his novels, it became part of his unique appeal: not only supplying the novelty of local colour to English readers, but giving his Scots readers a sense of national pride through its authenticity. Kurt Wittig remarks: 'Scott is truest to character in the case of his crofters and common people, as their speech is the most inherently dramatic.' Also, in *The Bride of Lammermoor* Scott himself 'defends his use of dialogue against the method of the painter, as literature is directed towards the ear'. These statements, however, apply only to his use of Scots. When he is obliged to make his Highland characters speak out, his not being a native speaker of Gaelic causes trouble: according to Wittig, 'his "Gaelic" style as a rule is altogether too Ossianic'.[31] Banim's method—'We follow the speaker in translation'—errs in the opposite direction, however: except for the phrase 'Pulses of my heart' (*cuisleanna mo chroí*), it stays too close to standard English. Not until much later did Douglas Hyde begin to solve the problem of translating literally—perhaps too literally—from spoken Irish; Synge, with the ear of a poet and musician, modified the literalism to provide rhythm and harmony; he may be said to have solved the problem as far as it is soluble. Synge had the advantage of not being fully committed to realism: as novelists attempting to reproduce the Irish-English of country folk, the Banims, Carleton, and even Griffin could not totally avoid the boggling, stammering, and absurdity present in their model. Carleton, in fact, revelled in it, making a virtue of necessity.

The 1825 series of three O'Hara *Tales* in three volumes was followed the next year by *The Boyne Water*, a three-volume historical novel written entirely by John Banim, who modelled it on Scott's *Redgauntlet*

---

[30] The O'Hara Family, *Crohoore of the Bill-Hook and The Fetches* (London & Belfast: Simms and M'Intyre, 1848), 87.

[31] Kurt Wittig, *The Scottish Tradition in Literature* (Edinburgh & London: Oliver and Boyd, 1958), 228.

(1824), according to Wolff. Though set in the seventeenth century and narrating events in the Williamite war, it was read at once as a tract for Banim's own times, urging the mutual tolerance between Protestant and Catholic that was promised by the Treaty of Limerick (1691). 'The Treaty of Limerick, will yet be kept', writes the Protestant hero to the Catholic one, his brother-in-law, who at the novel's end is in exile on the Continent.

The second series of *Tales* was also published in 1826, two of the three volumes being devoted to *The Nowlans*, a novel of contemporary Irish life, which John Banim seems to have based in part on his own early experience. He fell in love with the illegitimate daughter of a Protestant landlord, and she with him, but when he sought to marry her he was contemptuously rejected by her father, who prevented her from writing any further letters. John thought she no longer loved him, but when she died of tuberculosis in a matter of months, he learned the truth and was heartbroken. The hero of *The Nowlans*, a student for the Catholic priesthood, elopes with and marries the daughter of a Protestant landlord after he has taken vows: not only is he unable to support his wife, but he feels that their marriage is invalid. Even before this, he is sorely tempted by his cousin Maggy, one of the illegitimate brood of his profligate uncle. The scene of John Nowlan's attempted seduction of Maggy would have caused the novel to be banned in the Irish Free State a century later, let alone the later presentation of Maggy presiding over a brothel in Dublin.

Yeats admired *The Nowlans* enough to include it in his 1895 list of the thirty best Irish books, but part of its appeal for him must have arisen from the *lack* of any political content:

I do not think modern fiction has . . . anything more haunting than the description of the household of the spendthrift squireen, in the opening chapters of 'The Nolans,' or the account a little further on of the 'spoiled priest' taking the door from its hinges to lay upon it the body of his mistress and of the old men bringing him their charity.[32]

If *The Nowlans* made no political statement, it also contributed very little to the cause of reconciliation, showing deep suspicion of the Evangelicals in particular. A former priest named Horragan who has joined their ranks is the focus of Banim's satire. Wolff is perhaps unduly surprised by the bitterness of John Banim's next major novel, *The Anglo-Irish of the Nineteenth Century* (1828); so bitter was it that the publisher did not even issue it under the 'O'Hara Family' pseudonym, preferring anonymity, as no doubt the author himself did. The novel is

---

[32] Yeats, *Collected Letters*, i. 442.

essentially a disillusioned version of *The Absentee*: Banim has given up his 'hopes of conciliation and mutual respect between the English and the Irish people. . . . The note of hope at the end sounds falsely after the mood of despair that pervades the novel.'[33] One character whose presence suggests that *The Anglo-Irish* is a logical successor of *The Nowlans* is O'Hanlon, another 'renegade priest who has become "a stout biblical"'.[34]

In this same year of 1828, under the umbrella of the *O'Hara Tales*, Michael Banim published a three-volume historical novel, *The Croppy: A Tale of 1798*. Here at last is a novel about 1798 that penetrates to the centre of the inferno, County Wexford, scene of so many of the horrors that were outlined earlier. Although John and Michael Banim were too young to remember anything from this time, County Kilkenny borders on Wexford and had its own abortive rising, which was followed by an unusually brutal repression under Sir Charles Asgill.[35] The brothers must have heard many eyewitness accounts of the events of the year from all over south-east Ireland, and *The Croppy* may well be the most authentic novel written about the 'Boys of Wexford'. Politically, however, it remains faithful to the spirit of reconciliation that John seems to have abandoned. Wolff sums it up as follows:

Michael Banim faces his grim subject matter soberly and with what seems like extraordinary impartiality, only thirty years after the events. It was not until later that patriotic Irishmen could come to regard the rebels of 1798 as pure heroes of the nationalist struggle.[36]

John Banim's progressive illness, which led to his death at 44, may have been aggravated by his early struggle for recognition in London. Gerald Griffin, who went to London alone towards the end of 1823, shortly before his 20th birthday, spent three frustrating years there without ever quite gaining a footing in the theatre. A letter written to his parents in America on 12 October 1825 describes the worst part of this period of apprenticeship: 'It was a year such as I did not think it possible I could have outlived, and the very recollection of it puts me into the horrors.' Like many another son—rarely, of course, so innocent—he could not bear to write his parents while he had no good news to tell them. 'Until within a short time back I have not had since I left Ireland a single moment's peace of mind . . . trying a thousand expedients . . . only to meet disappointments everywhere I turned.'[37]

By February 1827, when he returned in temporary defeat to County Limerick, Griffin was damaged in both mind and body. He had developed

---

[33] Wolff, *Ireland*, 18.   [34] Murray, *Life of John Banim*, xxxiii.
[35] Thomas Pakenham, *The Year of Liberty: The story of the great Irish Rebellion of 1798* (London: Hodder and Stoughton, 1969), 282.
[36] Wolff, *Ireland*, 17.   [37] Griffin, *Life of Gerald*, 115.

an almost neurotic reluctance to accept help from other members of his profession, including the warm-hearted John Banim. Eventually he gave up literature altogether, joining the Irish Christian Brothers in 1836; he died of typhus in 1840. The tragedy *Gisippus*, on which he had pinned his hopes during his first year in London, was finally staged by Macready at Drury Lane in 1842 and 'received with the utmost enthusiasm both by the press and the public'.[38]

Few Irish writers can have shown less interest in politics than Griffin, either in his daily life or in his writings: this perhaps explains why his two full-length historical novels, *The Invasion* (1832) and *The Duke of Monmouth* (1836), were such failures, despite all the time and effort he devoted to them. Nevertheless, during his lifetime he achieved some of the acclaim for his prose fiction that he had vainly sought for his verse dramas and lyric poetry: his favourite writers when he was young were Shakespeare, Pope, Goldsmith, and Thomas Moore. Because he did not share the passionate urge to tell the truth about Irish life that inspired the Banims, Griffin oddly found himself even more at the mercy of the London publishers than they did.

Gerald's biographer, his brother Daniel, in discussing the popularity of the *O'Hara Tales*, gives full credit to 'the extreme originality, power, and truth' displayed in them, but he adds that 'the complete revolution' effected in the novel by Miss Edgeworth and Scott, 'and the attention then beginning to be bestowed upon Irish affairs, also in some degree contributed'.[39] No doubt influenced by similar considerations, Gerald published just before he left London a volume entitled *'Holland-Tide'; or, Munster Popular Tales*, written in great haste, which contained a novella and six shorter pieces, at least two of which are folktales; all were supposed to have been told at a 'Holland-tide' (Hallowe'en) party 'at the house of a respectable farmer in the west of Munster, upon whose hospitality chance threw the collector of these stories on the 31st of last October'.[40] He returned to London from County Limerick in August 1827 with a new three-volume work, *Tales of the Munster Festivals*, written in Ireland in just four months, which was published the same year also. The reviewers pointed out faults which they shrewdly attributed to hurried writing, but both books were well received by the British public.

The Banims, Griffin, and Carleton produced their early fiction at breakneck speed. Having discovered that it was artistically acceptable to use the local and national subject-matter nearest to their hands, John Banim and Gerald Griffin wrote with an ease and self-assurance which

---

[38] Griffin, *Life of Gerald*, 119.   [39] Griffin, *Life of Gerald*, 108.
[40] *'Holland-Tide'; or, Munster Popular Tales* (London: Simpkin and Marshall, 1827), 5–6.

they had never known before. The realization that one could write about one's own Irish society and its customs instead of those in aristocratic England or ancient Greece and Rome was almost akin to a religious revelation. Daniel Griffin says of his brother:

Though his turning himself to [prose fiction] was . . . *in a great degree compulsory and the effect of circumstances* [italics mine], he devoted himself to it with an ardour that fell little short of his passion for the drama, and this feeling grew upon him the more, when he observed it attended with a success which all his efforts in the other walk could not command. I have heard him say he thought . . . Shakespeare would have written novels if he had fallen on a novel reading time.[41]

Daniel rather naively complains that Gerald was inadequately paid for *Tales of the Munster Festivals* because 'the novel trade had declined'; for this he blames the London publishers, some of whom, 'when the taste for that species of writing became decided and strong, with a reckless and grasping spirit flung a quantity of mere rubbish into the market, in the shape of novels'. He does not pause to ask whether Gerald's own publisher was not actuated by the same spirit.

Unnerved by the critics, Griffin made two false starts on a second series of the *Tales*. 'He had intended', says his brother, 'to bestow more pains upon this series, and to render it if possible more deserving of public favour than the last', but because of the false starts Gerald found himself in November 1828 only half-way through the three-volume novel which he had promised his publisher for that month. As a result, half of *The Collegians* was written while the novel was going through the press: 'The printers overtook him about the middle of the third volume, and from this time forward it was a constant race between him and them.'[42] Nevertheless, *The Collegians* proved to be his masterpiece, the only work by which he is now remembered except among academics. When he was struggling to write one of his later books, to the surprise of Daniel, who reminded him of the ease with which he wrote *The Collegians*, Gerald would say, 'Oh, the Collegians was a story *that used to write itself.*'[43] The success of this novel, Daniel insists, is proof enough that Griffin did not enter the religious life because of thwarted ambition.

How little political motivation Gerald felt is demonstrated in a letter written to his older brother William on 11 April 1829. The tone is admittedly light and even humorous, but Daniel's introductory remarks assure us that in such letters, 'as in those of a more serious cast, he lays bare his heart fully'.

---

[41] Griffin, *Life of Gerald*, 221.   [42] Ibid. 223.   [43] Ibid. 274.

Gerald had been enjoying the hospitality of Mr (later Sir) Philip Crampton, Surgeon-General of Ireland, who not only appreciated his fiction but was able to tell him that Maria Edgeworth also admired it. Crampton was, of course, both a British official and a Protestant. Griffin wishes he could afford to spend another month in Dublin, 'in the first society'.

It would, after all, be a great advantage that people of rank and influence should know and be interested about one, and it is worth something to know what fashionable society is. *They are the people whom one writes to please* [italics mine], and it is well to know what pleases amongst them.

A few lines further on he says,

This, after all, is really the only rank in which I could ever feel *at home*—in which I could fling off the *mauvaise honte*—talk—laugh—and be happy . . . Why was I not born to a fortune?

If you were, says a little voice, you would never have known the Irish peasantry—nobody would know, nobody would care a fig for you.

Thank heaven, then, that I was born poor—but, oh! heaven, do not keep me so![44]

The dilemma so humorously expressed here is virtually as old as literature: if Maecenas were alive today, he would be blamed for raising Horace above his humble origin and doubtless accused of turning him into a 'lacquey of the ruling class'. Gerald Griffin was too politically naive to be of use to any government, but the same cannot be said of his older contemporary William Carleton (1794–1869).

The Ambiguities of William Carleton

Paradoxically, despite his almost complete independence of London publishers, Carleton was in some respects more at the mercy of magazine editors, book publishers, and readers than any of his predecessors in the history of Irish fiction. Barbara Hayley, the supreme authority on Carleton's infinitely complex bibliography, says that his 'forty years of writing produced eight distinct major collections of stories and thirteen novels, all but three of these being first published in Ireland'.[45] His dominant position in the Irish book trade, however, was partly the result of his willingness to shift 'his point of view opportunistically to suit the prejudices of his employers'.[46] Although Carleton began as an

[44] Ibid. 237–9.
[45] Barbara Hayley, 'A detailed bibliography of editions of William Carleton's *Traits and Stories* . . . , Pt. I', *Long Room*, no. 32 (1987), 31.
[46] Wolff, *Ireland*, 22.

anti-Catholic writer for the *Christian Examiner*, Wolff and Professor Hayley have both demonstrated that he toned down some of his *Examiner* stories for the republication in book format and removed further anti-Catholic passages in later editions. His first book, *Father Butler, The Lough Dearg Pilgrim* (Dublin: Curry, 1829), consisted of two *Examiner* stories: the first was too bitter ever to be reprinted, but the second, as amended, became part of the definitive 'New Edition' of *Traits and Stories of the Irish Peasantry* (Dublin: Curry; London: Orr, two vols., 1843–4), later known as the 'first series': this contained only one *Examiner* story, 'The Station', giving a portrait of an avaricious priest that must have offended many Catholics. There is nothing quite so offensive in the second series of the *Traits and Stories* (Dublin: Wakeman, three vols., 1883), although it includes four tales from the *Examiner*: among these is the wildly humorous 'Denis O'Shaughnessy Going to Maynooth', about a totally unfit candidate for the priesthood. Deliberately or not, Carleton balances against this story a new and sombre counterpart, 'The Poor Scholar', describing the struggles of a young man with a true vocation who eventually becomes a priest. Yeats concurred with many a common reader in finding this rather sentimental narrative among the most moving by Carleton.[47]

In 1834 Carleton returned to his original publisher, William Curry, Jr, whose list was designed to appeal mainly to Irish Evangelicals, of whom a number also figures in it as authors. Curry was, moreover, the proprietor and publisher of the *Christian Examiner*. In all probability both Curry and Carleton hoped to exploit the instant popularity of both series of *Traits and Stories*, but the rest of the volume passed into oblivion. Wolff says that 'The Death of a Devotee' and 'The Priest's Funeral' are 'perhaps Carleton's most virulently anti-Catholic stories'.[48]

The 'General Introduction' to the 1843–4 edition is of great importance and interest and says much that is true about Carleton and his Ireland, but, as often happens, its final paragraph is not its most veracious one:

In conclusion I have endeavoured, with what success has been already determined by the voice of my own country, to give a panorama of Irish life among the people . . . and in doing this, I can say with solemn truth that I painted them honestly, and without reference to the existence of any particular creed or party.[49]

Not only is this last phrase manifestly untrue of his early work, but he was soon to write a satirical novel in three volumes, *Valentine McClutchy*

---

[47] He included it in *Stories from Carleton* (London: Walter Scott, 1889).

[48] Wolff, *Ireland*, 23.

[49] William Carleton, *Traits and Stories of the Irish Peasantry*: a new edition, with an autobiographical introduction, I (Dublin: Curry; London: William S. Orr, 1843), xxiv.

The Irish Agent; or, Chronicles of the Castle Cumber Property (Dublin: Duffy, 1845), which was not only pro-Catholic but almost as hostile to Protestantism as his *Examiner* contributions had been to Catholicism.

The explanation of this about-face is, I fear, all too simple: Carleton had changed his publisher again. James Duffy, a Catholic from County Monaghan with a hedge-school education resembling Carleton's, had first prospered through buying up cheaply the English bibles given free to Irish Catholics by Evangelicals; these he sold at a profit in Liverpool. In 1845 Charles Gavan Duffy, the editor of *The Nation* newspaper, chose James Duffy as publisher of *The Spirit of the Nation*, the famous anthology, selected from early issues of the paper, which had become an instant best-seller when first published at the *Nation* office. Besides filling the need for reprints of the anthology, Duffy was soon entrusted with the monthly publication of a series of small, cheap, green-bound books entitled 'The Library of Ireland'. The twenty-two volumes published included a number of historical works and biographies of famous Irishmen written from a nationalist point of view. Literature was represented by five anthologies, a volume of verse by Thomas Davis, and three short novels by Carleton.[50]

One of these, *Art Maguire, or The Broken Pledge*, was in essence a temperance tract: it includes a brief preface, dated 4 July 1845, stating that the author proposes to write a series of 'Tales for the Irish people'; his 'object is simply to improve their physical and social condition'—a not very modest aim, which the famine in any case would soon thwart. He then goes on to reassure those of his readers 'who feel apprehensive that any thing calculated to injure the doctrinal convictions of the Catholic people may be suffered to creep into these Tales.'[51]

Since Carleton was then, and remained to the end of his life, a member of the Church of Ireland, this alone might be sufficient reason for such apprehensions; one cannot help thinking, nevertheless, that Carleton had few illusions about his reputation among Irish Catholics.

The fact remains that Duffy was delighted to have Carleton in his list from 1845 onwards: that year, he published, besides *Art Maguire*, *Rody-the-Rover* and *Parra Sastha* as volumes iii and v of the Library of Ireland, *Valentine McClutchy* and *Tales and Sketches Illustrating the Character of the Irish Peasantry*. More than half of the short pieces making up this last volume had appeared in the *Irish Penny Journal* (1840–1). The full title of the original edition of *Tales and Sketches* refers to 'usages,

---

[50] P. S. O'Hegarty, 'The "Library of Ireland" 1845–1847', in *Thomas Davis and Young Ireland*, ed. M. J. MacManus (Dublin: Stationery Office, 1945), 109–13. See also the account of James Duffy by 'Bibliophile', 116–18.

[51] William Carleton, *Art Maguire; or, The Broken Pledge: A Narrative*, Tales for the Irish People (Dublin: James Duffy, 1845), vii–viii.

traditions, sports and pastimes' as well as character, and many of the sketches resemble chapters in a handbook of social anthropology. They begin by outlining the social role of a country dancing-master, a match-maker, a midwife or a shanachie; Carleton then gives a character portrait of the most typical representative of each vocation that he has met and ends, usually, by relating an anecdote or two. The analytic power shown in some of these miniatures should increase our respect for everything he has to say about the political attitudes of the peasants.

Politics and religion were virtually synonymous for Carleton: having opposed Emancipation when a recent convert to Anglicanism, he aimed in his maturer years at a reconciliation between Catholic and Protestant. Like John Banim on the other side of the fence, he hoped to promote by his writings a better understanding of the Catholic point of view; he often sought to explain—though not to excuse—peasant violence ('agrarian crime' was the usual Victorian term) by drawing attention to the injustices and oppressions suffered by the peasantry. In the best of his early work, however, he lets events speak for themselves. 'Wildgoose Lodge', from the second series of *Traits and Stories*, restricts its moralizing to an epilogue of only three paragraphs: for that very reason it is Carleton's most convincing indictment of secret oathbound societies that take the law into their own hands. Based on a historical event that took place in County Louth in 1817/18, it describes with hideous vividness the burning alive of the entire family of an informer by a band of Ribbonmen, nearly thirty of whom were later hanged. The story is told in the first person by a reluctant eyewitness who is bound by his oath to be present but does not take part in the actual burning of the house or the thrusting back into the flames of men, women, and children: he is clearly an educated man, and his rather formal, precious narration makes the story almost unbearable to read.

Sixteen years later *The Tithe Proctor* (1849) told at much greater length a story based on the murder by Whiteboys of a family named Boland: it aroused the fury of, among others, D. J. O'Donoghue, Carleton's first biographer, who called it 'a vicious picture of the worst passions of the people, a rancorous description of the just war of the peasantry against tithes'.[52] He was not mollified by Carleton's depiction of the injustice and cruelty of the title character, employed by the Church of Ireland clergy to collect tithes from their involuntary parish-ioners, the Catholics. O'Donoghue, however, grudgingly concedes that 'As a study of villainy the book is convincing.' If Carleton's attitude to violence in *The Tithe Proctor* was not so consistent with that shown in

---

[52] Quoted in Stephen J. Brown, *Ireland in Fiction*, 2nd edn. (1st edn, 1919; Shannon, Ireland: Irish Univ. Press, 1969), 56.

'Wildgoose Lodge', one might suspect that the former had been concocted to please his Belfast publishers. As we have seen, however, Simms and M'Intyre published no further novels by Carleton after this one. One thing is certain: Duffy would not have dared to handle *The Tithe Proctor*, yet he was happy enough to publish several later titles by Carleton, including his most popular one, *Willy Reilly and his Dear Colleen Bawn* (1855), which Father Stephen Brown characterizes as 'practically free from political and religious bias, but . . . greatly inferior to his earlier works'.[53]

A number of critics have been puzzled and/or repelled by the doubtful morality and sinister politics of 'Phelim O'Toole's Courtship' (*Traits and Stories*, second series). I myself would choose this novella as Carleton's masterpiece in comedy, but I readily understand why its ambiguities are found disturbing. It is this very ambiguity of theme and moral that makes it a masterpiece. Carleton, like many better writers, knows how to have his cake and eat it too.

Phelim is a spoilt only child, up to every sort of roguery, for which his adoring parents always find an excuse. Aged 25, he makes advances to every unmarried woman of any age, if left alone with her for a moment. As a result, he finds himself engaged to three women at once, including the parish priest's elderly housekeeper. Hoping to escape them all, he arranges for his name to be 'called to' all three on the same Sunday. Instead of refusing to proclaim the banns, however, the priest does what he is asked by the relations of the three women, planning to teach both Phelim and his housekeeper a lesson. ' "It will also put the females of the parish on their guard against him," said [his] innocent curate, who knew not that it would raise him highly in their estimation.' Despite the priest's sarcasms—he nicknames Phelim 'the Patriarch'—the entire parish are so amused by Phelim's trickery that they forgive him, except of course for the friends and relations of the three 'damsels'. Soon afterwards, by a very stagy twist of the plot, Phelim finds himself in jail on suspicion of Ribbonism. Foodle Flattery, the father of one of Phelim's three fiancées, is easily persuaded to give evidence against him, and Phelim is lucky to be sentenced to transportation rather than hanging, having shared in many acts of terrorism, some perhaps on a par with that in 'Wildgoose Lodge'. It is Larry, Phelim's father, however, who has the last word, and a blackly humorous one it is: 'But sure the "boys" kep' their word to him, any how, in regard to shootin' Foodle Flattery. Myself was never betther plased in my life, than to hear he got the slugs into his heart, the villain!'

53 Stephen J. Brown, *Ireland*, 57.

After this grisly and unedifying conclusion, Carleton allows himself one paragraph of apology, in which he also seeks desperately for a moral that may satisfy at least some of his Protestant readers. I quote it in full because it contains, along with much that is equivocal, a sentence that sets forth unequivocally Carleton's views on political violence; I have taken the liberty of printing this sentence in italics.

We have attempted to draw Phelim O'Toole as closely as possible to the character of that class, whose ignorance, want of education, and absence of all moral principles, constitute them the shame and reproach of the country. By such men the peace of Ireland is destroyed, illegal combinations formed, blood shed, and nightly outrages committed. There is nothing more certain than this plain truth, that if proper religious and moral knowledge were impressed upon the early principles of persons like Phelim, a conscience would be created capable of revolting from crime. *Whatever the grievances of a people may be, whether real or imaginary, one thing is clear, that neither murder, nor illegal violence of any description, can be the proper mode of removing or redressing them.* We have kept Phelim's Ribbonism in the background, because the details could excite only aversion, and preferred exhibiting his utter ignorance of morality upon a less offensive subject, in order that the reader might be enabled to infer, rather than to witness with his mind's eye, the deeper crimes of which he was capable.[54]

This disclaimer leaves us wondering how many of Carleton's readers in fact regarded sexual immorality as 'less offensive' than illegal violence. Perhaps in 1833 they were still a majority, but fifteen years later their number would already have dwindled. Furthermore, the indulgence shown by the parish to Phelim's amorous exploits may imply a similar indulgence towards Ribbonism. Carleton's unwillingness to 'excite . . . aversion' suggests that he too feels a secret affection for Phelim and does not want to reduce his stature as folk hero. This is probably one reason why Phelim's Ribbonism is 'kept . . . in the background'. When it does finally emerge into the foreground, his stature is unexpectedly enhanced. I have already quoted the last words of the tale, expressing pleasure at the fate of the 'traitor' Flattery: Phelim's outburst when he finds he must stand trial is even more shocking to loyalist feelings, yet I am sure that Carleton felt a vicarious thrill as he wrote it:

'Our day will soon come, an' thin I'd recommend yees to thravel for your health. Hell saize the day's pace or happiness ever will be seen in this country, till laws, an' judges, an' gaols, an' gaolers, an' turnkeys, an' hangmen is all swep' out of it. . . . An' along wid them, goes the parsons an' prochtors, tithes an' taxes, all to the divil together. That day's not far off, ye d—d villians. An' now I tell yees, that if a hair o' my head's touched—ay if I was hanged to-morrow—

---

[54] William Carleton, *Traits and Stories of the Irish Peasantry*, Second Series (Dublin: William Frederick Wakeman, 1833), iii. 453.

I'd lave them behind me that 'ud put a bullet, wid the help an' blessin' o' God, through any one that'll injure me! So lay that to your conscience, an' do your best. Be the crass, O'Connell 'ill make you look nine ways at wanst for this! He's the boy can put the pin in your noses! . . . An', wid the blessin' o' God, he'll help us to put our feet on your necks afore long!'[55]

In actual fact, O'Connell was a staunch upholder of law and order, whose agent was active in putting down agrarian crime in County Kerry.[56] It was Carleton, not he, who once took the Ribbonmen's oath—doubtless under severe pressure from the young men of the neighbourhood, among whom he was renowned for his athletic prowess more than for his intelligence. Phelim's outburst is comic, of course; it summarizes the creed of a criminal, not that of a philosophic anarchist. Carleton, however, shares Phelim's view of tithe proctors, if not of parsons. To the very end, Carleton's psyche retained a hidden corner in which he remained loyal to the subversive oath taken in youth.

Nevertheless, in his list of thirty books published in the Dublin *Daily Express* (27 February 1895), Yeats found room for three books by Carleton—*Fardorougha the Miser*, *The Black Prophet*, and *Traits and Stories of the Irish Peasantry*—while insisting, 'I have excluded every book in which there is strong political feeling, that I may displease no man needlessly.'[57] Since Yeats knew the Carleton *oeuvre* thoroughly from the days when he compiled *Stories from Carleton* (1889), and scattered through his letters of 1888–95 what amounts to the best criticism of Carleton ever printed, I must respect this judgement even though I do not entirely accept it. Yeats also said, in submitting his list, that he had 'included only books of imagination of Ireland'. The prose fiction of William Carleton deserves inclusion under both of these categories: though it supports no political programme, it offers brilliant insights into the politics of its time.

A Synthesis—The Nation and Jail Journal

One might think that the contributors to *The Nation*, weekly newspaper of the Young Ireland movement from 1842 to 1843, had solved the problem of a synthesis between politics and literature, but this is only true if one accepts a very broad definition of literature. Thomas Davis does not seem to have taken himself seriously as a poet, though he responded promptly when Charles Gavan Duffy, editor of the *Nation*, asked for 'national ballads'.

---

55 Carleton, *Traits and Stories*, 2nd series, iii. 425–6.
56 His land-agent was his brother James O'Connell; see MacDonagh, 189–90.
57 Yeats, *Collected Letters*, i. 440.

Davis assured me he had never published a verse, though like most men of culture in the progress of self-education he had written and destroyed reams of paper covered with rhymes. Within a fortnight he brought me the 'Death of Owen Roe' . . . and week after week, for three years, he poured out songs as spontaneously as a bird.[58]

James Clarence Mangan is the one true poet associated with the *Nation*, but Roibeárd Ó Faracháin is surely correct in saying of him,

when he wrote strictly propagandist verse he scarcely bettered [the Young Irelanders'] other scribblers; indeed, Davis, who in general was very much his inferior as a poet, managed to give more quality to his propaganda in rhyme. Moreover, for the first three years of the *Nation's* existence, Mangan sent to it only his hastiest writings, reserving the real stuff for the *Dublin University Magazine*.[59]

It is his share in the rediscovery of Gaelic literature, of which he was supplied with literal translations by George Petrie, John O'Donovan, and John O'Daly, that gives Mangan his full stature, despite his baroque variations upon the originals. Nobody would dispute that 'Dark Rosaleen' is the most 'national' of his poems, though some scholars now believe that the original was in fact a love song, not a patriotic allegory. Samuel Ferguson, too, was a part of the Gaelic revival: his best translations of Irish songs date back to his *DUM* review articles on Hardiman's *Irish Minstrelsy* in 1834, when his youthful study of modern spoken Irish was still fresh in his mind. Much later, his acquaintance with Old and Middle Irish inspired the narrative poems in *Lays of the Western Gael* (1865), *Congal* (1872), and *Poems* (1880). His only literary contribution to the Young Ireland canon was the 'Lament for Thomas Davis' (1847), published not in the *Nation* but in the *DUM*.

The classic literature of '48, like that of '98, consists almost entirely of biography and autobiography; indeed, one might say that it consists of the works of John Mitchel: *Jail Journal* on the one hand, and on the other his vivid, unlamenting memoir of Thomas Francis Meagher, written in 1867 and never separately published.[60] Other writers sometimes achieved literature by accident: for example Michael Doheny in the last chapter of *The Felon's Track*, where he describes his wanderings in Cork, Waterford, and Kerry before finally escaping from Ireland. Probably because the '48 defeat was so ignominious and did not bring death in battle to a single leader, it inspired none of the elegiac poems in English or Irish that one associates with earlier defeats.

---

[58] Charles Gavan Duffy, *Young Ireland: A Fragment of Irish History 1840–1845*, Irish People's Edition (Dublin: M. H. Gill, 1884), 69.

[59] Roibeárd Ó Faracháin, 'James Clarence Mangan', in MacManus, 61.

[60] 'Mitchel on Meagher', in MacManus, 71–104: it was serialised in the Dublin weekly *The Shamrock* after Meagher's death in 1867.

When Mitchel 'was kidnapped, and carried off from Dublin, in chains', on 27 May 1848, he still hoped for a successful revolution in Ireland, but for the moment all political and military activity had become impossible for him. *Jail Journal* begins with a longish entry, ostensibly written that very day; whether it was or not, it contains no statement of Mitchel's purpose in keeping a diary, no promises of unprecedented frankness *à la* Rousseau—in short, no suggestion that Mitchel is undertaking a work of art. On the second day, in a parenthesis, he offers the only hint of his intentions ever granted the reader:

And now—as this is to be a faithful record of whatsoever befalls me—I do confess, and will write down the confession, that I flung myself on the bed, and broke into a raging passion of tears—tears bitter and salt—tears of wrath, pity, regret, remorse—but not of base lamentation for my own fate.[61]

Perhaps Mitchel's only conscious purpose was to pile up instances for British (or, with grim humour, 'Carthaginian') injustice to himself and his fellow convicts. Thomas Flanagan, in his brilliant essay 'Rebellion and Style: John Mitchel and the *Jail Journal*', while he follows Yeats in stressing the importance of Mitchel's very personal prose style, also refers several times to Mitchel's 'design'.[62] The term is ambiguous in that it can refer to both an artistic intention and a political one: that is what makes it peculiarly appropriate.

Perhaps the most powerful of the unifying ideas that make *Jail Journal* a work of art is Mitchel's condemnation of the British Empire. The picaresque adventures which he encounters during his largely involuntary journey round the world never leave him at a loss, because the empire upon which the sun never sets—already a cliché in his time—always manifests itself in fresh iniquities. Another fundamental idea is expressed by Mitchel's choice of the Greek quotation of his title-page, which means 'Numbered neither among the dead nor among the living'. The entire journal covers a gap in time during which the diarist exists only through his unspoken thoughts and his writing: otherwise he is without civil rights, as a felon, and makes it a point of honour to obey every command or restriction imposed on him.

The British Empire is to Mitchel what Moby-Dick is to Captain Ahab: Mitchel is our Irish Melville and, like him, delights to imitate Carlyle—not merely the sage's eccentric vocabulary and syntax but his mistrust of all nineteenth-century orthodoxies. Mitchel's mind had reached its full growth when he embarked on his reluctant voyages in his 33rd year, so that he learned little that was new from them;

[61] John Mitchel, *Jail Journal* (n.p.: Univ. Press of Ireland, 1982), 9.
[62] Reprinted from the *Irish University Review*, 1:1 (Autumn 1970), as the 'Critical Introduction' to the above edition of *Jail Journal*, vii–xxxv.

educated at Trinity, he had been a lawyer, a journalist, a politician; what is more, he had been married for a dozen years and was the father of a family. Melville's voyages, by contrast, made from his 20th to his 25th year, supplied the only higher education—the only Harvard and Yale, as he put it—that was open to him. Both Mitchel and Melville, however, in their different ways possessed the intellectual and emotional capacity to make sense of experiences that were wasted on tens of thousands of their contemporaries, whether 'felons' or seamen.

Jail Journal, then, is a unique synthesis of literature and politics, flawed—as much as Melville is flawed—by an egotism that takes for granted the reader's interest in every adventure and every thought that has occurred to its author. For once, there was no editorial restraint exercised by a publisher: *Jail Journal* first saw the light as a serial in *The Citizen*, a New York newspaper, in 1854. The editor of this periodical was none other than John Mitchel.

The limitations imposed on Irish writers by readers and publishers—in Ireland as well as England—will constantly reappear in the chapters that follow. Each time the restriction, real or imagined, will take a different form; each time, however, it will contain a political component, whether veiled or overt. By an imagined restriction I mean the exercise of self-censorship on the part of an author for fear of offending the supposed prejudices of readers. This is dealt with in the sub-chapter entitled 'The Morals of Deirdre', where for example we find Lady Gregory assuring the people of Kiltartan that she has bowdlerized the Ulster Sagas for fear of offending them: a wasted precaution, surely, since almost nobody in that impoverished County Galway village could have afforded *Cuchulain of Muirthemne*, published in London by John Murray, or even the Irish translation, published in Dublin by the Gaelic League. Perhaps it was the middle-class members of that organization whom Lady Gregory wished to reassure.

One of the more subtle intrusions of politics into publishing concerned the New Irish Library series which began publication in 1894. Yeats was planning a similar series when Sir Charles Gavan Duffy, back in Europe after a successful career in Australian politics, made his proposal to T. Fisher Unwin and was accepted. Yeats felt that Duffy's selections, beginning with an unpublished historical work by Thomas Davis, were a half-century out-of-date aesthetically as well as chronologically, but his attempts to reach a compromise on behalf of the new generation of writers were largely outmanoeuvred or ignored.

Much more spectacular were the famous riots at the Abbey Theatre against Synge's *Playboy of the Western World* in 1907 and O'Casey's *The Plough and the Stars* in 1926. The theatre survived these and many other shocks, but the attempt to create an equally enduring publishing house in Dublin failed, however nobly. Maunsel & Co., later Maunsel and Roberts, was founded in 1905 by Joseph Maunsel Hone, George Roberts, and Stephen Gwynn. Ironically, it is now best known for the non-publication of the first edition of Joyce's *Dubliners* in 1912, but the man responsible for the destruction of the sheets of that work was the printer, not the publisher. Maunsel's published Synge's *Collected Works* (1910) and a great many single plays and collections by the early Abbey dramatists, as well as poetry, novels, collections of essays, and political pamphlets. After the collapse of Maunsel and Roberts in 1925, London publishers faced little competition from their Dublin counterparts. Since only one Dublin-published volume, Frank O'Connor's translation of *The Midnight Court*, was ever banned by the Irish Censorship Board, it is possible to argue that a strong publishing industry in Dublin might have averted the worst effects of censorship on Irish writing. But it is doubtful whether the Dublin publishers would have mustered the courage to publish the books which the Board banned after they were issued in London.

3 Evangelical Revival in the Church of Ireland, 1800–69

Sons of the Clergy

It would be outrageous to suggest that the true purpose of the Irish Literary Revival was to provide alternative employment for the sons of clergymen after Disestablishment had reduced the number of livings provided by the Church of Ireland. Nevertheless the Revival, whose first stirrings can be felt in the decade after the Irish Church Act of 1869, did have this unintended side-effect. Among its founders, Standish James O'Grady and Douglas Hyde were clergymen's sons, while W. B. Yeats and J. M. Synge had clerical grandfathers. Yeats's paternal grandfather and great-grandfather were both rectors of country parishes; Synge's maternal grandfather, the Revd Robert Traill, rector of Schull, County Cork, died in 1847 of a fever caught while ministering to the famine victims among his parishioners. Although the Synges were a famous Irish clerical family, one has to go back to the dramatist's great-great-grandfather to find a clergyman in the direct male line.[1]

No doubt the quality of one's ancestors' churchmanship counts more in the long run than the number among them who have sought a livelihood in the Church. Precisely for this reason, one senses more than mere coincidence in the clerical antecedents of these four writers and others who later joined their movement. We expect writers and other artists to come from educated families, and virtually every clergyman of the Church of Ireland received a university education—of a kind which ensured that the immediate clerical ancestors of Yeats, Synge, Hyde, and O'Grady were more interested in scholarship than literature.[2] If they influenced their descendants' renewal of intellectual and artistic life in Ireland, it seems likely that the impulse came from their religious fervour rather than from any special gift for literature. The Church of Ireland as a whole, both clergy and laity, was powerfully affected

---

[1] For the Synge genealogy and much information about other persons mentioned here, see *Burke's Irish Family Records*, ed. H. J. Montgomery-Massingberd (London: Burke's Peerage, 1976).

[2] Joseph Hone, *W. B. Yeats 1865–1939* (New York: Macmillan, 1943), 5. But see Michael Sadleir, *Dublin University Magazine: Its History, Contents and Bibliography* (Dublin: Bibliographical Society of Ireland, 1938), 64. Sadleir says that Butt edited the magazine from August 1834 'until some time in 1838', but does not mention any 'co-editor'—Hone's description of the Revd William Butler Yeats, grandfather of the poet.

throughout the nineteenth century by the Evangelical Revival, which began in the Church of England during the last quarter of the eighteenth. Evangelicalism sought the same emotional response as Wesleyan Methodism, while taking a less optimistic view of human nature. There was at least an even chance that anyone ordained for the Irish Church between 1800 and 1850 would have undergone some Evangelical influence; those ordained in the second half of the century were virtually all Evangelicals.[3] There is, however, no need to rely on statistics or guesswork, since what used to be called the 'views' of our four authors' progenitors are well known.

The authenticity of Thomas O'Grady's vocation may be gauged by the fact that it came as a shock to his family, who regarded him as 'a "little wild"' for making the Church his profession instead of, like his brothers, the Army or the Navy. Hugh Art O'Grady writes:

When Standish was a child the evangelical movement was at its zenith, Cork was its stronghold, and between his father and the famous Bishop Gregg there was a deep friendship. Accordingly he was brought up in a religious atmosphere, whose only parallel today can be found in the Society of Friends.

Standish himself studied divinity for two years, but his outlook 'was too broad, too unconventional, for a Church of Ireland clergyman'. Nevertheless,

O'Grady grew to manhood with . . . a deep religious feeling, and a minute knowledge of the Bible. The religious feeling, which he never expressed in conversation, came out in his writings on social questions. To him the devil was very much alive in our great civilization.[4]

The Synge family, unlike the O'Grady clan, were staunch Evangelicals even as laymen. According to the gossipy *Recollections* of Revd Richard Sinclair Brooke, unofficial historian of Irish Evangelicalism, John Synge, the dramatist's grandfather, made Glanmore Castle available for clerical meetings at a time when these were a rallying point for the Evangelically inclined. Not only was he 'a skilled Hebraist', but his second son, the Revd A. H. Synge, became Brooke's 'able, pious and devoted assistant' at the Mariners' Church, Kingstown, built in 1836 under Evangelical auspices.[5] (Kingstown is now renamed Dún Laoire, and the church has

---

[3] On Synge's grandfather, the Revd Robert Traill, see David H. Greene and Edward M. Stephens, *J. M. Synge 1871–1909* (New York: Macmillan, 1959), 4. For Hyde's education, see Dominic Daly, *The Young Douglas Hyde . . .1874–1893* (Dublin: Irish Univ. Press, 1974), 1–2. On Thomas O'Grady, see Hugh Art O'Grady, *Standish James O'Grady: The Man and the Writer* (Dublin: Talbot Press, 1929), 23–9.

[4] O'Grady, *Standish James O'Grady*, 28–9.

[5] Richard Sinclair Brooke, *Recollections of the Irish Church* (London: Macmillan, 1877), 34–5. The 'second series' with the same title (Dublin: Hodges, Foster and Figgis, 1878) is hastily compiled and has not been quoted in this chapter.

become the Irish Maritime Museum.) This Alexander Synge was in 1851 'the first Protestant missionary' to the Aran Islands. In a letter written to one of his brothers he reported. 'I get on with the people so far very well, but how will it be when we begin to attack their bad ways, religion, *etc.*, I don't know.' Evangelicals being strict Sabbatarians, one of the 'bad ways' he soon denounced was handball-playing on Sunday: the parish priest began to demolish the handball court next day.[6] Irish Roman Catholicism tended to be influenced by Evangelicalism in two opposite ways: sometimes, as here, it imitated Evangelical puritanism; usually, however, it became more Catholic and, above all, more Roman.

The Revd Robert Traill, despite his exemplary self-sacrifice, also illustrates the bigoted aspects of Evangelicalism. He complained that his Bishop, 'who is well known as the enemy of all evangelical piety, objects to me on account of my religious sentiments'. Nor was the Bishop his only affliction:

I have waged war against popery in its thousand forms of wickedness, until my life had nearly paid the forfeit. . . . None but those who have had the trying experience can possibly know the state of inquietude and feverish anxiety in which the Roman Catholics . . . keep the man who boldly denounces their abominations.[7]

Although J. M Synge rejected not only Evangelicalism but all other forms of Christianity, he remained to the end of his life essentially Puritanical in morals and manners. His nearest brother in age, the Revd Samuel Synge, published a touching, ill-organized memoir whose burden is that the playwright's life deviated but little from the Evangelical norm. Samuel, as one might expect, managed to convince himself that John 'died looking to God, I feel sure'.[8] No wonder John wrote of Samuel to Molly Allgood, his fiancée: 'He is one of the best fellows in the world, I think, though he is so religious that we have not much in common'.[9] It is likely that Samuel believed his brother had undergone the conversion thought essential by Evangelicals when they both attended 'the Mission held by Rev. Marcus Rainsford in Zion Church', apparently in 1881.[10] As its name suggests, this church in Rathgar, Dublin, was built for Evangelicals. More conservative Anglicans might not have permitted the holding of such a 'mission'.

---

[6] David H. Greene and Edward M. Stephens, *J. M Synge 1871–1909* (New York: Macmillan, 1959) 75.

[7] Ibid. 4

[8] Revd Samuel Synge, *Letters to my Daughter* (Dublin: Talbot Press, n.d. [1931], 131.

[9] J. M Synge, *Letters to Molly*, ed. Ann Saddlemyer (Cambridge, Mass., Belknap-Harvard Univ. Press, 1971, 43.

[10] Synge, *Letters to my Daughter*, 20, 50.

This brief look at the families of O'Grady and Synge shows that Evangelicalism offered both attractive and repellent aspects and that its influence continued into the next generation. The clerical tradition in the Yeats and Hyde families predates the Evangelical dawn in Ireland: the four successive generations of clerical Hydes commenced in the first half of the eighteenth century, and the Revd John Butler Yeats, great-grandfather of the poet, was born in 1774.[11] It was the Revd William Butler Yeats, grandfather of the poet, who is said to have antagonized his rector by Evangelicalism while a curate at Moira, County Down; few who studied divinity at TCD in the early 1830s can have escaped Evangelical influence.[12] The group who founded the *Dublin University Magazine* in 1833 were all Conservatives in politics and usually Evangelicals as well. The first editor, the Revd Charles Stuart Stanford, remained sternly Evangelical throughout his life; Isaac Butt, who succeeded him as editor in 1834 and held the post for four years, shared Stanford's political and religious beliefs at the time, though he is now best remembered as the founder of the Irish Parliamentary Party. The Revd W. B. Yeats was a college friend of Butt's and, like him, seems to have modified if not abandoned his Evangelicalism as he grew older; he certainly was no bigot.[13] Two of his brothers, though laymen, were keen Evangelicals: of Matthew Yeats, the poet's father later wrote that 'Bible Christianity' did him 'a great deal of injury—it spoiled him, made him unhappy'. Nevertheless, he assured Matthew's eldest son, Frank, 'You ought to be proud of being descended from the Yeats—Of all the people I have known they were the most attractive and the most spiritually minded—you did not see them at their best.'[14] Despite his agnosticism, Yeats's father—the second John Butler—would have not hesitated to apply the phrase 'spiritually minded' either to himself or to any of his four children.

Douglas Hyde's attitude to the Church of Ireland in his youth was complicated by his feelings towards his father, the Revd Arthur Hyde. Douglas's eldest brother (who died in 1879) had been expected to become the fifth successive Arthur Hyde among the Irish clergy, but he turned agnostic, to the bitter regret of his father, who blamed the atmosphere at TCD. Douglas, however, seriously contemplated entering the Church— and even joining its foreign missions—from January 1877, when he

[11] John Butler Yeats, *Letters to his Son W. B. Yeats and others*, ed. Joseph Hone (New York: Dutton 1946), 214.

[12] William Michael Murphy, *Prodigal Father: The Life of John Butler Yeats* (Ithaca, NY: Cornell Univ. Press, 1978), 549, n.15.

[13] Sadleir, *Dublin University Magazine*, 61–3, 68–70. For Stanford's proselytizing, see James Godkin, *Ireland and her Churches* (London: Chapman & Hall, 1867), 199, 204. Brooke pays tribute to Stanford's culture, *Recollections*, 128.

turned 17; he took his BA in 1884, passed his final divinity examination in 1885, and may have been working towards the degree of Bachelor in Divinity when he changed to the study of law in October 1886. By 1883, however, father and son were disagreeing angrily about fundamental beliefs. Whatever his other tenets were, Arthur Hyde seems to have insisted upon a literal interpretation of the Bible: one night they 'had a terrible row. . . about belief in the Bible and about angels'.[15] Nevertheless, drinking and card-playing were permitted in the rectory; indeed, Douglas often felt that his father indulged in both to excess, so the moral tone of the family was far from Evangelical.

At this period the young Hyde was moving away not only from Evangelical literalism but from the Evangelicals' traditional Toryism. On 1 March 1885 he read a paper to the College Theological Society bearing the somewhat misleading title 'The Attitude of the Reformed Church in Ireland'. Here is part of the sympathetic report published in the *Dublin University Review* for April:

The latter part of the Paper gave the essayist's own opinions as to the position the Irish Church clergy ought to take up with regard to the present Nationalist movement. This position, according to Mr Hyde, should be one of approval, implicit if not avowed. Such opinions are not very common in the Theological Society [*an ironic understatement*], and their expression evoked against the essayist many hostile criticisms.[16]

Although he never left the Church of Ireland, Hyde was destined to become a missionary of the Gaelic Revival rather than the Gospel. If he had taken orders, he might well have risen to be a bishop or even Primate; instead, he was elected unopposed as the first President of Ireland under the 1937 Constitution.

One more founder of the Literary Revival must be mentioned in the context of Evangelicalism. Lady Gregory was the daughter of a layman and precluded by her sex from making the Church her profession, but her autobiography contains a very explicit account of her Evangelical upbringing and the conversion which set at rest her fears of hell. Because of Adam's sin,

there was no escape except being washed in the Blood of the Lamb, and that could not be unless you were converted, unless you believed while still in this earthly life; there was no place for repentance, no Purgatory. . . .

---

[14] Thomas S. W. Lewis, 'Some New Letters of John Butler Yeats', in *Modern Irish Literature: Essays in Honor of William York Tindall*, ed. Raymond J. Porter and James D. Brophy (New York: Iona College Press–Twayne, 1972) 343.

[15] Dominic Daly, *The Young Douglas Hyde* (Dublin: Irish University Press, 1974), 51.

[16] Ibid. 55.

So it was no wonder that she was troubled. Was she a believer? Lacking it, what must she do to be saved? . . . The restlessness of the mind increased. Then of a sudden one morning in the cottage on Lough Corrib her father had taken as a fishing lodge, she rose up from her bed at peace with God. All doubts and all fears had gone, she was one of His children, His angels were her friends. . . . His word, the Bible was her only book. She need no longer strive to do His will, it was her delight to do it.

Lady Gregory adds this characteristic and endearing comment: 'She was a little ashamed of this ecstasy, a little shy, unwilling to have it known.' At first she was satisfied to read only the Bible and religious books, 'the only ones of which there were a plenty in the house', but then she began to show discrimination, preferring George Herbert's poems and *The Imitation of Christ* to doctrinal hymns and books of sermons.

As an indication of how deliberately unliterary her family was, consider the following:

As to novels, she had been taught to consider them food unfit for the use of Christ's flock; and indeed the daughters of the house were forbidden to read even the Waverleys until they attained the age of eighteen. And for this she was afterwards grateful, for coming later they never won her heart and all her romantic sympathies were kept for Ireland.[17]

With the passage of time, her love of literature expanded beyond the limits of English, leading her eventually to the Irish folklore that surrounded her in Connacht and ultimately to literature in Irish. Her religious belief, like O'Grady's and Hyde's, persisted throughout her life, though it ceased to be all-engrossing. Her unswerving loyalty and unselfish devotion to all her 'causes' in later years—whether individuals like Yeats and Sean O'Casey, or cultural institutions like the Abbey Theatre, or issues of national significance like the return of her nephew Hugh Lane's picture collection to Ireland—bore the stamp of her early moral training. In her career as a dramatist and writer of narrative prose, however, we observe the paradox, also apparent in the work of Synge, that an unliterary—indeed an *anti*literary—religious orientation can adapt much of its intensity to the concerns of art. Many readers now object to what they feel is the false simplicity, mannered rather than spontaneous, of her writing in the Kiltartan dialect, but the passages just quoted from *Seventy Years* combine simplicity of diction with complexity of thought. They may also suggest that Evangelicalism's greatest gift to any writer was an intimacy with the language of the King James Bible and the Book of Common Prayer.

[17] Augusta Lady Gregory, *Seventy Years* (Gerrard's Cross: Colin Smythe, 1974).

From Evangelicalism to 'Souperism'

The founders of the Literary Revival tended to repudiate their Evangelical heritage because of its negative aspects, particularly the widespread though not universal hostility of Evangelicals to Roman Catholicism. A movement seeking a national cultural revival could not afford to alienate the great majority of the nation who were devoutly Catholic. Also, a movement that idealized the peasant and his culture, whether expressed in Irish or English, dared not be suspected of despising his religion. In their anxiety to deny the errors of Evangelicalism, the Revival writers first ignored and then forgot what they owed to its positive life-enhancing aspects.

The historian G. M Young characterized the parallel situation in England—less complicated there because Catholics formed a small minority instead of a large majority of the population—as follows:

On one of its sides, Victorian history is the story of the English mind employing the energy imparted by Evangelical convictions to rid itself of the restraint which Evangelicalism had laid on the senses and the intellect; on amusement, enjoyment, art; on curiosity, on criticism, on science.[18]

The Protestant writers of the Revival were very conscious of their need to liberate the senses and the intellect, but they also felt obliged to free themselves and others from ingrained political and religious prejudices. The greatest threat to their success, and one of which they seem never to have been sufficiently aware, was the association in the folk mind between Protestantism and some unscrupulous forms of proselytism. The blame for these must be laid squarely on certain groups of Evangelicals.

Before tracing how Evangelicalism came to be identified with 'souperism' in the popular mind, I must attempt to characterize the Evangelical movement as it manifested itself in Ireland, beginning with the testimony of a brilliant but somewhat hostile witness, the Revd Professor John Pentland Mahaffy, later Sir John and Provost of TCD. Recalling half a century later the 'popular preachers of Dublin in 1850', he noted that, unlike the early Puritans, they were content with the King James Bible and did not think an accurate knowledge of the Greek and Hebrew originals essential:

But so convinced were they of the vital importance of Scripture, that I have actually heard a clergyman . . . assert the verbal inspiration of the English Bible, on the ground that the same influence which guided the pens of the original writers could not have failed to guide . . . the translators. . . .

[18] George Malcolm Young, *Victorian England: Portrait of an Age* (London: Oxford Univ. Press, 1936), 5.

Regarding therefore the Bible, as they understood it, [as] the absolute rule of faith, they nevertheless . . . never quarrelled with the Book of Common Prayer; they read through the service devoutly every Sunday.

The 'real work of the day', however, was the sermon, often lasting three-quarters of an hour, in which it was the preacher's 'absolute duty to set forth the whole Gospel . . . , so that any stray person, or any member of the congregation in a contrite condition, might then and there attain conversion (which was always sudden) and find peace'. Furthermore, 'They did not hesitate to preach that all those who had not embraced the doctrine of justification by faith were doomed to eternal perdition.'

Mahaffy's final judgement on these men is rather severe:

Their logic was often at fault. . . . They boldly preached that while man was free to do evil, and therefore responsible for it, he was unable, owing to Adam's transgression, to do any good thing of himself. And yet they never doubted the benevolence of the Deity, though they called every conversion a miracle. They lived saintly and charitable lives, though they inveighed against the value of good works.

He does not deny that 'They were excellent and able men', but 'most philosophers would denounce' the creed which they proclaimed 'as a cruel and even immoral parody of the teaching of the Founder'.[19]

It would be hard to find a better witness for the defence than the Revd Richard Sinclair Brooke, already mentioned. I have characterized the style of his *Recollections* as 'gossipy', but even there he has moments of true eloquence. The following passage cannot be described as a logical definition of Evangelicalism; rather, it tries to convey the essence of evangelical teaching under ideal conditions:

wherever the Gospel of Christ is told forth with fervour, feeling, and simplicity, the people in this country, both high and low, throng to listen, and are never weary in so doing. Ritualism may dazzle the senses, Rationalism delight the intellect, but it is only a *full Christ*, all-sufficient in life for an holy example, all-sufficient in death for an atoning sacrifice, all-sufficient in glory to sanctify and help us by the impartation of His grace—it is only this Christ, like a full ocean breaking upon a thousand shores of feeling, and reaching and touching every realm of thought and life—it is this, and this only, that can, through the Spirit, go down and speak to the heart, and wake up its every pulse to the reception and enjoyment of a life which, begun then, will outlive death and last for ever.[20]

Stopford Augustus Brooke, Richard's son, made valuable critical contributions to the Literary Revival, but one could argue that the

[19] J. P Mahaffy, 'The Drifting of Doctrine', *Hibbert Journal*, 1 (1902–3), 504–5.
[20] Brooke, *Recollections*, 28–9.

father demonstrates a more purely artistic gift than his son's in *Poems* (1852).[21]

The above quotations emphasize four of the five essential doctrines of Evangelicalism: 'the utter depravity of unregenerate human nature, necessity for conversion, justification of sinners by faith, . . . and the divine inspiration, authority and sufficiency of Holy Scripture.'[22]

It was the fifth, 'free offer of the Gospel to all mankind', that led to division among Irish Evangelicals and ultimately caused all of them to be mistrusted by Irish Roman Catholics. This doctrine clearly implied the necessity of foreign missions to non-Christians; did it, however, also encourage the undertaking of missions to fellow-Christians who were not convinced of the sufficiency of Scripture or of justification by faith alone without good works? Those who gave a positive answer to this question eventually brought Evangelicalism into disrepute.

An early fruit of the Evangelical revival in England was the founding of the Church Missionary Society in 1799; its aim was to bring Anglican Christianity to the non-Christian world. Fifteen years later, the Revd Benjamin Williams Mathias and other leading Evangelicals, both clerical and lay, founded the Hibernian Church Missionary Society in Dublin for the same purpose. It is indicative of Mathias's sense of the priorities in Ireland that he had already founded the Hibernian Bible Society in 1806, only two years after its counterpart, the British and Foreign Bible Society. Before taking this step, Mathias had consulted fellow-Anglicans and the ministers of other Protestant denominations in Dublin. Among the Anglicans consulted, all presumably in sympathy with Evangelicalism, were Bernard Shaw, grandfather of the dramatist, and the Revd Walter Stephens. (One of G. B. S.'s uncles was christened Walter Stephens Shaw, though none of the younger Shaws seems to have known why.)[23] There was an urgent need for Bibles in English as well as in Irish because of the eighteenth-century torpor of the Church of Ireland.

Contrary to the probable intentions of Mathias, who might have been a Franciscan in an earlier century, several local branches of the Hibernian Bible Society became centres of aggressive Protestant propaganda, especially in the years just before the passage of Catholic Emancipation in 1829.[24] Another Evangelical foundation, the Irish

---

[21] Revd R. S. Brooke, *Poems* (Dublin, James McGlashan, 1852).

[22] 'Evangelical', *Everyman's Encyclopaedia*, 4th edn. (London: John Dent, 1958)

[23] *Brief Memorials of the Rev B. W Mathias, Late Chaplain of Bethesda Chapel* (Dublin: William Curry, Jun. 1842), 164.

[24] For the controversies stirred up by the Hibernian Bible Society and some of its local branches, see Desmond Bowen, *The Protestant Crusade in Ireland, 1800–70* (Dublin: Gill & Macmillan, 1978), 71–3, 98–103. The society was multi-denominational from its inception. In 1821 the Protestant Archbishops of Armagh and Dublin resigned from their posts in the society, though Church of Ireland Evangelicals continued to work with it (Donald Harman Akenson, *The Church of Ireland: Ecclesiastical Reform and Revolution, 1800–1885*: New Haven: Yale Univ. Press, 1971), 135.

Society (1818), went one step farther: its purpose was to teach Irish-speaking peasants to read the Scriptures in Irish to their neighbours. While insisting that it was not a proselytizing agency, the Irish Society had to stress the number of conversions to Protestantism that its activities fostered if it wished to continue to receive donations from its supporters in Britain and Ireland.[25]

It was in the 1830s that the more extreme Evangelicals began an overt campaign of proselytism among Roman Catholics in Ireland. The chief centres were two or three of the poorest parishes in Dublin City, where Stanford (former editor of the *Dublin University Magazine*) was a leader, and some impoverished areas on the Atlantic coast. Relatively successful missions were established by the Revd Edward Nangle, who learned Irish, on Achill Island, and by the Revd Charles Gayer, an Englishman, in the Dingle Peninsula; Gayer owed much to the help of one of the Moriarty brothers, three local Irish-speaking converts.[26]

In 1849 the most notorious and for a time the most successful of proselytizing agencies, the Society for Irish Church Missions to the Roman Catholics, was founded by the Revd Alexander Dallas, with headquarters in London at Exeter Hall, a hotbed of Evangelical societies. Dallas, an English parish clergyman, was chiefly occupied in fund-raising for the Society throughout the British Isles, but he had many Irish allies, especially in Counties Galway and Mayo; Alexander Synge, for example, was sent to Aran by Dallas. The great irony of the Connacht mission was that its converts, shunned by their neighbours and trained for white-collar occupations at the mission schools, found themselves obliged to emigrate to America or the British colonies instead of swelling the ranks of the Church of Ireland at home.[27] The long-term consequences of Dallas's campaign may well have included the prevailing Counter-Reformation spirit of Irish Catholicism for the rest of the century and beyond, and the advancing of the date for the inevitable Disestablishment of the Church of Ireland.

On the mythic level—the vital one for literature and folklore—as on the historical level, what Desmond Bowen calls 'The Protestant Crusade' had important consequences. That Dallas should have begun his missionary campaign while the Irish people, especially in Connacht, were still reeling from the Great Famine of 1845–7 made a very sinister impression.

[25] Lionel James, *A Forgotten Genius: Sewell of St Columba's and Radley* (London: Faber & Faber, 1945), 99.
[26] Bowen, *Souperism: Myth or Reality?* (Cork: Mercier Press, 1970) 83–8. The Revd Thomas Moriarty began his ministry in 1839, at the invitation of Gayer. The Revd William Sewell and his friends Viscount Adare and William Monsell believed that Moriarty was more of a High Churchman than an Evangelical. According to Monsell, 'The difference between Ventry and other places consisted in the Irish-speaking minister there and the Church principles which he advocated.'
[27] Bowen, *Souperism*, 88, 103.

The Evangelical missionaries were accused of bribing starving people with food, of tempting them to sell their religious birthright literally for a 'mess of pottage'. The term 'souper', meaning a convert to Protestantism, is said to have been in use in Dingle even before the famine.[28] From the reign of Elizabeth onwards, Gaelic poetry includes many satires against converts to Protestantism: all were believed to have renounced their faith because of the higher material and social status enjoyed by Protestants, especially when Catholicism was virtually proscribed by the Penal Laws. Douglas Hyde translated some of these in *The Religious Songs of Connacht*.[29] Not until the nineteenth century, however, were converts accused of bartering their faith for bare subsistence. In 1847, at the height of the famine, the Catholic clergy were overwhelmed by the duty of giving the last rites to the dying; thousands more might have died but for the soup kitchens, usually financed by Quaker relief organizations but operated by the local Church of Ireland clergy with their families. It is easy to see how charges of 'souperism' could arise in such circumstances. As Bowen says, the writings of Alexander Dallas make it hard to believe that 'souperism would never be considered by his followers as a tactic, after he publicly announced his intention to take direct advantage of the desperate suffering of the Irish people'; he warns us, however, that 'even with Dallas and his followers, souperism is difficult to prove'.[30] Dallas's movement, as we have seen, did not begin until the famine was over, but if Synge's grandfather, for example, had survived, he would have been peculiarly vulnerable to accusations of this kind because of his reputation for anti-Catholicism. Bowen gives several examples of clergymen whose conduct in 1847 was just as heroic as the Revd Robert Traill's, but who were later charged with souperism.[31]

Had it not been for the unfortunate timing and some of the dubious tactics of Dallas's campaign, the pervasive atmosphere of 'souls for soup' surrounding the Church of Ireland might have dispersed quite easily with the passage of time. Only those aware of this mythico-historical background can grasp the full significance of Yeats's *The Countess Cathleen*, which by coincidence rather than intentional symbolism became the first play performed by the Irish Literary Theatre (8 May 1899). In a pamphlet *Souls for Gold*, this play about demons buying Irish souls during a medieval famine was denounced as anti-Catholic and made the subject of a public protest by University College Dublin students. No Trinity students, however, seem to have protested against the identification of proselytizers with demons![32]

[28] Bowen, *Souperism*, 84.   [29] Daly, 118.
[30] Bowen, *Souperism*, 124.   [31] Ibid. 84.
[32] W. B. Yeats, *Autobiographies*, (London: Macmillan, 1955), 414–16. See also George Moore, *Hail and Farewell: Ave* (New York: Appleton, 1911), 127–8, 133–7.

The Intellectual Heritage

Besides its theological and mythological effects, the Evangelical Revival in Ireland, as in England, had moral, social, and, more surprisingly, intellectual consequences. Despite all the emphasis on faith at the expense of works,

Evangelical morality was the single most widespread influence in Victorian England. . . . it spread through every class and taught a clear set of values. The peremptory demand for sincerity, the delight in plain-speaking, the unvarying accent on conduct, and the conviction that he who has attained a Higher Truth must himself evangelise, leap from the pages of [Leslie] Stephen's books and proclaim him a child of the Evangelical tradition.[33]

In his brilliant analysis of Sir Leslie Stephen's thought and character, Lord Annan argues convincingly that certain members of the 'Bloomsbury' group—E. M. Forster and Stephen's two daughters, Vanessa Bell and Virginia Woolf—were linked to the Evangelical Clapham Sect not only by ties of blood but in some sense by intellectual tradition also. It is Annan's example, in fact, that has emboldened me to pursue similar connections in Ireland.

As regards moral tone, I think the most striking difference between the average nineteenth-century Irish Anglican and his eighteenth-century counterpart must have been the former's seriousness of manner, an outward and visible sign of mental and moral sobriety. No longer the roistering squires of Sir Jonah Barrington's *Recollections* or Maria Edgeworth's *Castle Rackrent*, many Church of Ireland laymen came to be perceived by their Roman Catholic neighbours as 'sourfaces' (D. P. Moran's term): a far cry indeed from Goldsmith's 'men of a thousand pound a year in Ireland' who 'spend their whole lives in running after a hare, drinking to be drunk, and getting every Girl with Child, that will let them'.[34]

A change in moral tone was not the whole story, however, as Annan notes:

The intellectual heritage of Evangelicalism has been too readily forgotten . . . it is too often assumed to be a religion with a theology simplified to the point of banality which calls men to action rather than strengthens their minds . . . It is true that no outstanding intellect emerges among the clergy of the Evangelical persuasion, but the histories of the movement . . . do not follow the sheep who

---

33 Noel Gilroy Annan, *Leslie Stephen: His Thought and Character in Relation to his Time* (London: MacGibbon & Kee, 1951), 110.
34 Oliver Goldsmith, *Collected Letters*, ed. Katherine C. Balderston (Cambridge Univ. Press, 1928) 10.

stray from the fold. Half the men and much of the enthusiasm of Tractarianism were of Evangelical origin; the most fervent recruits of rationalism came from Evangelical homes.[35]

Ireland, for fairly obvious reasons, supplied few recruits to the Tractarian/Oxford movement, but at least three outstanding rationalists came from Irish Protestant families. We cannot be sure how Evangelical the homes of John Tyndall and W. E. H. Lecky were, but J. B. Bury's father served the diocese of Clogher as curate, rector, and, eventually, canon. Two of the historian's brothers became clergymen: one died young, but the other must have been perturbed by *A History of the Freedom of Thought* or some of the eldest brother's work on the early history of Christianity.[36] Mahaffy, though not the intellectual equal of Bury, had a world reputation in his day for his work on Greek papyri. As we have seen, he was very much a Broad Churchman in later years, but his mother and his clergyman father were impeccably Evangelical.[37] Like Mahaffy, the Revd Stopford Brooke moved theologically far to the 'left' of his father—so far that he became a Unitarian, denying the divinity of Christ and therefore no longer a Christian according to the doctrine held by Richard Sinclair Brooke. Stopford Brooke's volume of lectures and sermons and his critical and historical works on English literature are now virtually forgotten; he is chiefly remembered as an early influence on Bernard Shaw and a probable model for the Revd James Mavor Morell in *Candida*. His maternal grandfather, the Revd Joseph Stopford, a Fellow of TCD 1790–1809, was revered as a pioneer Evangelical; a cousin, Alice Stopford, daughter of an Irish Archdeacon and his devoutly Evangelical wife, married the English historian J. R. Green, who had already given up Anglican orders, and herself won a reputation as a historian of Irish nationalism.[38]

Towering intellectually above all these, though incapable of the scholarship of a Bury or the scientific insight of a Tyndall, stands Bernard Shaw. It is impossible to comprehend fully his lifelong obsession with religion or his idiosyncratic moralizing versions of socialism unless one becomes aware of the deep commitment to Evangelicalism shown by the two generations of Shaws who preceded him. He makes no secret of the bigotry endemic in his family; what he fails to mention— perhaps does not even know about—is their close involvement with some of the more positive and innovative trends in Evangelicalism. His

[35] Annan, *Leslie Stephen*, 110.

[36] James B. Leslie, *Clogher Clergy and Parishes* (Enniskillen: Printed for the Author, 1929), 82–3.

[37] See William Bedell Stanford and Robert Brendan McDowell, *Mahaffy: A Biography of an Anglo-Irishman* (London: Routledge & Kegan Paul, 1971).

[38] Brooke, *Recollections*, 16.

grandfather Bernard Shaw's friendship with the pioneer Evangelical B. W. Mathias has already been noted, along with his somewhat eccentric approach to the naming of children: not only did he name Walter Stephens Shaw after a fellow Evangelical but he named another son after his own father-in-law, the Revd Edward Carr, rector of Kilmacow, while the dramatist's father, George Carr Shaw, was named after the relation who officiated at his parents' wedding. Incidentally, the Revd George Whitmore Carr was, like many Evangelicals, an enthusiast for temperance; less typically, he was broadminded enough to join Father Theobald Mathew in his famous crusade against alcohol. One hopes he never discovered that his namesake was for many years an alcoholic.[39]

In his anxiety to represent himself as a 'downstart', from a family in decline, Shaw was often evasive about the respectability of his father's brothers: he makes cruel fun of the religious mania displayed by his eldest uncle, William Bernard Shaw, in later years, but omits to mention that Uncle William (also known as Barney) was educated at TCD and took holy orders in the Church of Ireland.[40] Shaw also insists that none of his father's immediate family ever prospered, carefully ignoring his Uncle Henry, a generous benefactor of Evangelicalism, whose energy and wealth helped to construct 'that genteel suburban Irish Protestant church, built by Roman Catholic workmen who would have considered themselves damned had they crossed its threshold afterwards'.[41] This was Christ Church, Leeson Park, still a Dublin landmark, described by James Godkin in 1867 as 'the most splendid monument . . . of the power of the voluntary principle in the Establishment—a church built in the Gothic style, light, commodious, and elegant . . . and offering accommodation to 1,300 people, with an equally commodious asylum for the blind in the same style of architecture.'[42] It replaced the old chapel of the Molyneux Asylum for the Blind, situated in Peter Street, which had become a slum; the old buildings had in any case been ingeniously adapted from a circus! This early example of the flight of a middle-class congregation from the inner city was planned by the Revd Dr Charles Marlay Fleury, Chaplain of the Asylum and a powerful Evangelical preacher. One of Henry Shaw's daughters married a son of Dr Fleury, so that there were ties of blood as well as religion between the two families.[43]

The essay 'On Going to Church', already quoted, contains this memorable assertion: 'When I was a little boy, I was compelled to go to

[39] John O'Donovan: *Bernard Shaw*, Gill's Irish Lives (Dublin: Gill & Macmillan, 1983), 33.

[40] Charles MacMahon Shaw, *Bernard's Brethren* (New York: Henry Holt, n.d.) [1939], 47–8.

[41] 'On Going to Church', in *Selected Non-Dramatic Writings of Bernard Shaw*, ed. Dan H. Laurence (Boston: Houghton Mifflin, 1965), 386.

[42] Godkin, *Ireland*, 111.　　[43] Brooke, *Recollections*, 43–4.

church on Sunday; and though I escaped from that intolerable bondage before I was ten, it prejudiced me so violently against churchgoing that twenty years elapsed before, in foreign lands and in pursuit of works of art, I became once more a churchgoer.' The 9-year-old Shaw did not in fact engineer his own escape from bondage: as he tells us in a companion essay, 'In the Days of My Youth' (1898), his family 'broke with the observance and never resumed it' after they went to live in Dalkey—that is, after the nominal Catholic but professed atheist George John Vandaleur Lee joined the household. In his last revision of this essay, Shaw states unequivocally that the church he detested was 'the Molyneux in Upper Leeson Street'.[44] It seems clear that Shaw's father attended this church as well as sending his son there; in a late reminiscence, Shaw wrote: 'I can remember the ante-Lee period in Synge St. when my father, as sole chief of the household, read family prayers'.[45] Even if he had by then lost his father's Evangelical faith, George Carr Shaw still clung to its forms until he felt the impact of Lee's far stronger personality.

The young G. B. S. had a keen nose for middle-class snobbery among Evangelicals—all the more so because he was sometimes guilty of it himself, as he admitted in *Sixteen Self Sketches* (1949): for eighty years he kept it a secret that his parents, urged by Lee, had sent him to a Roman Catholic school for a few months in 1869 until he rebelled in 'shame and wounded snobbery'. His experiences in Leeson Park led him to say, 'What helped to make "church" a hotbed of all the social vices was that no working folk ever came there'.[46] It seems unlikely though not impossible that Shaw was granted this insight at 9 years old, but it is confirmed by James Godkin, a brilliant Irish amateur sociologist writing in 1867:

the free church [Evangelical] congregations are for the greater part far the most select, respectable, and fashionable, for they consist generally of those who are able to pay their way, and who prefer paying liberally for pews . . . into which no stranger may intrude. And it sometimes happens that the graduations of wealth and respectability are marked by the position occupied by certain families in the church . . . no doubt one cause of the success of these churches is that the worshippers may avoid unpleasant contact with people of inferior positions, some of whom may not be very well dressed, perhaps not over clean; or they may be offensive by the vulgarity of their manners.[47]

It is not surprising that someone from this social stratum should argue, in both the play *Major Barbara* and its preface, that 'the worst of our

44 Bernard Shaw, *Self Sketches*, 76.
45 G. B. Shaw, *Complete Prefaces*, (London: Hamlyn, 1965) 856.
46 Bernard Shaw, *Self Sketches*, 76.
47 Godkin, Ireland, 207.

crimes is poverty, and . . . our first duty, to which every other consideration should be sacrificed, is not to be poor.'[48]

Idealism Reborn and Redefined

Godkin makes clear that by the late 1860s Irish Evangelicalism had ceased to be a revolutionary, prophetic faith; like many such renewals of the spirit it was rapidly hardening into a dogma embodied in an institution—specifically the Disestablished Church of Ireland, as it was called after 1869. (Its official title from the Act of Union until Disestablishment had been the United Church of England and Ireland.) The economic organization of the Church was now controlled by middle-class laymen, who for a time seemed determined to change the Book of Common Prayer radically in the direction of Evangelical orthodoxy; in the end, the conservatism of the clergy prevailed.[49]

If the idealism and energy of earlier days were to survive, they must find new channels in the minds and hearts of the young; and find them they did. The Revd Charles Osborne, brother of the Impressionist painter Walter Osborne, has left us a perceptive account of the intellectual ferment in Protestant Dublin of the 1870s:

just when George Tyrrell was a youth in Dublin, various groups of thinking young men, whose parents were nearly always orthodox Protestants of the old-fashioned Low Church variety, were experiencing . . . disengagement of their minds from Puritan moorings. The direction taken was not the same in each case, but the liberating process was experienced, whatever the ultimate goal of the soul's barque might be.[50]

The most obvious direction led to some other form of religious observance—often High-Church Anglicanism, to be found in a few Dublin churches such as All Saints', Grangegorman, where the rector was a son of the Revd Charles Maturin, novelist, dramatist, sometime Evangelical and grand-uncle of Oscar Wilde. Of the young men who chose this way, Osborne says, 'some changed their minds or ceased to trouble about such matters, others left the country, generally to serve in the Anglican ministry in England or the Colonies; while a very few acknowledged Rome as the true end of their wanderings'.[51] The most famous and controversial among these last few was Father George Tyrrell; Wilde might have joined them in his twenties but lost courage

---

[48] Bernard Shaw, *Prefaces* (London: Odhams, 1938), 118.
[49] Akenson, 302–9; J. T. Ball: *The Reformed Church of Ireland* (1537–1886), 294–303.
[50] Maud Dominica Mary Petre, *Autobiography and Life of George Tyrrell* (London: Arnold, 1912), i. 145.
[51] Ibid., i. 146–7.

and put off his conversion until he was dying. One of his Portora contemporaries, John Haughton Steele, a son of the Headmaster, having been a Church of Ireland clergyman for many years, was received into the Roman Catholic Church in 1910 and became a secular priest in 1912. Another contemporary, Edward Sullivan, a friend of Wilde's, had a younger brother John who entered Portora two years after Wilde had left; he was converted in 1896 and ordained a Jesuit priest in 1907. These conversions may confirm the authenticity of Wilde's own: at the very least, they convey an atmosphere now largely forgotten.[52]

Christianity, in whatever form, was not to be the only religious option: by 1886 a Dublin Lodge of the Theosophical Society had been founded by Charles Johnston, friend of both Yeats and A. E. (George Russell).[53] Given the peculiar religious sociology of Ireland, the fact that Theosophy was non-Christian did not prevent it from holding almost exactly the status of a tiny Protestant sect. The principle defined by Annan as 'following the inner light wherever is shines' inhibited Protestants from objecting strongly to the cult, while official Catholicism rarely felt obliged to notice a group which in practice had no appeal for Catholics. John Eglinton (W. K. Magee), biographer and friend of A. E., claimed a greater role for Theosophy in the Literary Revival than seems justified. I agree with his premise that 'Probably there has never been in any country a period of literary activity which has not been preceded or accompanied by some stimulation of the religious interest.' Eglinton denies that in Ireland this stimulus was provided by either Catholicism or Protestantism; instead, one must look to 'the ferment caused in the minds of a group of young men by the early activities of the Theosophical Movement in Dublin'.[54] What this theory fails to explain is why Protestants and—with one or two exceptions—*only* Protestants, mainly from Evangelical Church of Ireland families, became Theosophists.[55] As I see it, both the interest in Theosophy and the 'period of literary activity' resulted from the stimulus of Evangelicalism.

Osborne does not suggest that all educated young Dubliners of the 1870s turned towards religion: many of the 'thinking students' at Trinity, he says, were influenced by the rationalism of John Stuart Mill. Also, despite the fact that Irish Evangelicals, in sharp contrast to their British counterparts, were traditionally Tories, Osborne recognizes the

---

[52] Annan, *Leslie Stephen*, 110.

[53] Henry Summerfield, *That Myriad-Minded Man: A Biography of George William Russell. 'A. E.'* (Gerrards Cross, Bucks.: Colin Smythe, 1975), 16.

[54] John Eglinton, *A Memoir of A. E., George William Russell* (London: Macmillan, 1937), 11.

[55] Edward Corbett, a Roman Catholic acquaintance of A. E.'s, became a Theosophist, at least for a time (Summerfield, 11). I know of no other Catholic converts in Ireland.

'distinct vein of national sentiment and aspiration, never entirely quenched among Protestant young men'.[56]

More significant for literature than a purely political nationalism were two tendencies peculiar to the Irish version of Evangelicalism: its interest, however narrow and utilitarian, in the Irish language, and its insistence on linking the post-Reformation Church of Ireland with the pre-Norman Celtic Church of St Patrick and his successors. The doctrine that the Reformation in Ireland had pruned away Roman corruptions and accretions, thus restoring the Church of Ireland to its Celtic purity, is by no means a nineteenth-century invention. It goes back to the great James Ussher, Anglican Archbishop of Armagh *ca.* 1575–1656, who stated it most succinctly in *A Discourse of the Religion Anciently Professed by the Irish and British* (1631) and supported it by collecting, editing, and publishing numerous early ecclesiastical documents.[57]

Ussher's arguments might seem more likely to appeal to High Church believers than to Evangelicals: one of the former, the Revd Robert King, did publish a history—of the 'Holy Catholic Church in Ireland'—based on Ussher's concepts and research; but priority in the nineteenth century belongs to the Evangelicals. Henry J. Monck Mason, an Evangelical layman who had helped to found the Irish Society and was its Secretary for many years, wrote a tract entitled *The Old Religion of St Patrick and St Columbkille*, no doubt in commemoration of the fourteenth centenary of Patrick's coming to Ireland in 432; by 1838, when the third edition, 'much enlarged', appeared under a somewhat different title, its author had published a related work, *Primitive Christianity in Ireland: A Letter to Thomas Moore, Esq.* (1836). This criticized the poet's treatment of the early Irish Church in the first volume of his *History of Ireland*. A note prefixed to *Primitive Christianity* promises to devote any profits to the printing and 'gratuitous circulation' of the third edition of the earlier work. Monck Mason was therefore clearly more of a pamphleteer than a scholar, and it need not surprise us that the 1838 volume, addressed to 'My Dear Fellow Countrymen', is in fact aimed at his Roman Catholic countrymen.[58]

Monck Mason, following Ussher, denied that the Celtic Church subscribed to any of the following doctrines: the supremacy of the Pope; transubstantiation and the real presence of Christ in the Eucharist; the offering of prayers for the dead and the related belief in Purgatory;

---

[56] Petre, 1, 145.

[57] *The Whole Works of the Most Rev. James Ussher*, ed. Charles Richard Elrington, 17 vols. (Dublin: Hodges & Smith, 1847–64). Vols. xiv and xvii were edited by James Henthorn Todd.

[58] Henry J. Monck Mason, *Primitive Christianity in Ireland: A Letter to Thomas Moore, Esq.* (Dublin: William Curry, Jun., 1836), 24. Bowen, *Protestant Crusade*, 51, mentions a pamphlet in similar vein by Edward Nangle, published in 1834.

the invocation of saints; the sacramental nature of penance; and the celibacy of the clergy.[59] As a staunch Evangelical, he further insisted that 'the great standard of faith referred to by the early Irish Christians was the Bible itself'; he has even succeeded in convincing himself that it 'was read . . . by all in their vulgar tongue'! More important still, certain passages in the *Epistle to Coroticus* prove to his satisfaction that St Patrick taught justification by faith alone.[60]

From the point of view of the Revival writers, this harking back to the period antedating both religious and ethnic divisions in Ireland had a positive merit: they were trying to create in the cultural domain a national unity that had become more and more elusive in the political arena. Standish O'Grady summed up their aims unforgettably: 'I have not come out from my own camp to join any other. I stand between the camps and call.'[61] For various reasons, including the influence of Theosophical ideas, the literary movement finally sought common ground not in any Christian century but in the pagan era, which Celtic scholars of many nationalities were rapidly bringing to light; the folklorists and language Revivalists were uncovering contemporary Irish survivals of paganism with equal rapidity!

As we have seen, the preservation of the Irish language was aided, though not exactly in good faith, by the Evangelically inspired Irish Society. Because of pressure from that body, under the guidance of Monck Mason, Trinity College was induced to found a Professorship of Irish in 1838, 'its endowment being at first provided largely by a fund raised for the purpose by public subscription'.[62] It is not surprising, then, that the first four holders of the Chair were Church of Ireland clergymen, at least one, the Revd Daniel Foley, being a convert from Roman Catholicism.[63] It was the fourth in line, the Revd James Goodman, who gave Synge his first lessons in Irish.

This and most of the other consequences of Evangelicalism discussed in this chapter must in the last analysis be viewed as accidental products of a particular historical situation. The essential point is that Evangelical renewal, though it may have encouraged some philistinism among the laity, brought to the clergy of the Church of Ireland spiritual gains far outweighing any putative intellectual loss. James Anthony Froude became disillusioned with Tractarianism during a stay of 'some months in

---

[59] Monck Mason, *Primitive Christianity*, 24–106.

[60] Ibid. 116.

[61] *All Ireland Review* 4 (1903). For a rather similar attitude see Yeats, *Autobiographies*, 101–2.

[62] *Trinity College Record Volume* (Dublin: Hodges, Figgis, 1951), 72.

[63] Brooke, *Recollections*, 55. The first holder of the chair, the Revd Thomas de Vere Coneys, had been Nangle's assistant at the Achill Mission, 1838–40 (Henry Seddall, *Edward Nangle: The Apostle of Achill* (London: Hatchards, 1884)), 117.

Ireland in the family of an Evangelical clergyman'. Part of his tribute to them deserves to be quoted here:

There was quiet good sense, an intellectual breadth of feeling in this household, which to me, who had been bred to despise Evangelicals as unreal and affected, was a startling surprise . . . Christianity at—[Delgany] was part of the atmosphere which we breathed; it was the great fact of our existence, to which everything else was subordinated.

The literary descendants of such clergymen were not always conspicuous for their quiet good sense, but intellectual breadth of feeling cannot be denied. It was no accident that the movement they initiated proved to be idealistic in the highest degree, a last towering wave of the great Romantic surge, for the beginnings of Romanticism in English literature had been intimately bound up with the revival of 'enthusiasm' in religion led by George Whitefield and John Wesley, and continued by the Anglican Evangelicals. Works once again gave way to faith, facts to myth, the truth of the head to the truths of the heart. Standish O'Grady wrote:

A nation's history is made for it by circumstances, and the irresistible progress of events; but their legends, they make for themselves. In that dim twilight region, where day meets night, the intellect of man, tired by contact with the vulgarity of actual things, goes back for rest and recuperation, and there sleeping, projects its dreams against the waning night and before the rising of the sun.
    The legends represent the imagination of the country; they are that kind of history which a nation desires to possess.[64]

No doubt Standish O'Grady saw the bourgeois Evangelical orthodoxy of his day as part of 'the vulgarity of actual things', with which he contrasts the ideal world of the imagination.
    One common form taken by the reaction against Evangelicalism is completely overlooked in Charles Osborne's essay: the substitution for it of the religion of Art. It is a strange omission on the part of the son and brother of painters; W. B. Yeats, with a similar family background, could not have been guilty of it:

I am very religious, and deprived by Huxley and Tyndall, whom I detested, of the simple-minded religion of my childhood, I had made a new religion, almost an infallible Church of poetic tradition, of a fardel of stories, and of personages, and of emotions, inseparable from their first expression, passed on from generation to generation by poets and painters with some help from philosophers and theologians.[65]

----

[64] Standish O'Grady, *History of Ireland: Critical and Philosophical* [all pub.] (London, Sampson Low, 1881), i. 41.
[65] Yeats, *Autobiographies*, 115–16.

The rapid conversion of Yeats, who was born in 1865, contrasts with that of Stopford Brooke. Brooke was born in 1832, a full generation before Yeats, and raised in the far from simple-minded version of Evangelicalism taught by the Revd R. S. Brooke. In L. P. Jack's biography of the younger Brooke we can trace a slow, steady evolution from his youthful Evangelicalism to an old age more concerned with art than with religion. Yet one can agree with Jack that Brooke,

> quite early in life, with little aid from others and in the face of much opposition, . . . had formed for himself an ideal of the Christian ministry which was to reconcile the two currents of his being in a deep synthesis of Art and Religion, of Nature and Spirit.[66]

The religion of Art, as understood in England in the 1890s, excluded morality: even of Stopford Brooke in his old age we read that 'Morality ceased to have any meaning for him save as the expression of love.'[67] Yeats, in an early letter, said of George Eliot that 'if she had more religion she would have less morals'.[68] Paradoxical as it sounds, this judgement could be approved by a believing Evangelical, for it stresses salvation by faith not works. Indeed, Irish churchmen of the old 'high-and-dry' school, who taught morality to the exclusion of almost everything else, were very suspicious of the morals of the early Evangelicals, who preached about nothing but faith. In fact, of course, the morals of the latter were excellent, and few of their literary progeny rebelled against their rules of conduct. The stereotype of the *fin-de-siècle* poet— drunkard, gambler, womanizer, suicide—simply did not exist in Protestant Ireland; among Irish exiles, the frugality,—perhaps even asceticism, of a Shaw effectively counter-balanced the self-destructiveness of a Wilde. Neither greed of gain nor more amiable vices distracted the Revival writers from their self-imposed task. If they had a besetting sin, it was amateurism, a reluctance to learn their trade as artists, or even as scholars, that can be found in Hyde, O'Grady, Russell, and numerous minor figures. In part it was due to the anti-intellectualism threatening every movement that values emotion more than thought: to prefer the one does not require us to hate the other—something the Evangelicals too often forget. Mainly, though, the amateurism suggests a belief in salvation by faith: so long as one's heart is in the right place, why be anxious about one's collected works? Synge never subscribed to this attitude, nor did Lady Gregory, but in *The Countess Cathleen* Yeats seems to suggest that the road to Heaven is paved with good intentions;

[66] Jack, i. 57–8. See also ii. 454: 'In later life he would quote with approval the saying of Blake "Art and Christianity are one".'

[67] Jack, ii. 454.

[68] *The Letters of W. B. Yeats*, ed. Allan Wade (New York: Macmillan, 1952), 50.

> The Light of Lights
> Looks always on the motive, not the deed,
> The Shadow of Shadows on the deed alone.[69]

In maturity he took a different view:

> The intellect of man is forced to choose
> Perfection of the life, or of the work,
> And if it take the second must refuse
> A heavenly mansion, raging in the dark.[70]

Perhaps both of these quotations affirm the same truth: salvation by works alone is impossible; in the second, therefore, Yeats accepts his own damnation. The doctrine is purely Evangelical.

---

[69] *The Collected Plays of W. B. Yeats*, 2nd edn. (London: Macmillan, 1952), 50.

[70] 'The Choice', in *The Collected Poems of W. B. Yeats*, 2nd edn. (London: Macmillan, 1950), 278.

4   *The Revival Begins*

The Later Ferguson

Although Samuel Ferguson is classified as a 'forerunner' of the Literary Revival in Boyd's *Ireland's Literary Renaissance*, I myself regard him as the first important figure of the movement. If the term 'Revival' or 'Renaissance' is to have any validity as a metaphor, those who accept and use it need first of all to be convinced that what is revived or reborn did once enjoy an independent existence of significant dimensions. The scholarly investigations described in the last chapter, while damaging to the inflated claims made by some Irish historians, were sufficient to convince unprejudiced readers that the literature of Old and Middle Irish—let alone that in Early Modern—deserved at least as much respect as the Norse mythology made famous by Wagner. The inclusion of a long article on Celtic literature—predominantly Irish of course—in the ninth edition of the *Encyclopaedia Britannica* proved that the subject had become intellectually respectable by 1870.

A modern scholar concerned with, say, the Italian Renaissance need not pause for a moment to ask himself what there was for that movement to revive; his real problem is quite other. To what extent was the painter or writer whom he is studying consciously trying to re-create the art of the past? Also, to what extent has he, whether consciously or unconsciously, produced a re-creation rather than a pastiche—or even a parody? Too great reverence for one's sources leads to pastiche; the irreverence endemic in Irish society finds its literary expression in parody. Of one thing we can be sure, however: the movement was self-consciously Revivalist—a term which incidentally recalls its Evangelical affinities—from the very beginning. Two books published in 1894 may be cited: *The Revival of Irish Literature* and *The Irish Literary Revival*. The first was a series of lectures by Charles Gavan Duffy, George Sigerson, and Douglas Hyde suggesting ways and means of bringing about a Revival, but the second—by W. P. Ryan, an Irish journalist in London—treated the revival as a *fait accompli*, although none of its recognized masterpieces had yet been published.

Still, by 1880 Ferguson had produced a body of work in the Revivalist mode that was far from negligible. As we have seen, in *Congal* (1872) he had used as sources two prose sagas translated by O'Donovan: 'They seemed to possess, in a remarkable degree, that largeness of purpose, unity, and continuity of action which are the principal elements of Epic Poetry, and solicited me irresistibly to the endeavour to render them into some compatible form of English verse.' This seems to mean that he hoped to produce an epic simply by versifying O'Donovan's translation, but he had to abandon the attempt because he 'found the inherent repugnancies too obstinate for reconcilement'. Again, it is difficult to be sure exactly what he means; perhaps O'Donovan gives us a clue when he points out that the *Banquet of Dun na n-Gaedh* is 'simpler, plainer, and more natural in its style, and less interrupted by flights of bombast' than the *Battle of Magh Rath*, to which it serves as an introduction. The story of the battle is nearly three times as long as that of the banquet because of its torrents of compound adjectives in descriptive passages and mountains of hyperbole lavished on the victor, Domnall, son of Aed, son of Ainmire. Myles Dillon, in *The Cycles of the Kings*, describes the text chosen by O'Donovan as 'a long and tedious narrative of the worst period. From the style and language it cannot be earlier than c.1300.' The *Banquet*, on the other hand, belongs to the eleventh century according to Dillon. It is a pity that O'Donovan did not choose to edit and translate the first recension of the *Battle*, which is shorter and less turgid: perhaps he found it too difficult, since it is mostly in Old Irish, 'and may date from the early tenth century'. It is summarized in *The Cycles of the Kings*.

Out of such promising materials did Ferguson construct his 'Poem in Five Books', which cannot be called an epic, though it often makes use of incidents and characters that would not be out of place in epic poetry. *Congal* is a highly idiosyncratic example of a typical Victorian genre, the moralized historical or mythical narrative poem, akin to Arnold's *Sohrab and Rustum* and to many individual poems in *Idylls of the King*. Lest we should be in any doubt about the moral nature of his enterprise, Ferguson offers us, immediately after his brief preface, the following:

THE ARGUMENT
Ambition, Anger, Terror, Strife and Death,
Each, here, its Book in Congal's story hath.

The ambition and anger are Congal's, but the supernatural terrors of Book III fail to deter him from seeking revenge on Domnall. The strife occurs at the Battle of Magh Rath (now Moira, County Down), which can be reliably dated AD 637 for Domnall was one of several historical Irish kings famous enough to have cycles of legends to their reigns, in the manner of Charlemagne. Although countless thousands supposedly die in the battle, the death of Congal is the main subject of Book V: as in O'Donovan's text and in Yeats's *The Herne's Egg*, the chief agent of death is a Fool, Congal's foster-brother Cuanna.

Ferguson offers no explanation for his choice of the treasonous, headstrong Congal as eponymous hero of the poem, but he obviously regards him as a tragic figure. Although many of Congal's grievances against Domnall are just, he refuses to submit them to arbitration and declares war immediately after the series of (possibly unintended) slights he receives at the start of the banquet. He is no better able to control his temper than Oedipus or Ajax. Ferguson also gives him historic and symbolic weight by presenting the battle of Moira as 'the expiring effort of the Pagan and Bardic party in Ireland, against the newly-consolidated power of Church and Crown'. This misinterpretation he owed to 'the late Dr Charles O'Conor', son of Charles O'Conor of Belanagare. In adopting it, Ferguson manages to overlook O'Donovan's footnote (p. 281): 'He [O'Conor] observes in a note, that 'This seems to have been a religious war between the Christian king Donald, and the Pagan Congal, 'an observation which is sufficient to show that Dr O'Conor never read, or at least never understood, the Battle of Magh Rath.' Congal's treason consisted in his going to Scotland to seek allies: his chief supporter, says Myles Dillon, was Domnall Brecc, 'king of Dál Riada, the Irish kingdom in Scotland, which at that time included a small territory in north-east Ireland . . . one result of the battle seems to have been the loss to the Scottish kingdom of its Irish territory.'

Ferguson's poem does not place great stress on the theme of Irish national resistance to the Scottish invaders in dealing with the actual battle, but Book III shows the old gods of Eire threatening Congal with disaster—described in the Argument as 'The Rising-out of Erin's guardian Ghosts'. One of the most fearsome passages—not found in the prose original—describes the Washer of the Ford:

> A ghastly woman it appeared, with grey dishevelled hair
> Blood-draggled, and with sharp-boned arms, and fingers
>   crook'd and spare
> Dabbling and washing in the ford, where mid-leg deep she stood
> Beside a heap of heads and limbs that swam in oozing blood,
> Whereon and on a glittering heap of raiment rich and brave
> With swift, pernicious hands she scooped and pour'd the crimson'd wave.

When Congal asks the giant hag what she is washing, she says:

> ' . . . the severed heads and hands
> And spear-torn scarfs and tunics of these gay-dressed, gallant bands

Whom thou, oh Congal, leadest to death. And this, the Fury said,
Uplifting by the clotted locks what seemed a dead man's head,
Is thine own head, oh Congal.'

One can't deny the effectiveness of this interpolation from another story, but all too often Ferguson merely indulges in needless erudition when he deviates from O'Donovan's text, especially the swift narrative of the *Banquet*: he sometimes even versifies one of O'Donovan's footnotes. His greatest break with his sources, however, consists of his introduction of a 'love interest': Congal is betrothed to Lafinda, sister of the King Sweeny (Suibne) who traditionally went mad and fled from the Battle of Moira—though Dillon points out that the earliest recension of the battle story, which 'appears to be of historical value', does not mention Suibne at all. Lafinda herself seems to be a pure invention of Ferguson's; she is a Christian, whereas Suibne, according to Ferguson, is an unrepentant pagan who drowns the hermit Erc in the River Boyne. St Ronan puts a curse on him for this sacrilegious murder, causing his madness. An entire separate tale, *Buile Shuibne* (The Madness of Sweeny), sometimes alluded to by Ferguson, recounts his adventures as a madman, his conversion to Christianity, and his death.

Lafinda's part in the narrative is minimal, although the poem begins with Congal's farewell to her on his way to the banquet. After his declaration of war, he returns briefly to tell her that their wedding must be postponed; she urges him to accept Christianity and make peace, but he refuses and departs for Scotland. In Book III, just after the apparition of the Washer of the Ford, Lafinda makes a more determined effort to restrain Congal, obeying a dream in which St Brigid of Kildare instructed her to intercept him and warn him to 'Turn back or perish'. When Congal refuses, Lafinda's old servant, Lavarcam, seems to become St Brigid herself, and their chariot gallops away. Congal sacrilegiously cries, 'Thou robber Saint, restore / My bride!' and vainly hurls his spear at Brigid. Lafinda soon afterwards becomes a nun, but Ferguson rather implausibly arranges matters so that she nurses Congal on his deathbed: his last words allow her to believe that he has died repentant. Just before this, however, he has been granted a glorious vision of the god Manannan, suggesting a possible opposite interpretation of his words.

The ambiguity of this ending raises the question of the state of Ferguson's religious belief at the time when he wrote *Congal*—'long since accomplished', according to the 1872 preface. His widow concludes her memoir of him with a chapter entitled 'His Attitude Towards Questions of Belief' that does little but quote the religious verses of his later years and the letters of condolence that she received on his death. The entire book leaves us uncertain whether he was brought up an

Anglican or a Presbyterian, though it is clear from his poem 'Westminster Abbey' that he was a practising Anglican after his marriage and had no scruples about attending the rather High Church services at All Saints', Grangegorman. Lady Ferguson's least equivocal statement is the following: 'Ferguson's mind was not uniformly orthodox. He thought for himself. He made difficulties; and long felt a repugnance to the doctrine of original sin.'

Whatever their motivation, *Congal* includes some hearty denunciations of the seventh-century Christian clergy; these are, of course, put in the mouths of pagans, where they seem on the whole to be in character. Nevertheless, at my first reading of the poem, I thought I detected an animus more appropriate to a later century: Congal and his uncle Kellach the Halt occasionally sound like Ulster Protestants denouncing the 'idolatries' of the Roman Catholic Church and the greed of her clergy; one can more easily sympathize with the resentment of Kellach's chief bard, Ardan, who has seen the privileges of his order restricted or usurped by Christian clerics. It is surprising to find that Ardan is a monotheist, and perhaps even an apologist for state religion when he speaks of 'my lawful King, / Image of God'. This again, however, would reinforce the analogy between paganism and one type of Protestantism.

After the intervention of St Brigid, already described, one of Congal's Christian allies suggests that she should be brought over to their side by the lavish endowment of 'a splendid cell' in her honour. Another ally, though obviously sceptical, agrees with him: since they no longer know the proper druidic rites to propitiate the land's 'patriot Ghosts', all they have is 'this sacrifice / The Clerics make pretence to make'. Congal, however, believes implicitly in the clergy's power to use such punishments as 'priest-imprecated fire' if 'but the smallest jot / Of blind obedience he denied.' Kellach's final speech, which almost immediately precedes Congal's edifying deathbed scene, denounces priestly maledictions: 'Of no good God are these the priests . . . / 'I ne'er sought evil Spirit's aid 'gainst any enemy.' He warns Domnal that 'ruin and dishonour still on priest-led Kings await', and his last words are 'them that come / 'Cursing, I curse'. At this, St Ronan Finn, 'upheaving high his bell, / 'Rang it, and gave the banning word:' Kellach instantly falls dead.

Ferguson surely wishes to enlist his readers' sympathy for Kellach against the persecuting Bishop Ronan, but I do not think he is prompted by anti-Catholic bigotry: here as elsewhere in the poem he is expressing an anti-clericalism that may be deep-seated. One wonders whether Ardan's final statement of belief does not best reflect Ferguson's views at the time it was written:

Then Ardan spread his hands to heaven, and said, 'I stand alone,
'Last wreck remaining of a Power and Order over-thrown,
'Much needing solace: and, ah me, not in the empty lore
'Of Bard or Druid does my soul find solace and comfort more;
'Nor in the bells or crooked staves or sacrificial shows
'Find I the help my soul desires, or in the chaunts of those
'Who claim our Druids' vacant place. Alone and faint, I crave,
'Oh God, one ray of Heavenly light to help me to the grave.'

This at first reads like agnosticism but seems to end with the Evangelical's need for a personal conversion.

Whatever the final religious—and political—intention of the poem may be, *Congal* is unequivocally an ambitious work in the Revival mode. On the one hand it reveals a deep and respectful study of its sources; on the other, it uses those sources to create a new work of art containing new meanings for its own time.

Not everybody, unfortunately, will agree with the description of *Congal* as a work of art, yet few could deny that it is a notable work of craftsmanship, as firmly designed as a Gothic cathedral, though perhaps with more than its share of gargoyles and grotesques. Ferguson's display of erudition in regard to genealogy and traditional 'history' includes a habit of using Gaelic words—often archaic or in a would-be phonetic spelling—without explanation. The notes supplied in the first edition are not nearly as useful as a glossary of such words would have been; a list of proper names in normalized Gaelic spelling could also have been included. 'Kellach' for 'Cellach' is particularly annoying, since there is no letter 'k' in the Irish alphabet; Ferguson was apparently afraid that his readers would use the pronunciation 'Sellach'. He need hardly have bothered, since they would also pronounce 'ach' as 'ack'! The chief obstacle to enjoyment of the poem, however, is surely his choice of metre: many people instinctively reject all verse written in 'fourteener' couplets, and it must be admitted that Ferguson does not handle the form with much skill; he seems to ignore even the limited opportunities for varying the rhythm that are available to him. The subtlety of ear shown in his early translations appears to have deserted him. Ferguson may have adopted the metre as appropriate for epic because of an admiration for Chapman's Homer: in a letter of thanks for an inscribed copy, the poet Denis Florence MacCarthy remarked, 'In the two books [of *Congal*] which I have read, Homer and his best interpreter, George Chapman, were ever present in my mind.'

Ferguson's *Poems* (1880) includes a sequence of five verse narratives in what I have called the Revival mode: 'Fergus Wry-Mouth', 'The Twins of Macha', 'The Naming of Cuchullin', 'Conary', and 'Deirdre'.

All of these, in varying degrees, are faithful to their sources, though Ferguson usually supplies a moral or a modern reference of some kind. 'Mesgedra', the poem immediately preceding them, contains more moralizing than narrative, like the group of poems which gives its title to his earlier volume, *Lays of the Western Gael* (1865). Ferguson defends his retelling of the grisly legend of Mesgedra in an introductory note which insists that the Ulster Cycle is superior to the Finn Cycle precisely because it is more primitive: its 'revolting features need no more repel us from seeing what is behind, than Medea's cauldron or the supper of Thyestes should induce us to ignore the materials supplied by the Classical Dictionary.' Most of the poem, however, is taken up with praise of the Liffey valley and the pleasures it offers to young sportsmen from Dublin. The moral lies in the poet's regret, as he addresses the river, that

> . . . thou, for them, alas! nor History hast
> Nor even Tradition; and the Man aspires
> To link his present with his Country's past,
> And live anew in knowledge of his sires;
>
> No rootless colonist of alien earth,
> Proud but of patient lungs and pliant limb,
> A stranger in the land that gave him birth,
> The land a stranger to itself and him.

These lines in fact define an important part of the Revival programme, reminding one of Yeats's wish for 'a mythology wedded to hill and rock and tree'. Long afterwards, John Hewitt was to appropriate the words 'No rootless colonist' as the title for an essay affirming his right to call himself Irish.

'Fergus Wry-Mouth' succinctly tells, in thirty-eight heroic couplets, a tragic version of the death of Fergus Mac Leide in battle with a sea-monster. Completely free of moralizing, it ends as abruptly as Yeats's 'Cuchulain's Fight with the Sea' did in its original (1892) version. Yeats undoubtedly modelled his poem of forty-three heroic couplets, called 'The Death of Cuchulain' until 1925, upon Ferguson's. 'Fergus Wry-Mouth' ends with this stark couplet:

> He smiled; he cast his trophy to the bank,
> Said, 'I survivor, Ulsterman!' and sank.

Yeats's final couplet in his original version was:

> For four days warred he with the bitter tide,
> And the waves flowed above him and he died.

This, I think, is the high-water mark of Ferguson's influence on Yeats's poetic technique.

'The Twins of Macha' also avoids moralizing: in his introductory note Ferguson writes, 'The original is a good example of that conciseness and simplicity united with dramatic power which characterises the *Dinnsenchus* class of poems.' His own poem deserves the same praise as its original, though not all poems dealing with place-name lore possess the virtues he attributes to them. The tragic myth which explains how the fortress of King Conor Mac Nessa got its name is retold by Ferguson in twenty-six heroic couplets, including a fair proportion of laconic dialogue. Note that the original is in verse, whereas the poems I have singled out from this volume are all based on prose originals. Ferguson's immediate source was a text and translation contributed by O'Curry to *The Ancient Churches of Armagh* (1860), a work by the Church of Ireland scholar Revd William Reeves, later Bishop of Down.

'The Naming of Cuchullin', a longer poem, mostly in blank verse, is far less satisfactory, though based on a charming anecdote that forms part of the boyhood deeds of the hero recounted early in the *Táin Bó Cuailnge*. Ferguson's decision to tell the whole story in dialogue, for which he has very little talent, might have been justifiable if he had abandoned the archaic vocabulary and syntax that his fellow Victorians thought appropriate for the translation or imitation of epic verse or prose. This style had already vitiated numerous passages in *Congal*, but its use in various speeches by the 7-year-old Cú Chulainn soon becomes ridiculous, especially if one happens to know how simply and even naively the hero speaks in the LU (Book of the Dun Cow) version of the tale.

'Deirdre', a much longer work in blank verse, again uses dialogue throughout. Ferguson describes it as 'a Monodrame; because, though the actors are more than one, the action is unbroken, and the principal figures remain in sight throughout, moving in a progressive scene . . . from . . . the Western Highlands of Scotland to . . . Emania [Emain Macha] . . . '. The appropriate modern medium for this hybrid genre would be film: at moments it is full of action; unfortunately, a sequence in the middle degenerates into travelogue as Deirdre asks the names of features of the Ulster landscape.

'Conary' is also a long poem in blank verse on a tragic subject—the untimely death of Conaire, one of the most famous among the legendary high kings of Ireland. The motifs which enhance the mood of tragic inevitability include Conaire's violation one by one of all the *geasa* (taboos) designed to protect him, and his having spared the lives of the evil foster-brothers who cause his defeat and death by leading British pirates in a raid on his kingdom. The original Middle Irish prose narrative vividly describes the night battle, stressing darkness, firelight, and the glare of houses set ablaze by the raiders. In an introductory note,

Ferguson acknowledges his debt to the original, *Togail Bruidne Da
Derga* ('The Destruction of Da Derga's Hostel'), making clear that as
usual he has not supplied 'a full reproduction' of it and has felt free to
include incidents from other sources. We should be grateful to him,
however, for adding to the Revival canon 'one of the longest and most
pathetic Irish sagas', which is furthermore one of the 'few complete
narratives of any great extent preserved from ancient Irish literature'.[1]

The standard translation by Whitley Stokes appeared in the *Revue
Celtique* (1901–2), fifteen years after Ferguson's death: it was W. M.
Hennessy who first made the poet acquainted with the tale, though he
did not himself publish a translation; O'Curry had, however, translated
long extracts in his *Manners and Customs*, Lecture XXV.

Ferguson makes skilful use of the repetitions and elaborate description in the original to delay the catastrophe and prolong suspense,
while omitting some of the grotesque exaggerations. One can see why
Yeats, in his two 1886 articles on Ferguson, admired 'Conary' only a
little less than 'Deirdre', his favourite. In the first article he singles out
for praise 'this poem's splendid plot,' apparently unaware that the plot
is not Ferguson's invention. My own feeling about the poem is that
while Ferguson deserves full credit for recognizing the power and
artistry of his original, it is these qualities, rather than anything of his
own, which retain our interest throughout a longish verse narrative;
they are equally present in Stokes's fairly literal translation. The last
complete reprinting of 'Conary' seems to have been that in Alfred
Perceval Graves's edition of *Poems of Sir Samuel Ferguson* (1916). Is it
because Ferguson's poem is a failure that no later playwright attempted
a tragedy based on the fate of Conaire?

As a poet, and indeed as a man, Ferguson's development reminds us
of Wordsworth's. We can pinpoint the year, if not the exact moment,
when his lyric gift deserted him; not unexpectedly, it roughly coincides
with the date at which he began to appreciate the comforts and privileges
of worldly success. In 1848, a year of abortive revolution, after a period
of growing discontent with British rule in Ireland, he addressed the
Protestant Repeal Association; yet it was in that very year that his
marriage to a member of the affluent Guinness family began his reconciliation with the Ascendancy. Yeats's review of his widow's memoir, *Sir
Samuel Ferguson in the Ireland of His Day* (two vols. 1896), links
Ferguson's social rise with his poetic decline: 'a hardness and heaviness
crept into his rhythm and his language from the dead world about him'.
To end the review, Yeats significantly quotes in full Ferguson's early

---

[1] T. P. Cross and Clark H. Slover, *Ancient Irish Tales* (London: Harrap, 1936; New York:
Barnes & Noble, 1936) 93.

translation, 'The Fair Hills of Ireland'. The hesitant rhythm of a line like 'There is dew at high noontide there, and springs i' the yellow sand', may have inspired similar effects in 'The Lake Isle of Innisfree'.

Whatever one's final assessment of Ferguson as a literary artist, his career is in one respect unique: having played an enthusiastic part in the rediscovery of the Irish past as a translator in his youth, he undertook in his maturity to create models for the revival of Irish literature. Let us not forget, either, that he contributed to Celtic scholarship throughout his life and in 1867 gave up a successful career at the Bar to become the first Deputy Keeper of the Records of Ireland. As R. F. Foster perceptively remarks, he was a 'bridge between the flowering of national studies in the 1830s and the literary renaissance of the 1890s'.

The Coming of Cú Chulainn

The title of this section derives from that of a book by Standish James O'Grady (1846–1928); characteristically, he persisted in misspelling the hero's name as 'Cuculain', for odd reasons which will appear later. Ernest Boyd called him 'The Father of the Revival', thereby casting doubt on the legitimacy of the entire movement. O'Grady's sole claim to the honour is that he was the first to retell in English the majority of the sagas associated with the Ulster hero: one must insist, however, that O'Grady's Cuculain is almost as much a literary forgery as Macpherson's Ossian. (One of Macpherson's shorter pieces, by the way, was 'The Death of Cuthullin [*sic*]: A Poem'.) As we saw in Chapter 3, scholars were reluctant to publish a translation of *Táin Bó Cuailnge* for several good reasons, of which the best was undoubtedly the sheer difficulty of the oldest text. Since O'Grady knew no Irish and had failed to pick up at Trinity even the dimmest conception of a scientific approach to language, none of these considerations deterred him in the least: like the fool he was, he rushed in where the angels of scholarship feared to tread.

In several phases of his erratic career, O'Grady proved himself, at least by worldly standards, a considerable fool: a noble fool, perhaps even a holy fool, an Irish reincarnation of Don Quixote—but still the sort of person who thinks one can achieve anything provided one's heart is in the right place. His Evangelical upbringing may have been partly to blame: once he felt the Lord was on his side, he disregarded the need for proper training and all other obstacles, material or human. One might sourly complain that his greatest folly was his hope of arousing the Anglo-Irish aristocracy to a sense of their duty to become leaders rather than exploiters of their country: objectively, however, his editorship of the *Kilkenny Moderator*, during which, despite his legal training, he brought on himself a shower of libel actions, actual or threatened, must be reckoned as the height of his foolishness. His blindness to the realities of editing a newspaper in an Irish country town, like other aspects of his career, makes it difficult to decide whether he was at heart an unpractical idealist or a practical joker.

For example, the first volume of his two-volume *History of Ireland*, published in 1878 and bearing the subtitle *The Heroic Period*, begins with a chapter on the Pleistocene era; this is followed by three chapters or the last Ice Age. The first sentence of the fifth chapter reads as follows: 'The earth is inhabited by eight distinct races of man—the Australian, the Negrito, the Maorie, the Red Indian, the Eskimo, and the African, the Mongol, the Scythian, and the Turanian.' It hardly matters where O'Grady found this aberrant ethnology: the arithmetic which supplies nine names for eight 'races' is surely his own. A page or two later, he informs us that the Gael is descended from the Scythian stock; from the Turanian stock come, among others, 'the Hindoo, the Arabian . . . the Phoenician and the Jew. Further west, the Pelasgian of Greece, the Etruscan of Italy, . . . the forgotten Berber, and the Basque.' In the next chapter he has the grace to admit, 'At what time the Basques took possession of Ireland cannot be determined with accuracy,' but he is convinced that they were the builders of the great tumuli in the Boyne Valley. Inevitably, a present-day reader wonders if O'Grady is offering these notions in all seriousness, and what, if anything, they have to do with the heroic period of Irish history.

In chapter vii, 'Dawn', O'Grady justifiably treats the pseudo-history of the *Leabhar Gabhála* (*Book of Invasions*) with the scepticism that he should also have applied to his own pseudo-scientific assertions: 'Early Irish history', he writes, 'is the creation mainly of the bards.' Having pointed to some of the evidence supporting this statement, he then asks, 'Why not pass on at once to credible history?' His answer to this very reasonable question shows that he is not in fact a historian but a mythologist: 'The legends represent the imagination of the country; they are the kind of history which a nation desires to possess.' For the remainder of this volume and all of the next, he is retelling myth and legend, drawing at first on the Mythological and Kingly Cycles and even on the Ossianic Cycle, which most scholars believe to be the latest of all. It is not until chapter XXIV, 'Boyhood of Cuchulain', that he focuses his attention on the Ulster Cycle, which he continues to draw on for the rest of the volume. The second volume, published in 1880, is subtitled *Cuculain and his Contemporaries*: chapters II–XXVIII complete the saga of the Ulster hero; his death is related in the final chapter.

One might have expected that O'Grady, when he discovered his true subject-matter, would have recast volume 1, eliminating most or all of the early chapters, but it is of a piece with the rest of his character that he should undertake such an ambitious book without careful planning and lack the patience to revise it. In 1882 he patched together the relevant chapters of both volumes into a single one, entitled *Cuculain: An Epic*. As he retained the original numbering of the pages he kept, the result is a bibliographer's nightmare. A short preface attempts to justify the application of the term 'epic' to this prose work and acknowledges that, whatever he once thought, 'History it is not'.

In the introduction that he wrote for *The Heroic Period* after completing the rest of the volume, O'Grady seems to waver between contradictory views of the historicity of his sources. The next year, however, he published an eighty-eight page pamphlet, *Early Bardic History, Ireland* (1879), in which he insists on the authenticity of the Cú Chulainn saga, at least: 'In the first volume . . . I have committed this error, that I did not permit it to be seen with sufficient clearness that the characters and chief events of the tale are absolutely historic.' The pamphlet was reprinted in full as the introduction to *Cuculain and his Contemporaries* (1880).

In 1881 O'Grady published a new work with the impressive title *History of Ireland: Critical and Philosophical,* vol. 1 (no further volume was published). Although the book contained 468 pages, the preface was confined to just one: in this brief space O'Grady outlined his plans for the future and made some admissions about the three books already completed. His first two volumes he now speaks of as portions of a longer work 'in which I propose to tell the history of Ireland through the medium of tales, epical or romantic'. In fact, no sequel to these volumes was ever published. The work for which he is writing the preface 'belongs to an altogether different order of historical composition, and is critical, not constructive or imaginative'. He then goes on to acknowledge unequivocally for the first time, 'Where I seem to quote, the quotations are literal translations supplied by competent scholars': this is the nearest he has yet come to admitting that he knows no Irish.[2] Finally, he informs us that he has transferred some of the material that seemed so incongruous in the earlier work—such as the chapters on the Ice Age—to the new book.[3]

One must constantly bear in mind that O'Grady was totally ignorant of Irish when he wrote *History of Ireland*: however, because of the close

---

[2] See, however, Standish O'Grady, *History of Ireland* (London: Sampson, Low, Searle, Marston & Rivington; Dublin: E. Ponsonby & Co., 1880), ii. 61.

[3] Yeats complains in *Autobiographies*, 201, that it was not reviewed 'by any periodical or newspaper in England or Ireland'.

resemblance of his name to that of Standish Hayes O'Grady, even those of his readers who did know Irish often mistook his work for that of his cousin. His first volume was given a respectful review in the *Revue Celtique* by E. Müller:

The work is almost entirely composed of translations . . . drawn for the most part from the *Leabhar na hUidhri*, the Book of Leinster, etc., which the author has studied very carefully. We think he would have done well, for the sake of the general reader, to add in a note . . . the place from which the translation is taken.

When O'Grady did supply some amateurish notes to the second volume, it at once became clear that his sources were themselves translations: some had been published, but others still survive in manuscript and may be studied in the library of the Royal Irish Academy.

According to a personal reminiscence published in his *All Ireland Review*,[4] a weekly that he produced almost single-handed from 6 January 1900 to December 1906, O'Grady began to learn Irish in the autumn of 1899. How little progress he made is demonstrated by the Irish lessons offered in the opening issue of *AIR*. O'Grady, as editor, insisted that they were the work of someone else, but only he seems capable of the comically unscientific and prescriptive attitude to language which is displayed in them. By the eighth issue the conductor of 'Our Gaelic Class' is announcing, 'I purpose . . . to pay less and less respect to contemporary elisions and aspirations, as practised by those who are too weak to keep alive the language that they speak.' This probably explains why O'Grady always spells 'Cuculain' without an 'h'. He seems blissfully unaware that aspiration has a vital grammatical and syntactical function in Old and Middle as well as Modern Irish.[5] Eventually, protests from readers persuaded the editor to hand over the 'class' to someone who actually knew Irish: T. W. Rolleston volunteered his services. Knowing O'Grady, one suspects that the publication of the absurd lessons was a humorous ruse to obtain such a volunteer.

Nevertheless, O'Grady's influence on Yeats, A. E. and many others is a matter of record and cannot be disputed. When Yeats alleged that 'every Irish imaginative writer owed a portion of his soul' to O'Grady, he was making a political comment that was highly subjective; but he continued thus:

In his unfinished *History of Ireland* he had made the old Irish heroes . . . alive again, taking them . . . from the dry pages of O'Curry and his school, and condensing and arranging, as he thought Homer would have. . . . Lady Gregory

4 'I started this paper in January, 1900, to a considerable extent as a means of corresponding with many friends', *AIR*, iii. 133.

5 'Cú Chulainn' means 'Hound of Culann'; the aspirate is a morpheme helping to indicate the genitive/possessive case.

has told the same tales, but keeping closer to the Gaelic text, and with greater powers of arrangement and a more original style, but O'Grady was the first, and we had read him in our teens.

(Yeats, *Autobiographies*, 221)

This passage, first published in 1922, when Yeats was nearly 60, expresses a more critical attitude than did his early reviews. Elsewhere in *The Trembling of the Veil*, he delivers this summary judgement: 'Standish O'Grady, whose *History of Ireland* retold the Irish heroic tales in romantic Carlylean prose'. Yeats was too young to review the *History* on its first appearance, but his enthusiastic 1895 article on *The Coming of Cuculain*, a reworking of part of it, makes full amends: indeed, Yeats's 30th year marks the peak of his reverence for O'Grady. In March 1895 he declined to reconsider the inclusion of six works by his idol in a list of the thirty best Irish books:[6]

I could do no other than give Mr O'Grady the lion's share, because his books have affected one [me?] more powerfully than those of any other Irish writer, and I know of no other criticism than a candid impressionism. I believe them to be ideal books of their kind, books of genius, but even if they were not, they would still contain more of ancient legend and circumstance than any other.[7]

Despite all the faults that have been indicated in the *History of Ireland*, it was for nearly twenty years (i.e. until the publication of Eleanor Hull's *Cuchullin Saga* in 1898) the only book available in which the cycle of Cú Chulainn, the pre-eminent folk hero of pagan Ireland, could be found in something like its full dimensions. Other, better English versions existed in manuscript, but O'Grady's was the first to reach print—because he dared to publish at his own expense. As it happened, in 1882 the poet Aubrey de Vere issued through his usual London publishers a long blank-verse poem, *The Foray of Queen Meave*: at one point in the volume, this work is subtitled 'The Tain Bo Cuailgne [*sic*]', but it is also described, more truthfully, as 'Five Fragments of an Ancient Irish Epic'—five separate poems, each with a different title. It is not an adequate presentation of the *Táin* in terms of either length or power. I wish that O'Grady rather than De Vere had had access to the manuscript translation of Brian O'Looney of both the LU and LL texts of the *Táin*. De Vere refers in his preface to 'Mr Standish O'Grady's brilliant bardic "History of Ireland"'; he also presented O'Grady with a copy of *The Foray* (now in my library). Did this prompt the publication of *Cuculain: An Epic* in the same year?

---

[6] *Letters of W. B. Yeats*, ed. Allan Wade, 247–8 (Macmillan: New York, 1955). The titles of the six books were: *The Bog of Stars*; *History of Ireland—Heroic Period*; *The Coming of Cuchullin*; *Fin and his Companions*; *The Story of Ireland*; *Red Hugh's Captivity*.
[7] John P. Frayne, *Uncollected Prose by W. B. Yeats*, i. 353.

Broadly speaking, O'Grady's narrative style is at its best when he has good sources to work on: I say 'work on' rather than 'work with' because he is rarely a humble collaborator. There is a passage in the introduction to *The Heroic Period* (pp. x–xiii) that ought to put us on our guard: in describing how he treats his sources, he speaks of 'do [ing] violence to the parts' so that 'the whole should be fairly represented'. He also claims that 'upon the realisation of the bards I have superadded a realisation more intensive, working closer to those noble forms . . .' (i.e. the heroes and heroines). The passage ends with a classic Victorian assertion: 'The nobler conception of any character, is, of course, to be preferred to the ignoble.' This comment will be recognized as being entirely in the spirit of the Revival mode.

Let me quote at length a passage that I found deeply moving at first reading—and still find so; it vividly illustrates most of O'Grady's strong and weak points. The dying Cú Chulainn has already tied himself to a pillar-stone, but the translation here followed by O'Grady is based on a later text than that by Whitley Stokes quoted in Chapter 1 (p. 31–2).

Now, as Cuculain stood dying, a stream of blood trickled from his wounds, and ran in devious ways down to the lake, and poured its tiny red current into the pure water; and as Cuculain looked upon it, thinking many things in his deep mind, there came forth an otter out of the reeds of the lake and approached the pebbly strand, where the blood flowed into the water, having been attracted thither by the smell, and at the point where the blood flowed into the lake, he lapped up the life-blood of the hero, looking up from time to time, after the manner of a dog feeding. Which seeing, Cuculain gazed upon the otter, and he smiled for the last time and said:

'O thou greedy water-dog, often in my boyhood have I pursued thy race in the rivers and lakes of Murthemney; but now thou hast a full eric, who drinkest the blood of me dying. Nor do I grudge thee this thy bloody meal. Drink on, thou happy beast. To thee, too, doubtless, there will sometime be an hour of woe.'[8]

The source for this motif is clearly indicated by a footnote on the previous page referring to 'RIA MS 23 E 4'. Up to now in the chapter O'Grady has essentially been following Stokes's version, according to which Laeg, Cú Chulainn's charioteer, is already dead, but the Early Modern Irish tale that O'Grady calls 'The Great Breach of Murthemney' makes Laeg (now spelled 'Laoidh') a witness of the other episode, as follows:

When Laoidh saw the plain evacuated, the carnage that had taken place, the living having fled, and Cuchulainn cooling himself and pouring water into his

[8] O'Grady, *History*, ii. 344.

deep and mortal wounds, he came towards him. When Cuchulainn saw him approach he became much rejoiced: and Laoidh began to dress his wounds and scars which poured forth blood in gory torrents into the pool of cold water. An otter came to drink the blood, and when Cuchulainn saw the dog licking up the substance of his body, he pulled a stone out of the brink of the ford, and making an aim at the dog, knocked it down lifeless. 'Bear victory and benisons,' cried Laoidh, 'O magnanimous Cuchulainn! you never made a truer aim than that aim, and the end of your life is not yet come—avenge yourself on the men of Ireland.' 'This is woful, O Laoidh,' replied Cuchulainn, 'I shall not kill either man or beast evermore after that dog: for it was the first feat I ever performed to kill a dog, and it had been foretold to me that the killing of a dog should also be the last feat I would perform.'

O'Grady deserves full credit for his appreciation of the charm of this episode but it is easy to guess his motives for the radical changes he has made. 'The nobler conception'—from a Victorian Christian viewpoint—must prevail. Prevention of cruelty to animals, a relatively new idea in O'Grady's time, is not the real issue here: rather it is the rejection of the law of revenge. Note that there is no mention in the source of Cú Chulainn's 'deep mind'. He is a man of action, and a pagan. We like to think nowadays that primitive peoples live more harmoniously with animals than we do, but the words put into the hero's mouth by O'Grady express a sensibility almost unknown before the late eighteenth century: compare Burns's 'To a Mouse'. The cause of Cú Chulainn's last smile was quite different in O'Grady's source, by the way: the hero's bowels were spilled on the ground, and a 'hungry-mouthed raven' came to eat them, but 'a turn of the bowels having caught around the feet of the raven, it fell down'. This was the macabre or grotesque event that lightened the hero's last moments. Since O'Grady refused to allow Cú Chulainn to kill the otter or 'water-dog', he also has to give up the motif that parallels the hero's first exploit—killing Culann the Smith's dog and taking its place and name—with his last one.

An artist certainly has the right to treat his sources with the utmost freedom: Shakespeare is the great exemplar in English; but was O'Grady an artist? The description of how the otter feeds convinces us with its visual detail, though perhaps a real otter would have been more shy of man, but when the hero opens his mouth to utter archaic claptrap, the illusion vanishes. Nicholas O'Kearney, the editor and translator of the source, was never admired for his mastery of English prose, yet I prefer his clumsy literalness to O'Grady's rhetorical flourishes. On the other hand, O'Grady was most unlucky in the only nearly complete translation of *Táin Bó Cuailnge* available to him. He calls it 'O'Daly's MS. Translation',[9]

9 Ibid. 110 n.

but in fact John O'Daly mentions several times in its pages that he is only the transcriber, whereas 'Mr Kelly' is the translator.[10] It appears to be a very inaccurate translation of a corrupt text related to the Book of Leinster *Táin*. One could justify almost any liberties taken with such a source; O'Grady, however, sometimes invents episodes, including a visit to 'the walled city of Ath-a-cliah', *c.* AD 9, when no such city existed.[11]

If anything, O'Grady's thought was even more Carlylean than his prose style. *History of Ireland* has for a subtext the first lecture in *On Heroes, Hero-worship and the Heroic in History*, 'The Hero as Divinity'. *The Story of Ireland* (1894), that most anomalous of all his works, can be read as a gloss on 'The Hero as King' and Carlyle's other writings on Cromwell. This man, traditionally regarded as one of the arch-villains of Irish history, is a hero to O'Grady, who tries to rehabilitate him in Irish opinion, devoting nineteen of his 213 pages to the task. The passage bristles with Protestant prejudice and Protestant myth:

> The Puritans were able to conquer Ireland for much the same reason that the Norsemen, and afterwards the Normans, were able to conquer it. They were bolder, sincerer, more true-hearted, more upright, and more united than those whom they overthrew.[12]

As history, the book is worthless: in a copy inscribed to John Quinn, O'Grady admitted, 'I wrote this outline of Irish History rapidly in less than a month; looking up no authority during its composition except for the Battle of the Boyne.' He justifies this method by adding, 'I wrote it thinking that the things I remembered because I felt an interest in them, might be interesting to the reader.' This statement puts *The Story of Ireland* almost on a par with that comic masterpiece *1066 and All That*, which outlines English history by setting down what we *think* we remember of it. At times O'Grady, unconsciously, is as funny as Sellars and Yeatman, but not often enough to dispel the odour of what we now call fascism. It will not surprise those who accuse Yeats of sympathy with totalitarianism to learn that *The Story of Ireland* was one of the six 'ideal books' by O'Grady on Yeats's list of recommended reading— twenty-five years before Mussolini's march on Rome: 'I would . . . make a great league of . . . the great landlords, the great manufacturers and the great merchants, and harness all Ireland under them, and abolish for ever and a day this absurd Irish democracy.'[13]

---

[10] Denis Henry Kelly is also mentioned as the translator of The Book of Fenagh: 'Revised, indexed and copiously annotated by W. M. Hennessy and done into English by D. H. Kelly, Dublin, 1875'; *Bibliography of Irish Philology* (Dublin: Browne & Nolan, 1913).

[11] O'Grady, *History*, ii. 184, 290–3

[12] O'Grady, *The Story of Ireland* (London: Methuen & Co., 1894), 140.

[13] *All Ireland Review*, iii. 147.

After 1882, O'Grady wrote only political works, historical novels and books for boys: *The Story of Ireland* invites classification under all these headings, having been apparently intended for boys from the start.[14]

His longest polemic, *Toryism and the Tory Democracy* (1886), modelled on Carlyle's *Past and Present*, casts Lord Randolph Churchill as the indispensable hero without whom no book of O'Grady's seems able to exist. Its most dogmatic sentence advocates both state capitalism and the regimentation of the working class: 'The State has a right to control the labour which it employs.' Later, he lost patience with the Tory Party and the Irish landlords—especially when the latter unheroically allowed themselves to be bought out under the various Land Acts. His last political writings were socialist, contributions to *The Peasant* and A. R. Orage's *The New Age*.[15] This dizzying change of direction had been foreshadowed by the astonishing brief chapter on 'James Fintan Lalor, the "Prophet"' in *The Story of Ireland*. Lalor (1807–49) advocated peasant ownership of land as a right to be claimed by violent revolution if necessary: 'The Land the People's, for that strip and bid Ireland strip.'[16] In 1894 O'Grady did not agree with Lalor but he recognized a heroic element in him:

From the brooding brain of the Tipperary recluse, from some fiery seed dropped there by the genius of the age, sprang forth suddenly an idea full-formed, clear, mature, clad as if in shining armour, and equipped for war. Something very new and strange, something terrible, as well as beautiful, there emerged.

Despite the hackneyed allusion to the birth of Athena from the head of Zeus, this is one of O'Grady's better flights of rhetoric. It may even be the origin of one of Yeats's most famous lines: 'A terrible beauty is born.'

There is still extant a letter in which O'Grady explains to an unnamed correspondent why he gave up writing about prehistoric Ireland:

My former works on Irish history I published at my own expense . . . I perceived that I could not go on upon those lines. England alone now buys books, Ireland does not. So I determined to work upon a period in which the English people took an interest & eventually fixed on the Elizabethan conquest of Ireland.[17]

The letter probably refers to *Red Hugh's Captivity* (1889), the first of four volumes of historical fiction (published between 1889 and 1897) set in the sixteenth and seventeenth centuries. O'Grady did not completely abandon his first love, however, publishing *Finn and his*

[14] Letter of 9 March 1893, 'Colby Library Quarterly' (1958): 298.

[15] Philip L. Marcus, *Standish O'Grady*, (Lewisburg: Bucknell University Press, 1970), 75.

[16] O'Grady, *The Story of Ireland*, 198.

[17] O'Grady letter, National Library of Ireland, accession date, 16 September 1930. The letter was found with the Nat. Library's copy of *Red Hugh's Captivity*.

Companions, with a preface clearly aimed at young readers, in 1892 and *The Coming of Cuculain: A Romance of the Heroic Age of Ireland* in 1894; this was a reworking of the hero's 'boyhood deeds'. Later he drew on *History of Ireland* for two further volumes about Cú Chulainn, reproducing selected chapters almost *verbatim* to complete the saga. *In the Gates of the North* (1901) is selected from vol. i and *The Triumph and Passing of Cuculain* [1920] from vol. ii. The Talbot Press reprinted the four last-named books and several others by O'Grady, including one that became perhaps his best-known book in his native country, *The Bog of Stars and Other Stories of Elizabethan Ireland* (1893). These reprints were obviously designed for use in schools in place of similar works by British writers, and several of his books were translated into Irish, both before and after 1928, the year of his death. A memorial volume, *Standish James O'Grady: The Man & the Writer* (1929), included memories and appreciations by, among others, A. E., Alfred Perceval Graves and Alice Milligan.

In an often-quoted reminiscence entitled 'A Wet Day', O'Grady relates how he stumbled on O'Halloran's history of Ireland one wet day in a country-house library, was fascinated by its fabulous account of the early period, and soon developed an obsessive desire to learn more. J. J. MacSweeney, librarian of the RIA, guided his further studies, with the results we know. Eventually,

though the professors and educated classes in general laughed at or ignored me, a good many young men and young women quite unknown to me did not; such as Miss Tynan, Miss Eleanor Hull, Mr Yeats, Mr Rolleston and others. The fact reminds me of a noble utterance of Finn. . . . 'Small, in sooth, was my consideration in Erin till my sons and my grandsons, and my gallant nephews and grand-nephews grew up around me.'

One might have thought that when these gallant sons and nephews—and daughters and nieces—began to adapt the heroic tales for the theatre, introducing them to a new and potentially wider Irish audience, O'Grady would have been immensely gratified. Not at all: paradoxical as always, he decried the performance of A. E.'s *Deirdre*, despite having serialised the play in the *All Ireland Review*:

I don't think A. E. ought to have dramatised the story of Deirdre at all. It is the one story in which the Captain of the Red Branch is exhibited as bad . . . Last year we witnessed the degradation of Finn [in *Diarmuid and Grania*, by Moore and Yeats]; this year that of Concobar Mac Nessa.

On the next page, he is found condemning not only these particular plays but *all* attempts to dramatize the Ulster cycle: 'The Red Branch ought not to be, and cannot be, staged. They are too great. . . . Will you . . . poetically and dramatically exhibit to the people Meave in her palace full of husbands.' Here once again is the age-old battle between art and morality: as in Greek tragedy, the myths that question or violate the accepted codes are precisely those that attract the artist. Despite O'Grady's partial rejection of his Evangelical upbringing, he decides any conflict between the demands of art and his nursery morality in favour of the latter. Because of this, if for no other reason, he could never be a true artist.

Yeats's Golden's Bridge

In contrast to O'Grady, William Butler Yeats, the son of a highly articulate painter who would almost as soon talk about his art as practise it, decided very early that his vocation was to be an artist. For a time, he studied to be a painter, but quickly recognized that his own gift was for poetry, an art that John Butler Yeats (1839–1922) greatly admired. 'My father', wrote W. B. Yeats later, 'had always read verse with . . . intensity and . . . subtlety', though his strong opinions about the intellectual context of poetry did not always agree with those of his elder son. 'It was only when I began to study psychical research and mystical philosophy that I broke away from my father's influence. He had been a follower of John Stuart Mill'; so had others of John Butler Yeats's Trinity contemporaries, as pointed out in Chapter 3 (p. 80). In reaction against Utilitarianism and what he called 'popular science', W. B. Yeats might have remained imprisoned for life by the ultimately sterile contemporary doctrine of 'art for art's sake'. Fortunately for him and for us, he was converted to Irish nationalism by one of his many surrogate fathers, John O'Leary (1830–1907), a Fenian leader, who returned to Ireland after five years of imprisonment and fifteen of exile. Whatever of Evangelicalism the poet had absorbed from his mother and grandparents responded positively to O'Leary's mixture of uncompromising patriotism and tolerant Catholicism: 'He had the moral genius that moves all young people and moves them the more if they are repelled by those who have strict opinions and yet have lived commonplace lives.'

O'Leary introduced Yeats to the patriotic poems of Thomas Davis and the Young Irelanders generally, but 'he did not, although the poems of Davis made him a patriot, claim that they were very good poetry'. For ten years (1885–95) Yeats devoted himself to studying what he called 'the tradition of Ireland'. Since his father and the rest of the family were chronically in need of money, he combined this self-education with the earning of a pittance by compiling several anthologies. For

Fairy and Folk Tales of the Irish Peasantry (1888) he received twelve guineas, and seven for *Stories from Carleton* (1889). Every anthology was to some extent an act of criticism by virtue of its choices and omission, but Yeats also spent those years writing dozens of articles, reviews and letters to the editor, in which he strove to establish a critical canon of Anglo-Irish writing. His first two recorded articles eulogize the poetry of Ferguson; they were both published in 1886, the year of the older poet's death. Yeats describes him as 'the greatest poet Ireland has produced, because the most central and most Celtic'. He 'was made by the purifying flame of National sentiment the one man of his time who wrote heroic poetry'. A paragraph near the end of this second—and most substantial—article echoes a belief held by both Ferguson and O'Grady:

Of all the many things the past bequeaths to the future, the greatest are the legends; they are the mothers of nations. I hold it the duty of every Irish reader to study those of his own country till they are familiar as his own hands, for in them is the Celtic heart.

Yeats's critical writings from this formative decade are mostly to be found in the first volume of his *Uncollected Prose* (ed. John P. Frayne, 1970). He followed the Ferguson articles with two similar assessments of poets already dead—Robert Dwyer Joyce (1830–83) and James Clarence Mangan (1803–49).[18] Soon he was invited to review poetry by living Irish authors: where possible, as with the collected edition of William Allingham's poems, he tried to cover the entire *oeuvre*. After 1888 he was given for review a number of books dealing—well or ill—with Irish folklore and was thus able to give public praise to Douglas Hyde's early work, especially *Love Songs of Connacht* (1893). He also praised William Larminie's one collection of folk-tales, though failing to appreciate the imitation of Gaelic assonantal rhyme in some of Larminie's poems.[19] It was not until many years later that Yeats began to employ this type of rhyme. When Kuno Meyer's scholarly edition and translation *The Vision of MacConglinne* came to Yeats for review, he was delighted with its 'sharp and glittering' satire, though, as we have already seen, his own version of the tale was to be sombre and defeatist in tone.

By 1894–5 Yeats was well enough known to be able to launch the reputations of A. E. as a poet and John Eglinton as an essayist with not entirely uncritical reviews in the London *Bookman*. A series of four articles (July–October 1895) in the same periodical, under the general heading 'Irish National Literature', present the fruits of ten years' reading in the form of a revised canon of nineteenth-century Irish

[18] 'The Poetry of R. W. Joyce', in *Uncollected Prose by W. B. Yeats*, ed. John P. Frayne (New York: Columbia Univ. Press, 1970), i. 104–119.
[19] Frayne, (ed.), *Uncollected Prose*, i. 229–30.

literature. His fourth article, subtitled 'A list of the Best Irish Books', contains forty-six titles—forty-eight if we include one work not yet published and one in French, H. d'Arbois de Joubainville's *Mythologie Irlandaise*. This list should be compared with that of thirty books published in a letter of his to the Dublin *Daily Express* earlier the same year. The last title in the new list is his own: *A Book of Irish Verse* (1895), which he compiled, he says, 'because I disliked those already in existence'. The recent publication of this book in London added authority to his list. Another anthology, for which he had culled the prose fiction of the century, also guided his choice: *Representative Irish Tales* (two vols., 1891).

The first article of the series, subtitled 'From Callanan to Carleton', defines 'national writers' as 'those who have written under Irish influence and of Irish subjects'. Yeats emphasizes the difficulty of trying to create an Irish literary tradition in English—'English-speaking Ireland is very new'—and understands the impatience of writers like Thomas Moore, Davis, and Mitchel, who borrowed ready-made English genres and styles in order to reach their audience quickly. He himself, however, prefers translators like J. J. Callanan and Edward Walsh among the early poets, and values the minor Young Ireland versifiers only because they built up an audience for 'four important poets': Aubrey de Vere has temporarily been admitted to the canon alongside Mangan, Allingham, and Ferguson. Among the early novelists, too, he values the painful struggles of the Banim brothers and Carleton to build up a native tradition of fiction in the English language more than the greater sophistication of Maria Edgeworth in all her novels except *Castle Rackrent*. The second and third articles, on contemporary prose writers and contemporary poets respectively, are less coherent: Yeats's personal relations with the authors, especially the women, lead to some decidedly eccentric critical judgements, including a preposterous defence of that preposterous book, O'Grady's *Story of Ireland*.

Yeats's contributions to Irish daily newspapers, and especially to *United Ireland*, which was uncompromisingly Parnellite even after Parnell's death, naturally had a more political—and polemical—tone than those written for British literary magazines. He lamented the unwillingness of the Irish to buy books, attacked the 'scholasticism'— 'Philistinism' would have been a better word—of Trinity College, and engaged in a controversy with Edward Dowden, the renowned professor of English there, on the relative merits of Irish and English writers. On the other hand, aware of Yeats's growing prestige as a poet and critic, the editor of *United Ireland*, John McGrath, sometimes gave him an opportunity to express more fully his philosophy of literature.

The most important of these statements of principle, 'Hopes and Fears for Irish Literature' (*United Ireland*, 15 October 1892), contrasts the attitude of his London friends in the Rhymers' Club with those of his literary friends in Dublin. To the former, 'Poetry is an end in itself; it has nothing to do with life, nothing to do with anything but the music of cadence, and beauty of phrase.' To the latter, as to Yeats himself, 'literature must be the expression of conviction, and be the garment of noble emotion and not an end in itself'. Sometimes, as in Ferguson's 'Conary', these beliefs have given rise to works 'beyond all praise and imitation'. Unfortunately, 'Here in Ireland the art of living interests us greatly, and the art of writing but little. We seek effectiveness rather than depth.' Irish poets must learn their trade. If they can adopt from their French and English contemporaries 'a little of their skill, and a little of their devotion to form, a little of their hatred of the common-place and the banal', Yeats has the highest hopes for them:

We have behind us in the past the most moving legends and a history full of lofty passions. If we can but take that history and those legends and turn them into dramas, poems, and stories full of the living soul of the present, and make them massive with conviction and profound with reverie, we may deliver that great new utterance for which the world is waiting. Men are growing tired of mere subtleties of form, self-conscious art and no less self-conscious simplicity. But if we are to do this we must study all things Irish.

(John P. Frayne, *Uncollected Prose by W. B. Yeats*, i, 250)

Clearly, Yeats would have felt too embarrassed to make such a passionately patriotic statement in any English periodical, even if the editor was willing to let it pass.

Yeats's own readiness to 'study all things Irish' did not, however, include the Irish language. In a letter to the editor of *United Ireland* (17 December 1892) he praised Douglas Hyde's recent lecture entitled 'The De-Anglicising of Ireland' but argued that Hyde's chief proposed means to that end, the revival of Gaelic, was impossible. He claimed that Hyde himself had admitted this, though the passage he quotes does not appear in the text as published in *The Revival of Irish Literature* (1894); perhaps the foundation of the Gaelic League had convinced Hyde that both 'men' and 'money' would be forthcoming for his great undertaking. Yeats also refused to accept one of Hyde's most powerful arguments—that the Irish language is 'the best claim which we have upon the world's recognition of us as a separate nationality'.

The poet's solution, perhaps dictated by an apparent inability to master any language except English—which may have been a necessary condition of his total mastery of that language—was to translate or retell 'all that is best of the ancient literature' in an English which should have 'an indefinable Irish quality of rhythm and style'. Stopford Brooke took up a very similar position in his inaugural address to the Irish Literary Society of London, rather prosaically entitled 'The Need and Use of Getting Irish Literature into the English Tongue', but he lacked any gift for the resounding phrase: it was Yeats who hoped that this process would make 'a golden bridge between the old and the new'.

5 Bernard Shaw: Irish
International

Shaw's Irishness: Protestant and Catholic Estimates

Although only two of his plays, *John Bull's Other Island* and *O'Flaherty, V.C.*, are directly concerned with Ireland, Shaw always made a point of his Irishness:

Really the English do not deserve to have great men. They allowed [Samuel] Butler to die practically unknown, whilst I a comparatively insignificant Irish journalist, was leading them by the nose into an advertisement of me which has made my own life a burden.[1]

As the quotation suggests, being Irish was part of a stratagem to confuse his English readers and keep them off-balance: 'the position of a foreigner with complete command of the same language has great advantages. I can take an objective view of England, which no English-man can.' This passage, from an interview granted at age 90, ends by showing the other side of the coin: 'I could not take an objective view of Ireland.'[2] The sheer bulk of Shaw's non-dramatic writing about Ireland, from which *The Matter with Ireland* gives us but a 300-page selection, sufficiently guarantees his sincerity in asserting his Irishness, even though he stated in his will that his 'domicile of choice is English.'[3]

No Protestant Irishman can deny Shaw's Irishness without denying his own. Even St John Ervine, anxious though he was to prove that Shaw was no longer a citizen of the Republic of Ireland when he died, makes sure to mention in the first paragraph of the foreword to his biography that Shaw said to him, 'You will understand the Irish side of me better than anybody who is not Irish.'[4] The other Irish Protestant writers of his time usually admired and understood Shaw, Yeats being the great exception. Everybody remembers Yeats's dream of being 'haunted by a sewing-machine, that clicked and shone, but the incredible thing was that the machine smiled, smiled perpetually'. What one forgets is

[1] Bernard Shaw, from the preface to *Major Barbara*, in *The Complete Prefaces* (London: Paul Hamlyn, 1965), 123.
[2] Bernard Shaw, *The Matter with Ireland*, ed. Dan H. Laurence and David H. Greene (New York: Hill and Wang, 1962), ix.
[3] St John Ervine, *Bernard Shaw: His Life, Work and Friends* (New York: William Morrow, 1956), 111.
[4] Ervine, *Bernard Shaw*, vii.

the conclusion of the passage: 'Yet I delighted in Shaw, the formidable man. He could hit my enemies and the enemies of all I loved, as I could never hit, as no living author who was dear to me could ever hit.' Yeats also repeated Wilde's epigram with glee: 'Mr Bernard Shaw has no enemies but is intensely disliked by all his friends', saying that he 'felt revenged [by it] upon a notorious hater of romance, whose generosity and courage I could not fathom'. The last clause shows that Yeats learned to appreciate the man, if not the work.[5]

Lady Gregory, on the other hand, recognized Shaw as a kindred mind and Mrs Shaw as one whose upbringing and idealism were not very different from her own. Lennox Robinson, himself a great admirer and sometimes imitator of Shaw, tells us in his selection from Lady Gregory's journals that 'In later years her best friends in England were Bernard and Mrs Shaw, and I think that I have recorded almost every word of her memories of them.'[6] Yeats and she had rejected *John Bull's Other Island* on the possibly specious ground that they had no actor to play Broadbent, but Robinson describes Shaw as 'a firm and faithful friend' of the Abbey Theatre, perhaps from the very day of his rejection. In 1909 the Abbey, disregarding the objections of the British Government in Ireland, produced *The Shewing-Up of Blanco Posnet*, which had been banned from the public stage in England on the ground of blasphemy. They were in a sense repaying Shaw for the rejection of *John Bull*, which was not performed at the Abbey until 1916, but their defiance of the Lord Chamberlain of course earned world-wide publicity for the Irish theatre movement. Among the many representatives of the foreign press on opening night was James Joyce, as acting correspondent for an Italian paper. Shaw later helped Lady Gregory in her campaign to have Hugh Lane's collection of paintings returned to Ireland and took part with Yeats in the founding of the Irish Academy of Letters. When the Abbey turned down Sean O'Casey's *The Silver Tassie* in 1928, Shaw wrote a scathing letter to Lady Gregory about Yeats's clumsy handling of the whole matter.[7]

As for O'Casey, a less typical Irish Protestant than the others, he seems to have both admired and loved Shaw, whom he called 'the second Saint Bernard', from the earliest days of his intellectual awakening. At a dinner just after the success of *Juno and the Paycock*, when modern playwrights were being discussed, 'Sean whispered the names of Shaw and Strindberg, which they didn't seem to catch.' Earlier, in 1923, O'Casey told Joseph Holloway that he 'loves Shaw's work because in the very

5 W. B. Yeats, *Autobiographies* (London: Macmillan, 1955), 133–4, 283.

6 Isabella Augusta, Lady Gregory, *Journals*, ed. Lennox Robinson (New York: Macmillan, 1947), 199.

7 Gregory, *Journals*, 110–11; Lane pictures, 289, 292–3; help for the Abbey, 66–7, 199; miscellaneous Shaviana, 199–216. Note Shaw's Anglo-Irish verses to the Gregory granddaughters, 18.

kernel of tragedy he can introduce something to make one laugh its sting away. [T. C.] Murray never does this; his tragedy is ever unrelieved.' In spite of some digs at Mrs Shaw, the chapter 'Shaw's Corner' in *Sunset and Evening Star* is perhaps the most generous in all six volumes of O'Casey's autobiographies.[8]

The published selection from Holloway's manuscript diary, 'Impressions of a Dublin Playgoer', reminds us that Dublin did not have to wait for an Abbey production to see some at least of Shaw's earlier plays. For instance, *John Bull's Other Island* was performed at the Theatre Royal, presumably by an English touring company, at some date prior to 30 November, 1907, for on the latter date Holloway mentioned 'the introduction of the sixty policemen on the first night'. The occasion for the remark was a discussion of the preface to *John Bull's Other Island* held at the Contemporary Club. In the year of the *Playboy* riots, 'policemen' was a ticklish word: 'W. B. Yeats was drawn at once, and up in arms against me', for he had brought police into the Abbey during the riots. If the Dublin première of *John Bull* occurred after that of *The Playboy of the Western World*, one can understand the presence of police at the Royal, since Shaw's play seemed much more likely than Synge's to inflame an Irish audience. From Holloway we also know that Forbes Robertson took *Caesar and Cleopatra* to Dublin in 1907. When *John Bull* was finally given its Abbey première on 25 September 1916, it played to packed houses. J. Augustus Keogh, who had succeeded the unpopular St John Ervine as manager, followed up this success by producing *Widower's Houses* and *Arms and the Man* in October. On 25 March 1917 Holloway said to Keogh, 'We have had far too much Shaw of late at the Abbey, and many are saying so to me'; *Man and Superman* had received its first performance there in February, but probably the trivial *Inca of Perusalem* in March proved the last straw. 'When I said that the Gaiety or the Royal were the proper places for Shaw's plays and not the Abbey, Keogh could have slain me on the spot.' One is hardly surprised to read on 9 May that 'J. A. Keogh has got his walking papers from the Abbey; a love of Shaw and a hatred for Irish drama and Irish acting were, I am sure, the cause.' *The Doctor's Dilemma* (26 May 1917) was the last Shaw piece to receive an Abbey première until *Androcles and the Lion* (4 November, 1919).[9]

[8] Sean O'Casey, *Autobiographies*, 2 vols., St Martin's Library (London: Macmillan, 1963), ii. 596–623; ii, 484; ii, 105. Joseph Holloway, *Joseph Holloway's Abbey Theatre: A Selection from His Unpublished Journal*, ed. Robert Hogan and Michael J. O'Neill (Carbondale: Southern Illinois Univ. Press, 1967), 220.

[9] Holloway, *Abbey Theatre*, 97, 277, 188, 191–2, 193. Dates of first performances from Brinsley Macnamara (pseud. of John Weldon), *Abbey Plays 1899–1948* (Dublin: Three Candles, n.d.). Note Holloway's letter to Miss Annie E. F. Horniman about the company she sent to Dublin in Shaw's plays, led by Ben Iden Payne, 109.

Holloway's distinction between Irish drama and the plays of Shaw need not be construed to mean that he thought Shaw was not Irish: Holloway viewed him correctly as an international dramatist, needing a more sophisticated style of acting than the Abbey could provide. One often feels that Holloway represents the lowest common denominator of the Abbey audience, but in fact he was closer to the *juste milieu,* and he was never anti-Shaw. Though Holloway never mentions Shaw's Dublin accent, perhaps because he was unaware of it, he could not possibly dismiss as un-Irish a man who spoke more or less like himself. Shaw did not have a Protestant accent—if such a thing exists—but a Dublin Southside accent, similar to that of James Joyce and J. F. Byrne, Joyce's 'Cranly'.[10] A lecture by Shaw in person was for Holloway, and surely for many Dubliners like him, 'one of those great exciting events in one's life'. Although he was too inclined to assume that everybody in any audience agreed with him, we may believe Holloway when he writes, 'all said they would not have missed it for anything'. Not everything Shaw said was agreed with, however: 'He was hissed for   a slighting reference to the Gaelic, and Dr McWalter contradicted his assertion that the Irish girls have bad teeth.'[11] Shaw's morality in general proved acceptable to his countrymen, and if he was a little suspect in the matter of sexual morality, at least he observed decorum. Arthur Griffith's daily *Sinn Féin* praised *The Shewing-Up of Blanco Posnet* and its performance at the Abbey, calling it 'a moral play' in the issue of 26 August 1909, but an article the following day took a different view:

We don't want this sort of play in Ireland just at present. We are not ready for it, and I can quite imagine it would be a happy condition of affairs if we were never ready for it. Let Mr Shaw keep on juggling to English audiences who have no such inconvenient thing as conviction. Mr Yeats has created a sensation in putting his play on at the Abbey Theatre. But he has done nothing whatsoever thereby for the movement towards a National drama that is slowly growing in this country. He has given us a taste of London monstrosities. That is all.[12]

Whether Griffith actually wrote this article or not, it is typical of his narrowly nationalist, philistine view of the arts—in public at least. As reported by Holloway, Patrick H. Pearse was much more tolerant, in private conversation:

The Abbey is a freak theatre and should be treated as such; if you don't like it, stop away. Pearse admires Yeats for his splendid pluck. He thinks Yeats the

[10] This opinion is based on recordings made by Joyce and Shaw, on conversations with J. F. Byrne in New York, and on overhearing Holloway in the Abbey Theatre foyer.

[11] Holloway, *Abbey Theatre,* 142.

[12] W. B. Yeats, *Memoirs,* ed. Denis Donoghue (London: Macmillan, 1972), 229n.

greatest talker in Ireland. Ireland has always had such men as Shaw, Yeats, Martyn, Russell, and Moore—irresponsible beings that help to keep life fresh.[13]

Curiously, the severest attack on Shaw for anti-nationalism and even for Protestant bigotry—I mean one made by a usually intelligent and responsible writer—came from Ernest A. Boyd, whom I have always assumed to be an Irish Protestant, perhaps from a Presbyterian family. While he admits that Shaw did not come from a 'narrow, puritan home'— Chesterton's phrase—he goes on to characterize it as 'a typically Irish Protestant home':

The father, an outwardly most respectable Civil Servant, the son educated at a veritable stronghold of Irish Protestantism, the social snobbery and hostility towards 'Papists'—nothing is wanting to provide the *mise en scène* which surrounds the peculiar development of what is known in Ireland as 'the loyal garrison.' All the circumstances point to Shaw's having been a potential supporter of the Union.[14]

All the circumstances pointed to the same conclusion about the man who baptized Shaw, his second cousin and uncle by marriage, the Revd William George Carroll, 'the first minister of the . . . Church of Ireland to become a Home Ruler and a Republican'.[15] Boyd could not of course have known that a nominal Catholic, George John Vandeleur Lee, formed part of the Shaw household from 1866, but he ought to have read 'In the Days of My Youth', first published in 1898, and given credence to the final paragraphs, in which the power of music to overcome religious and social barriers is illustrated by Shaw's mother's taking part as soloist in the Masses of Haydn and Mozart. These of course were sung in Roman Catholic churches: 'All of which led to the discovery . . . that a Roman Catholic priest could be as agreeable and cultivated a person as a Protestant clergyman was supposed, in defiance of bitter experience, always to be.'[16] Boyd ends by assuming what he is trying to prove: 'the Irish Protestant is deprived, in advance, of nationality, otherwise he would cease to exist. He is the artificial creation of English Government in Ireland, and knows only the patriotism of gratitude for benefits conferred.' This reads very strangely from a man who, though born in Dublin, received much of his education in Switzerland and Germany and served in the British Consular Service, 1913–20. A

---

[13] Holloway, *Abbey Theatre*, 151.

[14] Ernest A. Boyd, 'An Irish Protestant: Bernard Shaw; I, At Home', in *Appreciations and Depreciations: Irish Literary Studies* (Dublin: Talbot Press; London: T. Fisher Unwin, 1917), 105.

[15] Ervine, *Bernard Shaw*, 7.

[16] 'In the Days of My Youth' (original version), from *M. A. P.*, 17 September 1898, in *Selected Non-Dramatic Writings of Bernard Shaw*, ed. Dan H. Laurence (Boston: Houghton Mifflin, 1965), 436–7.

'sabbatical' from this service to study the Irish literary movement, about which he wrote several books, struck some of the leaders of the 1916 Easter Rising as a little too conveniently arranged.[17]

Despite Boyd's Scottish surname and his having worked for the then ultra-Protestant *Irish Times* (1910–13), he may well have been baptized a Catholic, being 'of Scottish, Irish, and Spanish ancestry': we may thus include him with Griffith, Holloway, and Pearse as examples of the Irish Catholic reaction to Shaw. One further voice from that side of the house demands to be heard—that of Joyce:

Shaw is a born preacher. His lively and talkative spirit cannot stand to be subjected to the noble and bare style appropriate to modern playwriting. Indulging himself in wandering prefaces and extravagant rules of drama, he creates a dramatic form which is much like a dialogue novel. He has a sense of situation, rather than of drama logically and ethically led to a conclusion.[18]

There speaks a writer whose favourite among Shaw's plays, doubtless because of its Ibsenite rigour, seems to have been *Mrs Warren's Profession*. Joyce's own striving after a 'noble and bare style' in *Exiles* sadly thwarted his natural gift for comedy. Unwilling to imitate Shaw, even if he were able to do so, Joyce kept a judicial eye on him throughout his life. One of the characteristics of Irish Protestant intellectuals like Shaw, Yeats, and A. E. aroused the deepest suspicions of this very suspicious man: having abandoned the 'illogical and incoherent' absurdity of Protestantism, they were all too ready to adopt some other belief, such as Theosophy, that seemed to Joyce an absurdity taken to the nth power; they might even embrace the 'logical and coherent' absurdity of Roman Catholicism.[19] He had hoped for better things from Shaw, but this is how he concluded his review of *The Shewing-Up of Blanco Posnet* in the Trieste newspaper *Il Piccolo della Sera*, 5 September 1909:

And may not this play reflect a crisis in the mind of its writer? Earlier, at the end of 'John Bull's Other Island', the crisis was set forth. Shaw, as well as his latest protagonist, has had a profane and unruly past. . . . And now, perhaps, some divine finger has touched his brain, and he, in the guise of Blanco Posnet, is shown up.

---

[17] Boyd, 'An Irish Protestant', 117–18. For biographical details see the article on Boyd in *Twentieth Century Authors*, ed. Stanley J. Kunitz and Howard Haycraft (New York: H. W. Wilson, 1942). Geraldine Dillon, sister of the executed leader Joseph Plunkett, is my informant about suspicion in regard to Boyd.

[18] James Joyce, 'Bernard Shaw's Battle with the Censor', in *The Critical Writings of James Joyce*, ed. Ellsworth Mason and Richard Ellmann (New York: Viking, 1959), 208.

[19] James Joyce, *A Portrait of the Artist As a Young Man*, The definitive text corrected from Dublin Holograph (New York: Viking, 1964), 244.

Joyce may first have learned of Ibsen's existence from *The Quintessence of Ibsenism*: at any rate the editors of his *Critical Writings* are convinced that he had read Shaw's important essay before writing 'Ibsen's New Drama', published in the *Fortnightly Review*, 1 April 1900, when he was barely 18.[20] The library he left behind him in Trieste on moving to Paris in June 1920 included these volumes by Shaw: *Cashel Byron's Profession*; *The Devil's Disciple*; *Getting Married* and *The Shewing-Up of Blanco Posnet*; *John Bull's Other Island*; *Love among the Artists*; *Major Barbara*; *Misalliance, The Dark Lady of the Sonnets, and Fanny's First Play*; *Mrs Warren's Profession*; *The Perfect Wagnerite*; *The Philanderer*; *Socialism and Superior Brains*; *Three Unpleasant Plays* (*Widower's Houses, The Philanderer, Mrs Warren's Profession*). One also finds other collections with Shaw's work in them: *Fabian Tracts*, nos. 1–173 (bound together) and Sidney Webb, *Socialism and Individualism*.[21] A later play that we know Joyce had seen or read is *Saint Joan*.[22] He congratulated Shaw on winning the Nobel Prize for Literature in a short letter dated 26 November 1926. In a letter to *Picture Post*, 3 June 1939, Shaw denied being disgusted by *Ulysses* and called it 'a literary masterpiece'. But Shaw's most moving tribute to Joyce occurs in his longest sustained autobiographical essay, the preface (1921) to *Immaturity*:

In 1876 I had had enough of Dublin. James Joyce in his Ulysses has described, with a fidelity so ruthless that the book is hardly bearable, the life that Dublin offers to its young men, or, if you prefer to put it the other way, that its young men offer to Dublin. No doubt it is much like the life of young men everywhere in modern urban civilization. A certain flippant futile derision and belittlement that confuses the noble and serious with the base and ludicrous seems to me peculiar to Dublin; but I suppose that is because my only personal experience of that phase of youth is a Dublin experience.[23]

In fact, many Dubliners, including Joyce, would endorse that phrase, 'peculiar to Dublin'.

The first book about Shaw written by an Irishman was the work, as one might expect, of a member of the Anglo-Irish gentry: John Stewart Collis, author of *Shaw* (1925), belonged to one of its most talented families. Of Shaw's Irish reputation at that time, just a year before his 70th birthday, Collis says, 'He is despised as a fool by the foolish, considered a crank by the more intelligent, and disliked by the jealous.'

[20] Mason and Ellmann (eds.), *Critical Writings*, 48, 208.

[21] Richard Ellmann, *The Consciousness of Joyce* (New York: Oxford Univ. Press, 1977), 108, 127–8, 132.

[22] James Joyce, *Letters*, ed. Stuart Gilbert (New York: Viking, 1957), 221.

[23] Shaw, *Complete Prefaces*, 673. Nobel Prize, James Joyce, *Letters*, ed. Richard Ellmann (New York: Viking, 1966), iii. 146; *Picture Post*, *Letters*, iii. 444n.

The sources of this attitude are twofold: 'First, because he freely criticises Ireland; second, because he is a successful man—two unforgivable sins to an Irishman. The Irish cannot bear criticism; for like all races who have been oppressed they are still without mental bravery.' The 'jealous'—or more accurately, the envious—cannot forgive Shaw his success outside Ireland. 'The Irish are the most jealous nation alive . . . the English are always ready to help a promising young man, but the Irish will deliberately baulk the career of a young man for no better reason than because he is promising.'[24]

Collis's study penetrates more deeply than its casual style may suggest, but its greatest virtue is its uninhibited youthful enthusiasm:

My qualification for writing this book is simply that when I was a schoolboy I saw *John Bull's Other Island* performed at the Abbey Theatre before I had ever heard of Shaw. Never will I forget that evening! I was sixteen—that frightful age, that no-man's-land between childhood and manhood when you don't know where you are or what you are, and look up for help and guidance to fools and bullies and liars and cheats. The play was acted by the best set of Irish Players that have ever worked together at the Abbey Theatre—perfect beyond perfection. I heard the voice of [Peter] Keegan; I listened to the heavenly music—and I knew at last I was feeling the real thing. I forgot that I was sixteen: I knew only that I was listening to words that I fain would have uttered, to thoughts which were surely mine. In that hour I saw straight into the soul of Bernard Shaw and the opinion of him which I then formed has ever since been increasingly justified.[25]

Note how different Collis's response to the last act of *John Bull* is from that of Joyce, yet both see the play as recording a crisis in Shaw's spiritual life; Joyce is more explicit and actually uses the word 'crisis', whereas Collis implicitly recognizes it by undergoing his own adolescent spiritual crisis.

There will be much more to say about Shaw's religion, but first I want to set down my own impressions of Shaw beside Collis's; I feel the more justified in doing so because my mother came from a clerical family very like that of Shaw's grandmother Frances Carr. My mother's maiden name was Charlotte Olivia Abbott; not only was her father the Archdeacon of Clogher in his later years, but two of his brothers were also clergymen of the Church of Ireland; so were one of her brothers and one of her brothers-in-law. I never met any of the older generation, but I think none of them was as Evangelical as the general run of the Shaws in their time. My father's family, who were all originally Methodists, showed much more of the Evangelical tone, though my father later joined the Church of Ireland and became a lay member of its General Synod. My introduction to Shaw was earlier and less romantic than

---

[24] John Stewart Collis, *Shaw* (London: Cape, 1925), 11, 12, 14.   [25] Ibid. 15–16.

Collis's: as a pre-adolescent of 10 I cynically enjoyed the anti-romanticism of *Arms and the Man* brilliantly played by an all-boy cast at Portora (*alma mater* of Oscar Wilde and Samuel Beckett). Although not yet aware that Shaw was Irish, I responded instantly to his wit and humour. My mother and my clerical Uncle Wilfred, among others, had brought me up in this Irish and Anglo-Irish tradition of joking about everything. My grandfather's rectory must have been full of it, what with his three Trinity-educated sons, his succession of curates, and his three pretty daughters, of whom my mother was perhaps the cleverest. The greatest humorist of all may have been my grandmother, Charlotte Elizabeth Church, daughter of a modest 'big house' in County Derry, of whose frivolity I was an eye-witness when she was in her seventies.

Coming from the more serious Methodist tradition, my father had little sense of humour, but he was demonstrative in matters of sentiment and religion; my mother was not. If Shaw believed that his mother was incapable of sentiment and had no religious convictions, my mother often gave the same impression, but it was a false one. One other trait of my mother's, doubtless learned from her own mother, helped me to appreciate Shaw very quickly: like Shaw (and indeed Swift), if a telling remark came into her head, she could not resist making it, no matter how inappropriate the company might be—especially if some of her shockable in-laws were present. She assumed that a lady who really was a lady could say whatever she liked, since she was far too well-trained ever to fit the action to the word. Gentlemen, in the presence of ladies at least, had to be more circumspect. I am sure, however, that Shaw's father, even in his drinking days, did not insist that he was a confirmed teetotaller out of mere hypocrisy: no matter how often he 'backslid', he held firm to an Evangelical conviction of the sinfulness of alcohol. It is not surprising that Shaw's comedies about the upper classes often present outspoken women and untrustworthy or hypocritical men: this is particularly true of *Heartbreak House*, which happens to be the first Shaw play I read, perhaps shortly before my 13th birthday; soon afterwards I became a convinced Shavian. None of the Portora masters shared my taste, but in the summer holidays just after my 15th birthday my former primary schoolteacher, Kathleen Thomson, lent me, volume by volume, all the plays and prefaces in her set of Shaw. In the autumn I wrote Shaw a long, admiring letter and received in return a postcard photograph of his splendid head, with the following message on the back: 'Well, go ahead and get it all over. You must tackle The Intelligent Woman's Guide. It will keep you going for months.'

Shaw was my intellectual salvation, for he transformed me from a smug little machine for passing examinations into someone who cared about ideas and was capable of feeling genuine concern about social and political justice. He taught me to cultivate my own originality, be it great or small, and to count remediable ignorance as a sin, especially where my knowledge of the arts was deficient; conformity with one's schoolmates and one's social class must be resisted by every possible means. My prose style, if I have one, is based on Shaw's 'Augustan Irish classical English',[26] reinforced by the public speaking of my father and the sermons of my friends and relations among the Church of Ireland clergy.

In later years, when he had mellowed towards his Evangelical upbringing, Shaw acknowledged other influences upon his style:

That I can write as I do without having to think about my style is due to my having been as a child steeped in the Bible, The Pilgrim's Progress, and Cassell's Illustrated Shakespear. I was taught to hold the Bible in such reverence that when one day, as I was buying a pennyworth of sweets in a little shop in Dublin, the shopkeeper tore a leaf out of a dismembered Bible to wrap them in, I was horrified, and half expected to see him struck by lightning.[27]

He was steeped in the Book of Common Prayer too, of course. A sentence in the preface to *London Music in 1888–90* completes the picture of the Shaw brothers' Evangelicalism sketched in Chapter 3 (p. 78): 'I can remember the ante-Lee period in Synge St. when my father, as sole chief of the household, read family prayers'. Shaw then quotes fairly accurately from the General Confession.[28] The sheer quantity of citations from the King James Bible and the Book of Common Prayer is particularly noticeable in a late work, *Everybody's Political What's What?* (1944), but Shaw's greatest *tour de force* with biblical language is the Revd George Lind's sermon in Chapter XI of *The Irrational Knot*, his second novel. The text is 'How can Satan cast out Satan?' (Mark iii.23).

Shaw as Novelist, 1878–88

Apart from *My Dear Dorothea*, a short piece which Shaw wrote at the age of 21 and which was not published until 1956, the novels are Shaw's earliest works. But anyone expecting to find them crammed with memories of Ireland will be sorely disappointed. The 23-year-old Shaw appears to have wanted to take up the English novel at the exact point which it had reached in 1878—roughly speaking, at the peak represented by George Eliot's *Middlemarch* (1872), 'which I read in my teens and . . .

[26] Shaw, *The Matter with Ireland*, 29.
[27] Bernard Shaw, *Everybody's Political What's What?* (London: Constable, 1944), 181. Abbreviated below as *EPWW*.
[28] Shaw, *Complete Prefaces*, 856.

almost venerated'.[29] This is high praise, since the teenage Shaw was not much given to veneration. As he explained in 1944, 'I began, as all serious artist-authors had to in the eighteen-eighties, by writing novels (the theatre being mentally dust and ashes)'. Many critics, including Shaw himself, have belittled his 'five jejune samples in that *genre*',[30] but I must beg to differ with him and them. Even the well-named *Immaturity* deserves a reading, if only for the grace and irony of its classical style. No English reader could have guessed, had it been published in 1880 instead of fifty years later, that its obviously youthful author had not been to a university. Note too that the title was not chosen in Shaw's seventies but is integral to the novel: Robert Smith, the observer of the action but no hero, is told in the brief epilogue, 'You are just a bad case of immaturity', and does not resent or question this judgement.[31]

The novelist unfortunately has not chosen any one far-off mundane event to which his whole creation moves; the total effect of the book is therefore anticlimactic, but Shaw has managed to create one truly memorable character, the Evangelical (but non-Anglican) preacher St John Davis, whose sense of predestination seems almost more Muslim than Calvinist. As he tells Smith, who was instrumental in his meeting Harriet Russell, the independent Scots dressmaker who is the heroine (if any) of *Immaturity*, 'Other men had their souls to think of; but I hadn't. Mine was saved; and I well knew it. I knew I was doing God's will when I fell in love. It's ordained in the Bible that we should. I didn't obey the Bible by halves, Mr Smith.'[32] When Harriet marries Cyril Scott, a painter, Davis, disillusioned, gives up preaching for the musical stage; in the chorus at some private theatricals, he sees Harriet in the audience and creates a disturbance. As the ever-obliging Smith leads him gently away, Davis insists that his last meeting with Harriet shows 'the hand of Destiny'; he then retells each incident of his little tragedy, which he sees as foreordained. Smith finally protests: 'But what on earth use is such a belief? It simply amounts to saying that whatever is, is'[33] Just after they part, Davis, in the last stages of tuberculosis and half-crazy from disappointment, collapses in the street. The police, thinking he is drunk, put him in a cell for the night; in the morning he is dead. The novel should have ended here instead of dragging on for another hundred inconclusive pages.

[29] Bernard Shaw, 'Postscript: After Twentyfive Years', in *Back to Methuselah*, The World's Classics, no. 500 (London: Humphrey Milford, Oxford Univ. Press, 1945), 299. Also in Bernard Shaw, *Complete Plays with Prefaces* (New York: Dodd, Mead, 1962), ii. pp. cv–cvi.

[30] Shaw, *EPWW*, 188.

[31] Bernard Shaw, *Immaturity*, Standard Edition (London: Constable, 1931), 423.

[32] Shaw, *Immaturity*, 128.

[33] Ibid. 317.

Shaw seems not to have been sure whether he wanted to refute Calvinism or to exemplify the would-be-scientific refutation of free will which he afterwards claimed to have found in *Middlemarch*. Fifty years on, he characterized his first three novels thus:

The first two I wrote on lines of the science of that time, the hero of the second being a complete Rationalist practising electrical engineering as a profession. Then, finding I could get no further in this direction, I quite deliberately and consciously abandoned it, and made the hero of my next novel a totally unreasonable . . . composer like Beethoven.[34]

I wonder how deliberate and conscious the shift from a rational to an intuitive hero actually was at the time: the aging Shaw admitted that the whole world was then beginning, perhaps unconsciously, to value intuition once more. Of one thing I am sure: Edward Conolly, the allegedly rational hero of *The Irrational Knot*, is granted free will by his creator, exercising it both to reach the top of the engineering profession and to contract a singularly unwise marriage with a young society lady, Marian Lind, who quickly bores and is bored by him. Although the title is clearly intended by Shaw to apply to the institution of marriage as a whole, the reader seems more likely to regard this particular union, or disunion, as 'the irrational knot'. Marian become pregnant by a former suitor, Sholto Douglas, but soon loses patience with him and is willing to return to Edward if he wants her. At his sister's death-bed, he speaks harshly to Marian as never before:

'Is it utterly impossible for you to say something real to me? Only learn to do that, and you may have ten love romances every year with other men, if you like. Be anything rather than a ladylike slave and liar. There! As usual, the truth makes you shrink from me. As I said before, I refuse further intercourse on such terms.'[35]

In effect, though the scene goes on for three or four more pages, this is the end of the marriage and of the novel.

Edward's sister, Susanna, shows some of her brother's power of will in rising to the top of *her* profession as a singing and dancing star of the blatantly sexual musical entertainment then known as burlesque. She leads the life of a 'free woman' until she falls in love with Marian's cousin Marmaduke Lind, who genuinely loves her but is forbidden by his social code from marrying her. She bears him a daughter, and her enforced idleness as mistress and mother encourages her evident tendency to

---

34 Shaw, *EPWW*, 188–9; but see 'Mr Bernard Shaw's Works of Fiction: Reviewed by Himself', in *Selected Non-Dramatic Writings*, 312, where Shaw tentatively attributes the change to an attack of smallpox he suffered in 1881 while writing this novel. The 1892 article need not be any more trustworthy than the 1944 memories, of course. In *Cashel Byron's Profession* the hero and Lydia Carew, the heroine, also provide examples respectively of intuition and rationalism.

35 Bernard Shaw, *The Irrational Knot*, Standard Edition (London: Constable, 1931), 332.

alcoholism. Marmaduke finally loses patience with her and decides to marry Lady Constance Carbury, the bride his family approves of. Susanna goes to New York, where Marian has also fled with Sholto, in a futile attempt to revive her stage career; she soon dies of drink there, Marian visiting her bedside from time to time during her last illness. Is free will, then, merely a temporary and abnormal condition?

Despite the unattractiveness of Edward, its focal character, *The Irrational Knot* is easily the best of Shaw's novels, destined sooner or later to find its place in the history of the English novel. Shaw himself called it 'a fiction of the first order. . . . one of those fictions in which the morality is original and not ready-made'. In the same 'PS' to his preface for the first authorized American edition (Brentano's, 1905), he compares himself with Ibsen:

I seriously suggest that The Irrational Knot may be regarded as an early attempt on the part of the Life Force to write A Doll's House [1879] in English by the instrumentality of a very immature writer aged 24.[36]

Much of *The Irrational Knot*—and indeed the other novels—is written in tense, self-conscious dialogue as the characters, like their immature creator, struggle to defend their individuality and undermine one another's pretentions. The smaller, more closely knit cast of characters in *The Irrational Knot* and the relative brevity of the book produce a concentrated effect that accentuates by contrast the diffuseness of *Immaturity* and *Love among the Artists*, Shaw's third novel. The latter does not represent as radical a change in philosophy as Shaw after-wards claimed for it. When we compare Owen Jack, its composer-hero, with Edward Conolly, we certainly find Jack's habitual behaviour more colourful and outrageous than the more circumspect Conolly's; Jack, too, being unaware of his own anti-social traits, accuses others of lying about them; nevertheless, he knows himself better than to marry *anyone*, however congenial she may seem. Furthermore, if Jack sacrifices everything and everybody to his music, to which he feels an instinctive spiritual devotion, the supposedly rational Conolly behaves and feels similarly about science, theoretical or applied. For him, Shaw has simply taken the Romantics' conception of the Artist and refurbished it as the Engineer; he would have called it the Scientist had he dared, but his experience, gained with the Edison Telephone Company of London, had been confined to engineers.[37]

Shaw did not always limit himself, however, to matters in which he could lay claim to expertise: though still five or six years away from the celebrated loss of virginity on his 29th birthday (1885), he accepted the

---

[36] Shaw, *Irrational Knot*, xix.   [37] Ibid. vi–viii.

obligation of all novelists to deal at length with love and marriage. Although Smith himself is too immature to fall in love or marry, many of his fictional friends and acquaintances in *Immaturity* do either or both, especially in Books Three and Four, 'Courtship and Marriage' and 'Flirtation'. In chapter 10 James Vesey, an older man clearly brought into the narrative for the sole purpose of being an advisor, gives some wise counsel to Cecil Scott about 'the folly of prudent marriages'. Himself 'the fruit of an unsuitable marriage between two quite amiable people',[38] Shaw obviously thought he was an expert on marriages prudent and imprudent, several of which are observed with irony in his first three novels, perhaps the saddest being that in *Love among the Artists* between Adrian Herbert, a second-rate painter, and Mlle Szczympliça, a first-rate pianist.

Shaw does not really convince me that he has penetrated the creative part of Jack's mind; his accounts of the effect of Jack's music on the hearer are no better than, say, E. M. Forster's impression of Beethoven's Fifth Symphony in *Howard's End*. Shaw's superior knowledge of music becomes useless when he is writing for the layman, who by definition is ignorant of musical notation and other technicalities: he falls back on metaphors drawn from natural phenomena, perhaps leaving the musical ignoramus under a misapprehension as total as Shaw's own about algebra: 'I guessed for myself that a + b was shorthand for Eggs and Bacon.'[39] It is easier to describe the formation of an interpretative artist than that of a creative one: for me, the most fascinating part of *Love among the Artists* describes the transformation into a professional actress of the genteel Magdalen (Madge) Brailsford. Owen Jack is her voice coach; she wishes to marry him out of gratitude, but he wisely declines. Shaw must have picked up his early knowledge of backstage life from his elder sister, Lucy, who became a professional singer in light opera during 1881, the year *Love among the Artists* was written. Madge's vocal training under the painstaking if somewhat eccentric care of Jack found its real-life counterpart in the training of Shaw's mother and sister according to the 'Method' of G. J. Vandeleur Lee, who, as we have seen, shared a house with the Shaw family in Dublin; he eventually left there for London, where he was soon followed by Shaw's mother and sisters.[40]

Lee incidentally freed the young Shaw from Protestant bigotry in two ways: in public he was a Roman Catholic, as were most of his pupils

---

[38] Shaw, *EPWW*, 75.   [39] Ibid. 182.

[40] John O'Donovan, *Shaw and the Charlatan Genius: A Memoir* (Dublin: Dolmen, 1965), *passim*. Shaw's own first mention of Lee occurs in the preface to *London Music in 1888–90* (London: Constable, 1937): see *Complete Prefaces*, 852–67.

and other musical associates, so that Shaw's mother sang Mass with them in Dublin churches; in private he declared himself an atheist, creating a climate in the Shaw home that made it possible for G. B. S. to give up church-going before his 10th birthday. What other influence Lee had on the formation of Shaw's character is and will be the subject of endless disputes.

These three novels, then, indicate the scope and quality of the literary culture Shaw brought with him from Ireland. Despite all he was to write about the futility of his classical education, studying Latin has produced its customary side-effects: he had learned how to write precise, grammatical English as a result of practice in translating from an archaic language into a modern one; also, it had made him aware of the language in the abstract, as the study of any non-native language almost necessarily does if the student is intelligent. He was taken away from the Wesleyan Connexional School just as he was about to be introduced to Greek. Under Lee's influence he was then sent to the Central Model Schools, which he left after seven months from mixed motives of snobbery and renascent bigotry. Though the great majority of the students at this supposedly non-denominational school were Roman Catholics, Latin seems not to have been required. Shaw's last school, the Dublin English Scientific and Commercial Day School, suited him better, since it was Protestant and taught no Latin—as the word 'English' in its lengthy title was intended to convey.[41]

Cashel Byron's Profession (the 'profession' is bare-knuckle prize-fighting), Shaw's fourth novel, delighted Robert Louis Stevenson and narrowly escaped making Shaw 'a successful novelist at the age of twenty-six'.[42] Although it failed to boil the pot then, we can classify it now with, in Shaw's own words, 'such shameless potboilers as Pygmalion, Fanny's First Play, and You Never Can Tell'.[43] Still, it is worth noting that Cashel too is an intuitive hero, a true artist of the prize ring. When the heiress Lydia Carew tries to find reasons for marrying Cashel, which she has already made up her mind to do, she offers the following rationalization:

'As to our personal suitability, I believe in the doctrine of heredity; and as my body is frail, and my brain morbidly active, I think my impulse towards a man strong in body and untroubled in mind a trustworthy one. You can understand that: it is a plain proposition in eugenics.'[44]

---

[41] Ervine, *Bernard Shaw*, 25–33. For Shaw's view of classical education, see *EPWW*, 159–60.
[42] Bernard Shaw, *Cashel Byron's Profession*, Standard Edition (London: Constable, 1932), v.
[43] 'Postscript: After Twentyfive Years', 289; *Complete Plays with Prefaces*, (New York), ii. p. xcvi. (See note 29 above.)
[44] Shaw, *Cashel Byron's Profession*, 223.

In the final chapter we are told that 'Her children . . . proved to her that heredity is not so simple a matter as her father's generation supposed.' The only further point to make is that in this novel, as in *The Irrational Knot*, a character dies of drink: the final paragraph describes the sad end of William Paradise, once Cashel's only credible rival for the championship of England. Shaw is paying homage once again to his Evangelical ancestry.

An Unsocial Socialist, the fifth and last of the novels, seems to be chiefly responsible for the stereotype of Shaw the Novelist. Sidney Trefusis, the title character, has inherited from his father, a 'king' of industry, a fortune which he cannot give away: by selling his cotton mills and other property, he would only be giving his employees and tenants a change of masters; if he followed the advice of Jesus and gave all the proceeds to the poor, he would only lower wages and raise rents for them. Instead, he uses his income to help create 'a vast international association of men pledged to share the world's work justly, to share the produce of the work justly'.[45]

Trefusis also happens to be what Victorians called a 'bounder' and a flirt as well. Shaw gloried in his hero

because, without losing his pre-eminence as hero, he not only violates every canon of propriety, like Tom Jones or Des Grieux, but every canon of sentiment as well. In an age when the average man's character is rotted at the core by the lust to be a true gentleman, the moral value of such an example as Trefusis is incalculable.

Sidney deserts Henrietta, his beautiful and loving but conventional wife, because her constant demands for amorous or affectionate attention interfere with his socialist mission, or so he claims; in fact, when she is absent, he wastes an equal amount of time on flirtations with other women. Meeting Henrietta by accident near the cottage where he is hiding under the transparent disguise of Jefferson Smilash, a 'common' labourer, he gives her and the reader a long lecture on socialism, such as Shaw reserved later for his prefaces. Henrietta unfortunately lacks the skill of Ann Whitefield in deflating the male idealist: hence the whole chapter (no. V) becomes one-sided and boring, even for Shavians, as do several of the following chapters too.

Trefusis/Smilash flirts with three boarding-school girls, all of whom fall seriously in love with him: despite his immense conceit, he does not

---

45 Laurence (ed.), *Selected Non-Dramatic Writings*, 61. The editor tells us (xiv): 'The text of *An Unsocial Socialist* is set from the first edition (1887) and the Appendix from the "cheap" edition (1888).' These dates suggest that Shaw is referring retrospectively to the First International, which was founded in London by Marx and Engels in 1864; the general council was moved to New York in 1872, and in 1876 the moribund organization was formally dissolved at a conference in Philadelphia. On the other hand, Shaw may have been aware of activity already in progress which resulted in the founding of the Second International in 1889.

realize the damage he has done, being apparently even more incapable of love than his immature creator. Yet it is Shaw's own affectionate, carefully differentiated portraits of these handsome, healthy, not-too-sentimental English girls that prove his continuing potential as a novelist. They reappear as young women in Book Two, but Shaw quickly loses interest even in Agatha Wylie, their leader, who is already the Shavian New Woman in embryo; she agrees to marry Trefusis after Henrietta's death (essentially of a broken heart), but we cannot believe that Agatha, as we know her, could possibly accept Sidney: Shaw would have had to devote fifty pages to their courtship in order to convince us. As he later explained:

I resolved to give up mere character sketching and the construction of models for improved types of individual, and at once to produce a novel which should be a gigantic grapple with the whole social problem. But, alas! at twenty-seven one does not know everything. . . . I broke down in sheer ignorance and incapacity.[46]

Unbelievable characters and an excess of propaganda for socialism or other 'advanced' doctrines form the leading accusations in the critics' travesty of the Shavian novel. So well-founded, however, were their attacks on his last novel that Shaw felt obliged to publish two separate apologias for *An Unsocial Socialist*. The later one, from which I have already quoted twice, appeared in 1892 as part of an article. The earlier took the form of a 'Letter to the Author from Mr Sidney Trefusis' appended to the issue in a cheap binding of the remaining sheets of the unsuccessful first edition. In 'correcting a few misapprehensions', Trefusis reveals the charges brought against the novel by readers as well as critics. 'In noveldom woman still sets the moral standard'; consequently Trefusis has been characterized as a heartless brute by women readers. 'Hence some critics have been able plausibly to pretend to take the book as a satire on Socialism.' Sidney's behaviour at Henrietta's death was considered particularly heartless; 'but the truth is that I was greatly affected at the moment; and the proof of it is that I and Jansenius [her father] . . . behaved in a most unbecoming fashion, as men invariably do when they are really upset.' Chapter V, with its Marxist lecture on surplus value, 'as an account of what actually passed between myself and Hetty . . . is the wildest romance ever penned. Wickens's boy [who saw 'her a kissin' of you'] was far nearer the mark.' Trefusis's parting shot is a paragraph beginning, 'In conclusion, allow me to express my regret that you can find no better employment for your talent than the

---

[46] This and the preceding quotation come from 'Mr Bernard Shaw's Works of Fiction: Reviewed by Himself', *Selected Non-Dramatic Writings*, 313. Des Grieux is the hero of Prévost's *Manon Lescaut*, but Shaw is probably thinking of Massnet's opera *Manon*, based on the novel. Shaw's self-review first appeared in a London periodical called *The Novel Review* (February 1892).

writing of novels.'[47] When these words first met readers' eyes in April 1888, Shaw had begun yet another novel but definitively abandoned it in January 1888.[48]

Realism and the Muses, 1885–98

If *The Irrational Knot* had been offered to Henry Vizetelly, Zola's English publisher—there seems to be no evidence one way or the other about this—and if it had been accepted by him, as several of George Moore's early works were, to be published under the rubric of 'A Realistic Novel', it would have attracted an already existing 'advanced' readership created by the Zola translations and made fanatical by the imprisonment of their publisher. Moore gained a notoriety, by Vizetelly's publication of *A Mummer's Wife*, *A Drama in Muslin* (set in Ireland), and other novels, that Shaw would have been glad of; he could surely have developed into at least as good a novelist as Moore—though *Esther Waters* might have proved beyond him. Inevitably, like Moore, he would sooner or later have burst the bonds of Realism, but it is surprising how long he wore the badge of Realist even after becoming a playwright.[49]

The great weakness of *The Quintessence of Ibsenism* (1891) lies in Shaw's insistence on Ibsen's realism and anti-idealism, even when he is dealing with *Peer Gynt*; it was not until he had written several plays in what he believed to be the Ibsen manner that he began to grasp the broad humanity and even humour of his Norwegian master. The three *Plays Unpleasant* are not so named ironically, yet Shaw, even more than his audience, must have felt that they were truly Ibsenite, especially *Mrs Warrens' Profession*. This play, like *Ghosts*, explores the social evil of female prostitution, but the blame for it is now laid not on the narrow morality of Evangelical religion but on the entire capitalist economic and social system. Furthermore, Shaw's play uses the classic Ibsen technique, derived from Aeschylus and Sophocles, of a gradual unveiling of the sins and crimes of the past—those of a mother, this time, instead of a father, a Clytemnestra who is not quite a match for Ibsen's Oedipal Captain Alving. *Arms and the Man* is not only Shaw's first 'pleasant' play but his first humane one, a worthy immediate predecessor of *Candida* (1895). After all the contempt for the womanly woman expressed in *The Quintessence of Ibsenism* and in his second play, *The*

---

47 'Appendix: Letter to the Author from Mr Sidney Trefusis', *Selected Non-Dramatic Writings*, 199–203.

48 Bernard Shaw, *An Unfinished Novel*, ed. and introd. by Stanley Weintraub (London: Constable; New York: Dodd, Mead, 1958), 19.

49 See 'A Dramatic Realist to His Critics', reprinted from *The New Review*, London, July 1894, in *Selected Non-Dramatic Writings*, 323–40.

Philanderer (written 1893), here she is, in the person of Candida, straight out of Wordsworth:

> A perfect Woman, nobly planned,
> To warn, to comfort, and command;
> And yet a Spirit still, and bright
> With something of angelic light.[50]

However suspect the biographical approach to literary criticism may seem, a critic cannot reject an insight which forces itself on him no matter where it comes from. The three works in *Plays Unpleasant* were written during or immediately after Shaw's liaison with the widowed Mrs Jenny Patterson, a friend of his mother and his sister Lucy. I have always tended to think of Shaw's sexual initiation as an amusing birthday present, given to 'an absolute novice' by a passionate and experienced woman at least twelve years older than himself; but when one looks at the dates supplied by Shaw's diary, the affair becomes almost sordid, dragging on for nearly eight years, during most of which Shaw was also involved with other women. Begun on 26 July 1885, it lasted until 4 February 1893, when Mrs Patterson, mad with jealousy, 'burst in on' Shaw and the actress Florence Farr in the latter's rooms 'very late in the evening'. Shaw's diary continues: 'There was a most shocking scene, J. P. being violent and using atrocious language. At last I sent F. E. [Florence Farr was Mrs Florence Emery] out of the room, having to restrain J. P. by force from attacking her.' This event not only terminated the relationship between Shaw and his jealous mistress: it provided him with half the first act of *The Philanderer*, written later the same year.[51] Jenny's jealous bad temper—possibly in part due to the menopause— had already suffused the character Blanche Sartorius in *Widowers' Houses* (1892), a part which, ironically, Florence played (very badly) in the première. One wonders that Shaw did not cast Florence Farr as Grace Tranfield, the character modelled on herself, in the long-delayed first performance of *The Philanderer*, which she actually stage-managed, in 1905![52]

Perhaps Jenny also haunts the third unpleasant play, *Mrs Warren's Profession*, where *all* the characters are so thoroughly nasty to each other. True, Vivie Warren, the most unpleasant of all to my mind, is the antithesis of Mrs Patterson in almost every way: rather, the bitter after-taste is caused by the revelation of Vivie's parentage, she being the sour

---

[50] William Wordsworth, *The Poetical Works*, A New Edition, 6 vols. (London: Edward Moxon, 1857), ii. 106.

[51] Ervine, *Bernard Shaw*, 145–6, 152–3, 166–7, 251.

[52] Josephine Johnson, *Florence Farr: Bernard Shaw's 'New Woman'* (Gerrards Cross: Colin Smythe, 1975), 55, 116.

fruit of a mercenary relationship between 'Miss Vavasour' (Mrs Warren) and 'Sam Gardner, gone into the Church! Well, I never!' Shaw ought to have been—perhaps was—thankful that his own loveless though non-mercenary high jinks did not have such a serious result.[53]

Who then is the tutelary goddess of *Plays Pleasant*? Who released Shaw from his nearly 40-year-old mistrust of women? His contempt for their claims to intelligence, all-pervasive in the novels, has disappeared from his third play, where Mrs Warren and her daughter show themselves far superior in intelligence as well as sheer brute cunning to any of the men. None of the first three plays, however, contains a likeable woman—unless she be Grace Tranfield. Yet at the very beginning of *Arms and the Man* we encounter the adorable Raina, dreamily watching the stars but, as we soon discover, intelligent enough to wonder whether she and her fiancé, Sergius, 'perhaps . . . only had our heroic ideas because we are so fond of reading Byron and Pushkin'. This character and this play, so markedly different from their predecessors, convince me that Florence Farr had become Shaw's benign Muse as well as his intellectual friend and lover. After all, *Arms and the Man* had been written for her at her own request: Shaw recorded in his diary for 26 November 1893 the start of 'a new play—a romantic one—for F. E'.[54] Although the part of Raina was indeed written for Florence with love and gratitude, Shaw was so appalled by her performance of the leading role in the Anglo-Irish Dr John Todhunter's *A Comedy of Sighs* that he persuaded her to take the part of the servant Louka in his own play, 'without any sacrifice to her dignity'; the role she should have played went to the more professional Alma Murray. In those days at least, Shaw the Realist never confused life with art. *Arms and the Man* replaced the Todhunter play on 21 April 1894 and ran for over eleven weeks, rescuing Florence's brief season at the Avenue Theatre both financially and artistically.[55] Three of her playwrights were Anglo-Irish, for Yeats's *The Land of Heart's Desire* had its première as the curtain-raiser for *A Comedy of Sighs* and was retained on the playbill until 12 May, after which a new curtain-raiser was put on to lure the critics back to the theatre.[56]

Unfortunately, by 1895 Shaw had lost patience with Florence's dilettantism: he seems to have believed that, if she would only give up her dabbling in other arts and concentrate upon acting, she could become the greatest serious actress of her day. Then, perhaps, he would have written all his plays for her and their artistic partnership might even

[53] *Mrs Warren's Profession*, Act I 'curtain'; Act III, just prior to curtain.
[54] Johnson, *Florence Farr*, 59.   [55] Johnson, *Florence Farr*, 61–2.
[56] W. B. Yeats, *The Letters*, ed. Allan Wade (New York: Macmillan, 1955), 230 n.

have ripened into marriage.[57] In spite of this disappointment, Shaw never reverted completely to his old distrust of women: Candida manipulates men, but her protective flattery of her husband, Morell, has really enabled him to make the fullest use of his talents, though it is shocking to discover that she has succeeded in hiding her lack of sympathy with the religious beliefs of this enlightened clergyman. Shaw nevertheless once said that 'Candida . . . is the Virgin Mother and nobody else.'[58] Her motherhood, though Shaw wisely keeps her children off-stage, helps to confirm my belief that this part was not only written with Ellen Terry in mind but supplies an idealized portrait of her: the famous platonic correspondence between actress and playwright had begun in 1892. Poor Ellen Terry, by the way, manipulated nobody: almost her entire stage career was shaped to fit that of Henry Irving. Not until 1906, after his death, could she appear in a Shaw play, as Lady Cicely Waynflete in *Captain Brassbound's Conversion*, a part written for her in 1899. Through another of the ironies common in the history of the theatre, the role of Candida was created, in the English provinces, by Janet Achurch, Shaw's letters to whom often consisted of lectures on her drink and drug habits.[59]

Shaw's two actress-Muses brought him relatively unscathed through the four *Plays Pleasant* and *Three Plays for Puritans*, though evil or untrustworthy women still occur in the *dramatis personae*. Louka, for example, is a young girl on the make, or seems so, until she proves to be even more of a romantic than Raina. Similarly, the Strange Lady in *The Man of Destiny* (1896) seems a consummate manipulatrix, until we discover that Napoleon is more than a match for her because he has no gentlemanly scruples whatever. In the end he acknowledges defeat: she completes her romantic mission of saving the unfaithful Josephine from scandal. Note that her age is given as 'The right age, excellency'— not 17 but 30. If Henry Irving, for whom the play is written, had fulfilled his promise to appear in it, presumably Ellen Terry would have played opposite him; Shaw certainly hoped so, or he would have made his heroine an *ingénue*. Ellen was in fact 49 in 1896 and therefore just ready to play 30-year-olds. She continued to be Shaw's Muse.

57 Johnson, *Florence Farr*, 64.

58 Letter to Ellen Terry, 6 April 1896, in Bernard Shaw, *Collected Letters 1874–1897*, ed. Dan H. Laurence (London: Max Reinhardt, 1965), 623.

59 Shaw told Richard Mansfield—*Collected Letters 1874–1897*, 486—that *Candida* was written for Janet Achurch, but I find this hard to believe. On drink and drugs, see for example *Collected Letters 1874–1897*, 583–4, 626, 687, 827–8.

Shaw As Playwright: The Dublin Tradition

You Never Can Tell (1897), fourth of the pleasant plays, was, as we have seen, called a pot-boiler by Shaw and therefore required no Muse. Nevertheless, it deserves attention as Shaw's first moderately successful attempt at comedy of manners, a genre that he later explored and expanded to fit his genius in *Man and Superman, Misalliance, Pygmalion,* and *Heartbreak House.*[60] One cannot escape the feeling that in *You Never Can Tell* Shaw was trying to supply the place of a once immensely successful fellow-Irishman, Oscar Wilde, who in 1897 was completing his two-year sentence in Reading Gaol. Furthermore, there seems to be some conscious imitation of *The Importance of Being Earnest*, a work which Shaw, both as moralist and as dramatic critic, professed to despise.[61] The only even mildly threatening woman in Shaw's play, Mrs Clandon, becomes a cipher when compared with Wilde's Lady Bracknell. Rather, her invasion of England backed by two daughters and a son whose educations have been quite unconventional suggests Lucinda Shaw's invasion of London with a similar family. Crampton (*sic*), Mrs Clandon's ultra-conventional deserted husband, unlike Shaw's father, will be allowed to enjoy the company of his two younger children as long as he consents to be their friend rather than their forbidding parent. The treatment of Mrs Clandon in this light-hearted play implies that Shaw has ceased to fear his own mother, even unconsciously, and has forgiven her for not being able to love him. In fact, the experience of being loved by another woman may have taught him that one can have too much of a good thing.

In accordance with an antithetical pattern that manifests itself throughout Shaw's artistic career and has already been observed in the novels, his next play, *The Devil's Disciple* (also 1897), contains what is arguably the wickedest woman he ever created, Mrs Dudgeon. Shaw claimed that she is 'a replica of Mrs Clennam' in Dickens's *Little Dorrit,* but I feel that she is more cruel: her version or perversion of Presbyterianism brings her no happiness; it merely enables her to make others miserable. Her son Dick, the title character, early decided that if this was Christianity, he was of the devil's party. His supposedly diabolical morality, which makes him befriend his illegitimate cousin, Essie, is contrasted with his mother's; Mrs Dudgeon keeps reproaching the orphan for her father's sin and insists that her position in society must therefore be among the lowest of the low. Nevertheless, with the fairness that he

---

[60] See Vivian Mercier, 'Shaw and the Anglo-Irish Comedy of Manners', *New Edinburgh Review*, no. 28 (March 1975), 22–4.

[61] Bernard Shaw, 'Oscar Wilde', in *Pen Portraits and Reviews, Collected Works*, Ayot St Lawrence Edition (New York: Wm. H. Wise, 1932), 29. 301–2.

habitually shows towards his characters, Shaw hints that much of Mrs Dudgeon's bitterness springs from her thwarted love for her brother-in-law, Essie's natural father.

To his own dismay, Dick Dudgeon finds himself capable of a spontaneous act of self-sacrifice when he is arrested as a rebel American by British troops who mistake him for Anthony Anderson, the local Presbyterian minister; the latter's pretty young wife, Judith, thinks Dick is sacrificing himself for love of her. The play's first audience, familiar with Dickens's *A Tale of Two Cities* and Freeman Crofts Wills's adaptation of it for the stage, *The Only Way* (1890), doubtless shared her misunderstanding, especially as they may have thought Dick a greater blackguard than Sydney Carton, who at least was not a self-proclaimed atheist. The third act must have bewildered them, especially when Dick says to Judith:

What I did last night, I did in cold blood, caring not half so much for your husband, or . . . for you . . . as I do for myself. I had no motive and no interest: all I can tell you is that when it came to the point whether I would take my neck out of the noose and put another man's into it, I could not do it. I don't know why not: I see myself as a fool for my pains; but I could not and I cannot.

Dick is rescued from the gallows in the nick of time—after a comic court-martial scene—by the Revd Anthony Anderson, who is now an American militia captain; he suggests that Dick should take over his pulpit. When Dick says, rather shamefacedly, 'I should have done for you what you did for me, instead of making a vain sacrifice', Anderson replies rather condescendingly, 'Not vain, my boy. It takes all sorts to make a world—saints as well as soldiers.' Institutionalized religion seems alien to Dick's temper, but his last cry on the scaffold, when he still thinks he is about to die, 'Amen! my life for the world's future!' promises some kind of vocation, be it religious or secular.

The court-martial scene, in which the accused, certain that the verdict will go against him however innocent he may be, baits his British captors and judges and in general plays the fool, would obviously have a different resonance in Dublin than in London: as perhaps in New York, where the first production of *The Devil's Disciple* took place (giving Shaw his first great box-office success), patriotic cheers would mingle with the laughter and jeering at British failure to muddle through. What's more, an Irish audience would cite another model than *The Only Way*, namely *Arrah-na Pogue or The Wicklow Wedding* (1864), by the Anglo-Irish dramatist Dion Boucicault, nephew of the poet George Darley. (Because of his popularity as actor and playwright among the Catholic Irish, Boucicault's Protestant upbringing and descent through his mother from the Darley and Guinness families tend to be forgotten.) Two other popular Victorian dramatists, the brothers Wills, were also

Anglo-Irish in the narrow sense and had attended Trinity College, Dublin. F. C. Wills has already been mentioned as the author of *The Only Way*; his brother had a professional career in both painting and literature. William Gorman Wills (1828–91) kept Henry Irving so well supplied with adaptations from literary classics such as *Olivia* (from Goldsmith's *The Vicar of Wakefield*) and shapeless original plays like *Charles I* that, with the help of 'the right happy and copious industry' of Shakespeare, the great but half-literate actor never felt the need to turn to Ibsen or Shaw, though he briefly thought of producing *The Man of Destiny*.[62]

David Krause gives the best brief summary of Boucicault's career, pin-pointing Shaw's debts to *Arrah-na-Pogue* and knowledge of other works by him.[63] He does not, however, mention Shaw's admission that 'the stage tricks by which I gave the younger generation of playgoers an exquisite sense of quaint unexpectedness, had done duty years ago in Cool as a Cucumber, Used Up, and many forgotten farces and comedies . . . , in which the imperturbably impudent comedian . . . was a stock figure.'[64] I owe to Dr Krause himself the information that *Used Up* (1844) was written by Boucicault in collaboration with the comic actor Charles Mathews.[65] Shaw was probably referring to *Arms and the Man* and *You Never Can Tell*, but he created many another imperturbably impudent character before he died, the most remarkable of all being, of course, himself. He is being impudent at the very moment when he writes these words in the preface to *Three Plays for Puritans* (1900), twitting the New York critics for describing *The Devil's Disciple* as 'novel—*original*, as they put it—to the verge of audacious eccentricity'. He has pointed out a few lines before that the play:

does not contain a single even passably novel incident. Every old patron of the Adelphi pit would . . . recognize the reading of the will, the oppressed orphan finding a protector, the arrest, the heroic sacrifice, the court martial, the scaffold, the reprieve at the last moment, as he recognizes beefsteak pudding on the bill of fare at his restaurant.[66]

Not only was the Adelphi Theatre the home of melodrama in London for decades, it was also a theatre in which Boucicault played during visits to England: for example, *The Colleen Bawn* enjoyed a long run there in 1860–61.[67]

---

[62] Preface to *Ellen Terry and Bernard Shaw: A Correspondence* (1931), *Complete Prefaces*, 780–95; 'Wills' is mentioned on p. 790. See also Freeman Wills, *W. G. Wills: Dramatist and Painter* (London, New York & Bombay: Longmans, Green, 1898), *passim*.

[63] David Krause, 'The Theatre of Dion Boucicault: A Short View of His Life and Art', in *The Dolmen Boucicault*, ed. Krause (Dublin: Dolmen Press, 1964), 9–47.

[64] Shaw, *Complete Prefaces*, 745.   [65] Krause, *Dolmen Boucicault*, 248.

[66] Shaw, *Complete Prefaces*, 745

[67] Krause, *Dolmen Boucicault*, playbill reproduced on endpapers.

Shaw was being thoroughly unjust to his critics: *of course* there is originality in *The Devil's Disciple*, in *Arms and the Man*, in *The Man of Destiny*, all of which adhere to the formulas of melodrama up to a point, only to lay them in ruins at last: *The Devil's Disciple* simply sticks to its formula longer than the others. Shaw repeated the trick just once more in a 'serious' play, *The Shewing-Up of Blanco Posnet*, subtitled 'A Sermon in Crude Melodrama'. Throughout his life, but especially in his early plays, Shaw defied the Gospel warning by putting new wine in old bottles. Sometimes the wine burst the bottle, as we were told it would, so that for instance Act III of *Man and Superman*—when performed at all—is usually done as a separate play called *Don Juan in Hell*. The old bottle on this occasion was Da Ponte's libretto for *Don Giovanni*, which could not be persuaded to scale the heavens or descend into hell without the assistance of Mozart's music, cleverly smuggled by Shaw into his Act III.

Why, though, did he as a modern dramatist choose those particular old bottles: melodrama and farce and what can only be called 'costume drama', since tragedy it is not? The answer is a simple one: Shaw used these apparently obsolete formulas because they were the ones he knew best, and he knew them best because he grew up in Dublin, where everything was behind the times according to London clocks: 'the theatre had hardly altered, except for its illumination by coal gas, since the eighteenth century'. Shaw seems to have been a regular visitor to the Theatre Royal from his 15th year, when he first began to earn money as a clerk, until he left Ireland at 20. In that time he saw an incredibly large number of plays, usually performed badly because of the stock-company system. The duties of the resident company were 'to support the stars who came to Dublin on their touring circuits, and to perform the Christmas pantomime and keep the house open in the occasional weeks left unfilled by the stars'. To provide a background for his correspondence with Ellen Terry, published in 1931, he gives a generalized description of the old stock companies, insisting that 'my own plays are written largely for the feats of acting they aimed at'. This fascinating passage includes a personal reminiscence:

At my first visit to the theatre I saw on the same evening Tom Taylor's three-act drama Plot and Passion followed by a complete Christmas pantomime, with a couple of farces as *hors-d'oeuvre*. Tom Taylor's Joan of Arc [N.B.] had Massinger's New Way to Pay Old Debts as a curtain raiser. Under such circumstances serious character study was impossible.[68]

---

[68] Shaw, *Complete Prefaces*, 786; the three preceding quotations are from p. 785.

'Of the English-speaking stars,' Shaw continues, 'incomparably the greatest was Barry Sullivan, who was in his prime when I was in my teens, the last of the race of heroic figures which had dominated the stage since the palmy Siddons-Kemble days.'[69] If he had grown up in London, Shaw could not have studied the art of this great Irish actor, who made a fortune by avoiding West End theatre rents and touring the provincial cities; he is buried in Dublin, with a statue over his grave.[70] Shaw also had an opportunity to study the grand style in acting as practised by women when Adelaide Ristori (1822–1906) visited Dublin with her Italian stock company, which soon became 'even more unbearably stale than an English one'. Fortunately the great male performer Tommaso Salvini played opposite her, so that Shaw had a standard with which to compare Sullivan. He also saw Henry Irving as Digby Grant in Albery's *The Two Roses* when the entire London production was brought to Dublin shortly before Irving began his thirty-year association with the Lyceum Theatre, London, in 1871; Shaw, though only 14 or 15 at the time, 'instinctively felt that a new drama inhered in this man'. Somewhat earlier, a visit to Dublin by 'Madge Robertson, who came with Buckstone and the entire Haymarket company from London', had 'struck the first shattering blow at our poor old stock company'.[71]

There is also, I must admit, a less simple answer to my question about the choice of seemingly obsolete vehicles for new ideas—new to the stage at any rate. In the preface to *Three Plays for Puritans* Shaw insists that he does not profess to write better plays than Shakespeare—though many readers have misunderstood him to say the opposite:

The writing of practicable stage plays does not present an infinite scope to human talent; . . . The summit of [this] art has been attained again and again. No man will ever write a better tragedy than Lear, a better comedy than *Le Festin de Pierre* or *Peer Gynt*, a better opera than *Don Giovanni*, a better music drama than *The Niblung's Ring* or, for the matter of that, better fashionable plays and melodramas than are now being turned out. . . . *It is the philosophy, the outlook on life, that changes, not the craft of the playwright* [italics mine].[72]

The counterpoint between the new ideas and the old techniques dazzled Shaw's early critics and audiences, giving them the impression of

[69] Shaw, *Complete Prefaces*, 787.

[70] For photographs of Sullivan and of his statue as Hamlet in Glasnevin Cemetery, see Christopher Fitz-Simon, *The Irish Theatre* (London: Thames & Hudson, 1983), 104. Note also Shaw, *Complete Prefaces*, 788: 'Had I passed my boyhood in London. . . .'

[71] Shaw, *Complete Prefaces*, 789; the preceding quotations are from pp. 788–89. For Salvini, see p. 791.

[72] Shaw, *Complete Prefaces*, 750.

startling originality. Nowadays, when Shaw's ideas are seen as either not new or not true, his plays still hold the stage by virtue of their time-tested plots and their repertory of comic techniques.[73] First unconsciously, then consciously, the young Dublin playgoer and opera addict made use of a native critical gift—sharpened by the sceptical conversation of Lee and his own family—and a capacious, though not totally accurate, memory to master the living theatre and traditional stage lore. At 20 he was already reviewing opera and concerts for a London periodical, *The Hornet*, without disgrace. By 1900, when the preface to *Three Plays for Puritans* was written, he had been, first, the leading London music critic (on *The World*, 1890–4), and second, the leading theatre critic (on *The Saturday Review*, 1895–8). He had crowned his critical campaign on behalf of Wagner's music with *The Perfect Wagnerite* (1898), just as he had begun his critical campaign for Ibsen's plays with *The Quintessence of Ibsenism* (1891).[74] On 22 May 1897 he published an article in the *Saturday Review* entitled, without hyperbole, 'Ibsen Triumphant'; he meant that Ibsen, already triumphant in so many other capitals, had finally conquered insular, once-Evangelical London. Much of the credit for this victory belongs to courageous actresses, actors, and theatre managers, but critics like Shaw and William Archer fought valiantly too. Is it any wonder that a playwright so gifted, so knowledgeable, so stage-struck, so familiar with everything that goes on before and behind the curtain, should have made himself the greatest master of the craft of comedy since Molière?

Religions, New and Old

In 1874 Shaw informed his boyhood friend Matthew Edward McNulty that 'he no longer aspired to become a painter: he wished to found a new religion'. McNulty, 'with tears in his eyes', begged him not to do so, on the ground that 'there were far too many religions in the world already'. Shaw obligingly gave up this idea and 'to please McNulty, he consented to become a literary genius'.[75] McNulty's boyish faith in Shaw's capacity to achieve anything he set his heart on is both comic and touching. What sort of religion, though, did Shaw, 18-year-old atheist, envisage as possible? It seems highly likely, to me at least, that it

---

[73] Shaw did not expect this to happen: 'the novelty of the advanced thought of my day . . . will assuredly lose its gloss with the lapse of time, and leave The Devil's Disciple exposed as the threadbare popular melodrama it technically is'. *Complete Prefaces*, 746.

[74] See however John O'Donovan, *Bernard Shaw*, Gill's Irish Lives (Dublin: Gill & Macmillan, 1983), 77. O'Donovan asserts that the notion of Shaw as 'a lone fighter for the cause of Wagner in London . . . is nonsense', and gives chapter and verse to prove this.

[75] Ervine, *Bernard Shaw*, 49.

was the same religion of compromise and consensus that he described thirty-three years later in a lay sermon delivered on 16 May 1907:

When I last stood on this platform, I said there was not a single established religion in the world in which an intelligent or educated man could believe. . . .

I want to see whether there is any possibility of our arriving at a religion on which we can agree, because it is very important we should have a religion of some kind. I know that that is quite a fashionable opinion, but we have got out of the habit of thinking that we ought to believe in the religion we have. Hardly any person in London believes in the religion he professes.[76]

Shaw, who had made a career of attacking fashionable opinions, half-apologizes for uttering a platitude about the importance of religion, even when it is qualified by the deflatory phrase 'of some kind'. Nevertheless, his belief in the necessity of holding to some religion was sincere enough: his art required it. In the final paragraph of the preface to *Immaturity* he would write, looking back at 65 on himself as a tyro novelist, 'I had the intellectual habit; and my natural combination of critical faculty with literary resource needed only a clear comprehension of life in the light of an intelligible theory: in short, a religion, to set it in triumphant operation.' The first 'intelligible theory' that Shaw discovered was in fact socialism, successively in the versions advocated by Henry George, Karl Marx, and the Fabian Society. Susanna (*The Irrational Knot*) can be viewed as the first victim of the capitalist system in Shaw's works to bear a name and display a unique personality—as opposed to the anonymous millions of sufferers. Capitalism has forced her to debase her arts of song and dance in order to earn a living. *Widowers' Houses* reveals the futility of trying to be a moral property owner under an immoral or, at best, amoral system. Mrs Warren's profession of brothel-keeper makes her as legitimate an *entrepreneuse* as many another woman capitalist, rendering absurd the old melodramatic idea of the 'fallen woman'.

In the end, socialism was not enough, but Shaw, unlike Saul on the road to Damascus, met with no instant blinding revelation of what he was forced to call the 'New Theology', for want of a better name, as late as May 1907. Fortunately for Shaw, in that year Henri Bergson—who adopted the concept of the 'Life Force' under the name of *l'élan vital*—published *L'Évolution créatrice*. At last, after twenty years, Shaw had found the perfect name—indeed, the perfect advertising slogan—for 'Lamarck-Butlerian' evolution (as opposed to the Darwinian version):

[76] 'The New Theology', in *The Portable Bernard Shaw*, ed. Stanley Weintraub (New York: Penguin Books, 1977), 304–5. Perhaps because of his experience as a Protestant pupil at an overwhelmingly Catholic school, Shaw thought that any children who were educated together needed to share the same religion and the same standard of morality: see *EPWW*, 151–2.

'Creative Evolution'. He did not in fact use this slogan in any major work prior to the preface of *Back to Methuselah* (1921), where it occurs on every second or third page, yet it must have enriched his religious thought and helped him to understand better his own *Man and Superman*. Whether he ever read Bergson's masterpiece, even after its translation into English, is far from certain.[77]

Anyone who reads Shaw's account of his first impressions of the Lamarckian theory, in a review for the *Pall Mall Gazette*, must be struck, not by his passionate acceptance of the new doctrine but by its lukewarm rejection.

Shaw admires 'the exceptional ability with which [Butler] has stated his case', but concludes that

It is not expedient to discuss here the main point raised by Mr Butler, particularly as he is evidently quite capable of writing another book on the scientific attainments of the *Pall Mall Gazette*, if provoked by contradiction. Let it suffice to acknowledge his skilful terseness and exactness of expression, his frank disdain of affected suavity, his apparently but not really paradoxical humour, his racy epigrams, and the geniality of his protest against 'a purely automatic conception of the universe as something that will work if a penny be dropped into the box'.[78]

Clearly Shaw recognized a kindred spirit, and his description of Butler's style in *Luck or Cunning?* could well be applied to his own style of ten years later; but did any new religion ever have so casual and negative a birth as Creative Evolution? Even in its maturity, Shaw did not claim too much for it: the last paragraph of his 1921 preface to *Back to Methuselah* admits that he is doing the best he can at his age: 'My powers are waning; but so much the better for those who found me unbearably brilliant when I was in my prime.' This and the preceding paragraph are combined and drastically revised in the 1944 version, so that we hear nothing of age or waning powers and the tone of the whole passage is optimistic.[79] A more typical view, I feel, is expressed in the preface to *On the Rocks* (1933); after passages bearing the cross-headings 'STANDARD RELIGION INDISPENSABLE' and 'ECLECTIC RELIGIONS' follows one headed 'IMPORTANCE OF FREE THOUGHT'. It includes these remarks:

[77] I have not been able to determine when Shaw first used the phrase 'Creative Evolution', which gained currency in English after being used as the title for the translation of *L'Évolution créatrice* in 1911. British philosophers were slow to recognize Bergson (1859–1941) as a seminal thinker; the 11th edn. of the *Encyclopaedia Britannica* (1910–11) contains no separate article on him and indeed only two passing references. More to the point, his name does not occur in the meticulous index of the *Complete Prefaces*.

[78] *The Pall Mall Gazette: An Evening Newspaper and Review*, 31 May 1887, 5.

[79] Compare Shaw, *Complete Prefaces*, 545–6, with the corresponding passage in the World's Classics edn. of *Back to Methuselah* (see note 29 above), lxxxvi–lxxxvii. The only American edition with this change seems to be *Back to Methuselah*, The World's Classics Galaxy Edition (New York: Oxford Univ. Press, 1947), lxxiii–lxxiv.

I, . . . being the son of an Irish Protestant gentleman, found myself, at the dawn of my infant conscience, absolutely convinced that all Roman Catholics go to hell when they die, a conviction which involved not only a belief in the existence of hell but a whole series of implications as to the nature and character of God. Now that I am older I cannot regard this as anything more than a provisional hypothesis which, on consideration, I must definitely reject. As the more pious of my uncles would have put it, I have lost my religious faith and am in peril of damnation as an Apostate. But I do not present my creed of Creative Evolution as anything more than another provisional hypothesis. It differs from the old Dublin brimstone creed solely in its greater credibility: that is, its more exact conformity to the facts alleged by our scientific workers, who have somehow won that faith in their infallibility formerly enjoyed by our priests.[80]

Most religious people would surely argue that the basic flaw in Creative Evolution is implicit in Shaw's definition of 'religion': all religions worthy of the name do offer a 'comprehension of life', whether 'clear' or not, but surely most would deny that this was the consequence of 'an intelligible theory'? A mystical experience of unity with the divine, a sudden surge of irresistible faith, 'being reborn' or 'seeing the light'— experiences that are usually the product of a long period of prayer and meditation, of self-denial, of visiting holy places or studying holy books, of sharing in oft-repeated rituals—it is to these that the religious attribute their sense of 'something understood', their comprehension of life, their belief in their own immortality.

To return to the 1800s for a moment: Shaw did not meet Samuel Butler for the first time until November 1889, two and a half years after his review of *Luck or Cunning?* By then, Lamarckian theory—which saw evolution as the product of conscious effort (cunning) rather than blind chance (luck)—had probably become 'intelligible' to Shaw, and indeed part of his daily thinking. In these years too he may have read earlier works by Butler that he never tired of quoting: *Erewhon* (1872), in which illness is treated as a crime and criminal behaviour as an illness; also *Life and Habit* (1878), in which Shaw found his favourite Butler quotation, which accused Darwin of having 'banished mind from the Universe'.[81] Shaw can hardly have been set on fire by contact with the humorous yet reserved personality of Butler himself, but the Lamarckian theory must have grown to seem more all-embracing, more aesthetically attractive, and far less mechanistic than socialism. As a biological rather than an economic theory, it was linked to those human passions that are the stock-in-trade of dramatists: passions of which, as we have already seen, Shaw became fully conscious only in the decade

---

[80] Shaw, *Complete Prefaces*, 367.
[81] Preface to *Heartbreak House*, *Complete Prefaces*, 381; see also 'Mr Gilbert Cannan on Samuel Butler', *Pen Portraits and Reviews*, 71; and *EPWW*, 157.

1885–95. On 1 August of the seminal year 1887 Shaw completed the short story 'Don Giovanni Explains', his most remarkable single piece of prose fiction, apparently not published until 1930. There he attributes to the Da Ponte / Mozart hero some of his own experiences of love and sex, gathered in the previous two years; even more interesting is Don Giovanni's account of heaven and hell as places that one can enter and leave at will, often expressed in phrases identical with those assigned to Don Juan in the third act of *Man and Superman* a decade and a half later. The narrator of the story is by her own account 'a very pretty woman' who was returning home alone in a railway compartment after attending a performance of *Don Giovanni* when the Don materialized before her. He tells her the story of his life—and afterlife, of course—giving his own Shavian view of himself, the devil, and all the Mozart characters just as they were to appear in *Man and Superman*; of the Superman, however, we hear nothing: Shaw's mind has not yet encountered Nietzsche's.[82]

Nor do we hear of Lamarckian Evolution: Shaw did not fully grasp its importance until Nietzsche had convinced him that the logical next step in evolution was to produce a new breed of human—call him / her the Superman / woman if you wish. The true purpose of 'the Revolutionist's Handbook', appended to *Man and Superman* as the work of John Tanner, the play's leading male, and frequently maligned by critics, is to insist that eugenics *is* evolution. Though Butler, Lamarck, and Creative Evolution are never mentioned in play, epistle dedicatory, or appendices, Shaw later described *Man and Superman* as 'a dramatic parable of Creative Evolution'. Unfortunately, 'nobody noticed the new religion in the centre of the intellectual whirlpool', and Shaw had to wait twenty years before finding himself 'inspired to make a second legend of Creative Evolution without distractions and embellishments', namely *Back to Methuselah*.[83]

Creative Evolution, then is an optimistic creed to the extent that Shaw believed mankind can control its own destiny for good; but after the World War of 1914–18 he had become painfully conscious that it could also control its destiny for evil. It seemed a matter of extreme urgency to warn the human race of the choices to be made immediately in order to avert a catastrophe towards which choices already made were leading. This explains why Shaw, at the age of 65, undertook the enormous task of writing *Back to Methuselah*; in doing so, he 'threw

---

[82] 'Don Giovanni Explains', *Short Stories, Scraps and Shavings*, Standard Edition (London: Constable, 1934), 95–118. In the retitled and repaginated edn., *The Black Girl in Search of God and Some Lesser Tales*, Standard Edition (London: Constable, 1934), the story appears on pp. 167–90.
[83] Shaw, *Complete Prefaces*, 545–6.

over all economic considerations, and faced the apparent impossibility of a performance during my lifetime'.[84] The pentalogy of plays—or, as Shaw called it, 'A Metabiological Pentateuch'—is unsatisfactory, not because of the 'waning powers' mentioned in the preface but because he set himself an impossible task. It seems to me that he had never had a specifically religious experience, though from puberty to his early thirties he had undergone several 'peak experiences', as some psychologists call them: natural scenery, music, sexual excitement were their inspirations. Even if Shaw had been capable of religious experience, he could scarcely have succeeded where all but Aeschylus and Sophocles—and Euripides in the *Bacchae*—have failed. Everybody since—Dante, Milton, Goethe included—has been far too self-conscious to write a truly religious poem. As for Shelley, I am not convinced that *Back to Methuselah* stands on a lower level than *Prometheus Unbound*. Set as it is between two of Shaw's masterpieces, *Heartbreak House* and *Saint Joan*, the pentalogy forms an integral part of Shaw's second peak period: most dramatists are not granted more than one, but Shaw may claim two, and even three if one reckons *Plays Pleasant* and *Three Plays for Puritans*—a run of brilliance beyond the reach of most writers—as the first. His second peak would then consist of three plays written between 1901–05; *Man and Superman*, *John Bull's Other Island*, and *Major Barbara*, each concerned with religion in a different aspect. If Shaw had died at 60, his reputation would rest on these three, all somewhat eclipsed by the too-popular *Pygmalion* (1913).

Irish Religions: John Bull's Other Island, *1904*

In turning from *Man and Superman* to the problems of Ireland, with its deep division between Catholic and Protestant, symbolized in part by an uneasy partnership of Larry Doyle and Tom Broadbent, Shaw was compelled to revive his memories, good and bad, of Irish Catholicism as seen from the outside. Whereas the dream scene in *Man and Superman* had ignored the mystical side of Spanish Catholicism—of which Shaw could well have been totally unaware—in favour of the mysticism of the Life Force, he may have thought the Abbey Theatre audience would expect an atmosphere of 'Celtic mysticism' from *all* its playwrights, not just from Yeats alone. At any rate, Peter Keegan, the 'silenced' priest, voices an Irish mysticism that is partly Roman Catholic and partly pagan Celtic, with a tilly of Hinduism thrown in for good measure. Keegan, because of his ambiguous status, has of course no right to

---

[84] 'Postscript: After Twentyfive Years', 289; New York edn. (see note 29 above), xcvi.

speak for Roman Catholicism, but most audiences assume that he is speaking for the author. Shaw thus neatly escapes the accusation that he, like Bob Williamson in the famous Orange ballad, 'turned Papish himself and forsook the old cause/That gave us our freedom, religion and laws', though his flirtation with what some of his Shaw ancestors would have called 'The Scarlet Woman' (i.e. the Roman Catholic Church) continued for a score of years. It culminated in the play *Saint Joan*, which with its preface (1924) attempted to prove that Sainte Jeanne d'Arc (canonized 1920) was really a Protestant!

In linking mysticism and Catholicism, Shaw is also influenced by the crude stereotype of the Catholic/Protestant opposition which he owed to his upbringing: although *John Bull's Other Island* scoffs constantly at the equally crude stereotype of the practical Englishman versus the dreamy, impractical Irishman, Shaw complacently assumes that, between Irishmen, the Protestant will always turn out to be more practical, more commonsensical, more up-to-date and go-ahead, a better statesman and a better citizen than his Catholic countryman. Like many an Irish Protestant even today, he is prepared to grant to Irish Catholics only what he regards as feminine virtues: spirituality (a more accurate word than 'mysticism'), intuition, sympathy, tenderness, love of children and other kin, marital fidelity. Even in his vices, the Protestant feels superior to the Catholic male: though many Protestants still are teetotallers, one who drinks may pride himself on being able to hold his liquor better; a more puritanical Protestant's sense of his own virility might make him feel that, if he *should* happen to leap over the traces, all those willing Catholic girls would hurry to grant him the favours they withhold from their own men. These are admittedly the attitudes of a self-imagined *Herrenvolk*, of conquerors towards the conquered; let me hasten to add for the reassurance of my Catholic friends and relations that they are now mostly unconscious. (They do however help to explain the sickening fact that Protestant terrorists, in sharp contrast to their Catholic opponents, do not hesitate nowadays to kill, maim, and torture women.) In Shaw's time, the more respectable of these attitudes were not merely part of every Protestant consciousness, male and female, but were given frequent expression in speech and writing. Shaw's two prefaces to the play are full of them, and his greatest tribute to Irish Catholicism is riddled with unconscious arrogance:

'The island of the saints' is no idle phrase. Religious genius is one of our national products, and Ireland is no bad rock to build a Church on. Holy and beautiful is the soul of Catholic Ireland: her prayers are lovelier than the teeth and claws of Protestantism, but not so effective in dealing with the English.[85]

[See opposite for n. 85]

Most surprisingly, *John Bull's Other Island* does not include a single Irish Protestant in its large cast: Broadbent and his valet, Hodson, both English, are the only even nominal Protestants included. Perhaps this strange omission means no more than that Shaw thought he needed no spokesman for Irish Protestantism in the play because as author he would be using all his dramatic skills and tricks of the trade to convey his own views both implicitly and explicitly. In thus identifying Protestant Ireland with himself, he made the Southern Irishman's common mistake of forgetting the North of Ireland or misunderstanding it. The *Collected Works* text (1930) of *John Bull's Other Island* very honestly begins with his apology for this gross error, in the form of a passage in italics prefixed to 'Preface to the Home Rule Edition of 1912', which he describes as an *'interim preface'*, reprinted *'after much hesitation'*, because it was based on *'two confident political assumptions that have since been not merely disproved but catastrophically shattered'*. One of these concerned Parliament, while the other was *'that Ireland was politically one and indivisible'*. Shaw had never dreamt of Partition nor of the possibility that:

Belfast Protestantism should accept Home Rule for itself in a concentration camp and thus abandon its co-religionists outside the camp to what must then inevitably become a Roman Catholic Home Rule Government of the rest of Ireland. (p. 3).

If Shaw had included even one Belfast Protestant in his *dramatis personae*, his imagination would never have allowed him to ignore that whole dimension of the problem: I suspect he was never in Belfast in his life, but he might have persuaded himself into paying the city a visit in the name of Realism and thus have come face to face with certain realities hitherto unguessed at by a confirmed Dubliner. It is understandable but unfair that he should end his retraction on a note of bitterness: '*I guessed ahead, and guessed wrongly, whilst stupider and more ignorant fellow-pilgrims guessed rightly.*'

In the original 'Preface for Politicians' (1906), now printed *after* the 1912 one, there is only a single passage that can be construed as prophetic of what actually happened in Northern Ireland. Having mentioned 'the sturdy conviction of the Irish Protestant that he is more than a match for any English Government in determination and intelligence', Shaw continues:

Here, no doubt, he flatters himself; for his advantage is not really an advantage of character, but of comparative directness of interest, concentration of force

[85] *The Collected Works of Bernard Shaw*, Ayot St Lawrence Edition, ii: *John Bull's Other Island, How He Lied to Her Husband, Major Barbara* (New York: Wm. H. Wise, 1930), 37. All further references to this volume appear in the text.

on one narrow issue, simplicity of aim, with freedom from the scruples and responsibilities of world-politics. (p. 35)

The Unionists of the North clung to this one advantage, with the results we know; furthermore, unlike the Irish Free State and, of course, the Republic, the Stormont Government was prevented by its constitution from having any world-wide responsibilities, let alone any 'scruples' of that kind. Foreign Affairs and Defence were among the concerns retained by the Westminster Parliament.

Another illustration of Shaw's unconscious Protestant 'male chauvinism' towards Catholic Ireland can be found in his cast of characters: not only is it almost exclusively male, but the two Irishwomen included—Nora and Aunt Judy—are both presumed virgins.[86] It is not clear whether any of the Irishmen, even Barney Doran, is married: Cornelius, Larry Doyle's father, has of course been married, but he is now a widower; Keegan and Father Dempsey keep their priestly vows of celibacy: Matthew Haffigan is wedded to his little bit of land; unless Patsy Farrell is given some land too, he has no hope of marrying. If Larry ever marries, his bride will surely be one of those buxom Englishwomen ('animated beefsteaks' in Broadbent's phrase) he likes to have affairs with: the supposed tie between him and Nora is an Irish tangle of calf-love, nostalgia, injured pride, bad faith, shame, unsophistication, and mere boredom, presented by Shaw with great sympathy and understanding. Yet it is Broadbent, the all-conquering Protestant from England, who cuts the Gordian knot and carries off Nora, the 'heiress'. At 36, she is not too old to bear him children: he says to Larry, 'I must feed up Nora', and their relationship seems in any case the only potentially fruitful one Rosscullen has to show. If the Broadbents raise a family, one can't help feeling that it will be a far more remarkable achievement than making 'a Garden city' of Rosscullen, something Broadbent also plans to do.

God help Ireland, we may well say, if Broadbent is really her only hope: seen through Shaw's unconscious prejudices, Rosscullen has no natural leader except the parish priest, who certainly cannot become the next Member of Parliament. The former Protestant landlord, 'poor Nick Lestrange', has been turned out of house and home by the foreclosing of his mortgage; the villains are the syndicate headed by Doyle and Broadbent. Doyle is rather taken aback, 'for I liked the old rascal when I was a boy and had the run of his park to play in. I was brought up on the property.' Broadbent answers inexorably, 'But he wouldn't

---

[86] On the other hand, Mrs O'Flaherty, the Irish mother in *O'Flaherty, V. C.*, is a hot-tempered, domineering woman. See *Collected Works* (New York: Wm. H. Wise, 1931), xv. 199–227.

pay the interest. I had to foreclose on behalf of the Syndicate'. (p. 84) Shaw was still enough of a Marxist to know that Lestrange and his class—to which he himself partly belonged—gave up their political power when they sold their estates under the various Land Acts, of which Wyndham's (1903) was the last. Many of them, like Lestrange, soon lost their parks and big houses as well through bad management. No one would any longer be foolish enough to elect such incompetents. When Larry Doyle offends the kingmakers by his socialism and what looks like anti-clericalism (but is not), Broadbent is chosen as candidate because of his power as a financier, despite what the Irish see as his extreme eccentricity, almost verging on madness. Nothing like this could happen in real life: despite his prejudices, Shaw must have known that a shift of economic power in Ireland would produce new *Irish* leaders. By 1920 Barney Doran might have become a respected if daredevil officer in the War of Independence and gone on to vote for the Treaty setting up the Irish Free State in 1922, having refused to take his seat at Westminster after being elected as a Sinn Féin candidate in 1918.

Shaw's ignorance of history encourages his Protestant prejudices; one sympathizes with Larry's cry, 'When people talk about the Celtic race, I feel as if I could burn down London. That sort of rot does more harm than ten Coercion Acts. Do you suppose a man need be a Celt to feel melancholy in Rosscullen?' (p. 85) However, when he goes on to say that 'Ireland was peopled just as England was; and its breed was crossed by just the same invaders' (pp. 85–6), the obvious answer is 'not in the same proportions!' Without going into nice distinctions between P-Celts and Q-Celts, one may well ask whether Shaw thought the Romans invaded Ireland, let alone the Angles, Saxons, and Jutes (before their genes had got hopelessly intermingled). It is not Shaw but one of his most hot-tempered characters who is speaking, of course; nevertheless, Shaw is capable of arrogant ignorance when speaking in his own person. Writing about the evil effect on Irish culture of the nationalism provoked by British rule, he said in 1906:

The great movements of the human spirit which sweep in waves over Europe are stopped on the Irish coast by the guns of the Pigeon House Fort. Only a quaint little offshoot of English pre-Raphaelitism called the Gaelic movement has got a footing by using Nationalism as a stalking-horse, and popularizing itself as an attack on the native language of the Irish people, which is most fortunately also the native language of half the world, including England. (p. 41)

This really takes one's breath away: as Shaw was no linguist, we cannot expect him to have studied Modern Irish, let alone the earlier language, but we can surely ask him to open his constant companion, the ninth edition of the *Encyclopaedia Britannica*, and read there in perfect English W. K. Sullivan's account of Irish literature in the old language.[87] He might even have been persuaded by it that one of 'the great movements of the human spirit' enabled Johann Kaspar Zeuss and his successors—German, French, and Irish—to raise Old Irish from the dead (see Chapter 1, pp. 1–2), thus allowing Yeats and his friends to make current once again the oldest vernacular literature in Europe.

It is in an earlier passage of the original preface, however, entitled 'A Fundamental Anomaly', that Shaw perpetrates his most shocking historical 'howler': one on which both Marxists and more orthodox historians can agree. The offending passage runs as follows:

Now nothing can be more anomalous, and at bottom impossible, than a Conservative Protestant party standing for the established order against a revolutionary Catholic party. The Protestant is theoretically an anarchist as far as anarchy is practicable in human society: that is, he is an individualist, a freethinker, a self-helper, a Whig, a Liberal, a mistruster and vilifier of the State, a rebel. The Catholic is theoretically a Collectivist, a self-abnegator, a Tory, a conservative, a supporter of Church and State one and undivisible, an obeyer. (p. 26)

One can hardly expect Shaw to have known Dante's views about the separation of Church and State, but he must be obtuse not to have noticed that the appeal of Protestantism to Henry VIII lay partly, if not chiefly, in the opportunity it gave him to become Head of the English Church as well as the English State. The early Quakers seemed like anarchists, but Pennsylvania had some stringent laws. So too did Massachusetts in the early days. And what are we to say about Calvin's Geneva or John Knox's Edinburgh? Friedrich Engels, with Marx's approval, pointed out in his *The Peasant War in Germany* that, whatever the Anabaptists led by Thomas Münzer may have encouraged in the way of rebellion and anarchy, Luther was quick to support the Protestant princes against their rebellious subjects.[88] As Shaw's long-term analysis was so faulty, it is not surprising that his short-term prediction was equally so: the Northern Ireland set up by the Government of Ireland Act (1920) showed numerous similarities to the petty German Protestant states and some of the New England colonies.

Most of what has been said so far concerns Shaw's prefaces to *John Bull's Other Island* rather than the play itself: when we turn to the latter, wondering just how it is going to handle the numerous themes

---

[87] 'Celtic Literature', *Encyclopaedia Britannica*, 9th edn.
[88] Friedrich Engels, *The Peasant War in Germany*, transl. from the original German by Moissaye J. Olgin, ed. & introd. D. Riazanov (London: Allen & Unwin, 1927), *passim*; see especially ch. II, 50–73. Shaw of course may not have had access to an English translation in 1904.

suggested in the original preface, Act I presents us with two red herrings
for our pains. Although Shaw insists that the play was written 'at the
request of Mr William Butler Yeats', the last thing a Dublin audience,
especially the select one at the Abbey Theatre, needed to see was a
demonstration of the absurdity of the Englishman's stereotype of the
witty, drunken, cajoling Irishman—and the venality of the Irishman
or pseudo-Irishman who flatters English prejudice by playing the role
for all it is worth in free whiskey and even five-pound notes. When
Larry Doyle, a real Irishman, comes into the office he shares with Tom
Broadbent, he soon drives Tim Haffigan of Glasgow off the stage and
out of the play. From the point of view of Yeats and Lady Gregory, still
only at the beginning of their campaign to abolish the 'stage Irishman',
Tim should never have been there in the first place.[89] During the rest of
Act I, Shaw tries to set up a new stereotype, the reverse of the old,
according to which English Broadbent is warm-hearted, outgoing,
impulsive, and entirely guided by emotion, whereas Irish Doyle is cold,
reserved, calculating, and entirely controlled by reason. The late Hilton
Edwards and Micheál MacLiammóir, founders of the Dublin Gate
Theatre, were the only people I ever knew who even partly exemplified
this Shavian stereotype in real life: it was a pleasure to see them play
Broadbent and Doyle in America, but they felt it would be trespassing
on Abbey territory to play these parts in Dublin. London audiences no
doubt found the whole of Act I new and delightful: it is generally
accepted that this play once and for all established Shaw's reputation as
a dramatist in England. Numerous Cabinet Ministers sought to learn
about Ireland by attending the Royal Court Theatre, and King Edward
VII greatly enjoyed a Command Performance.[90]

The only indispensable information conveyed in Act I consists of
Broadbent's motive for visiting Rosscullen—to see what can be done
with the newly acquired Lestrange property—and Doyle's reasons for
not wishing to accompany him. Not having bothered to go home for
the past eighteen years, Larry is somewhat dismayed by the prospect of
renewing ties with his father and his boyhood sweetheart. Shaw could
have explained these matters quite economically in what is now Act II.
The length of the play as we have it—a performance took three-and-a-
half hours—proved a nuisance to Edwardian audiences and even to
Shaw himself. C. B. Purdom writes, 'The play was in fact severely cut,

---

[89] In a letter to Shaw, Yeats commented: 'I thought in reading the first act that you had
forgotten Ireland, but I found in the other acts that it is the only subject on which you are entirely
serious. . . . It astonishes me that you should have been so long in London and yet have remembered
so much.' Quoted by Terence de Vere White, 'An Irishman Abroad', in *The Genius of Shaw: A
Symposium*, ed. Michael Holroyd (London: Hodder & Stoughton, 1979), 34.

[90] Ervine, *Bernard Shaw*, 337.

and the printed text is part only of what was originally written; even that was cut.'[91]

For an Irish audience, the play really begins only when the curtain rises on Act II. A totally unexpected character—unknown to Doyle and therefore not mentioned by him in Act I when he lists the Rosscullen people he would just as soon not meet again—occupies the stage. Dressed in black, he is talking, '*in a brogue which is the jocular assumption of a gentleman and not the natural speech of a peasant*', to a grasshopper: that is to say, he is interpreting, in consonance with his own mood, the chirps of the insect. 'I suppose now,' he says, 'you've come out to make yourself miserable be admyerin the sunset?' The grasshopper '*sadly*' replies, 'X. X.' (p. 97). They soon agree that the sunset, to both of them, represents the gate of Heaven: 'but tell me this, Misther Unworldly Wiseman: why does the sight of Heaven wring your heart an mine?' The grasshopper declines to answer this question, but when the man asks, 'Which would you say this country was: hell or purgatory?' his response is monosyllabic. 'Hell! Faith I'm afraid youre right. I wondher what you and me did when we were alive to get sent here.' (p. 98)

When the grasshopper has fallen silent, a younger labourer, Patsy Farrell, appears from hiding and begs 'Father Keegan', as he calls him, to protect him against the insect which said 'it was a divil out o hell' (p. 99). The man in black insists that he is no longer a priest and that Patsy must pray for him by the name of Peter Keegan, but Patsy insists in his turn that Peter is a saint. A moment later, when Nora comes to consult Keegan about the likely effects of living abroad upon Larry's feelings, he reminds her of the story about himself, that he 'confessed a black man and gave him absolution', whereupon the black man 'put a spell on me and drove me mad'. In his youth he travelled widely in pursuit of his students: to Salamanca, Rome, Paris, Oxford, Jerusalem, and the island of Patmos. 'From that I came to Ireland and settled down as a parish priest until I went mad.' (p. 102)

In the first scene of Act IV he tells the true story to Doyle and Broadbent: he was at the deathbed of an elderly Hindu,

who told me one of those tales of unmerited misfortune . . . which sometimes wither the commonplaces of consolation on the lips of a priest. But this man did not complain of his misfortunes. They were brought upon him, he said, by sins committed in a former existence. Then, without a word of comfort from me, he died with a clear-eyed resignation that my most earnest exhortations have rarely produced in a Christian. (p. 154)

---

[91] *Bernard Shaw's Letters to Granville Barker*, ed. C. B. Purdom (New York: Theatre Arts Books, 1957), 43.

As a result of this experience, 'the mystery of this world [was] suddenly revealed to me': this world is hell. We remember the scene with the grasshopper and also what has just happened at the very beginning of Act IV: during the hysterical laughter over Barney Doran's account of the death of the unfortunate pig which Broadbent absurdly tried to deliver to its buyer alive and loose in the back of his motorcar, Keegan suddenly said *'with intense emphasis'*: 'It is hell: it is hell. Nowhere else could such a scene be a burst of happiness for the people.' (p. 148)

Clearly, Peter Keegan has been—and still remains, in Shaw's view— the priest of a Catholic Church and a redeemer whose kingdom is not of this world. Throughout the play he is contrasted with Father Dempsey, the parish priest of Rosscullen, who seems very much at home in this world and rules his parish like a little king. He is no saint; neither is he an unscrupulous exploiter of his position. Shaw describes him in a longish stage direction, part of which runs as follows:

He is a priest neither by vocation nor ambition, but because the life suits him. He has boundless authority over his flock, and taxes them stiffly enough to be a rich man. The old Protestant ascendency is now too broken to gall him. On the whole, an easygoing, amiable, even modest man as long as his dues are paid and his authority and dignity fully admitted. (p. 104)

The word 'boundless' represents Protestant ignorance and 'taxes' per- haps Protestant malice, but on the whole it is a fair description of an average parish priest, vintage 1904. He loses dignity only once in the play, when he rebukes Pasty Farrell thus: 'Father Keegan indeed! Cant you tell the difference between your priest and any ole madman in a black coat?' (p. 109).

Note how careful Shaw is not to put two priests onstage together: a confrontation would force him to be unfair to one or the other; not until *Saint Joan* did he possess the skill and the temerity to allow the Saint to confront the Inquisitor, while managing to be fair to both. Even then, at the peak of his fame, he would scarcely have dared this *coup de théâtre* without the support of the convincing historical documents edited by Quicherat. Nevertheless, the discretion and skill shown in *John Bull's Other Island* are of a high order. Father Dempsey is men- tioned by name three times in Act I, where it is made quite clear that his Catholicism is the Catholicism of Larry Doyle's father but not that of Larry himself: 'My Catholicism is the Catholicism of Charlemagne or Dante, qualified by a great deal of modern science and folklore which Father Dempsey would call the ravings of an Atheist.' (p. 91) Act II, as we have seen, introduces Keegan without preliminaries: although he leaves the stage before Dempsey appears, his spirit dominates the rest of the act and may even be thought to have something to do with Broadbent's falling in love with Nora at the Round Tower, which Dempsey has tried to deprive of its 'Celtic' glamour earlier in the act.

As for Act III, totally preoccupied as it is with the economics and politics of *this* world, Keegan does not appear in it at all, for he has no business there. Father Dempsey, on the other hand, is very much present as an important—the most important—member of the informal committee gathered to choose a new candidate for the Imperial Parliament instead of the sitting Member. The other committee men are Cornelius Doyle, who dearly hopes Larry will be chosen, Barney Doran, and Matthew Haffigan. This act provides the 'discussion scene', which Shaw insists is the hallmark and the great novelty of the New Drama that he has created. Though it appears static when compared with the action-crammed Act II of *Major Barbara*, it fulfils the same end of providing a socialist or Marxist object-lesson in the functioning of capitalist society. As Shaw was thoroughly aware, it is also a haven for good character actors, just like its counterpart in *Major Barbara*:

The two parts in this dialect set [of six] which will be coveted, and create jealousy as to the lead in that line, are Matt. Haffigan, an old, small, peat faced, leathery man with a very deep plaintively surly voice, and Barney Doran, a coarse, red haired reckless man of barbarous humor. Haffigan has his chance in the third act (he does not reappear); and Doran has what will be professionally considered the fattest bit—the story of the pig in the first scene of Act IV.[92]

Any critic who is still the dupe of the generalization that every character in a Shaw play is simply the author in disguise should read and ponder this letter and similar ones in the Shaw-Barker correspondence, besides taking another look at the scenes already mentioned. Some of the finest actors then living played their most memorable parts in Gabriel Pascal's film version of *Major Barbara* (1941).

In fact, every character present 'has his chance' in Act III, but Matthew Haffigan with his constant lament about 'me sufferins' gets the 'fattest' part of all. Every one of the other Irish characters tries to shut him up, without success; it is not until an Englishman, Hodson, turns on him and says that his sufferings are as nothing compared with those of the English lower-middle class that he seems likely to be silenced. Even then, however, after Hodson says that the long-suffering English can behave themselves without Coercion Acts or removable magistrates, Matt thinks he has found the last word: 'Bedad youre right. It'd ony be waste of time to muzzle a sheep'. (p. 142) Only the fear of being driven at 40 miles an hour in Broadbent's car makes him quit the stage—at a

---

[92] Purdom, *Bernard Shaw's Letters*, 27.

run. It is the frequency of such comic reversals of the situation, created by the opposing or juxtaposing of characters, that keeps Shaw's audience entertained. Meanwhile the socialist lesson keeps driving home a single point: the class war does not end when a limited group of tenants are turned into peasant proprietors; on the contrary, it is intensified as the new 'landlords' close ranks against the proletariat (in Irish terms, landless labourers like Patsy Farrell). When Larry is offered the candidacy, he asks why the committee want to replace their present Member of Parliament.

MATTHEW (*breaking out with surly bitterness*) Weve had enough of his foolish talk agen lanlords. Hwat call has he to talk about the lan, that never was outside of a city office in his life?

CORNELIUS. We're tired of him. He doesn't know where to stop. Every man cant own land; and some men must own it to employ them. It was all very well when solid men like Doran and Matt were kep from ownin land. But hwat man in his senses ever wanted to give land to Patsy Farrll an dhe like o him? (p. 127)

Larry loses all hope of being chosen when he promises:

If I get into parliament, I'll try to get an Act to prevent any of you from giving Patsy less than a pound a week (*they all start, hardly able to believe their ears*) or working him harder than you'd work a horse that cost you fifty guineas. (p. 131)

This is one of the rare moments at which Matthew is struck speechless; in the words of the stage direction, he '*turns openmouthed to the priest, as if looking for nothing less than the summary excommunication of Larry*'. At this point the discussion does turn into a duel between Father Dempsey and Larry, but the priest is somewhat disarmed by Larry's wish to see the Catholic Church become established in Ireland, as the Anglican Church once was. He would also like to 'have Ireland compete with Rome itself for the chair of St Peter and the citadel of the Church; for Rome . . . is pagan at heart to this day, while in Ireland the people is the Church and the Church the people' (p. 133). Dempsey is '*startled, but not at all displeased*' by such novel ideas: his final words to Larry are, 'Young man: you'll not be the member for Rosscullen; but dheres more in your head than the comb will take out' (p. 134). After this, the priest shows no objection to Broadbent as a candidate on the ground of his being a Protestant, so long as his politico-economic views are satisfactory. As he leaves the stage, he has only one doubt about the qualifications of the new candidate:

You might find out from Larry, Corny, what his means are. God forgive us all! it's poor work spoiling the Egyptians, though we have good warrant for it; so I'd like to know how much spoil there is before I commit meself. (pp. 137–8)

On this characteristic note he disappears from the play for good: the religious aspects of Act IV are entrusted to Peter Keegan.

The opening of Act IV is the most Swiftian passage in the entire *oeuvre* of Shaw. In later years he stressed the fundamental optimism of Creative Evolution, representing pessimists like Swift and Shakespeare as having been made obsolete by the onward march of the Life Force. Forty years after *John Bull's Other Island* he was to say, 'Had Swift seen men as creatures evolving towards godhead he would not have been discouraged into the absurdity of describing them as irredeemable Yahoos enslaved by a government of horses ruling them by sheer moral superiority.'[93] It is pointless to quarrel with Shaw's interpretation of Swift, though if the Yahoos really were men instead of man-like animals without souls or reason, Swift as a Christian could not have regarded them as 'irredeemable'. The point is rather that Shaw was capable of writing in Swift's own vein:

This world, sir, is very clearly a place of torment and penance, a place where the fool flourishes and the good and wise are hated and persecuted, a place where men and women torture each other in the name of love; where children are scourged and enslaved in the name of parental duty and education; where the weak in body are poisoned and mutilated in the name of healing, and the weak in character are put to the horrible torture of imprisonment, not for hours but for years, in the name of justice. It is a place where the hardest toil is a welcome refuge from the horror and tedium of pleasure. . . . Now, sir, there is only one place of horror and torment known to my religion; and that place is hell. Therefore it is plain to me that this earth of ours must be hell, and that we are all here . . . to expiate crimes committed by us in a former existence. (p. 155)

These words are of course Peter Keegan's, echoing speeches that I have already quoted, but the rise of the curtain on Act IV has already presented us with a visual and aural image of Barney Doran and a half-dozen of his friends behaving like Yahoos—a very 'modern' stage effect. '*They are screaming with laughter, doubled up, leaning on the furniture and against the walls, shouting, screeching, crying*' (p. 145). The whole of this indoor scene exemplifies the volatility of mood that came to be associated in critics' minds with the finest plays of the Abbey Theatre: *The Playboy of the Western World* or *Juno and the Paycock*, for example. This volatility, notable also in the works of Chekhov, comes in the first place from the authors, who veer from low comedy to pathos to savage indignation to irony, and even to tragedy, with a suddenness that catches most audiences by surprise. An Irish audience, on the other hand, especially when given a hint or two by an Irish acting company, is

---

[93] 'Postscript: After Twentyfive Years', 300; *Complete Plays with Prefaces* (New York), ii. p. cvi. (See note 29 above.)

off on the new tack almost at once. To judge by Boucicault's Irish plays, Dublin audiences were already quick to follow in his time, but English audiences, until quite recently, had lost the knack, which they certainly possessed in Shakespeare's day. As for American audiences, the content of a play has to be very close to home before they can respond readily to its humour or pathos.

Shaw runs the gamut of virtually all the stage moods or modes within his power during this scene: first we have Doran and his grinning shrieking Yahoos, going off into fresh fits of cruel laughter as he repeats details of the pig's saga for the fourth time since he entered the house. Aunt Judy and Nora try to quiet him, if only for the sake of Keegan's outraged nerves. Then Keegan himself lashes out in bitter sarcasm which abruptly turns to Hindu (or Franciscan) compassion: 'Tell us again how our brother was torn asunder.' When Doran has established who the brother is, he responds with a non-vegetarian example of Shavian low comedy: 'Bedad I'm sorry for your poor bruddher, Misther Keegan; but I recommend you to thry him wid a couple o fried eggs for your breakfast tomorrow.' (p. 147) This remark is so completely in character that Shaw need offer no apology for it: Swift had written far crueller sentences in his own person and in cold blood, so to speak. What follows Doran's narrative is an example of high comedy at its purest: Broadbent enters, miraculously unhurt after the accident to his car; quite unaware of the hilarity it has provoked, he treats the whole matter with great seriousness, while turning it to political account by making a speech about 'the gravity of the peril through which we have all passed' and his hope that it 'will prove an earnest of closer and more serious relations between us in the future' (p.149). With true Irish politeness the laughers, having managed to repress their sense of absurdity or vent it in cheers, withdraw in orderly fashion. Broadbent follows them to say goodnight while Larry assures Cornelius that the candidate won't 'be laughed out of the town' (p. 151). When Broadbent returns, he is delighted to be introduced to such an influential person as Keegan. An amusing dialogue at cross purposes follows between the two, modulating into Keegan's story of the Hindu's death and his own conversion to the belief that this world is hell. Keegan is amazed to learn that Broadbent feels at home in the world; in answer to Broadbent's question, he emphatically states that he himself does not—whereupon Broadbent prescribes phosphorus pills for his overworked brain!

Keegan, Broadbent, and Cornelius then go their different ways, leaving the still unfinished scene to pass into yet another mood. Larry finds himself alone with Nora for the first time in eighteen years; it is soon clear to them both that he has nothing to say to her. With unconscious cruelty, he assumes that she has nothing to say to him either: indeed, he seems quite relieved that she hasn't. He is hardly gone from the room when she '*gives way to a convulsion of crying*' (p. 151). Broadbent, returning, finds her in this state and tries to comfort her, providing a natural modulation into the scene's *finale*, a half-passionate, half-comic love duet. At its end the triumphant Broadbent, having won his bride, '*sweeps her out into the garden*' saying, 'I want the open air to expand in' (pp. 167–8). A critic might complain that the scene, besides being far too long, lacks all unity of tone and is in fact an appalling farrago of discordant emotions. Having already mentioned Shakespeare, I will suggest only one further comparison to the outraged critic: let him take any scene or act of *The Marriage of Figaro* and maintain that Mozart and Da Ponte—or at least the latter—are not guilty of the same supposed faults as Shaw. If Mozart's music gives Da Ponte an unfair advantage, the same comparison may be more justly made with the original work by Beaumarchais.

Act IV, Scene 2, has for its *raison d'être* the final confrontation between Keegan on the one hand and the partnership of Doyle and Broadbent on the other; Shaw, nothing if not thorough, has a few i's to dot and t's to cross before that, however. Candidate Broadbent has tired and displeased Nora by announcing their engagement and introducing her to those whom she considers 'the lowest of the low' in Rosscullen, all in the name of democracy. She refuses to 'say something nice' to Keegan, who would see through her 'as if I was a pane o glass' (p. 169). As Broadbent hurries off to greet Peter with his news, Larry comes up the hill full of good advice for Nora: she ought to marry Broadbent. When Nora anticipates him by announcing her engagement with a hint of triumph, he is careless enough to admit that this is what was in his mind: she will be a far more important person to him and everyone else as Mrs Tom Broadbent that she ever was as Nora Reilly. Piqued, she reminds him of her 'fortune' of forty pounds a year; he very ungraciously tells her that it won't pay her cook's wages in London. She answers bravely that 'if the worst comes to the worst, we can always come back here an live on it' (p. 171). Telling Larry that she is done with him forever, she turns her back on him and goes.

Meanwhile, Broadbent is '*energetically*' telling Keegan of his plans to lay out a golf links and build a hotel on the ex-priest's favourite hillside. It has been pointed out—for example by John Stewart Collis[94]—that *Major Barbara* (1905), Shaw's next major play, presents what Yeats would call a 'counter-truth' to its predecessor. The final scene of each

[94] John Stewart Collis, 'Religion and Philosophy', in *The Genius of Shaw*, 91, 93.

play shows an entrepreneur, Broadbent or Undershaft, singing the siren song of capitalism to a God-seeker, Keegan or Barbara, who has become at least temporarily disillusioned with his or her faith. Undershaft doesn't have to promise Barbara heaven on earth: in so far as it is possible, he has already created it at Perivale St Andrews; all she has to do is go and see. In Cusins's words,

Everything perfect! wonderful! real! It only needs a cathedral to be a heavenly city instead of a hellish one ['hellish' because the site of an arms factory]. (p. 326)

Broadbent's siren song, on the other hand, is more than a little comic and consists of promises that may never be fulfilled:

I shall bring money here: I shall raise wages: I shall found public institutions: a library, a Polytechnic (undenominational, of course), a gymnasium, a cricket club, perhaps an art school. . . . the round tower shall be thoroughly repaired and restored. (p. 176)

Barbara accepts her father's invitation to join him, not because of material wealth but because of:

all the human souls to be saved: not weak souls in starved bodies, sobbing with gratitude for a scrap of bread and treacle, but fullfed, quarrelsome, snobbish, uppish creature. (p. 348)

Keegan, on the contrary, feels that the people of Rosscullen already have their feet on the way of salvation; Doyle and Broadbent's gospel of efficiency can only bring them the damnation that in his opinion the partners have already incurred themselves:

Standing here between you the Englishman, so clever in your foolishness, and this Irishman, so foolish in his cleverness, I cannot in my ignorance be sure which of you is the most deeply damned. (p. 180)

One thing we the audience can be sure of, however, is that those who identify Bernard Shaw with Larry Doyle are deeply mistaken. Certainly it would be out of character for Keegan to preach Creative Evolution just before the final curtain as Barbara does:

(*She is transfigured*). I have got rid of the bribe of bread. I have got rid of the bribe of heaven. Let God's work be done for its own sake: the work he had to create us to do because it cannot be done except by living men and women. (p. 349)

Nevertheless, after all the talk about hell and damnation, Shaw will not let us leave the theatre without giving us his vision of heaven through the lips of Peter Keegan:

In my dreams it is a country where the State is the Church and the Church the people: three in one and one in three. It is a commonwealth in which work is play and play is life: three in one and one in three. It is a temple in which the priest is the worshipper and the worshipper the worshipped: three in one and one in three. It is a godhead in which all life is human and all humanity divine: three in one and one in three. It is, in short, the dream of a madman. (p. 181)

6   *W. B. Yeats: Master Craftsman*

Let us try to look with the eyes of an early reader at the first edition of *Poems* (1895), the volume which made Yeats's reputation as an Irish poet secure and, in a series of revised reprintings, kept it green—too green for the author's taste—throughout three decades. As early as 1906 he confessed to finding 'especially in the ballads, some sentimentality and triviality':[1]

When the poems in this book were first written they had the merit, hard to discover now, of a novel simplicity. Swinburne was dominant; the blank verse of 'The Countess Cathleen' was less rhetorical than recent dramatic verse, and it was not yet clearly apparent that, in avoiding rhetoric and complications, I had fallen into sentimentality.[2]

In fact, however, by 1895 the battle against sentimentality and other weaknesses—some perhaps imaginary—had already begun. The preface says that the author has 'revised, and to a large extent, re-written, *The Wanderings of Usheen* and the lyrics and ballads from the same [1889] volume', but passes silently over his definitive rejection of eighteen of these. The poet has also 'expanded, and, he hopes, strengthened *The Countess Cathleen*'. He expresses regret at having, in his present stage of skill, 'been compelled to leave unchanged many lines he would gladly have re-written'.[3]

All this may have sounded like false modesty to the 1895 reader, but it was Yeats's first acknowledgement of the lifelong habit of revision that made him a supreme master of his craft. Ironically, he later marred, even ruined a few of these early poems by revising them forty years after they were first composed. The general reader today, who owns the *Collected Poems* and *Collected Plays*, must perforce content himself with all of Yeats's poems in their final versions; the scholar, running his eye up and down—especially down—the pages of the Variorum editions, can follow the long, meticulous process of revision; it is the student of Yeats's manuscripts, however, who can best judge and marvel at

[1] *The Variorum Edition of the Poems of W. B. Yeats*, ed. Peter Allt and Russell K. Alspach (New York: Macmillan, 1957), 851; hereafter cited in the text as *VPO*, followed by the appropriate page number.
[2] Allan Wade, *A Bibliography of the Writings of W. B. Yeats* (London: Hart-Davis, 1951), 155.
[3] *VPO*, 845

What wounds, what bloody press,
Dragged into being
This loveliness.[4]

After noting the dedicatory poem, 'To Some I Have Talked with by the Fire', with its promise of 'Danaan rhymes', implying a mixture of the Celtic and the occult, the Victorian reader no doubt followed Yeats's own ordering of the poems and plunged directly into *The Wanderings of Usheen*. Whatever one may think of this poem today, it was well received at its first appearance in 1889, conferring prestige not only on its young author but on the nascent Irish literary movement. In attempting a longish (over 900 lines) narrative/allegorical poem, Yeats consciously or unconsciously invited comparison with the greatest living English poet: the more so because Tennyson had recently based *The Voyage of Maeldune* (1879) on an early Irish Christian narrative belonging to the same otherworld-journey tradition as *The Wanderings of Oisin*.[5] A measure of the success of his audacious challenge is the fact that on Tennyson's death in 1892 Yeats was one of 'four distinguished poets' invited by the editor of the London *Bookman* to say 'whether in their opinion the laureateship should be continued, and if so, on whom it should be conferred'.[6]

Why did Yeats succeed in capturing the imagination of his mainly English readers with an Irish tale when Ferguson—not to mention the plodding Aubrey de Vere—had failed to do so?[7] In the first place, he was unhampered by a classical education: while he apparently thought he was writing an epic, he was actually weaving a romance. The Finn cycle lends itself more naturally to romantic treatment than the Ulster cycle; also, Yeats's most immediate source was an eighteenth-century poem by a known author whose relationship to the anonymous Fenian lays resembled that of Sir Walter Scott to the Border ballads.[8]

---

[4] *The Variorum Edition of the Plays of W. B. Yeats*, ed. Russell K. Alspach and Catharine C. Alspach (New York: Macmillan, 1966), 531; hereafter cited in the text as *VPL*, followed by the appropriate page number.

[5] Tennyson's source was 'an early copy' of Patrick Weston Joyce's *Old Celtic Romances*, also first published in 1879; see Alfred Perceval Graves, *Irish Literary and Musical Studies* (London: Elkin Mathews, 1913), 8–10. Graves, who obtained the advance copy for Tennyson, had hoped that the Laureate would choose 'Oisin in Tirnanogue' as the subject for a poem; Yeats may have known this. Yeats used the phonetic spelling 'Usheen' only in the 1895 *Poems*; in the second edition, 1899, he reverted to 'Oisin'; Macpherson's spelling was of course 'Ossian', while the standard Modern Irish is 'Oisín'. 'Danaan' means for Yeats 'of the Tuatha Dé Danann'; in earlier English usage it meant 'Greek', from Latin 'Danaus'.

[6] *The Letters of W. B. Yeats*, ed. Allan Wade (New York: Macmillan, 1955), 218 n.; hereafter cited as *Letters*.

[7] Aubrey de Vere, *The Foray of Queen Meave and Other Legends of Ireland's Heroic Age* (London: Kegan Paul, Trench, 1882) contains 'The Sons of Usnach' and 'The Children of Lir' as well as the title poem, based on key passages of the *Táin Bó Cuailnge*, but even these classic Irish tales did not capture the public ear in his versions. Ferguson has been discussed in an earlier chapter.

[*See opposite for n. 8*]

Furthermore, the Pre-Raphaelite pictorial element in the poem must have attracted rather than repelled all but the most avant-garde readers. Rossetti, Hunt and Millais had been Tennyson's most brilliant and faithful illustrators a generation before. Yeats, like Oscar Wilde, infinitely preferred their work to that of the French Impressionists—then being praised in London by George Moore, among others—and he had learned to share Rossetti's admiration for Blake.[9] It was only natural that he should describe Niamh, his heroine, thus:

> A pearl-pale, high-born lady . . .
> And like a sunset were her lips,
> A stormy sunset on doomed ships;
> A citron colour gloomed in her hair.
>
> (*VPO*, 3)

The 1895 version introduced Niamh more swiftly than did the earlier one; also, the hostility between St Patrick and the aged Oisín, who recites his own youthful adventures, is made clear from the start, preparing us for Oisín's fierce rejection of Christianity at the end of the poem. Yeats's revisions have tightened the whole work, but the fundamental structure was always sound.

Each 'Book' narrates a journey to and sojourn in a different island, those of Dancing, Victories and Forgetfulness: nobody knows 'which of these / Is the Island of Content?' (*VPO*, 46). In his old age Yeats described them as 'three enchanted islands, allegorical dreams, / Vain gaiety, vain battle, vain repose' (*VPO*, 629). Understandably, the prolonging for a hundred years of any human activity, however normal, reduces Oisín to a state of boredom and homesickness, whereas Niamh and her fellow-immortals of the Tuatha Dé Danann never tire of their pleasures. The moral of the poem as a whole resembles that of Tennyson's 'Tithonus': a goddess should not lightly bestow immortality on her human lover, since their natures are so different. A Victorian reader would also be reminded of Tennyson's 'The Lotus-Eaters' by the Island of Forgetfulness. Although Yeats does not blatantly insist on it, the Island of Dancing is in fact the Island of Love, presided over by Aengus, to whom the Literary Revival

---

8 *Laoi Oisín ar Thír na nÓg* ('Lay of Oisin on the Land of Youth') is universally acknowledged as the work of Micheál Coimín (d. 1760), but the anonymous ballads on which it is modelled belong to the period 1200–1600. *Duanaire Finn* ('The Poem-Book of Finn'), the most important manuscript collection of these, was compiled in 1626–7. See Myles Dillon, *Early Irish Literature* (Chicago: Univ. of Chicago Press, 1948), 40–1, 48–50, 150.

9 W. B. Yeats, *Essays and Introductions* (London: Macmillan, 1961), vii. 'When I was thirty I thought the best of modern pictures were four or five portraits by Watts (I disliked his allegorical pictures—had not allegory spoiled Edmund Spenser?); four or five pictures by Madox Brown; four or five early Millais; four or five Rossetti where there are several figures engaged in some dramatic action; and an indefinite number of engravings by William Blake who was my particular study.' For the Pre-Raphaelite illustrations to Tennyson, see his *Poems* (London: Edward Moxon, 1857).

assigned the role of Cupid or Eros in a misleading Celtic pantheon. Here, if anywhere, the love of Oisín and Niamh must have reached a physical consummation that still lay outside Yeats's experience in real life; long afterwards he described himself in 'The Circus Animals' Desertion' as 'starved for the bosom of his [Oisín's] faery bride' (*VPO*, 629).

Aengus, holding up a sceptre that Yeats may have consciously intended as phallic, sings in praise of 'joy', which

> wakes the sluggard seeds of corn,
> And stirs the young kid's budding horn,
> And makes the infant ferns unwrap,
> And for the peewit paints his cap,
> And if joy were not on the earth,
> There were an end of change and birth
> (*VPO*, 18)

Yeats's pagan paradise was unlikely to shock any Victorian: Niamh insists that she is a virgin when she comes to lure away Oisín; in her homeland 'broken faith has never been known, / And the blushes of first love never have flown' (*VPO*, 8). Though Aengus proclaims that 'here there is no law nor rule' (*VPO*, 19), his islanders preserve a pre-lapsarian innocence. So, perhaps, do the characters in the original Ossianic ballads, but their sexual promiscuity with both mortals and immortals is taken for granted.

In other respects too, Yeats was no slavish follower of Irish tradition: though he took the basic plot of Oisín's exile and return from Michael Comyn, the three islands are his own invention. After a hundred years in the Island of Dancing, Oisín finds on the shore 'a staff of wood / From some dead warrior's broken lance' (*VPO*, 24). This sets him thinking of the Fianna's battles, so that Niamh feels it is time to bring him to the Island of Victories. As she and Oisín ride away on her fairy horse, he hears those he has left behind singing—in the anapaestic rhythm that later almost became synonymous with Celticism—of mortality and immortality:

> 'But we are apart in the grassy places,
> Where care cannot trouble the least of our days,
> Or the softness of youth be gone from our faces,
> Or love's first tenderness die in our gaze.
> The hare grown old as she plays in the sun. . . .
>
> And the kingfisher turns to a ball of dust,
> And the roof falls in of his tunnelled house.
> But the love-dew dims our eyes till the day
> When God shall come from the sea with a sigh
> And bid the stars drop down from the sky,
> And the moon like a pale rose wither away.'
> (*VPO*, 27–8)

In Book I, at least, lyric passages like these are handled with far greater skill than the narrative verse.

Determined to make each part of his poem as different as possible from the others, Yeats changes both his metre and his décor in Book II, using as his basic pattern the heroic couplet rather than the octosyllabics on which he played variations in Book I, and substituting 'Mananan's dark tower' for the 'winding thicket' and 'grassy places' of Aengus's realm. Appropriately, the interior of the sea-god's tower is like that of an ocean cave. In it Oisín and Niamh find 'A Lady with soft eyes like funeral tapers' (*VPO*, 33), chained between two old eagles; she is in the power of a demon. Oisín instantly promises to fight and conquer her oppressor: although insisting that the task is impossible, she gives him the sword of Mananan (Manannán in Modern Irish). Surprisingly, the demon looks unworthy of his opponent: he is 'dry as a withered sedge' and paradoxically both 'Bacchant and mournful' (*VPO*, 39). Nevertheless, he fights doughtily for a time,

> But when at withering of the sun he knew
> The druid sword of Mananan, he grew
> To many shapes; I lunged at the smooth throat
> Of a great eel; it changed, and I but smote
> A fir-tree roaring in its leafless top;
> I held a dripping corpse, with livid chop
> And sunken shape, against my face and breast,
> When I had torn it down
>
> (*VPO*, 40–1)

Eventually, Oisín kills the demon and throws him into the sea; he then feasts and sings for three days with the two women:

> On the fourth morn
> I found, dropping sea foam on the wide stair,
> That demon dull and unsubduable;
> And once more to a day-long battle fell
>
> (*VPO*, 43)

The next hundred years continue in the same way; with the demon turning up punctually every fourth morning: 'an endless feast, / An endless war' (*VPO*, 44). When Oisín is at length reminded of his father, Finn, by a beech-bough cast up from the sea, Niamh decides to bring him to the Island of Forgetfulness.

The allegorical meaning of Book II has puzzled the critics.[10] While the impossibility of a human life entirely devoted to love can be

---

[10] For examples of two sharply contrasted views, see John Unterecker, *A Reader's Guide to William Butler Yeats* (New York: Noonday, 1959), 49. 'Or perhaps both are right. The battle was against both father and sex, each reared its ugly head every four days or so and each, somehow, had to be subdued.'

accepted as the primary meaning of Book I, it seems a little obvious to make the same point about war in Book II. The dullness and sordidness of the demon suggest the unending demands made on the ascetic by his bodily appetites or on the average human by ugly economic necessity. Oisín seems proud of the strength which enables him to drive off the demon, even if only temporarily, and jeers at what he regards as St Patrick's inability to defeat evil by milder methods:

> In what land do the powerless turn the beak
> Of ravening Sorrow, or the hand of Wrath?
> For all your croziers, they have left the path
> And wander in the storms and clinging snows,
> Hopeless forever.
>
> (*VPO*, 42)

Possibly the maiden chained to the eagles is a victim of Sorrow, while the demon personifies Wrath. As the lovers leave the second island, a 'monotone, / Surly and distant'—the voice of the demon—utters ten lines of lyric verse, ending thus:

> I wage
> War on the mightiest men under the skies,
> And they have fallen or fled, age after age:
> Light is man's love, and lighter is man's rage;
> His purpose drifts away.'
>
> (*VPO*, 45)

This encourages the simplest possible interpretation of Books I and II, without necessarily precluding more complex ones.

Book III introduces a third metre, being made up entirely of hexameter quatrains: the rhythm is predominantly anapaestic. The landscape changes also, this time to a deep valley overarched by towering trees, where Oisín and Niamh see:

> Under the starlight and shadow, a monstrous slumbering folk,
> Their naked and gleaming bodies poured out and heaped in the way . . .
> And each of the huge white creatures was huger than
>   fourscore men;
> The tops of their ears were feathered, their hands were
>   the claws of birds.
>
> (*VPO*, 48–9)

There is no exact precedent for such creatures in Irish mythology, but giants and bird-men are both common. The chief figure—unnamed—on the Island of Forgetfulness holds a branch covered with bells in his hand. When Oisín wakens him by blowing Niamh's horn, the giant shakes the bell-branch and puts the hero and his beloved to sleep for a century.

While he sleeps, Oisín dreams not only of the Fianna but of the heroes and heroines of the Ulster cycle:

> So lived I and lived not, so wrought I and wrought not,
> > with creatures of dreams,
> In a long iron sleep, as a fish in the water goes dumb
> > as a stone.
>
> > (*VPO*, 53)

Occasionally the sleepers would half awaken; at one such moment Oisín catches sight of an Irish starling alighting and is reminded of an early morning hunt with the Fenians. (Had Yeats been more faithful to tradition, he would surely have chosen the blackbird, a creature most dear to Finn.) At once the fairy horse comes to him; Oisín tells Niamh he must see Finn and the rest, if only for half a day: 'Ah, sweet to me now were even bald Conan's slanderous tongue!' Niamh reluctantly lets him go with the starling in his hand:

> 'O wandering Usheen, the strength of the bell-branch
> > is naught,
> For there moves alive in your fingers the fluttering
> > sadness of earth.'
>
> > (*VPO*, 55)

She warns him against touching, even for a moment, the soil of Ireland.

When Oisín arrives in his own land, he quickly becomes disillusioned with its present state under Christian rule:

> Much wondering to see upon all hands, of wattles
> > and woodwork made,
> Your bell-mounted churches, and guardless the sacred
> > cairn and the rath,
> And a small and a feeble populace stooping with mattock
> > and spade.
>
> > (*VPO*, 58)

Not only the Fianna but their gods are a long time dead. He decides to return to Niamh, but on the way unwisely helps two puny church-builders struggling with a bag of sand:

> The rest you have heard of, O croziered one—how, when
> > divided the girth,
> I fell on the path, and the horse went away like
> > a summer fly;
> And my years three hundred fell on me, and I rose
> > and walked on the earth,
> A creeping old man, full of sleep, with the spittle
> > on his beard never dry.
>
> > (*VPO*, 60)

Having told his story Oisín returns to a question which the saint failed
to answer in Book I: Where are his old companions of the Fianna?

> ST PATRICK. Where the flesh of the footsole clingeth on the burning
> stones is their place;
> Where the demons whip them with wires on the burning stones
> of wide hell.
>
> (*VPO*, 61)

Oisín immediately decides to make his way to Hell and lead the Fenians
to victory over the demons, but St Patrick says this is impossible: 'None
war on the masters of hell', and Oisín must instead kneel:

> . . . and pray for your soul
> that is lost
> Through the demon love of its youth and its godless and
> passionate age.
>
> (*VPO*, 63)

Oisín rejects this: what is the point of going to Heaven if none of his old
friends will be there? With a Protestant flourish he throws away his rosary
('the chain of small stones') and proclaims defiantly,

> when life in my body has
> ceased,
> I will go to Caoilte, and Conan, and Bran, Sceolan,
> Lomair,
> And dwell in the house of the Fenians, be they in
> flames or at feast.
>
> (*VPO*, 63)

The poem thus ends with a moment of intense drama, but Yeats has not
stressed the allegorical meaning of the third island. Nevertheless, it
seems clear enough: humans cannot love for ever or be angry for ever,
but nothing can keep them from remembering. Under the influence of
the bell-branch, Oisín can forget 'realistic' details, such as 'How the
fetlocks drip blood in the battle, when the fallen on fallen lie rolled'; he
can forget his society's technology. 'That the spear-shaft is made out of
ashwood, the shield of osier and hide'; what he cannot exorcize from
his dreams are the mythological and legendary figures of his people—
'all who are winter tales' (*VPO*, 52–3). What have the giant figures of
the Island of Forgetfulness achieved? They do not know, because they
have forgotten; we do not know, because they do not appear in our
myths. Wisely, Yeats chose as the hero of his poem one whom the Irish
have never forgotten; the poem, in turn, has introduced to the English-
speaking world an archetype full of symbolic meaning—*Oisín i ndiaidh
na Féinne* ('Oisin after the Fianna' or 'in the Wake of the Fianna'). *The*

Wanderings of Usheen, when read aright, contains both precept and example for the revival of Irish myth and legend.

II

The 1895 volume continues with *The Countess Cathleen*, a work planned as a 'counter-truth' and complement to *The Wanderings of Usheen*. Yeats's intentions in writing this play are partly set forth by the preface to *The Countless Kathleen and Various Legends and Lyrics* (1892):

> The greater number of the poems in this book as also in 'The Wanderings of Oisin' (1889), are founded on Irish tradition. The chief poem is an attempt to mingle personal thought and feeling with the beliefs and customs of Christian Ireland: whereas the longest poem in my earlier book endeavoured to set forth the impress left on my imagination by the Pre-Christian cycle of legends. The Christian cycle being mainly concerned with contending moods and moral motives needed, I thought, a dramatic vehicle. The tumultuous and heroic Pagan cycle, on the other hand, having to do with vast and shadowy activities and with the great impersonal emotions, expressed itself naturally—or so I imagined—in epic and epic-lyric measures. No epic method seemed sufficiently minute and subtle for the one, and no dramatic method elastic and all-containing enough for the other.
>
> (*VPO*, 845)

Although Yeats in the end rejected Christianity, it must always be remembered that the most powerful influence on his religious life came from the Order of the Golden Dawn, to which he belonged from 1890 to 1922. Membership of the Order was never regarded by its adepts as incompatible with a total commitment to Christianity; on the contrary, it seems to have been founded partly for the purpose of reconciling Christianity and occultism. Yeats himself was conscious of this purpose throughout the 1890s: in the later years of the decade he dreamt of founding a specifically Irish order, based on the Castle Rock in Lough Key, whose worship 'would unite the radical truths of Christianity to those of a more ancient world'.[11] Also, he must have realized that he would alienate many of his fellow-Irish, Protestant as well as Catholic, if he wrote too often in the vein of the last lines of *The Wanderings of Usheen*. It is ironic that *The Countess Cathleen*, his gesture of reconciliation, should have been attacked as anti-Catholic in 1899.

In his 1892 preface Yeats speaks of the Pagan and Christian traditions as a 'double fountainhead' for a future 'great distinctive poetic literature' (*VPO*, 845). Not much attention has been paid to the Christian

---

11 W. B. Yeats, *Memoirs*, ed. Denis Donoghue (London: Macmillan, 1972), 124. For the Order of the Golden Dawn, see George Mills Harper, *Yeats's Golden Dawn* (London: Macmillan, 1974), *passim*.

aspect of the Revival, yet it is far from negligible. Katherine Tynan's inspiration was primarily Catholic, and Yeats early suggested that she write a Nativity play: his wish was later fulfilled by Hyde in Irish; Lady Gregory translated Hyde's play and wrote 'The Travelling Man' and *The Story Brought by Brigit*; both she and Hyde made available in English much material from the Irish saints' lives.[12] Hyde's *The Religious Songs of Connacht* is as valuable in its way as his *Love Songs of Connacht*. Yeats himself later wrote four notable miracle plays: *The Hour Glass, Calvary, The Cat and the Moon*—and most astonishing in its paradoxical orthodoxy—*The Resurrection*. *The Countess Cathleen* remains, however, the most determinedly Irish and Catholic of his Christian plays—'not less national, Celtic, and distinctive' in feeling than Ireland's 'many moving songs and ballads', as the 1892 preface claims. (*VPO*, 845)

Nevertheless, I have reluctantly reached the conclusion that *The Countess Cathleen* never, in any of its published versions, fulfilled Yeats's intentions for it. (Even the folk-tale on which it is based turned out to be French not Irish, though Yeats had included it in *Fairy and Folk Tales of the Irish Peasantry* [*VPL*, 170–3].) The chief stumbling-block was that these intentions were too numerous and some of them were mutually contradictory. As the 1892 dedication states, the play was 'planned out and begun' in 1889 at the suggestion of Maud Gonne, who was to have played the title role.[13] The play would also, unknown to her, be an allegory of her spiritual condition as it then appeared to Yeats:

> I thought my dear must her own soul destroy,
> So did fanaticism and hate enslave it . . .
>
> (*VPO*, 63)

Most dangerous of all these conflicting purposes, conscious and unconscious, which the play came to serve was Yeats's urge to write himself into the play as the unhappy poet-lover of the Countess. Kevin, the prototype, plays a minimal part in the 1892 version: he is the author-composer of the song 'Who will go drive with Fergus now'; apart from that he is memorable only because he cannot sell his soul to the demons, having already surrendered it wholly to the Countess.[14] In the 1895 and later versions his name has become Aleel and he plays a

[12] 'The Nativity', translated from the Irish of Douglas Hyde, is in Lady Gregory's *Poets and Dreamers* (1903; rpt. Port Washington, N.Y.: Kennikat, 1967), 244–54; see also 'The Lost Saint', 236–43. Lady Gregory compiled *A Book of Saints and Wonders* (1906–7) and Hyde *Legends of Saints and Sinners* (1915). 'The Travelling Man' (1909) and *The Story Brought by Brigit* are in *The Collected Plays of Lady Gregory*, ed. Ann Saddlemyer (Gerrards Cross: Colin Smythe, 1971), iii.

[13] Nevertheless, in a letter of 1 February 1889, two days after his first meeting with Maud Gonne, Yeats wrote: 'Dowden . . . urged me to write a poetic drama with a view to the stage. I have long been intending to write one founded on the tale of 'Countess Kathleen O'Shea' in the folklore book. I will probably begin one of these days.' *Letters*, 108.

[See opposite for n. 14]

larger and larger part—but to very little purpose, since the Countess can no more love him than Maud Gonne could love his creator. As Yeats presents him, abject in devotion, the audience cannot believe even for a moment that he will be able to persuade the Countess not to sell her soul. In fact, given what we know of her, it seems mathematically certain that, once the demons have stolen all her remaining possessions, she will instantly sell her soul to the highest bidder in order to keep her poor vassals alive through the famine. Yeats has a Protestant's rigid view of Catholicism: whereas any Irish Catholic audience, and any Irish Catholic theologian worth his salt, would be ready to damn the Countess if she *didn't* sell her soul.

I see in the play no subtle conflict of 'moral motives' such as Yeats postulated in his preface: a poetic drama of beleaguered conscience does not appear in Ireland until the first plays of Austin Clarke. What Yeats achieved in the 1892 and 1895 versions resembles rather a medieval fresco of the Last Judgement: at the right hand of 'the Light of Lights' stand the Countess, her devoted servants, and those among the peasants who remained loyal to their faith, with the angelic choirs hovering above; at His left hand are the two demons disguised as merchants along with their reluctant helpers from Irish folk fantasy—the 'sheogues', 'sowlths,' and 'thivishes' of Yeats's would-be phonetic spelling—and their peasant victims, constrained by famine to sell their own souls for gold.[15]

Nevertheless, the scene in which some of the peasants and then Cathleen herself sell their souls is dramatically effective and survives in the definitive version; so too does the final moment when an angel announces the carrying of the Countess's soul to Heaven. But the most satisfying feature of the play, as Yeats himself indicated, is its 'less rhetorical' ('more subtly rhetorical' might be a truer description) handling of blank verse. The most moving passages owe their effect to simple, powerful images conveyed in what appear to be the simplest of words. Among the most familiar lines in all Yeats are those given to Oona, the Countess's old nurse, at the final curtain:

> OONA. Tell them who walk upon the floor of peace
> That I would die and go to her I love;
> The years like great black oxen tread the world,
> And God the herdsmen goads them on behind,
> And I am broken by their passing feet.
>
> (*VPL*, 169)

---

[14] *The Countess Kathleen* [*sic*] (1892) differs so widely from the final version published in *The Collected Plays of W. B. Yeats* (London: Macmillan, 1952) that the two texts have been printed on facing pages in *VPL*, 2–169.

[15] Modern Irish sióg, fairy, *pl.* sióga; samhailt, phantom, *pl.* samhailteacha; taibhse, ghost, *pl.* taibhsí.

The image of 'great black oxen' has captured the imagination of count-less readers, much in the way that Marvell's 'Time's winged chariot' does. When read aloud, the phrase invites a full stress on each of the first three syllables, slowing the line and enhancing its effect. In contrast to the preceding one—a mere monosyllabic sing-song with an unpleasant internal rhythm—this great line reveals the sheer power of the mono-syllable, when correctly used, in English verse.

One justification for the simplicity of language throughout the play is immediately obvious: most of the speakers are peasants, while the more sophisticated characters spend much of their time speaking *to* peasants. Even when Cathleen is addressing Aleel, or the two demon merchants are plotting together, the level of discourse hardly rises at all. Cathleen never communes with herself, thus making it almost impossible for the audience to detect any conflict of motives within her: I cannot really understand why Yeats rejects the convention of soliloquy while retaining many of the other conventions of Shakespearean drama. As a result, Cathleen's speeches constantly verge on sentimentality when they do not fall into it. Take for example her dying speech, the famous passage quoted by Joyce in *A Portrait of the Artist*:[16]

> Bend down your faces, Oona and Aleel:
> I gaze upon them as the swallow gazes
> Upon the nest under the eave, before
> He wander the loud waters: do not weep
> Too great a while, for there is many a candle
> On the high altar though one fall.

> (*VPL*, 163)

Every reader must judge for himself, but I feel that the image of the swallow bidding a long farewell to his nest (*her* nest when Yeats later revises 'He' to 'She') is sentimental, whereas that of the fallen altar candle is appropriate. In the intense moments of the play Yeats was remarkably successful in adapting blank verse to Irish country speech, as he was also in *The Land of Heart's Desire* (1894).

Let us try to imagine the reactions of a cultivated London audience—attracted, some of them, by a Beardsley poster—on 29 March 1894, when the curtain rose on the 'curtain-raiser' at the Avenue Theatre to reveal '*The kitchen of Maurteen Bruin's house. An open grate with a turf fire is at the left side of the room*' (*VPL*, 181). More than seventy-five years of Abbey Theatre plays (1904–) have accustomed world audiences to many almost identical settings, but this first one must

---

[16] James Joyce, *A Portrait of the Artist As a Young Man*, the definitive text, corrected from the Dublin holographs by Chester G. Anderson and ed. by Richard Ellmann (New York: Viking, 1964), 225.

surely have been received with a gasp or two. As in so many later Irish peasant plays, the first speaker is the woman of the house, the wife and mother. Like the other characters, says the 1895 text, she is '*supposed to speak in Gaelic*', but it is English blank verse that the audience hears:

> Because I bade her go and feed the calves,
> She took that old book down out of the thatch
> And has been doubled over it all day.
> We would be deafened by her groans and moans
> Had she to work as some do, Father Hart,
> Get up at dawn like me, and mend and scour;
> Or rise abroad in the boisterous night like you,
> The pyx and blessed bread under your arm.
>
> (*VPL*, 181–2)

How many in the theatre actually recognized the medium as verse is hard to guess, especially since the content offers prosaic details like the feeding of the calves. Nevertheless, whether in prose or verse, *The Land of Heart's Desire* must soon have revealed itself as a poetic realization of a universal folk theme, the human stolen by beings of another world. (*The Wanderings of Oisin* is but a heroic elaboration of the same theme.) The action of the play on May Eve (30 April), known to ancient Ireland as *Bealtaine*, and like *Samhain* (Hallowe'en), a time at which the other world has exceptional power over this one. The fairies 'may steal new-married brides / After the fall of twilight on May Eve' (*VPL*, 186).

Reading in a manuscript book of Gaelic tales and poems compiled by her husband's grandfather, Maire, the daughter-in-law of Bridget (the first speaker), is fascinated by the story of the Princess Edain, wooed away from a human life by Midir, her former lover in the other world. Maire herself would like to go to this 'Land of Heart's Desire'. As it turns out, everything she does on this unlucky night puts her more in the power of the fairies. When she strews the traditional flowers on the threshold for good luck, a fairy wind sweeps them away; later, she breaks two May-eve taboos by giving milk to an old woman and fire to an old man who wants to light his pipe. Worse still, in a fit of a pique, she cries,

> Come, faeries, take me out of this dull house!
> Let me have all the freedom I have lost;
> Work when I will and idle when I will!
> Faeries, come take me out of this dull world,
> For I would ride with you upon the wind.
>
> (*VPL*, 192)

After Shawn, her young husband, has taken her aside and told her once again of his deep love, she seems reconciled to her lot; moments later, however, a child is heard singing an eerie song outside. Maire begs Shawn to 'cling close' to her because she has said 'wicked things to-night' (*VPL*, 194). From this point onwards she is full of fear, though Maurteen, her father-in-law, Father Hart, and even the mistrustful Bridget receive the child with great kindness. When the child is frightened by the crucifix on the wall, the priest removes it to an inner room, promising her that he will instruct her 'in our blessed Faith'; she will soon learn a more correct opinion of the Cross. Against the priest's obtuseness Maire insists that 'Some dreadful fate has fallen' (*VPL*, 202). Soon the child reveals herself as 'of the faery people'; because the crucifix is no longer in the room, her power exceeds that of the priest. He and she call on Maire to make her own choice between the two worlds; at length she says to the child, 'I will go with you' (*VPL*, 207). Although Shawn almost wins her back by his pleadings, she dies a minute or two afterwards. Father Hart, who regards the fairies as fallen angels, sums up:

> Thus do the evil spirits snatch their prey
> Almost out of the very hand of God
> (*VPL*, 210)

As the curtain falls, a voice offstage is singing the uncanny song heard before the child's entrance:

> The wind blows out of the gates of the day
> The wind blows over the lonely of heart
> And the lonely of heart is withered away
> (*VPL*, 210)

The Land of Heart's Desire defies criticism: one must either accept it wholly or reject it wholly. (The London audience and critics accepted it, while rejecting John Todhunter's *The Comedy of Sighs*, which was the *pièce de résistance*. Yeats's play was retained as the curtain-raiser for some weeks of the first run of Bernard Shaw's *Arms and the Man*, after Todhunter's had been taken off.) From the moment Maire is revealed reading the old book—and especially from the moment shortly afterwards when the audience learns that she is reading of the enchantment of Edain 'on a May Eve like this'—the action speeds inevitably towards tragedy. Either one has to dismiss all the foreshadowing incidents as absurd 'pishogues' and the fairy child as a dramatic device obsolete for two centuries, or one has to suspend disbelief for the sake of an intense emotion. It hardly matters whether one afterwards decided that the emotion was disproportionate to what provoked it, and therefore sentimental: the play has aesthetic unity and preserves a consistent tone throughout. No doubt a great deal of the success of any performance depends on the skill of the young actress playing the child: Yeats wrote the role—and indeed the play—for Dorothy Paget, niece of Florence Farr, director of the Avenue Theatre season.[17] Nevertheless, *The Land of Heart's Desire* is the definitive expression of a whole phase of Yeats's work, the product of both conscious thought about the occult world and unconscious longing. As early as 1888, in a letter to Katherine Tynan, he had expressed dissatisfaction with this phase, but apparently it had to run its course:

I have noticed some things about my poetry I did not know before, in this process of correction; for instance, that it is almost all a flight into fairyland from the real world, and a summons to that flight. The Chorus to the 'Stolen Child' sums it up—that it is not the poetry of insight and knowledge, but of longing and complaint—the cry of the heart against necessity. I hope some day to alter that and write poetry of insight and knowledge.[18]

III

Insight and knowledge were what Yeats sought from his membership of the Order of the Golden Dawn: it is likely that in giving the title of 'The Rose' to the next section of *Poems* (1895), he was claiming to have attained some share of these qualities. At any rate, the title can be read today as an unmistakable allusion to the Rosicrucian basis of the Order's teaching. In the 1895 preface, using the third person, he gave the following explanation of the sub-titles under which the lyric poems of this volume were grouped:

[The writer] has printed the ballads and lyrics from the same volume as *The Wanderings of Usheen*, and two ballads written at the same time, though published later, in a section named *Crossways*, because in them he tried many pathways; and those from the same volume as *The Countess Cathleen* in a section named *The Rose*, for in them he has found, he believes, the only pathway whereon he can hope to see with his own eyes the Eternal Rose of Beauty and of Peace.   (*VPO*, 845–6)

This last phrase expresses the significance of the Rose symbol more clearly than any other overt prose statement by Yeats. If we want to learn more, we must look to the poems themselves or to the poet's esoteric writings, published and unpublished.

The title of the introductory poem in *The Rose*, 'To the Rose upon the Rood of Time', evokes the basic symbol of Rosicrucianism—the Rose affixed to the junction of the Cross; it also suggests that while the

---

[17] W. B. Yeats, *Autobiographies* (London: Macmillan, 1955), 280–3.
[18] Yeats, *Letters*, 63.

Cross is temporal, the Rose is eternal. As Ellmann has pointed out, the poem expresses a complex and ambivalent attitude towards the Rose, which is at first asked to 'Come near me, while I sing the ancient ways': these ways include on the one hand ancient legends of Cú Chulainn and Fergus and on the other hand 'thine own sadness'.[19] Yeats's studies and experiments in magic and mysticism were inextricably linked with his explorations of Irish myth and folklore, because he believed both lines of research to be part of the one pathway leading to the ancient and eternal wisdom. The Order of the Golden Dawn, in his view, was struggling to revive knowledge that the Druids had taken for granted. The first stanza of this invocation of the Rose as Muse ends as follows:

> Come near, that no more blinded by man's fate,
> I find under the boughs of love and hate,
> In all poor foolish things that live a day,
> Eternal beauty wandering on her way
>
> (*VPO*, 101)

This needs no gloss: it has always been the poet's business to seek in the temporal that which is eternal.

In the second stanza, however, the poet surprises us by asking the Rose, in effect, not to come *too* near,

> Lest I no more hear common things that crave;. . .
>
> But seek alone to hear the strange things said
> By God to the bright hearts of those long dead,
> And learn to chaunt a tongue men do not know.
>
> (*VPO*, 101)

He seems to fear his pursuit of occult knowledge will dehumanize him and make him an unworthy singer of old Eire. One cannot be sure whether the misgivings are Yeats's own or those of John O'Leary, his mentor in Irishness, and perhaps also Maud Gonne's—though she shared some of his esoteric interests and belonged to the Golden Dawn for a short time.[20] Neither in this poem nor in his prose preface to the entire volume has Yeats been quite frank about the content of *The Rose*. There is another theme besides those of mysticism and Irish tradition— his love for Maud Gonne. Sometimes she becomes the modern incarnation of the Eternal Rose of Beauty, sometimes a symbol of Ireland, so that it is hard to characterize a particular poem as mystic or Irish or

---

[19] Richard Ellmann, *Yeats: The Man and the Masks* (1948; rpt. New York: W. W. Norton, 1979), 140–2.

[20] See the defence of his study of magic in a letter to O'Leary, *Letters*, 210–11. For Maud Gonne's connections with the Theosophical Society and the Golden Dawn, see Maud Gonne MacBride, *A Servant of the Queen* (1938; rpt. Dublin: Golden Eagle Books, 1950), 246–50.

simply a love poem. In the valedictory poem of *The Rose*, 'To Ireland in the Coming Times', Yeats apologizes for this tendency:

> Know, that I would accounted be
> True brother of that company
> Who sang to sweeten Ireland's wrong,
> Ballad and story, rann and song;
> Nor be I any less of them,
> Because the red-rose bordered hem
> Of her, whose history began
> Before God made the angelic clan,
> Trails all about the written page;
> For in the world's first blossoming age
> The light fall of her flying feet
> Made Ireland's heart begin to beat.
> (*VPO*, 137–8)

Here, he is saying that his preoccupations are the same as those of the ancient bards; nobody seems to have objected to this claim, but when, in the second stanza, he updated it and asked, for similar reasons, to 'be counted one / With Davis, Mangan, Ferguson' (*VPO*, 138), he was attacked as presumptuous and had to defend himself in a letter to *United Ireland*: 'I did not in the least intend the lines to claim equality of eminence, . . . but only community in the treatment of Irish subjects after an Irish fashion.[21] The third stanza insists upon the poet's sincerity—'I cast my heart into rhymes'—but the opening lines, and indeed the stanza as a whole, suggest ambiguities:

> While still I may, I write for you [Ireland]
> The love I lived, the dream I knew.
> (*VPO*, 139)

Are his love and his dream concerned with Ireland and her future, or have they more to do with Maud Gonne and everything symbolized by the Rose? In a note published with the first printing of 'To the Rose upon the Rood of Time', Yeats explicitly stated that 'of course' he did not use the Rose as a symbol of Ireland, though, for example, De Vere and Mangan had done so. (*VPO*, 798–9).

Although only about half of the poems in the 1895 arrangement of *The Rose* can be unequivocally classified as Irish, these do include some of his best work to date. Now overshadowed by *On Baile's Strand* and the other Cuchulain plays, 'The Death of Cuhoollin' ('Cuchulain's Fight with the Sea') is an anti-rhetorical narrative poem in the best Ferguson tradition.[22]

[21] Yeats, *Letters*, 213.
[22] Compare e.g., Sir Samuel Ferguson, 'Fergus Wry-Mouth', in *Poems* (Dublin: McGee; London: Bell, 1880), 44–7.

Like *On Baile's Strand*, it tells how the hero slew his own son, but the poem dispatches its subject in fewer than fifty heroic couplets. The 1895 version—except for its appalling would-be-phonetic spelling of Cú Chulainn—seems to me a better poem, or at any rate more consistent in style, than that in *Collected Poems*. The latter is a patchwork of early and late styles resulting from a revision in 1925. With an eye to his last play, *The Death of Cuchulain* (long planned but only published in 1939), Yeats changed the title of the poem to 'Cuchulain's Fight with the Sea' and suppressed the laconic final couplet giving the alternative version of the hero's death:

> For four days warred he with the bitter tide;
> And the waves flowed above him, and he died.
>   (*VPO*, 111)

'The Man who Dreamed of Faeryland' is an equally remarkable poem, containing a narrative element but essentially lyrical. Even in the original version Yeats handled his twelve-line stanza with ease and power. This poem has survived a more drastic revision (1929) than the Cuchulain one: the passages describing Faeryland have become both less Irish and less close to the sentimental. For instance, the *Collected Poems* text contains no mention of 'a Druid twilight' or 'A Danaan fruitage', but the fortunate result of these changes has been to make the poem more faithful to its original inspiration. The first three lines of each stanza have remained virtually unchanged since the original publication in W. E. Henley's *National Observer* (7 February 1891), and the four cardinal points—the concluding lines of each stanza—have been oriented to true north from that date. (*VPO*, 126–8). Desires for a woman, money, revenge, and peace after death are the subjects of the four stanzas; in each, a creature singing of Faeryland distracts the man from his attainable human goal. The respective lines recording his disillusionment with each goal in turn are:

> The singing shook him out of his new ease.   (1.12)
>
> And at that singing he was no more wise.   (1.24)
>
> The tale drove his fine angry mood away.   (1.36)

And, finally,

> The man has found no comfort in the grave.   (1.48)
>   (*VPO*, 126–8)

Nowhere has Yeats treated his favourite early theme with greater skill, and nowhere has he suggested so poignantly how his own mundane ambitions were thwarted by his poetic and mystic vocation. The four

Sligo/Leitrim place-names in the poem surely invite us to identify the 'man' with Yeats himself.

'Fergus and the Druid' takes a character from the Ulster Cycle and places him imaginatively in a situation which does not form part of the traditions about Fergus. Yeats's note in the 1899 edition of *Poems* gives an unusual view of Fergus and points to one of its sources: 'He was the poet of the Red Branch cycle, as Oisin was of the Fenian. He was once king of all Ireland, and, as the legend is shaped by Ferguson, gave up his throne that he might live in peace hunting in the woods.' (*VPO*, 795) Samuel Ferguson, in 'The Abdication of Fergus Mac Roy' was the first to suggest that, instead of being tricked out of his Kingship by his step-son, Conor, Fergus had given it up freely because the administration of justice bored and puzzled him.[23] The strain of hedonism in Yeats's Fergus—so evident in the famous lyric 'Who goes with Fergus?'—is an important part of the original legend.

In 'Fergus and the Druid' we see another side of the ex-King. He has become bored with feasting, yet he still feels the crown upon his head. In order to 'be no more a king', he wants to learn the Druid's 'dreaming wisdom'. The Druid tries to dissuade him, stressing the deterioration of his own body through excessive cultivation of the mind: 'No maiden loves me, no man seeks my help, / Because I be not of the things I dream' (*VPO*, 103). Eventually the Druid consents to give him 'this small slate-coloured bag of dreams', and Fergus experiences yet another disillusionment:

> I see my life go dripping like a stream
> From change to change! I have been many things:
> A green drop in the surge, a gleam of light
> Upon a sword, a fir tree on a hill,
> An old slave grinding at a heavy quern,
> A king sitting upon a chair of gold;
> And all these things were wonderful and great
> But now I have grown nothing, being all.
>
> (*VPO*, 104)

Except for changing the first line to 'I see my life go drifting like a river', Yeats made no major revisions in this passage afterwards: the series of vivid images and the steady onward sweep of the blank verse—except perhaps for the pedestrian rhythm and language of the second-last line—must satisfy the most exacting critic or self-critic. In its triple disillusionment, the poem reminds one of *The Wanderings of Oisin*, but it is decidedly more philosophical: the active life, both responsible and

---

[23] *Lays of the Western Gael, and Other Poems* (London: Bell and Daldy, 1865), 27–35.

irresponsible, is abandoned for the contemplative life, which is then shown to harbour a new kind of danger. Like 'The Man Who Dreamed of Faeryland' and 'To the Rose upon the Rood of Time', this poem symbolizes Yeats's awareness of the risks involved in a total commitment to the dream world of the imagination or to esoteric studies.

All the other Irish poems in *The Rose* except 'The Lake Isle of Innisfree' are open to charges of triviality and sentimentality. I have discussed the distinctive rhythm of 'The Death of Cuchulain' in Chapter 4 (p. 92) but I did not there draw the conclusion that the unique rhythm presupposes a unique emotion. Yeats's letters of the time, some of his journalism, and the novel *John Sherman* show clearly how much he detested London and longed for Sligo. The poem is *not* sentimental, being the exact expression of a profound emotion. Furthermore, Yeats has imagined with great preciseness just what a retreat from modern material civilization entails. Two or three of the finest lyrics in Old and Middle Irish voice the clerical poet's similar longing for a hermitage and contain similar mundane details. Then, 'clay and wattles' were the most readily available building material, honey the only sweetener, beans a staple of diet in the absence of the still unknown potato, given a soil and climate unsuited to cereals. All these materials could still be used today. Yeats was no farmer, yet enough of a gardener to grow beans, as passages in his letters and one or two poems clearly attest. But why go on defending what needs no defence? Like Dr Johnson on Gray's *Elegy*, I rejoice to concur with the common reader.

Among the undistinguished Irish poems which remain, 'A Faery Song' and 'A Cradle Song' ought surely to have been omitted, while 'The Lamentation of the Old Pensioner' has in fact been replaced in *Collected Poems* by a totally new work of 1925 vintage, masquerading under the same title. (*VPO*, 131–2) 'The Dedication to a Book of Stories selected from the Irish Novelists' (i.e. *Representative Irish Tales*) reveals Yeats adapting a poem to changed political conditions. The beautiful and healing lines with which it ends in *Collected Poems* were written in 1924, soon after the Irish Civil War, perhaps at the instigation of A. E., in whose *Irish Statesman* they first appeared:

> We and our bitterness have left no traces
> On Munster grass and Connemara skies.
> (*VPO*, 130)

The traditional Irish image of the soothing bell-branch, already used in *The Wanderings of Oisin*, is common to both versions, but the last three lines in 1895 ran:

> They [the bells] bring you memories of old village faces;
> Cabins now gone, old well-sides, old dear places;
> And men who loved the cause that never dies.
>
> (*VPO*, 130)

In 1924 Yeats may have felt that this last line was sentimental, as well as anachronistic now that the Irish Free State was in being.

The love poems in *The Rose* lack resonance compared with many that Yeats was to write in later years; they seem to have been inspired by the 'intoxication of pity' that he felt when he saw Maud Gonne, after an interval of several months, in July 1891:

She did not seem to have any beauty, her face was wasted, the form of the bones showing, and there was no life in her manner. As our talk became intimate, she hinted at some unhappiness, some disillusionment. The old hard resonance had gone and she had become gentle and indolent. I was in love once more and no longer wished to fight against it. I no longer thought what kind of wife would this woman make, but of her need for protection and for peace.[24]

Not many days afterwards, for the first time, he asked her to marry him and was refused. Out of such feelings must have come 'The Pity of Love', with its insistence that all things on earth 'Threaten the head that I love' (*VPO*, 119), and the original version of 'The Sorrow of Love', revised beyond recognition in 1925; here is the second stanza of the latter as it was n 1895:

> And then you came with those red mournful lips,
> And with you came the whole of the world's tears,
> And all the sorrows of her labouring ships,
> And all the burden of her myriad years.
>
> (*VPO* 120)

In 'The White Birds', there has awakened in the hearts of the lovers 'a sadness that may not die': the speaker longs for them to escape like Oisín and Niamh or the Children of Lir when turned into swans:

> I am haunted by numberless islands and many
> a Danaan shore,
> Where Time would surely forget us, and Sorrow
> come near us no more;
> Soon far from the rose and the lily, and fret of
> the flames would we be,
> Were we only white birds, my beloved, buoyed
> out on the foam of the sea!
>
> (*VPO*, 122)

---

[24] Yeats, *Memoirs*, 45.

Similarly, the best—and best-loved—of these early poems to Maud Gonne quickly turns towards a sadness quite alien to the famous sonnet by Ronsard on which it is based;

> But one man loved the pilgrim soul in you
> And loved the sorrows of your changing face.
>
> (*VPO*, 121)

As we all remember, 'When You Are Old' ends with a gentle regret at the departure of love, instead of Ronsard's incitement, 'Cueillez dès aujourd'hui les roses de la vie'.[25]

The beauty of Maud Gonne, nevertheless, was crucial for Yeats: the key line in both the revised and the original form of 'A Dream of Death' is 'She was more beautiful than thy first love' (*VPO*, 123). It may sound impossibly romantic nowadays, but her incomparable beauty was for him sacramental, the outward and visible sign of an inward and spiritual grace: somebody so endowed by the Creator must have a great destiny to fulfil. He soon realized that she was unfitted for great intellectual or artistic achievement, but he still hoped that she might lead Ireland to freedom or—better still—become the prophet and central symbol of a new religion. If my words seem extravagant, look at Yeats's own:

I had never thought to see in a living woman so great beauty. It belonged to famous pictures, to poetry, to some legendary past. A complexion like the blossom of apples, and yet face and body had the beauty of lineaments which Blake calls the highest beauty because it changes least from youth to age, and a stature so great that she seemed of divine race. Her movements were worthy of her form, and I understood at last why the poet of antiquity, where we would speak of face and form, sings, loving some lady, that she paces like a goddess.[26]

When a Romantic poet thinks of a woman in these terms, it is hard for him not to identify her with the Eternal Rose of Beauty and to hope that she will also become one with the Eternal Rose of Peace, though Yeats saw in Maud Gonne, almost from the first, 'a mind without peace'.[27]

'The Rose of the World', is, on one level, a mystical poem: in the first stanza, 'these red lips' of a living woman are also those of Deirdre and Helen of Troy, suggesting the changes of successive reincarnations. The second stanza, on the other hand, suggests a permanence in 'this lonely face' by comparison with which even 'the passing stars' are transitory, mere 'foam of the sky'. Unfortunately, the third stanza falls into sentimentality, describing Eternal Beauty as 'Weary and kind' and the Creator as making 'the world to be a grassy road / Before her wandering feet'

---

[25] Pierre de Ronsard, *Poésies choisies*, ed. Pierre de Nolhac and Françoise Joukovsky (Paris: Garnier Frères, 1969), 127.
[26] Yeats, *Memoirs*, 40.   [27] Ibid. 42.

(*VPO*, 111–12). A. N. Jeffares tells us, on the authority of E. R. Dodds quoting A. E., that the poem originally consisted of two stanzas composed after Yeats and Maud Gonne 'had returned from walking a long distance in the Dublin mountains. Yeats was worried because she had been exhausted by walking on the rough mountain roads, and added the third stanza, much to George Russell's disapproval.'[28] 'The Rose of Peace', whether viewed as a love poem or a mystical poem, is more sentimental still: we are asked to believe that the archangel Michael would forget his duties as 'leader of God's host' at the mere sight of 'you'; eventually, as a result, God would 'softly make a rosy peace, / A peace of Heaven with Hell' (*VPO*, 113).

'The Rose of Battle' is a less self-indulgent poem than 'The Rose of Peace', but like the latter it is concerned with 'God's wars', which cannot be won yet must be fought unceasingly. Those fitted to fight these wars are 'The sad, the lonely, the insatiable', and to them 'Old Night shall all her mystery tell'; the speaker of the poem is clearly one such, whereas:

> Danger no refuge holds, and war no peace,
> For him who hears love sing and never cease.
> (*VPO*, 114)

Surprisingly, the 'Rose of all Roses, Rose of all the World!' to whom the poem is addressed belongs also with God's warriors:

> Beauty grown sad with its eternity
> Made you of us, and of the dim gray sea.
> (*VPO*, 115)

It was passages like this, no doubt, that prompted Yeats's comment in 1925:

I notice upon reading these poems for the first time for several years that the quality symbolised as The Rose differs from the Intellectual Beauty of Shelley and of Spenser in that I have imagined it as suffering with man and not as something pursued and seen from afar.   (*VPO*, 842)

If Yeats meant to refer to poems where the Rose seems all too clearly Maud Gonne, this contempt would be disingenuous, but I think he had in mind poems like 'To the Rose upon the Rood of Time' and the present one. The most successful religious lyric in *The Rose* is not a Rose poem at all but a song originally written for *The Countess Cathleen*, now known as 'The Countess Cathleen in Paradise' but entitled 'A Dream of A Blessed Spirit' in 1895 (*VPO*, 124–5). Its traditionalism—a

---

[28] A. Norman Jeffares, *A Commentary on the Collected Poems of W. B. Yeats* (Stanford California: Stanford Univ. Press, 1968), 30–1.

blend of Christian humility with Christian triumphalism—is the secret of its success in both early and later versions. For all Yeats's insistence on the great antiquity of the Rose as a symbol, he is in fact constructing its 'tradition', poem by poem. (Had he read the article on 'Rosicrucianism' in the ninth edition of the *Encyclopaedia Britannica*, he might have been startled at the dubious origins of some of his interpretations of the Rose.) By referring to traditional symbols very familiar to his readers—those of 'Leda and the Swan', for instance—he wrote some powerful though uncharacteristic lyrics at various stages of his career: 'The Countess Cathleen in Paradise' is one of these.

Of all the poems in *The Rose*, 'The Two Trees' is the one that may most justly be claimed to express insight and knowledge. Though it was partially revised for *Selected Poems* (1929) in accordance with Yeats's new symbolic jargon, so that 'Tossing and tossing to and fro' became 'Gyring, spiring to and fro', its fundamental symbolism remained unchanged:

> Beloved, gaze in thine own heart,
> The holy tree is growing there;
> From joy the holy branches start,
> And all the trembling flowers they bear. . . .
>
> There, through bewildered branches, go
> Winged Loves borne on in gentle strife,
> Tossing and tossing to and fro
> The flaming circle of our life.
> When looking on their shaken hair,
> And dreaming how they dance and dart,
> Thine eyes grow full of tender care:
> Beloved, gaze in thine own heart.
>
> (*VPO*, 134–5)

The tree in this first stanza is unmistakably the Tree of Life, whereas that in the second stanza, 'With broken boughs, and blackened leaves, / And roots half hidden under snows', is at least partly the Tree of Knowledge: instead of 'Winged Loves', it is the 'The ravens of unresting thought' which fly through the branches. 'The Two Trees' is not anti-intellectual, however; its message is much subtler: when reflected in 'the bitter glass' held up before humanity by the demons, the Tree of Life can become distorted into a Tree of Death. This 'glass of outer weariness,' / Made when God slept in times of old', (*VPO*, 135), can also give us the knowledge of good and evil. The ravens are described as:

> Peering and flying to and fro,
> To see men's souls bartered and bought.
> When they are heard upon the wind,

And when they shake their wings; alas!
Thy tender eyes grow all unkind:
Gaze no more in the bitter glass.

(*VPO*, 136)

The whole poem recalls Yeats's judgement on Maud Gonne as he first knew her:

mixed with this feeling for what is permanent in human life there was something declamatory, Latin in a bad sense, and perhaps even unscrupulous. She spoke of her desire for power, apparently for its own sake, and when we talked of politics spoke much of mere effectiveness, or the mere winning of this or that election.[29]

The entire poem admonishes Maud Gonne and all its readers that 'only the means can justify the end': 'She [Maud Gonne] meant her ends to be unselfish, but she thought almost any means justified in their success.[30] An attitude like hers leads to 'men's souls [being] bartered and bought'— and women's souls too, as *The Countess Cathleen* reminds us. In the words of 'The Circus Animals' Desertion':

I thought my dear must her own soul destroy,
So did fanaticism and hate enslave it.

(*VPO*, 630)

Often, in reading the poems of *The Rose*, one is led to doubt the boast made in 'To Ireland in the Coming Times':

My rhymes more than their rhyming tell
Of the dim wisdoms old and deep,
That God gives unto man in sleep.
For the elemental beings go
About my table to and fro.

(*VPO*, 138)

Nevertheless, if Ellmann is right in claiming that the imagery of 'The Two Trees' derives from the Kabbalah rather than the Book of Genesis, then we ought to be grateful for Yeats's preoccupation with 'the dim wisdoms'.[31] What I have written about this poem only suggests a tithe of the riches to be drawn from its symbolism. 'The Two Trees' is simultaneously a love poem, a mystical poem, and a philosophical poem. Its multiple intentions do not mar it as, for instance, *The Countess Cathleen* was marred, and its multiplicity of meanings points forward to the great lyrics of Yeats's maturity.

[29] Yeats, *Memoirs*, 41.
[30] Ibid. 42.
[31] Richard Ellmann, *The Identity of Yeats* (New York: Oxford Univ. Press, 1954), 76.

IV

In the arrangement of *Poems* (1895), as we have seen, Yeats put his earliest poems at the end, under the title *Crossways*. It is always a little disconcerting to open *Collected Poems* at the beginning, where *Crossways* is now placed, and find this group of lyrics and ballads, most of which one has forgotten and some of which one has never really known. Yet 'The Song of the Happy Shepherd'—with its youthfully arrogant assertion that 'words alone are certain good'—makes a fitting introduction to the quintessence of a master of words. Even at their first appearance in the *Dublin University Review* (October 1885) the opening lines had the ring of true poetry, written by one who had not yet found his own style but had read with care Spenser and Milton's poetry[32] and much else:

> The woods of Arcady are dead,
> And over is their antique joy
> (*VPO*, 64)

A poet, too, who could already construct a verse paragraph that leads on, thought by thought and image by image, to a satisfying, if not necessarily logical conclusion:

> The very world itself may be
> Only a sudden flaming word,
> 'Mid clanging space a moment heard
> In the universe's reverie.
>
> (*VPO*, 65)

Adequate as these four lines must have seemed in 1885, by 1895 three of them had been revised into their final form; the second has remained unaltered ever since its first printing.

'The Sad Shepherd' suggests by its title that it was deliberately written to contrast with the preceding poem—an 'Il Penseroso' to follow a 'L'Allegro'—but in fact it had an independent origin. Its first title was 'Miserrimus' ('the most unhappy man'), and the different metres of the two poems also suggest that they were not intended as companion pieces. As in 'The Cloak, the Boat and the Shoes', the poet seems obsessed by the idea—perhaps even the reality—of Sorrow with a capital 'S'. The play 'The Island of Statues', of which 'The Cloak, the Boat and the Shoes' originally formed a part, does end happily, but it is full of the sorrow of love. (*VPO*, 644–79) So is the little tragedy *Mosada* (1886), the first of Yeats's works to be separately published

---

[32] The pastoral atmosphere is from Spenser and Milton's early poems, but note the phrase 'optic glass' from the famous passage on Galileo in *Paradise Lost*, Book iii.

(*VPO*, 689–704). Several others among the eighteen poems omitted from *Crossways* are also tragic or at least pathetic. 'Love and sorrow, one existence' (*VPO*, 647) is treated as axiomatic in them. Thus, several years before his meeting with Maud Gonne, Yeats was already writing poems of unhappy love: temperament, as well as literary convention, was preparing him for his fate.

May it not have been experience rather than temperament? Yeats tells us in *Reveries over Childhood and Youth* that he was very unhappy as a child, but 'There was no reason for my unhappiness'. Later in the same passage he acknowledges that 'Some of my misery was loneliness and some of it fear of old William Pollexfen my grandfather.'[33] He was lonely of course because often separated from the rest of his family; as a petted eldest child, he naturally missed his parents most of all. His biographers say much about his relationship with his father—certainly well documented on both sides—and its psychological effects. It may, however, have been his relationship—or lack of it—with his mother that decisively moulded the poet and made his childhood unhappy. Separated from her for many months at a time, soon after the births of siblings, he must have felt that the separation was somehow his own fault: though indeed the loss of her presence and her support against his frightening maternal grandfather was sorrow enough to bear, without any additional feeling of guilt. Because of his mother's reticence even when they were together, it was only after her death that he realized 'she had great depth of feeling'.[34] When he was reunited with her in London, she had already become a stranger: 'My memory of what she was like in those days has grown very dim'.[35] In 1887, when he was 22, she had two strokes and never fully regained even the uncertain health she had known before. He may have unconsciously felt then that she had abandoned him once more. The depression evident in much of his early poetry, along with his later willingness to stay committed to a woman who had rejected him, may be attributable to his unhappy feelings about the first woman in his life.

These two autumnal poems, 'Ephemera' and 'The Falling of the Leaves', exude weariness as well as sorrow, though the last lines of 'Ephemera' already express the belief in reincarnation that Yeats was to find greatly reassuring in his old age. In contrast, two of the group of three 'Indian' poems, 'Anashuya and Vijaya' and 'The Indian upon God' are cheerful but inept. The third, 'The Indian to His Love', must be taken more seriously. On close inspection it may possibly have to be dismissed as a twopence-coloured version of the penny-plain 'To an Isle

---

[33] Yeats, *Autobiographies*, 6.   [34] Ibid. 31.   [35] Ibid.

in the Water', but the bravura of the opening stanza can still take one's breath away:

> The island dreams upon the dawn
> And great boughs drop tranquillity;
> The peahens dance on a smooth lawn,
> A parrot sways upon a tree,
> Raging at his own image in the dim enamelled sea.
>
> *(VPO, 77)*

The assured march of the lines suggests that this stanza must be vintage Yeats or the result of a late revision, but it is not. Except for the excision of the word 'dim', Yeats could find no fault with it after 1895.

Apart from 'The Song of the Happy Shepherd' there are only four poems in *Crossways*, all Irish, that are entirely successful. One is 'Down by the Salley Gardens'—'an attempt to reconstruct an old song from three lines imperfectly remembered by an old peasant woman in . . . Ballysodare, Sligo' *(VPO, 90)*. Assuming that the first three lines were hers, I feel that the remaining five have caught the spirit of folk poetry—English, perhaps, rather than Irish—almost to perfection. The image from personal observation, 'as the grass grows on the weirs', seems no less appropriate than the traditional/conventional one, 'as the leaves grow on the tree'. A poem so nearly anonymous cannot be accused of sentimentality, even by so stern a critic as Yeats himself. 'The Meditation of the Old Fisherman'—'founded upon some things a fisherman said to me while out fishing in Sligo Bay' *(VPO, 797)*—shares the same anonymous quality. If the man did not actually use the words of the refrain, 'When I was a boy with never a crack in my heart', they are certainly not beyond the range of Irish country speech, except, oddly enough, that 'never' would have been pronounced 'ne'er' in many parts of Ireland, including my own county, Offaly. The first stanza, with its apostrophe to the waves and its self-conscious line, 'Though you glow and you glance, though you purr and you dart', seems a little 'arty', but the second stanza rings true, especially the line about the cart 'That carried the take to Sligo town to be sold'. The most authentic touch—because Yeats is totally unconscious of it—is the use of 'pebbly' as a trisyllable (no doubt his own pronunciation) in the last stanza *(VPO, 90–1)*. In comparison with these two poems, the three ballads at the end of *Crossways* and 'The Ballad of Father Gilligan' in *The Rose* fail to catch the folk note. When they are naive, they seem to me naive in the wrong way, and when they are stilted—as almost every folk-song is in places—they are so in too literary a manner.

'To an Isle in the Water' must be judged trivial for the same reasons as 'A Faery Song' in *The Rose*. 'The Stolen Child', on the other hand, although Yeats cited it as typical of the 'flight to fairyland' in his early work, cannot be ignored. It is a poem that nobody else could have written, not even the Ferguson of 'The Fairy Thorn', and that no one afterwards could successfully imitate, though literally scores must have tried. What is inimitable is the refrain of the first three stanzas (modified to fit the narrative by slight changes in the fourth):

> Come away, O human child!
> To the waters and the wild
> With a faery, hand in hand,
> For the world's more full of weeping
> Than you can understand.
>
> (*VPO*, 87–8)

D. G. Rossetti doubtless revealed to Yeats the cumulative power of a refrain, but the younger poet, throughout his career, was to put it to uses undreamed of by the elder one. One must also recognize touches reminiscent of Christina Rossetti's 'Goblin Market' in the first stanza:

> There we've hid our faery vats,
> Full of berries
> And of reddest stolen cherries.
>
> (*VPO*, 87)

These echoes become irrelevant once we grasp how firmly three of the four stanzas are placed in the Sligo landscape: the first mentions an island in Lough Gill, near Slewth Wood; the second, 'The dim gray sands. / Far off by furthest Rosses'; the third, 'the hills above Glen-Car' and its waterfall. Yeats's fairies are local, almost earth-bound, not mere conventions, and the 'solemn-eyed boy' whom they carry off in the end seems reluctant to leave such concrete images of home as 'the kettle on the hob' or 'the brown mice . . . round the oatmeal chest' (*VPO*, 89). This is not folk poetry, as 'Down by the Salley Gardens' almost seems to be, but it is folk-inspired poetry of a remarkable kind.

For me, 'The Madness of King Goll' is the best poem in *Crossways*. Though it had not quite reached its final form in 1895, it had already profited by three revisions, resulting in a stronger, harsher poem than the first version published in *The Leisure Hour* (September 1887). Lines like these have a Fergusonian ring:

> I called my battle-breaking men
> And my loud brazen battle-cars
> From rolling vale and rivery glen
>
> (*VPO*, 83)

The great triumph of this poem, however, is the hypermetric refrain which closes each of the six twelve-line stanzas:

> They will not hush, the leaves a-flutter round me, the beech leaves old.
>
> (*VPO*, 82–6)

King Goll tells his story, which Yeats found in O'Curry's *MS. Materials of Irish History*, (*VPO*, 857)[36] in the first person and past tense, but the present-tense refrain reminds us that he is still mad, still unfit for the company of men, still alone in the open air with winter coming on.

Despite the great potential of 'The Two Trees', with its foretaste of greater poems to come, passages in it like 'alas! / Thy tender eyes grow all unkind' confirm Yeats's own charges about sentimentality masquerading as simplicity. In the end, it was some of the most specifically Irish poems that gave *Poems* (1895) not only popularity but enduring strength. Impressive as the longer works may have seemed at the time, I find that certain lyrics which combine the Sligo landscape with Irish folk themes remain to this day neither sentimental nor simple: 'The Stolen Child', for example, and above all, 'The Man Who Dreamed of Faeryland'. Yeats's capacity for fusing narrative and lyric elements into a unique whole is also demonstrated by these two poems and by others like 'Fergus and the Druid' and 'The Madness of King Goll'. If Yeats wrote in his early days 'to sweeten Ireland's wrong', Ireland in her turn gave his poetry roots in her landscape and the strengths that come from working in an old tradition—even though that tradition had become severely eroded in the process of transfer from Irish into English. In 1892 he had asked

Can we not build up a national tradition, a national literature, which shall be none the less Irish in spirit from being English in language?. . . Can we not write and persuade others to write histories and romances of the great Gaelic men of the past . . . until there has been made a golden bridge between the old and the new?[37]

If *Poems* (1895) cannot be described in its entirety as forming such a bridge, at least it does contain poems of enduring worth in which the artistic values of the 1890s fuse with tougher, purer metal drawn from an ancient hoard.

The Great Comedian

The 'Great Comedian' in the poem 'Parnell's Funeral' was, as we know, Daniel O'Connell. Yeats gave him grudging admiration as an 'old

---

[36] This information is omitted from the first two printings of *VPO*.

[37] 'The De-Anglicising of Ireland', in *Uncollected Prose by W. B. Yeats*, ed. John P. Frayne (New York: Columbia Univ. Press, 1970), i. 255.

Rascal' whose sexual prowess made him fit to stand alongside Nelson and Parnell in 'The Three Monuments'. Nevertheless, he professed to despise the 'gregarious humour of O'Connell's generation and school.[38] It is to Yeats himself, however, that I here apply the title of Great Comedian. Not that I agree entirely with the view he once expressed in a letter to his father, 'I am really essentially a writer of comedy'. Nor did Yeats himself, in fact. This half-joking self-appraisal must have been prompted by a surprising discovery recorded in the same letter, 'I find that my talent as a stage manager is in the invention of comic business'.[39]

I should admit at once that I consider Yeats's two greatest plays to be *Purgatory* and *The Resurrection*—the one a tragedy and the other a miracle play. On the other hand, my two next favourites among his plays are *The Player Queen*, almost a true comedy, and *The Herne's Egg*, a tragicomedy or 'black' comedy. We have Yeats's own word for it that *The Player Queen* began as a tragedy in verse, only to end as what he unfairly terms 'a farce' in prose. This movement from tragedy to comedy, from high seriousness to humour, is for me a recognizable motif in the pattern of Yeats's entire development as an artist. On this point George Moore made a typically shrewd reflection in *Ave*: 'the thought suddenly struck my mind that the *cocasseries* [comicalities] of Connaught were more natural to [Yeats] than the heroic moods he believes himself called upon to interpret. His literature is one thing and his conversation is another, divided irreparably. Is this right?[40] The later Yeats, who laid so much stress on 'unity of being', would certainly have agreed that it was *not* right. As he grew older, more and more of his 'conversation' found its way into his 'literature'. The mature artist found it possible to express in his work more and more facets of his many-sided personality, including the sense of humour that had always been present in his conversation—and also in his correspondence. Yeats sometimes perceived the change himself, as when he tells Lady Gregory with some excitement, in a letter of 5 March 1913, that he has just finished 'The Three Hermits'—'my first poem which is comedy or tragi-comedy'.

Yeats's humour can be most readily documented from his letters. The vast majority of these were spontaneously composed and harshly written or, in later life, dictated: they are in consequence a better index to his conversational style and natural humour than the alleged records of his talk produced by the faulty memories and lively imaginations of Moore, Gogarty, and other memorists. The 'General Introduction' to

---

[38] Yeats, *Autobiographies*, 195.
[39] Yeats, *Letters*, ed. Allan Wade (New York: Macmillan, 1955), 524.
[40] George Moore, *Ave* (New York, 1917), 281.

the 1986 *Collected Letters* draws attention to this 'rare spontaneity' on the part of 'such a fastidious craftsman' and notes that 'the correspondence presents [Yeats] as gregarious, chatty, amusing, inquisitive, and even scandalous'.[41] So far as I recall, there is only one letter published by Wade[42] in which Yeats admits that his motive for writing it is 'a desire to gossip', but internal evidence shows that the same urge underlay many and many another letter, particularly to his women friends and to John Quinn. Joyce's letters, to women compare unfavourably with Yeats's; we miss in Joyce's the subtle mixture of *galanterie* and intellectuality that Yeats shares with some of the *philosophes* of the eighteenth century. Joyce gives either sheer eroticism (as in his letters to Nora) or sheer intellectuality (as in those to Harriet Weaver).

There is no reason to suppose that Yeats's conversation with women friends was any more straitlaced than his letters. In an apologetic letter to Edmund Dulac (1 December 1922), he writes:

Those last two nights when I dined with you I was very tired and overflowed, as almost always when tired, in phantastical scandalous patter, a patter made all the worse from having lunched with a woman friend brought up like myself under the shadow of England's first emancipation in 1890 or so. It is my refuge from logic, and passion, and the love of God and charity to my neighbours and other exhausting things.[43]

In a letter to Olivia Shakespear, possibly the lunch companion referred to, Yeats once remarked: 'you will see that I am still of opinion that only two topics can be of the least interest to a serious and studious mind—sex and the dead'.[44]

Obviously I have just been referring to the mature Yeats and his conversation or correspondence with sophisticated women like Florence Farr, Mabel Beardsley, Mrs Shakespear, Ethel Mannin, and Dorothy Wellesley. He did not write anything really scandalous to his sisters or to Katherine Tynan or Lady Gregory, but he did give free rein to his sense of humour in letters to these intimate though less sophisticated correspondents. As for Maud Gonne, the evidence is missing, virtually all of his letters to her having been destroyed. I would assume, however, that since she had no sense of humour, he would rarely have risked a joke. It may be significant, too, that we find little humour in the letters published by Wade for the decade succeeding the poet's first meeting with her in 1889. The only other comparable dearth of humour in Wade occurs during and around the First World War.

[41] W. B. Yeats, *Collected Letters*, vol. I, ed. John Kelly and Edward Domville (Oxford: Clarendon Press, 1986), xxxix–xl.
[42] Wade, *A Bibliography*, 883. (To Dorothy Wellesley, 18 February 1937.)
[43] Ibid. 693.   [44] Ibid. 730.

Disappointingly, the first volume of letters edited by Kelly and Domville supplies hardly any new examples of this aspect of Yeats: here is one, however, addressed to his brother's wife; 'Please give my thanks to Jack for the ciggarette [sic] holder. It has helped many a cigarrette to resolve it self [sic] into verses.'[45] One of the more dubious charms of this quotation is that under the ground rules of the *Collected Letters* it contains two different spellings of 'cigarette'—both incorrect. I must admit, however, that in turning the pages of the new edition I came upon some very characteristic pieces of humour that I had somehow overlooked in Wade. Best of all is the letter of 16 December, 1894, to his sister Lily,[46] whose sense of humour so closely resembled his own; he had just returned from a stay in Lissadell:

I lectured in the School House on Fairy lore chiefly to an audience of Orangemen. It was a novel experience. I found that the comic tales delighted them but that the poetry of fairy lore was quite lost on them. They held it Catholic superstition I suppose. However I had fortunately chosen nothing but humourous [sic] tales. The children were I beleive [sic] greatly excited. Mr Jones of Roughley said afterwards that now there should be another lecture to put my lecture 'on a sound religious basis' for he feared it may have sent away many of the audience with the idea that the fairies really existed.

Yeats never drags out these little anecdotes, but he makes sure not to stop until he has included all the details that will amuse his reader. Farther on in the same letter he shrewdly characterizes various members of the Gore-Booth family, including the fifth baronet: 'Sir Henry Gore Booth thinks of nothing but the north pole, where his first officer to his great satisfaction has recently lost him self & thereby made an expedition to rescue him desirable.'

I may be wrong, but I think that this kind of understated humour is not really native to Ireland; it could even be one of our invisible imports from the neighbouring island. Humour is regarded as so purely English that the French have borrowed the English word for it, making a sharp distinction between *l'humour* and *l'humeur*. Samuel Beckett's French publisher, Jérome Lindon, insists, by the way, that although the French use the word they still do not understand what humour is: they equate it with stories about cuckolds (*des histoires de cocus*). Yet when Thackeray wrote a book entitled *The English Humorists of the Eighteenth Century*, most of the subjects turned out to be more or less Anglo-Irish, among them Swift, Sterne, and Goldsmith. My private term for this genre is 'Church of Ireland rectory humour'. Though not myself a clergyman's son, I grew up in the heart of the tradition. My mother was an archdeacon's

---

45 Kelly & Domville (eds.), *Collected Letters*, 452.   46 Ibid. 9 418–19.

daughter: she possessed a lively sense of humour, shared with at least two of her brothers, one himself a clergyman. Looking back I see that it was no accident that I felt drawn to write *The Irish Comic Tradition*.

The Anglo-Irish who had social pretensions tended to cultivate a cruel type of wit, but those who were contented with life in a country rectory excelled in genuine humour and passed on their taste to their more ambitious sons and grandsons. George Farquhar and his more successful disciple, Oliver Goldsmith, were sons of clergymen, as were Henry Brooke, the highly moral imitator of Sterne in *The Fool of Quality*, and Douglas Hyde, whose work has been surveyed in Chapter 3 (pp. 64, 67–8) and who was the author of a brilliant lampoon on the Trinity College Fellows who opposed the study of the Irish language.

One might have supposed that the solemn nature of the Evangelical movement would have deprived the Irish Anglicans of their collective sense of humour, but both Synge and Yeats, grandsons of Evangelical clergymen, refute that idea. Shaw, as has been pointed out, was the grandson of a leading Evangelical layman, married to a clergyman's daughter. As for Wilde, we all know about his erring father but ignore the fact that Sir William Wilde had two brothers and a brother-in-law who were clergymen. The humorists who were themselves in holy orders are exceptions that prove the rule: we think of Swift primarily as a bitter satirist, forgetting *Cadenus and Vanessa*, for example, or even the gentler moments of *Gulliver's Travels*. Swift's punning friend, the Revd Thomas Sheridan, encouraged the Dean's flair for amiable nonsense, besides passing on the humorous tradition to his grandson the dramatist. It is a pity that the Revd Laurence Sterne can only be counted as an honorary Irishman—though the title is well earned by his influence on James Joyce and Flann O'Brien. Despite his over eighty books, Canon Hannay (George A. Birmingham) seems puny beside Swift: nevertheless he is in the same tradition. There should be a country rectory somewhere in William Trevor's background—his father was a bank manager. Perhaps there is some similarity in the relative positions of these two occupations, especially in country towns and villages, which would produce a like effect on their offspring.

Looking more closely at Yeats's letters, it is possible to construct from them a sort of profile of his humour in its most natural expression. This is very different from the wit that predominates in his poetry. Yeats himself differentiated between the two ideas, as is demonstrated by his first reaction to Shaw: 'Last night at Morris's I met Bernard Shaw, who is certainly very witty. But, like most people who have wit rather than humour, his mind is somewhat wanting in depth.'[47] Even in the moments

---

[47] Wade, 59.

when the Yeats of the *Letters* sounds like Oscar Wilde, it is humour rather than wit that animates his paradoxes. His comment on the suicide of Richard Pigott, the forger of letters allegedly written by Parnell, might have gone into *The Importance of Being Earnest*: 'Poor Pigott! One really got to like him, there was something so frank about his lies. They were so completely matters of business, not of malice.'[48] This was not intended for any eye but Katherine Tynan's; when Yeats wrote a letter for publication, however, he sometimes strove for and achieved a conscious wit. The well-known letter to the *Gael* on 23 November 1887 is worth quoting once again:

Dear Sir, I write to correct a mistake. The curious poem in your issue of the 19th inst. was not by me, but by the compositor, who is evidently an imitator of Browning. I congratulate him on the exquisite tact with which he has caught some of the confusion of his master. I take an interest in the matter, having myself a poem of the same name as yet unpublished.[49]

The Yeats of this early period showed a dangerous facility in his newspaper prose. Some of the material written for the *Providence Journal* and the *Boston Pilot* has the amusing triviality of a literary gossip column. For instance, there is the account of an autograph sale at Sotheby's in which, after a moving quotation from a letter by Blake that was for sale, Yeats goes on:

A letter by George Meredith was put up and sold for five pounds. A dealer who had bid five shillings seemed greatly surprised. Meredith was a new star. 'Who is he?' he muttered. 'He must be bidding himself.' Among the letters were several from kings and princes. On the whole, potentates went dirt cheap. As I came into the room the auctioneer was crying out, 'Any advance on eight shillings for Joseph Bonaparte?[50]

This anecdote illustrates one characteristic of Yeats's humour—the power of observation underlying it. He is too often thought of as directing all his attention inwards upon himself, but when he directed it outwards, as he very often did, he could see more clearly than the average man. Here is a little comedy of manners involving Yeats and a man-servant:

You would have been much amused to see my departure from Oxford. All the while I was there, one thing only troubled my peace of mind—the politeness of the manservant. It was perpetually 'Wine, Sir? Coffee, Sir? Anything, Sir?' At every 'Sir' I said to myself, 'That means an extra shilling, in *his* mind, at least.' When I was going, I did not know what to give him, but gave him five shillings. Then suddenly thought I had given him too little. I tried a joke. My jokes had

[48] Ibid. 112–13.   [49] Ibid. 55–6
[50] *Letters to the New Island*, ed. Horace Reynolds (Harvard Univ. Press, 1934), 94.

been all failures so far with him. It went explosively and I departed sadly knowing I had given too much.[51]

In those days, Yeats was of course young (23) and poor, and therefore more conscious of what others thought of him than he was in later life. But after he became an Irish Senator, he showed a sly awareness of the new deference paid him:

I find that everybody is very polite to a senator, and if there are any that want his money or his life—which is probable—they do not show by daylight. At my club people come and turn up the electric light for me if I forget to do so myself; and quite a number of persons with very slight conversational powers come and talk to me in public places.[52]

Often, this power of humorous and ironic observation was focused upon strong, vivid personalities who fully deserved such attention: Madame Blavatsky or William Morris, for instance. When Yeats's sister 'Lilly' was studying embroidery with May Morris, she used to keep him supplied with Morris anecdotes, which he would pass on to Katherine Tynan. Yeats's own observations of Morris and his circle deal more in irony and less in slapstick than his sister's:

He [Morris] talks freely about everything; called the English 'The Jews of the North', and seems greatly worshipped by those about him; by young Sparling especially, who carries it so far that, when he was telling Rhys about his engagement to Miss Morris, he said, 'She is very beautiful. Morris, you know, says so,' taking Morris's opinion as final in all matters—as, indeed, the only opinion. Meanwhile Morris denounces hero-worship, praises the northern gods at the expense of the Greek, because they were so friendly, feasting and warring with the men and so little above them.[53]

The unstressed juxtaposition of Sparling's hero-worship with Morris's denunciation of it is beautifully ironic. Throughout his life, Yeats excelled at this—so much so that many of his readers and acquaintances have thought him without humour. Jack Yeats, his painter brother, had the same quality, both in writing and in speech. No doubt every member of the family had it. With an audience so alert as the father, sisters, and brothers, no one needed to signal a joke in advance or to laugh at his own witticisms. Monk Gibbon quotes a very characteristic letter from Lily in her old age: 'I did enjoy the drive—your mother and Mary are both quick-minded—I find people you have to say even unimportant things [to] several times over before they take it in very exhausting— but *they* take up one's note at once.'[54]

[51] Wade, *A Bibliography*, 87.   [52] Ibid. 696–7.   [53] Ibid. 44.
[54] Monk Gibbon, *The Masterpiece and the Man* (London: Hart-Davis, 1959) 215.

Though there was little of the stage Irishman about Yeats, he occasionally exploited the fact that most of his favourite correspondents were English. During the Civil War, and again in Blueshirt days, there is a certain bravado about some of his humour, an exploitation of the English person's fear of the 'wild Irish'. In 1922 he tells Charles Ricketts; 'We left Gort about five weeks ago and the day we left had two feet of water on our kitchen floor as the blowing up of our bridge had dammed the river. The neighbourhood is now I hear quite peaceful as there are no bridges left.'[55] Later, when as a Senator he had an armed guard, he told Olivia Shakespear: 'My armed guard now very much on the alert just now (many republicans are I think in town for a conference) and I was challenged last night on the stairs. I was in my stocking feet so as not to wake the children'.[56] He then adds, with careful nonchalance, 'I give my guard detective stories to train them in the highest tradition of their profession.' In 1933 he told the same correspondent, 'The chance of being shot is raising everybody's spirits enormously.' He occasionally enjoys twitting our Irish hypersensitivity or deviousness, for the benefit of an English correspondent, as when he explains to Florence Farr why the actress Miss Darragh is not popular with the Abbey company:

She says such things as, 'Why do you not get that castor screwed on to the table leg?' instead of making enquiries and finding out that the castor cannot be screwed on because the woman who washes the floors and the stage carpenter have quarrelled about it—and the stage carpenter would sooner die than screw it on.[57]

Yeats was naturally fully aware of what he calls 'our Irish cruelty' and might as well have called our malice. In commenting on his first impressions of Joyce's *Ulysses*, he writes: 'A cruel, playful mind like a great soft tiger cat—I hear as I read, the report of the rebel sergeant in '98: 'O he was a fine fellow, a fine fellow. It was a pleasure to shoot him'.[58]

How much of this malice and mental cruelty did Yeats himself share? Not very much, really; for all his mentions of his own bitterness, he seems in his letters a magnanimous man, though some of his behaviour towards fellow poets hardly qualifies for that adjective. Only about George Moore is he undeviatingly 'catty', as in the story which ends with Moore saying to Walter Sickert's mistress, plaintively, 'But Sickart [*sic*] and I always share'.[59] Yeats did not, it is true, invent this story, but he was happy to pass it on to John Quinn. He also relished a posthumous story about Swinburne that he passed on to Mrs Shakespear.

[55] Wade, *A Bibliography*, 692. [56] Ibid. 698.
[57] Ibid. 481. [58] Ibid. 679.
[59] Ibid. 509–10.

Adah Menken [the American actress] was given £5 a week by Prinsep and others to seduce Swinburne. She said at the end of a couple of weeks that she had always been an honest woman and could not accept the money. 'We have been constantly together for two weeks and nothing has happened except that he has bitten me twice'.[60]

He follows this with an unusual flash of wit, partly at the expense of Ezra: 'She [Adah Menken] had some talent, wrote a sort of free verse (the American vice).

Turning from these rather disillusioning examples of his humour, we find some that illustrate his poetic imagination, beginning with his description of his plans for the arrangement of the portraits made of him for the 1908 collected edition. The passage ends as follows:

I am going to put the lot one after the other: my father's emaciated portrait . . . beside Mancini's brazen image, and Augustus John's tinker to pluck the nose of Shannon's idealist. Nobody will believe they are the same man. And I shall write an essay upon them as all the different personages that I have dreamt of being but have never had the time for.[61]

I wonder if this was the origin of the doctrine of the Mask and the Anti-Self.

Another example is the description of his 'large white dog' at Thoor Ballylee in 1927, 'which has a face like the Prince Consort, or a mid-Victorian statue—capable of error but not of sin'.[62] Even when his imagination exercised itself in dreams, it could be humorous. He tells Mrs Shakespear of

a dream I had about a certain Betty Duncan who has just run off for the third time, and her father Jim Duncan. Betty Duncan kept shooting off rockets, and whenever a rocket exploded Jim Duncan picked up the stick and baptised it out of a soap dish. He is devoted to his grandchildren.[63]

Almost from the beginning of the *Letters* there are moments when Yeats applies his deadpan irony to those occult phenomena in which he most wants to believe. Perhaps the earliest example occurs in a letter to Katherine Tynan on 12 February 1888: 'A sad accident happened at Madame Blavatsky's lately, I hear. A big materialist sat on the astral double of a poor young Indian. It was sitting on the sofa and he was too material to see it. Certainly a sad accident!'[64] In 1902 he tells Lady Gregory, 'My alchemist . . . has just made what he hopes is the Elixir of Life. If the rabbits on whom he is trying it survive we are all to drink a noggin full—at least all of us whose longevity he feels he could honestly

---

[60] Ibid. 825.   [61] Ibid. 502.   [62] Ibid. 725.
[63] Ibid. 777.   [64] Ibid. 59.

encourage'.[65] One is reminded of that late poem, 'The Apparitions', which has as its refrain:

> Fifteen apparitions have I seen
> The worst a coat upon a coat-hanger.

The ultimate measure of a man's sense of humour is his capacity to laugh at himself. Yeats possessed this ability from the start, nor did it atrophy as he grew old and famous. In the very first letter printed by Wade, 'probably not later than 1884', when the poet was 19, Yeats sends 'the shortest and most intelligible' of his poems to Mary Cronin, saying, 'I am afraid you will not much care for it—not being used to my peculearitys [sic] which will never be done justice to until they have become classics and are set for examinations.'[66] Obviously this is self-mockery not boasting. Nearly fifty years later he writes to L. A. G. Strong after reading the latter's *A Letter to W. B. Yeats*,

My dear Strong, Fable and rumour were I believe goddesses and some of the charming stories you tell about me are doubtless their handiwork . . . I shall take an early opportunity of making some of those telling retorts my own in very deed. I thank you very much for your essay. My wife reminds me—I am dictating this to her—that I said to her when I came downstairs after reading it 'You must treat me with great reverence tonight.' I was seeing myself as your essay sees me.[67]

Again some lines of 'The Apparitions' come to mind:

> I can sit up half the night,
> With some friend that has the wit
> Not to allow his looks to tell
> When I am unintelligible.[68]

It seems to me that a similar scepticism is the impulse—conscious or unconscious—underlying *The Player Queen* and *The Herne's Egg*.

Any discussion of *The Player Queen* must start with these words from Yeats himself:

I began in, I think, 1907, a verse tragedy, but at that time the thought I have set forth in *Per Amica Silentia Lunae* was coming into my head, and I found examples of it everywhere. I wasted the best working months of several years in an attempt to write a poetical play where every character became an example of the finding or not finding of what I have called the Antithetical Self; and because passion and not thought makes tragedy, what I made had neither simplicity nor life . . . At last it came into my head all of a sudden that I could get rid of the play if I turned it into a farce; and never did I do anything so easily.[69]

[65] Ibid., 365.   [66] Ibid., 30.   [67] Ibid., 787.
[68] Yeats, *Collected Poems* (New York: Macmillan, 1956), 332.
[69] Yeats, *The Variorum Edition*, ed. R. and C. Alspach (New York: Macmillan, 1966), 761.

The Antithetical Self is still omnipresent in the final, farcical version of *The Player Queen*, but I will not discuss that aspect of the play here. I want to examine this play *The Herne's Egg* as exercises in systematic desecration—products of our Irish gift for anticlimax, for parody, for antithesis, for burning what we used to adore, in André Gide's phrase: Gide put it in the mouth of Ménalque in *The Immoraliste*, a character clearly modelled on an Irishman, namely Oscar Wilde. I do not just want to stress that the unicorn, which symbolized 'virginal strength' in *The Unicorn from the Stars*, is represented in *The Player Queen* as copulating with the dim but virginal Queen; after all, we have only the word of a 'night rambler' for that, and 'boys are liars'. Nor do I just mean that if a unicorn did in fact couple with the Queen, it was in parody of Yeats's great historical theme, the intercourse between a divine being and his human bride. Nor that 'the new order of the ages' finds its prophet in the Old Beggar who was once a donkey; when his back itches and he lies down and rolls and brays, 'the crown changes', or the gyres reverse.

No, the desecration is far more personal than that. The 'triangle' in the play consists of Septimus, a romantic but not a popular poet; Decima, a *femme fatale*, who torments and betrays him; and Nona, the quiet but genuinely 'sexy' woman who loves and comforts Septimus. Admittedly, the part of Decima was written for Mrs Patrick Campbell, so that her profession of actress and her flamboyant personality could be regarded as paralleling Mrs Pat's. But was not Maud Gonne an actress too, at least in *Cathleen Ni Houlihan*? And did she not flout the conventions with a ruthlessness that Mrs Pat could never match? Who but Maud Gonne could pass off her illegitimate daughter as adopted and get away with it? The Nona of the play could be Mrs Shakespear, or she could be Florence Farr, who was herself an actress. Septimus *needs* his 'bad wife' to hurt him into poetry, as Yeats seems to have needed 'mad Ireland' or Maud Gonne, but some of the best poems are composed with Nona's naked back as a writing desk, a detail stolen by Yeats from Laclos's *Les Liaisons Dangereuses*. The mood of the play is very much that of 'The Circus Animals' Desertion':

> Those masterful images because complete
> Grew in pure mind, but out of what began?
> A mound of refuse or the sweepings of a street,
> Old kettles, old bottles and a broken can,
> Old iron, old bones, old rags, that raving slut
> Who keeps the till.

For once at least, in *The Player Queen*, 'that raving slut' became a 'masterful image' and yet remained a raving slut.

Let me just pin-point a few instances of Yeatsian self-parody in *The Player Queen*. The crucial problem for anybody wishing to direct a performance of this play seems to me to lie in the character of Septimus. Nona and Decima are largely from stock, but how seriously are we to take the drunken Septimus? How much *veritas* is there in his *vino*? I would suggest that we have to take him very seriously indeed at times, but those commentators who take him seriously *all* the time are going too far. His self-pity about his bad wife becomes more than a little specious after we learn of the consolation he has been receiving from Nona; nevertheless he tries to convince himself that his sufferings are Christlike:

others have had bad wives, but others were not left to lie down in the open street, under the stars, drenched with cold water, a whole jug of cold water, shivering in the pale light of the dawn, to be run over, to be trampled upon, to be eaten by dogs.[70]

Then he says, 'Bring me to my stable—my Saviour was content with a stable.' All this is excessive, obviously. We become sure of this when he says, after being knocked down, 'it is necessary that I shall die somewhere where my last words can be taken down'.[71]

Because the Unicorn is so transparently a symbol, commentators hang on to every word that Septimus has to say about it. Undoubtedly, if the Unicorn gave up chastity and begot a new race, this would be a portent similar to the hatching of the third egg laid by Leda:

> And what rough beast, its hour come round at last,
> Slouches towards Bethlehem to be born?

When Septimus says, 'I announce the end of the Christian Era, the coming of a New Dispensation, that of the New Adam, that of the Unicorn',[72] he is surely in deadly earnest, or at least the poet who created him is; but when he adds, 'but alas, he is chaste, he hesitates, he hesitates', then we ought to feel just a little wary. The idea is too clever by half: did Zeus hesitate to approach Leda, did the Holy Ghost hesitate? And it is permissible to feel uneasy at the description of the Unicorn as 'that noble, milk-white, flighty beast'. It is Septimus who is 'flighty' rather than the Unicorn.

Septimus is arrogant towards 'bad, popular poets' like Happy Tom and Peter the Purple Pelican ('called . . . after the best known of my poems', says Peter), and they retort, 'You would be a popular poet if you could.' Yeats, or any other good poet, might well answer '*Touché*'! But is the swaggering, whining Septimus entitled to be arrogant? I think perhaps he is, if only as the author of the song in the play that begins,

70 Yeats, *Collected Plays* (London: Macmillan 1960), 390.   71 Ibid. 401.
72 Ibid. 416.

> 'He went away,' my mother sang,
> 'When I was brought to bed.'
> And all the while her needle pulled
> The gold and silver thread.[73]

For me this is among the most beautiful songs that Yeats ever wrote.

On the other hand, when Septimus has the stage properties tied on his back, he indulges in a passage of Yeatsian rhetoric that sounds magnificent, yet begs so many questions as to be meaningless: 'It is necessary that we who are the last artists—all the rest have gone over to the mob—shall save the images and implements of our art.'[74] *Are* they the last artists? And if they are, can they save their art merely by saving its images and implements? Surely Yeats intended the self-parody there, although when Septimus says something really difficult a few lines later—'Man is nothing till he is united to an image'—we know that Yeats meant it from the depths of his being, for we have read *A Vision*, not yet published when this speech was written.

One final example of Yeats's mockery of his fundamental beliefs occurs in the brief scene between the Old Beggar and Decima. She is trying to commit suicide:

OLD BEGGAR. No, no; don't do that. You don't know what you will be put to when you are dead, into whose gullet you will be put to sing or to bray . . .

DECIMA. I have been betrayed by a man, I have been made a mockery of. Do those who are dead, old man, make love and do they find good lovers?

OLD BEGGAR. I will whisper you another secret. People talk, but I have never known anything to come from there but an old jackass. Maybe there is nothing else. Who knows but he has the whole place to himself?[75]

If Yeats believed in anything, he believed in reincarnation and in another world peopled with spirits—yet here he is making fun of the former and expressing scepticism about the latter.

The union of the divine with the human is mocked at in Decima's last song:

> Shall I fancy beast or fowl?
> Queen Pasiphae chose a bull,
> While a passion for a swan
> Made Queen Leda stretch and yawn.

To put Leda's relations with Zeus on a par with Pasiphae's guilty lust for a mere animal is pretty cavalier on Yeats's part, though he never quite achieved the urbane scepticism of Oliver Gogarty's 'Leda and the Swan':

---

[73] Ibid. 406.   [74] Ibid. 419–20.   [75] Ibid. 425.

> Of all the tales that daughters
> > Tell their poor old mothers,
> Which by all accounts are
> > Often very odd;
> Leda's was a story
> > Stranger than all others.
> What was there to say but:
> > Glory be to God?

I should add that 'Well, glory be to God!' accompanied by a pious raising of the eyes to heaven is the supreme expression of Irish incredulity.

But it is to *The Herne's Egg* that we must turn for Yeats's expression of the ultimate blasphemy against the concept of the Divine Marriage, accompanied by his further mockery of reincarnation. It is worth noting that although Yeats wrote gleefully to Dorothy Wellesley that there would be 'uproar' when the Abbey played *The Herne's Egg*, he was 'greatly relieved' when the decision to put it on was rescinded. And he had adapted the original play to eliminate all Christian reference except by implication. In the Gaelic source, *Fled Dúin na nGéd* (The Feast of Dunangay) the eggs of contention were goose eggs that belonged to an Irish saint, whereas the priestess Attracta is unambiguously a pagan devotee of the Great Herne or heron-god,[76] even though her name is also that of a Christian saint. Not much else about the play is unambiguous. We can never be sure whether Attracta received the sevenfold attentions of the Great Herne or was raped by seven mortal men; even if the latter version were true, they might have served as vessels or instruments of the god's power. Whatever be the truth, the Herne's vengeance falls upon Congal, and the Fool is its instrument. A terrible vengeance it is, too, for although Attracta is forgiving enough to wish to lie with her own servant, Corney, in order to avert Congal's fate, the luckless king meets his ordained end of reincarnation as a donkey.

There are moments when ambiguity turns into double meanings. Robert Speaight once told me that he was present at a reading of the play by Yeats, who was hoping that Speaight might produce it. When the poet had read the final lines of Scene II,

> She lies there full of his might,
> His thunderbolts in her hand,

he burst into peal upon peal of Rabelaisian laughter.

Not only is Congal destined to be reborn as a donkey, but his new progenitor, the life-size toy donkey pulled along by Corney, is himself the reincarnation of a 'rapscallion Clareman':

---

[76] Apart from the typical Irish pronunciation of 'heron' as 'her'n', Yeats would have found this word in the first line of Tennyson's 'The Brook': 'I come from haunts of coot and herne.'

> What if before your present shape
> You could slit purses and break hearts,
> You are a donkey now, a chattel,
> A taker of blows, not a giver of blows.[77]

The ennobling possibilities of reincarnation are ignored, and the danger of being pushed *down* the ladder

> Into cat or rat or bat,
> Into dog or wolf or goose.

is stressed instead.

The Herne's Egg has broadly comic aspects too, such as the one-word speeches of Mike or the mincing reluctance of James to lie with Attracta:

> I am promised to an educated girl.
> Her family are most particular,
> What would they say—O my God!

Some of these touches may seem blemishes, belonging to a lower order of humour altogether than the moonshine madness of the play, but I think Yeats knew exactly what he was doing. He wanted to keep the audience continually off balance, utterly confused. Is the joke on Congal or is it on the Great Herne? I think it is certain that the bird-god triumphs, but Yeats the conjuror so distracts the listener with his 'scandalous patter' that we cannot be sure whether or not we saw the rabbit pop out of the hat. The subtle mixture of obscenity and poetry, of the grotesque and the macabre, makes *The Herne's Egg* a remarkable foreshadowing of the plays of Samuel Beckett as well as an extraordinary work of art in its own right. Before he wrote *The Herne's Egg*, Yeats told Dorothy Wellesley of his hopes for it: 'as wild a play as *Player Queen*, as amusing but more tragedy and philosophic depth'. Once again the tragedy eluded him, and the finished play seemed a farce, but one cannot confidently assert that the philosophic depth is lacking.

These two plays, when read with the kind of exhaustive attention that one can give them in a seminar, are seen to be in fact inexhaustible. A final resolution of their conflicts escapes us: where most tragicomedy ultimately tips its scale towards either comedy or tragedy, *The Player Queen* and *The Herne's Egg* continue to seesaw ironically in our mind long after we have finished seeing or reading them. Yeats, as one might expect of the author of *A Vision*, can burn what he used to adore and still go on adoring it. The diagram of the Great Wheel shows us that opposites need never be reconciled nor destroy each other. As Yeats once wrote, 'the spring vegetables may be over, they have not been

---

[77] Yeats, *Collected Plays*, 647.

refuted'. South does not refute North, for as the Wheel spins, South in its turn becomes North again. In the same way, Comedy does not refute Tragedy—the tragicomic wheel simply keeps turning.

The great majority of what may roughly be called Yeats's humorous poems are tragicomic in this ironic way. 'John Kinsella's Lament for Mrs Mary Moore' begins with tragedy and ends in comedy; 'The Friends of his Youth' begins with comedy and ends in tragedy; and so on. Some of the brief satirical epigrams are all of a piece, but I can think of only two poems—and those among his last—that I would dare to call unequivocally humorous. These are 'The Pilgrim' and 'The Statesman's Holiday'. The first of these mocks at religion, the second at politics, but without any bitterness. Yeats, having devoted the best energies of his mind to one or both of these subjects over a period of over fifty years, suddenly unwinds. Having felt so passionately and thought so deeply about them, he comes to realize that he can now, in the familiar phrase, either take them or leave them alone. In these two poems written in his seventies, he has finally given the freest possible rein to that sense of humour which Moore had diagnosed forty years before. In one of them, 'The Statesman's Holiday', an old man's rambling 'conversation' has indeed become 'literature', as it has in a more serious poem, 'The Apparitions', where he speaks of an old man's joy:

> When a man grows old his joy
> Grows more deep day after day.

Joy, gaiety—

> Gaiety transfiguring all that dread.

these are the dominant notes of the *Last Poems*, written in the face of his own imminent death and what he believed to be the imminent downfall of western civilization. If we had any doubt about the sincerity of Yeats's belief in personal immortality and in the cyclic renewal of human history, surely his mood in his last years and in those last poems must have removed those doubts forever. He is so sure of his beliefs that he can laugh at them and at himself, and he can say, without any more than our usual Irish exaggeration:

> Laughter not time destroyed my voice
> And put a crack in it.

7 John Millington Synge: Devil or Saint?

In *An Claidheamh Soluis,* one of the official newspapers of the Gaelic League, the editor, Pádraic Pearse, on 9 February 1907 denounced the entire Anglo-Irish dramatic movement for 'the spoiling of a noble poet in Mr Yeats, and the generation of a sort of Evil Spirit in the shape of Mr J. M. Synge'. In *Irish Freedom,* June 1913, Pearse made an indirect apology: 'When a man like Synge, a man in whose heart there glowed a true love of Ireland, one of the two or three men who have in our time made Ireland considerable in the eyes of the world, uses strange symbols which we do not understand, we cry out that he has blasphemed and we proceed to crucify him.'

The first of these comments appeared exactly a fortnight after the first night of *The Playboy of the Western World* in the Abbey Theatre, at a moment when the deepest suspicions of the Nationalist and Catholic press about the supposedly pro-British and anti-Catholic tendencies of the literary movement seemed to be confirmed once for all by this blasphemous and satiric presentation of Irish rural ways. Synge had been under suspicion ever since his début with what was in fact his second play, *In the Shadow of the Glen* (8 October 1903), despite the moral and artistic success of his first, *Riders to the Sea,* less than five months afterwards.

The reasons for the hostile reception of *The Playboy* will be examined later: what concerns us at the moment is Pearse's second judgement, conferring not only sainthood but the Messiahship that he himself is nowadays sometimes accused of seeking. Before taking this piece of hyperbole too seriously, let us remember that Synge had at that time been four years in his grave: we Irish always speak well of the dead. Also, it may have been comforting to feel that no further embarrassing masterpieces could explode upon the Irish from that 'fine and private place'. Furthermore, Synge's last, unfinished play, *Deirdre of the Sorrows,* produced posthumously at the Abbey (13 January 1910), treated the greatest love-story in Irish folklore almost without irony. We ought to treasure the phrase 'a true love of Ireland' as the perfect refutation of those Irish critics who even today reject Synge's work as un-Irish; they are the very people for whom Pearse's lightest word is law. His other phrases about Synge are more open to question: the dramatist showed a stout heart rather than a sad one when his finest play was attacked, and the use of strange symbols might more justly have been attributed to Yeats.

Synge himself showed a wry consciousness of the paradox stated in such an extreme form by Pearse. Years before his fame and notoriety, he said to Cherry Matheson (who rejected his proposal of marriage in 1896), 'It is very amusing to me coming back to Ireland to find myself looked upon as a Pariah, because I don't go to church and am not orthodox, while in Paris among the students I am looked upon as a saint, simply because I don't do the things they do.'[1] Much has already been said in Chapter 3 (pp. 64–5, 66) about the Synge family's Evangelicalism; here, Synge embodies a general truth about ex-Evangelicals, namely that they find it easier to shake off their families' religious beliefs than the accompanying moral and social codes. Synge's remark to Miss Matheson, a member of the Plymouth brethren, was doubtless intended to convince her that his sexual morality was impeccably orthodox, though his views on religion were not. It also suggests to me that his 'love affair' with his fiancée (unceremoniously called 'Molly' Allgood by his biographers) was never physically consummated. The tramps, beggars, and tinkers of *The Shadow of the Glen*, *The Tinker's Wedding*, and *The Well of the Saints* either spurn wedlock or are indifferent to its formalities, but Synge was consciously a gentleman by birth and upbringing. At 35, when he first met Miss Mary Allgood, he might have allowed himself liberties with a woman of his own age and class who happened to love him, but with a girl still in her teens he had too much integrity to play the role of 'seducer'. His self-image would have suffered too much damage; also, in the small, tightly-knit artistic world of Dublin he could not have escaped detection and censure. What's more, as a putative Protestant, higher in economic and social status than his Catholic beloved, he would have been regarded as a traitor by both confessional groups for different reasons. This all sounds dreadfully old-fashioned, and Professor Robin Skelton for one would laugh me to scorn, but Ireland, Protestant as well as Catholic, was old-fashioned for thirty or forty years after Synge's death, as I can testify from personal experience.

Most of the tensions in Synge's life and work arise from this Puritan-in-Paris syndrome. If, for example, we interpret the title character of *The Playboy* as an idealized portrait of the artist as a young man, we are soon faced by the paradox of Christy's dual nature. When he first appears, the stage direction describes him as '*a slight young man, . . . very tired and frightened and dirty*'. As the other characters proceed to

---

[1] C. H. H.: 'John Synge as I knew him', *Irish Statesman*, 5 July 1924.

question him about his reasons for being a fugitive, he is shocked at the suggestion that he might have been guilty of rape: 'Oh, the saints forbid, mister. I was all times a decent lad.' His own considered summation of his early life runs as follows: 'Up to the day I killed my father, there wasn't a person in Ireland knew the kind I was, and I there drinking, waking, eating, sleeping, a quiet, simple poor fellow with no man giving me heed.' The opposition between Christy One and Christy Two is most emphatically stated in Act III:

WIDOW QUIN [*to* MAHON, *with a peculiar look*]. Was your son that hit you a lad of one year and a score maybe, a great hand at racing and lepping and licking the world?
MAHON [*turning on her with a roar of rage*]. Didn't you hear me say he was the fool of men.

Which is the 'real' Christy? One might think that Pegeen Mike's '*wild lamentations*' at the final curtain had the last word in a philosophical as well as a literal sense: 'Oh my grief, I've lost him surely. I've lost the only playboy of the western world.' Yet she has said not long before that Christy's supposed murder of his father was 'a dirty deed'. Why should the last words we are allowed to hear her speak carry any special authority? *The Playboy* presents a group of simple people—or so we like to think; by 'simple' we mean both 'uncomplicated' and 'unsophisticated'. Its author, however, was very sophisticated, even avant-garde, in literary matters at least, keenly aware of the complicated relationship between illusion and reality and doubtless sceptical about the possibility of ever drawing a hard and fast line between them. He once said to Cherry Matheson, 'I am a poor man, but I feel that if I live I shall be rich. I feel there is that in me which will be of value to the world.' At the time this must have sounded like the purest illusion, the very stuff of dreams, yet barely ten years later he could be certain that he possessed something 'of value to the world', having had plays performed all over the British Isles and in Berlin and Prague—with German and Czech translations made by distinguished men of letters. Illusion had become reality, even riches seemed possible, but death, the ultimate reality, intervened.

It is worth noting that the character in *The Playboy* named after Synge—Shawn (i. e. John) Keogh—is a physical and moral coward, convention-bound and priest-ridden. His surname, like Synge, is pronounced as a monosyllable: to a native Irish speaker it would suggest *ceo* ('mist', 'fog', or, in a different context, 'anything' or 'nothing'; it may also mean 'blot' or 'blemish'). There are two equivalents of the name John in Irish, Sean and Eoin; Owen, the enigmatic character in

Act II of *Deirdre of the Sorrows*, bears the latter name: described in the *dramatis personae* as 'Conchubor's spy', he goes mad for love of Deirdre and jealousy of Naisi and commits suicide by cutting his throat with what was intended to be Conchubor's knife. Yeats's brief preface (April 1910) is chiefly concerned with this character:

He [Synge] felt that the story, as he had told it, required a grotesque element mixed into its lyrical melancholy to give contrast and create an impression of solidarity, and had begun this mixing with the character of Owen, who would have had some part in the first act also.

Shawn's timidity and Owen's insane jealousy are stronger traits in Synge's own character than the wild bravura of Christy Two. When we recall that the role of Deirdre, like that of Pegeen Mike, was specifically written for Máire O'Neill (Mary Allgood's stage name) and created by her at its first performance, Owen's mixture of grovelling with jealous rage takes on a new significance. A similar entanglement of life with art has been hinted at by scholars in Otway's *Venice Preserv'd* and in more than one Molière comedy.

Ann Saddlemyer has in effect added a seventh play to the Synge canon, *When the Moon Has Set*. In one act, this is the first dramatic work he ever completed, though it was never published or performed during his lifetime. In it we find the starkest expression of the basic Syngean conflict, for the very good reason that the technique lacks subtlety: instead of characters divided within themselves, we are offered Sister Eileen as the embodiment of Puritan rejection and fear of life, while her agnostic cousin, Colm Sweeny, represents the forces of earth and acceptance of life. Synge no doubt still had in mind his rejection as an unbeliever by Cherry Matheson, though the rigid Protestant girl has been unfairly transformed into that operatic cliché, the Catholic nun torn by the conflict between her love and her vow of chastity. Dr Saddlemyer's reasons for publishing *When the Moon Has Set*, though 'with reluctance', are cogently stated in the introduction to *Collected Works*, vol. iii Though I agree with them, it cannot be denied that the finished play, revised repeatedly by Synge from a two-act original, suggests by its very brevity a parody of Ibsen's mature technique. (Dr Saddlemyer has noted[2] that Synge's diaries during the 1890s 'record only two visits to the theatre, in September 1892 to see Beerbohm Tree's *Hamlet* in Dublin, and in March 1898 to see a production of Ibsen's *Ghosts* by Antoine's theatre in Paris'. Colm Sweeny's uncle has just died after twenty years of living as a recluse. When Colm reports to the

---

[2] J. M. Synge: *Collected Works*, ed. Ann Saddlemyer, Oxford: Oxford Univ. Press, 1968), iii, p. xii.

young servant Bride his puzzling conversation with a madwoman in a graveyard, Bride quickly tells him, in the time it takes her to 'settle' the turf fire, that Mary Costello went mad many years ago; she then shows him a portrait on the wall of Mary in her youth. Bride is surprised that Colm's uncle never told him the whole story. Sister Eileen then enters and, soon after, answers Colm's questions with a cold, flat statement: 'He [the uncle] wanted to marry her although she was beneath him, but when it was all arranged she broke it off because he did not believe in God.' It was soon after this break that Mary became insane and spent ten years in an asylum. The neophyte Synge takes only four pages to unfold a twenty-year-old tragedy where Ibsen in *Ghosts* is still examining facets of his characters' past lives in the concluding act of a long play. By the end of the fifth page, Colm has jumped to conclusions about the lesson implicit in these far-off events which have just been narrated to him. He says to Sister Eileen that their uncle's death 'is far from enough if it has not made you realize that in evading her impulses this woman did what was wrong and brought this misery on my uncle and herself'.

If this play had been written some twenty years later, one would assume that its author had been reading D. H. Lawrence and Freud. As things are, he seems more likely to have been reading Browning:

> And the sin I impute to each frustrate ghost
>
> Is—the unlit lamp and the ungirt loin,
> Though the end in sight was a vice, I say.
> > 'The Statue and the Bust'

Or he might have been thinking of Blake: 'Abstinence sows sand all over / The ruddy limbs and flaming hair.' With arguments like the one already quoted, he tries to browbeat Eileen into abandoning her vows and marrying him. She gives him what she believes is her final answer: 'It is only those who do the will of God who are happy; that is all I know.' She has barely said these words when, with undeniably powerful dramatic irony, '*A burst of hysterical laughter is heard outside and then a sob and a scrap of singing*'. A moment afterwards Mary Costello appears: she is hostile to Eileen because she is a nun, and expresses contempt for all clergy and religious. She is indifferent to the death of her former fiancé, but anxious about the lives of the five children who should have been hers, 'five children that wanted to live, God help them, if the nuns and the priests with them had let me be'. Rather illogically, she then begs for the crucifix Eileen wears, giving her in exchange two rings that she has found in a bureau drawer, together with a green dress. As she moves towards the door, she makes a speech reminiscent in rhythm and content of many that Synge was afterwards to write:

'I'll be going now I'm thinking, for I've a long way and this [the crucifix] will be keeping me company in the dark lane through the wood. God save you kindly the two of you. There's great marrying in the world but it's late we were surely, and let yourselves not be the same. Let you mind the words I was saying, and give no heed to the priests or the bishops or the angels of God, for it's little the like of them, I was saying, knows about women or the seven sorrows of the earth.

It might almost be old Mary Byrne of *The Tinker's Wedding* speaking, but one would like to know what are the seven sorrows of the earth. Perhaps they have some connection with the sorrows of the Virgin Mary?

Colm tells Eileen that at dawn, in half an hour, he will ask her to be his wife and she will accept him because she has 'a profound impulse for what is peculiar to women'. In the meanwhile she is to exchange her nun's habit for the green silk dress: 'I am not in the humour for blasphemy.' She meekly goes out and soon returns, wearing the dress: Colm, rather patronizingly, says, 'It is the beauty of your spirit that has set you free, and your emancipation is more exquisite than any that is possible for men who are redeemed by logic. You cannot tell me why you have changed. That is your glory.' One would like to think that Synge had heard rumours in Paris of Bergson's views on intuition, but when Colm speaks to himself as 'the male power' in the final speech of the play, it seems more likely that Synge has been reading *Thus Spake Zarathustra*, whether in the original or in translation. Putting Mary's ring on Eileen's finger, he speaks the closing words of the play: 'In the name of the Summer, and the Sun, and the Whole World, I wed you as my wife.'

Obviously this forced resolution will not do, neither artistically nor in real life. In *The Playboy*, Christy abandons Pegeen and promises in his last speech of the play never to settle down but to 'go romancing' through a romping lifetime from this hour to the dawning of the judgment day'. Despite his jealous possessiveness about Molly, Synge himself was never to marry: his fatal illness was but the last of many not entirely compelling reasons why he should not take this irrevocable step. The devil's advocate and would-be emancipator was not himself emancipated.

Tramp or Bourgeois?

In the middle classes the gifted son of a family is always the poorest—usually a writer or artist with no sense for speculation—and in a family of peasants, where the average comfort is just over penury, the gifted son sinks also, and is soon a tramp on the roadside.[3]

3 J. M. Synge, *Collected Works*, ed. Alan Price (London: Oxford Univ. Press, 1966), ii. 202.

As this passage reveals, Synge not only sympathized with tramps but actually identified himself with them. In his correspondence with Molly Allgood he frequently signed himself 'Your Old Tramp', though this was partly an allusion to the fact that Molly's first good Abbey role was that of Nora, who elopes with the tramp at the end of *The Shadow of the Glen*. The sociological generalization in the above excerpt from 'The Vagrants of Wicklow' is probably unverifiable, but it is clearly what Synge would have wished to be true. After giving a series of anecdotes at first and second hand about the striking behaviour of tramps and tinkers—including his own eyewitness account of a drunken flower-woman who tore off her clothes and challenged the police to a fight—he begins the last paragraph of the essay thus:

In all the circumstances of this tramp life there is a certain wildness that gives it romance and a peculiar value for those who look at life in Ireland with an eye that is aware of the arts also. In all the healthy movements of art, variations from the ordinary types of manhood are made interesting for the ordinary man, and in this way only the higher arts are universal.

Deeply concerned in his Evangelical way to assert the wholesomeness of art—something he will do more successfully in the preface to *The Playboy*—he sharply distinguishes it from 'another art . . . founded on the freak of nature.' Although he does not use the word 'decadent', he makes Huysmans a scapegoat, as in the *Playboy* preface: 'To be quite plain, the tramp in real life, Hamlet and Faust in the arts, are variations; but the maniac in real life, and Des Esseintes and all his ugly crew in the arts, are freaks only.' Synge's plays about tramps, tinkers, and beggars, therefore, are his 'versions of pastoral', though they tend to shade off quickly into what William Empson named 'mock-pastoral', in which the protagonist is to some extent an enemy of society—a cheat or a thief like Macheath in *The Beggar's Opera*—rather than a 'gentle shepherd'.

   The Synge character who best fills the role of the shepherd in the old Romantic spirit of pastoral is the Tramp in *The Shadow of the Glen*, which seems a sordid enough piece of realism until his last three speeches, all to Nora. We suddenly realize that he is, in effect, saying:

> Come live with me and be my love,
> And we will all the pleasures prove
> That hills and valleys, dales and fields,
> Woods or steepy mountain yields.

What matter that the pleasures he has to offer are 'feeling the cold and the frost, and the great rain, and the sun again, and the south wind blowing in the glens'. At the very least, these sensations will make Nora fully aware that she is alive. In this ironic pastoral or anti-pastoral, dare we overlook the fact that her unsatisfactory old husband Dan Burke ('farmer and herd') and her unsatisfactory young lover Michael Dara ('a young herd') are both shepherds, while the tramp emphatically is not?

Samuel Beckett, born thirty-five years after Synge, shares his preoccupation with tramps, beggars and others who live on the margins of established society. There may be some direct influence here, since Beckett has expressed admiration for *The Well of the Saints* and included an ultra-Syngean tramp in one of his early short stories. As I have shown elsewhere, however, Beckett's Murphy, Watt, Molloy, Malone, Vladimir and Estragon—to name no others—all seem to have begun life as more-or-less gifted scions of the middle classes, though when they appear before us they have already fallen into destitution. Jacques Moran in *Molloy* illustrates the ease with which one can be reduced from bourgeois comfort to almost total deprivation by a series of misfortunes. Paradoxically, he comes to regard this process as a liberation: Synge's Tramp suggests that Nora may come to view her expulsion from home in the same light. Except for Murphy and Moran, however, Beckett's characters do not enjoy their freedom and, especially in *Waiting for Godot*, cherish vain hopes of reintegrating themselves with the bourgeoisie.

I would suggest that the reason why Synge and Beckett are so fascinated with these marginal figures can be traced to their suburban upbringing. One tends to view Anglo-Irish literature as either claustrophobically rural (Yeats, Synge, Somerville and Ross) or agoraphobically urban (Joyce, O'Casey, O'Faolain). In fact, however, Yeats, Joyce, Synge and Beckett were born in the suburbs of Dublin. These suburbs, like those of nineteenth-century cities in general, were made possible by new developments in the technology of transport. The very first railway in Ireland (1834) ran from Dublin to Kingstown, already a port and summer resort, which promptly became the home of many year-round commuters; Synge lived there off and on from 1890 until his death. Before 1890, he and his mother lived mainly in Rathgar, a suburb created by horse-drawn buses and trams, later to be served by electric trams and motor buses. The Dublin and Wicklow Railway, which ran from its Harcourt Street terminus in Dublin after 1859, is almost a live character in some of Beckett's works; his home station at Foxrock, with Leopardstown Racecourse close by, is the setting for his first radio play, *All That Fall*.

The flight to the suburbs in the second half of the nineteenth century, with its concomitant building of Evangelical Protestant churches described in Chapter 3 (p. 77) was principally a Protestant one. Hence the middle-class constrictions of suburban life, notoriously galling to the artistic temperament, were intensified by the rigours of a voluntary ghetto—an involuntary one as far as children and young adults were concerned. Beckett did not escape its Evangelical and philistine pressures until he took up rooms in Trinity. Synge enjoyed a temporary liberation every summer, when his mother and he moved to one or another house in County Wicklow. Here began his cult of tramps, tinkers and beggars— forerunners of the Aran and Blasket islanders whose Gaelic speech and unbroken cultural tradition earned his respect in a way the Wicklow vagrants never could. Even in Wicklow, ironically, the ghetto pursued him: Ann Saddlemyer notes that in December 1889, aged only 18, he informed his mother that he would no longer attend church, 'except during summers in County Wicklow'. If he was absent from his parish church in a Dublin suburb, the other parishioners could assume that he was attending a city church; this was not possible with the small congregations and scattered churches in Wicklow. Synge was a hypocrite in offering this compromise, just as his mother was in accepting it, but they cared for each other enough to want to avoid at least one source of constant irritation.

The break with Evangelical Christianity occurred very early, forming the second stage of Synge's break with suburbia; the first, before he ever went to school, began with his becoming 'a worshipper of nature'; later, he developed an 'interest in natural science'. Before he abandoned science — in favour of music, especially, and also literature—it rendered him:

an important service. When I was about fourteen I obtained a book of Darwin's. It opened in my hands at a passage where he asks how can we explain the similarity between a man's hand and a bird's or bat's wings except by evolution. I flung the book aside and rushed out into the open air—it was summer and we were in the country—the sky seemed to have lost its blue and the grass its green. . . . My studies showed me the force of what I read, [and] the more I put it from me the more it rushed back with new instances and power. Till then I had never doubted and never conceived that a sane and wise man or boy could doubt. I had of course heard of atheists but as vague monsters that I was unable to realize. It seemed that I was become in a moment the playfellow of Judas.[4]

A period of 'misery' followed, whether 'a few weeks' or merely a few days, after which 'I regained my composure, but this was the beginning'. By the time he was 16 or 17 he had renounced Christianity. 'For a while I denied everything, then I took to reading Carlyle, [Leslie] Stephen, and Matthew Arnold, and made myself a sort of incredulous belief that illuminated nature and lent an object to life without hammering the intellect.' Curiously, Synge was so unclubbable, at least so far as his own sex was concerned, that even at university he did not find anybody who shared his unbeliefs:

4 Ibid. 10–11.

This story is easily told, but it was a terrible experience. By it I laid a chasm between my present and my past and between myself and my kindred and friends. Till I was twenty-three I never met or at least knew a man or woman who shared my opinions.[5]

This 'chasm' between the artist and his suburban ghetto is like the 'great gulf fixed' between Dives and Lazarus. Synge and Beckett could always return home physically to visit their mothers, but spiritually speaking 'they which would pass from hence to you cannot'.

Even the brief 'Autobiography'[6] constructed by Alan Bliss from manuscript fragments reveals that Synge fell in love with more than one suburban maiden; fortunately, they confirmed their suburbanity sooner or later by rejecting him. It might have been artistically appropriate for him to marry some Aran beauty among the many he admired, but the marriage could hardly have survived the 'culture shock' felt by this not-impossible woman after a few days in Dublin; Synge would have had to settle in the Gaeltacht. Whatever else Molly may have been, she was emphatically not suburban. Elizabeth Coxhead, in frank, racy style, gives this highly credible summary of her personality:

By temperament she was a rebel, unwilling to submit to any discipline except that which was self-imposed. She would work like a demon to make herself a better actress, but for literature and culture as such, or for the social position and acceptance which meant so much to Sally, she did not give a damn.[7]

In the first year of their relationship, Synge belied his Aran emancipation by revealing that his suburban roots went much deeper than he had imagined. Reading between the lines, one senses his anxiety lest Molly appear vulgar or at any rate unladylike. Eventually he learns to compliment her upon her good points instead of lecturing her on her faults, but he seems unable to avoid a patronizing tone:

By the way I've a compliment for you. The last Sunday that you came I happened to see you passing from my top window, and you *walked* very prettily indeed. Quite charmingly. Keep to your low heels now, and don't spoil it, there is nothing so charming in a woman as an easy and graceful walk, and there is nothing more rare! So my dear old love you may be proud of yourself. I wonder if this will seem a nice letter to you.?[8]

Some months earlier (27 August 1906), he had mingled jealousy, puritanism, and snobbery in a poignant letter from Kerry:

5 Ibid. 11.   6 Ibid. 3–15.
7 Elizabeth Coxhead: *Daughters of Erin*. Gerrards Cross: Colin Smythe 1979), 177–8.
8 *Collected Letters of John Millington Synge*, ed. Ann Saddlemyer (Oxford: Clarendon Press, 1983), i. 310.

This perfectly fresh wild beauty of the sea and sky is a delight to me, but it makes me sick when I think that you are left behind, and of all the more or less vulgar or beastly talk of Mac, and his friends that you are more or less forced to listen to. Read your Arthur [Malory's *Morte D'Arthur?*], that will keep your mind full of wild beautiful things.[9]

In a recent letter he had expressed a more legitimate concern:

I hope you'll read steadily when I'm away. I hate to preach at you or school-master you,—I like you so perfectly as you are—but you must know, that it will make life richer for both of us if you know literature and the arts, the things that are of most interest to me and my few personal friends, that you'll know one of these days.[10]

Alas, this was immediately followed by a letter in which he paid her a truly suburban compliment. 'Will it make you vain if I tell you I felt proud of my little chang[e]ling she looked so pretty and quiet and nice.[11] Fortunately, however she may have looked on this occasion, Molly was soon to create the part of Pegeen Mike, a girl whom nobody could describe as pretty or quite or nice.

A Cosmopolitan Education

The artistic career of Synge is too often presented as a nine years' wonder: from 1898 (first visit to Aran) until 1907 (*The Playboy*). The years 1907–9 are seen as those of failing powers and approaching death, while the thrice-nine years 1871–98 are shrugged off as largely irrelevant. Many photographs and portraits of his powerful head and craggy features give us an impression, conscious or unconscious, of something primitive in him, waiting to be aroused by a stimulus equally primitive. There are others, however, that might be mistaken for studies of a Parisian man of letters in serious mood. The two photographs on page 83 of *Letters to Molly*, edited by Ann Saddlemyer, illustrate the contrast almost perfectly.

The truth as I see it runs more like this: the stimulus of the Aran experience would have elicited little response had not Synge spent most of his earlier life preparing for it. I don't know why so many of us today are still surprised—as Yeats and Lady Gregory were—that *The Playboy* was the first work of world-wide importance produced by the fledgling literary movement. Synge was far better educated, both formally and informally, than either of them: he had travelled more

9 Ibid. 193–4. (Ironically, the 'Mac' referred to, Francis Quinton McDonnell, who acted under the name of Arthur Sinclair, was to become Molly's unsatisfactory second husband.)
10 Ibid. 191.   11 Ibid. 191–2.

widely in Europe and possessed a better knowledge of its languages than Lady Gregory, despite his poverty, though he may not have read as widely in English literature as Yeats. His knowledge of science, however superficial, and of music far surpassed theirs, while his awareness of painting ancient and modern, though not derived from practice as Yeats's was, reached almost the same level. He could not match Wilde's knowledge of Greek and Latin, of course, nor Shaw's of music, nor Moore's of painting, but his range of education was far wider than theirs. As Nicholas Grene puts it in his extremely valuable introduction to *The Synge Manuscripts in the Library of Trinity College Dublin*, referring to the period which began with his first visit to Paris in January 1895:

His language study and his reading notes have the methodical conscientious quality of a student completing a self-imposed higher degree in European letters.

This autodidactic period lasted for at least five years. To quote Grene once more,

his preoccupation is still very much with French contemporary letters and he continued to work on *Etude Morbide* and *Vita Vecchia* until 1900, for there are drafts of both typed with the machine he bought in that year. It was probably not until after his third visit in 1900 that Synge decided to draw together his Aran experiences into a book, and the first typescript must date from the period 1900–1.[12]

Synge's formal education began *c.*1881 at Mr Harrick's school in Upper Leeson Street and continued at Aravon House School, Bray. His poor health made his attendance at both schools irregular, but the secondary education begun at Aravon was continued adequately by thrice-weekly private tutoring at home, 1884–8. In 1888, just two months after his 17th birthday, he passed the relatively easy entrance examination of Trinity College, Dublin: as for many years thereafter, it required a modest knowledge of Latin. The examination was intentionally made easy because Irish secondary schools could not afford the intensive teaching possible in English sixth forms: Irish students entered the University at an earlier age than English students and normally spent four years at Trinity instead of the three years required for a BA at British and other Irish universities. Synge was perhaps a year younger at entrance than most of his classmates but, like them, he took his degree in 1892. He had begun to study the violin in 1887 and in November 1889 began to study violin, musical theory, and composition at the Royal Irish Academy of Music; in 1890 he was accepted there for advanced study in counterpoint also. His musical studies thus took

[12] *The Synge Manuscripts in the Library of Trinity College, Dublin*, ed. Nicholas Grene; 12–13.

more and more of his time and energy during his undergraduate years; nobody need wonder that he contented himself with a 'pass' BA. Not having taken the difficult entrance scholarship examination, he would probably not have been accepted in an Honours course anyway.

Synge rather airily sums up his formal education in 'Autobiography': 'I ran through history, chemistry, physics, botany, Hebrew, Irish, Latin, Greek, something of French and German and made a really serious study of the history and theory of music. English literature also I read with much care.'[13] The oppositions 'ran through' / 'made a really serious study' and 'ran through' / 'read with much care' suggest how superficial his contact with many of the first-mentioned subjects must have been. For example, prior to 1892 he had read the usual Latin school-authors: Caesar, Livy and Cicero in prose; Virgil and Horace in verse. I assume that he read only the usual selections from those, amounting to a few hundred lines of verse and perhaps no more than 200 small pages of prose. More significant for the dramatist he was later to become are Sophocles' *Antigone*, Euripides' *Hecuba*, and Aeschylus' *Prometheus Bound*. No doubt the choruses in these tragedies were omitted because of their linguistic difficulty—a traditional practice—but Synge could have derived pleasure as well as instruction from the not-so-difficult Attic Greek of the dialogue. We know that in Trinity he attended T. K. Abbott's lectures on the *Medea* of Euripides, though one is a little dismayed to read a diary note of 24 April 1892 referring to 'Church's *Stories from the Greek Tragedies*'. The only Greek and Latin authors not usually read in Irish secondary schools of the period that we find among Synge's jottings are Epictetus, Juvenal, and Erasmus—quoted in the original Latin.[14]

Though his winning of prizes in Irish and Hebrew indicates Synge's latent powers, too much store ought not to be set by these achievements. Such prizes were awarded in a particular term on the basis of an examination dealing with that term's work only. Synge was not above studying old examination questions, as two of his notebooks reveal.[15] Also, we do not know whether his classmates offered any serious competition. Synge's original motive for studying Hebrew may have been a desire to confirm his religious scepticism, but we have seen in Chapter 1 that at least one lay member of his clan had set a precedent for this study. His only Hebrew reading would have been in the Old Testament. As for the New Testament, *koiné* Greek seems easy to anyone with some training in the classical language; only in the twentieth century have scholars proved how mistaken this view can be.

Synge's serious reading in biology, economics, sociology, and philo-

---

13 Synge, CW, ii. 13.   14 Ibid. 386.   15 Synge MSS., items 4370 & 4371.

sophy belongs to his postgraduate years, though he had earlier read John Stuart Mill's *On Liberty* and caught that glimpse of Darwin's thought which affected him so profoundly. It was not until 30 September 1895 that he began a consecutive reading of *The Origin of Species*; he also read its successor, *The Descent of Man*. In the same year he read *First Principles* and *Principles of Psychology* by Herbert Spencer, then at the height of his reputation. In 1896 his reading focused more on the politics and economics of communism and socialism: Marx's *Capital* in German, the *Communist Manifesto* in French, writings on socialism by William Morris and E. Belfort Bax. At the end of this year, however, we find him reading *The Imitation of Christ*. His reading for the three following years introduced him to, among other works, A. R. Wallace on Spiritualism, Frazer's *The Golden Bough*, and, in French, *The Way of Perfection* by St Theresa of Avila. All these details are from Synge's pocket diaries, but two notebooks from the same period, manuscripts 4379 and 4380, amplify the record. In aesthetics he read Ruskin's *Stones of Venice* and Taine's *Philosophie de l'art*, while his more strictly philosophical reading included 'Nietzsche, Spinoza, Comte, Hegel (in German).[16] He also looked into the work of that shameless charlatan Mme Blavatsky, who temporarily fascinated Yeats and A. E. but not Joyce nor, I imagine, Synge.

It is high time to examine the range of his familiarity with literature in the modern languages, obviously the most significant influence on the development of any twentieth-century writer. Although he attended the lectures of Edward Dowden, the distinguished Shakespeare scholar who held the chair of English at Trinity, the diaries show him broadening and deepening his knowledge after graduation. It would be foolish to pick out any standard English author, from Chaucer, Spenser, and Milton, to Tennyson, Wordsworth, Shelley and Browning, and assert positively that Synge had not read him or her. Blake was only being discovered in Synge's lifetime, but he began to read Blake after his meeting with Yeats in 1896. I have not found a mention of Pope, but 'Augustan' poetry was out of fashion at the time: in the preface to Synge's *Poems* we find a judgement, 'in the town writing of the eighteenth century, ordinary life was put into verse that was not poetry', which reminds us of Matthew Arnold's inclusion of Pope among 'classics of our prose'.[17] (CW, i, p. xxxvi). On the other hand, Arnold shared his enthusiasm for Burns, whom Synge couples with Villon and Herrick as poets who 'used the whole of their personal life as their material'.

---

[16] Ibid. 41.
[17] J. M. Synge, *Collected Works*, ed. Robin Skelton (London: Oxford Univ. Press, 1962), i. p. xxxvi.

Among the dramatists, Shakespeare appears most frequently, as he should: Synge had read at least twenty of the plays, as well as the sonnets. *As You Like It* was perhaps the most often reread, an index of his feeling for the pastoral. I imagine that his careful reading of Coleridge's *Lectures on Shakespeare* was prompted by Dowden. Less expectably, he began to read the plays of Ben Jonson shortly before graduation in 1892 and continued broadening his knowledge of them in the years following: he notes a rereading of *Volpone* in 1897. Altogether, he read at least ten of the plays: in his 1907 preface to *The Tinker's Wedding* he was to say that 'the best plays of Ben Jonson and Molière can no more go out of fashion than the blackberries on the hedges'. He was almost as familiar with the French comic playwright as with Jonson and also read some Corneille, but if the name of Racine occurs, I have failed to find it, although Yeats specifically mentions him in writing of Synge. Apart from this strange lacuna, Synge's knowledge of the French classics, read in the original, was impressive: Villon, Rabelais, Montaigne, Ronsard, Malherbe, La Fontaine, Pascal, Voltaire, Rousseau, Diderot's *Le Neveu de Rameau*, Beaumarchais. From the nineteenth century come the poetry of Hugo, the letters of George Sand, the fiction of Balzac, Mérimée, Flaubert, Daudet, Zola, and Anatole France: he also read Renan's *Vie de Jésus* and *St Paul*, the criticism of Sainte-Beuve and Taine's *Histoire de la littérature anglaise*.

Many French writers of his own time and just before the Symbolists and Décadents—remained unknown to him until the third of his annual winter visits to Paris, a series that began in 1895. Among his reading for 1897–8 we find three plays by Maeterlinck, the poetry of Verlaine and his master Baudelaire, two references to Villiers de l'Isle Adam, and what may be the first mention of Huysmans; he read Pierre Loti's *Pêcheur d'Islande* and *Le Mariage de Loti* in 1898. Just when he began to read Mallarmé is not so clear, but manuscript 4382, a notebook 'from the period 1897–8', includes a draft of an essay on the poet, as does manuscript 4393, which also includes a draft of an essay on the Symbolists.[18] This second notebook can hardly have been started before 1900. As for Huysmans, whom Synge couples with Mallarmé in his preface to *The Playboy*, we can be sure that his erudite journey from despairing atheism to a half-reluctant Catholicism temporarily wooed Synge away from the more congenial scepticism of Anatole France and the neo-Romanticism of Loti. The reference to Des Esseintes implies at least a nodding acquaintance with *À rebours* (1884); Synge may not have read *Là-bas* (1891), the first book of the Luc Durtal tetralogy—

---

[18] Synge MSS., 42, 45.

though Joyce did—or its successor *En route* (1895), but he must have tackled *La Cathédrale* (1898) virtually on publication, for manuscript 4378, a notebook 'mostly used during the period 1898–99', contains 'an analysis of the symbolism in . . . *La Cathédrale*'. (*Synge MSS*, p. 40) No doubt this work, together with *À rebours*, prompted Synge's wonder at 'the fantastic erudition of Huysmans'. In calling Huysmans 'the literary oblate', Joyce implicitly mocked *L'Oblat* (1903), the last novel of the cycle; it is difficult to gauge Synge's opinion of the same book from his review in *The Speaker* (18 April 1903). Contrasting Huysmans with Loti, whose *L'Inde sans les Anglais* he was also reviewing, Synge begins his article thus: 'In Huysmans we have a man sick with monotony trying to escape by any vice or sanctity from the sameness of Parisian life, and in Pierre Loti a man who is tormented by the wonder of the world.'[19] Both are found wanting because both cause 'a feeling of unreality' in the reader: Anatole France is preferred to either for his 'Half-cynical optimism' and 'socialistic ideals', which go to form a 'practical philosophy . . . that is fearless and perfectly healthy'. Only the word 'sanctity' above is addressed specifically to *L'Oblat*, though the review also provided an outline of the action of the novel.

Synge's reading in the other languages he has studied, German and Italian, was not very extensive. Goethe he knew thoroughly, having read *Faust*, *Werther*, *Wilhelm Meister* and the lyrical poetry. Heine was another favourite. Schlegel is mentioned once, and so is Lessing's *Laokoon*, which Joyce knew well enough to quote in German. In Italian, Synge had read at least passages from the *Divina Commedia*, but it was the *Vita Nuova* first read in July 1896, that inspired his own medley of prose and verse, *Vita Vecchia*, found in manuscript after his death. Boccaccio and Petrarch (some of whose sonnets he translated) are the only other Italian authors named in the sources I have used. Although he did not learn Norwegian as Joyce did, the diaries mention at least six plays by Ibsen, several of which he may have read in German. *The Master Builder* he certainly did, for it is noted as *Baumeister*.

The late Alan Bliss included in his edition of the prose a manuscript draft, entitled, 'A Tale of Comedians', an article on Anatole France in which Synge, as never before perhaps, speaks like one having authority on the subject of literature. One is immensely grateful for this unpublished fragment, though it seems a mistake to attach it to the published 'Loti and Huysmans' review under a title supplied by Bliss, 'Three French Writers'.[20] Synge reviews France's *Histoire Comique*,[21] placing it in the tradition of Molière's *Tartuffe* and Voltaire's *Candide* and praising

[19] Synge, CW, ii. 395.　　　[20] Ibid. 395–6.　　　[21] Synge MSS., 45.

the 'mastery of the Paris dialect' shown in it: neither Flaubert nor Balzac, 'with all their talent, had . . . this supremely fine sense for the shades of other languages'. Synge continues:

It is interesting to notice how many of the more important writers of the last quarter of a century have used dialogue for their medium, and thus kept up a direct relation with the spoken language, and the life of those who speak it. How much more effective, for instance, has been the varied treatment of dialogue by Maeterlinck, Oscar Wilde, Anatole France, Ibsen and others, from any elaborate prose produced during the same period. With Flaubert and Pater elaborate prose reached a climax after which only two developments were possible: one has given us Huysmans and Mallarmé who make pitiful attempts to gain new effects by literary devices, the other gives us a simple dialogue such as is seen in Anatole France.[22]

Truly these are sweeping generalizations, modestly stated as if they were truths, but Synge, now 30 or so, has earned the right to generalize. France was perhaps an unfortunate choice as the fulcrum of this earth-shaking argument—Synge expresses his own doubts in the next paragraph—but the argument will reappear in the preface to *The Playboy* with Synge himself as a much more satisfying *point d'appui*. The paragraph just quoted anticipates in theory Synge's own later practice.

It is shrewd of Grene to suggest that Synge's 'later violent rejection of "Des Esseintes and all his ugly crew" was most likely a reaction against an earlier admiration'.[23] Among the evidence adduced by Grene is the 1897–8 notebook (MS 4382) containing extracts from Huysmans and others:

A passage imitated from *Salammbô* suggests that Synge read these authors as models for his own creative work. His notes on Mallarmé and the Symbolists are not essays in literary criticism; but attempts of a creative artist to produce an aesthetic theory to suit his own work. *Etude Morbide* and *Vita Vecchia* were both written out of strong personal emotion—Synge's sense of isolation and loss following his rejection by Cherry Matheson. But the autobiographical element should not conceal the fact that in these early works Synge is imitating his French decadent masters.[24]

In mentioning the occasional similarities between Synge's reading and Joyce's above—I could have noted many more—I had in mind the possibility that Synge might have become, as Joyce did after taking up his (unintended) permanent residence in Paris in 1920, or in Zurich earlier, a cosmopolitan artist writing for an international intelligentsia rather than in the first place for his own countrymen. (Note, by the way, Joyce's early mastery of Dublin dialogue in stories like 'Grace' and

[22] Ibid. 396.   [23] Ibid. 12.   [24] Ibid.

'Ivy Day in the Committee Room'; Synge, if he had lived, would surely have admitted Joyce to a place beside Anatole France in this respect, while deploring his abandonment of the 'initial style' part-way through *Ulysses*.) Synge, however, made a conscious choice—doubtless an unconscious one too—which he was able to defend intellectually in 'Three French Writers' and elsewhere: he would become, like France, a local and a national artist. Thanks to his Aran experience, he was already beginning to see how this could be done. In September 1905, with *Riders to the Sea*, *The Shadow of the Glen*, and *The Well of the Saints* already behind him, he would write to Max Meyerfeld, his German translator, saying: 'I have given up Paris and give all my time to writing for the little Theatre we have in Dublin.'[25]

The Morals of Deirdre

I

It is what I have tried to do, to take the best of the stories, or whatever parts of each will fit best with one another, and in this way to give a fair account of Cuchulain's life and death. I left out a good deal I thought you would not care about for one reason or another.

This quotation comes from the 'Dedication of the Irish Edition to the People of Kiltartan', as given in the first English edition of *Cuchulain of Muirthemne*.[26] Lady Gregory makes clear what is meant by 'the Irish Edition' later in the dedication, saying, 'My friend and your friend the *Craoibhin Aoibhin[n]* has put Irish of to-day on some of these stories that I have set in order, for I am sure you will like to have the history of the heroes of Ireland told in the language of Ireland.'[27]

There follows immediately, in the English edition, that famous preface of Yeats's which begins:

I think this book is the best that has come out of Ireland in my time. Perhaps I should say that it is the best book that has ever come out of Ireland; for the stories which it tells are a chief part of Ireland's gift to the imagination of the world—and it tells them perfectly for the first time. Translators from the Irish have hitherto retold one story or the other from some other version. . . . But few of the stories really begin to exist until somebody has taken the best bits out of many manuscripts. Sometimes, as in Lady Gregory's version of Deirdre, a dozen manuscripts have to give their best before the beads are ready for the necklace.[28]

As we know, Yeats had been reading widely in scholarly and literary translations from the Irish before he ever met Lady Gregory: vol. i of

[25] Synge, *Collected Letters*, i. 127.
[26] Lady Gregory, *Cuchulain of Muirthemne: The Story of the Men of the Red Branch of Ulster Arranged and Put into English* (London: John Murray, 1902), v–vi.
[27] Ibid., p. vi.   [28] Ibid., p. vii.

his *Uncollected Prose,* written between 1886 and 1896, proves this conclusively. Yet it is often hard to say whether Yeats has read a particular translation, unless it tells a unique tale or contains a unique image that he could have found elsewhere—a condition rarely fulfilled by any literature so close to folklore as the Irish is. It is as though Yeats were in such a hurry to forget the learned translator's style that he forgot his name as well. Some of Yeats's judgements on style were odd, in any case: he speaks of Standish Hayes O'Grady's 'hateful Latin style', whereas the late David Greene admired it for preferring always the Teutonic word to the Romance word. Whitley Stokes, whose countless translations, says James F. Kenney, show 'an accuracy, felicity and conciseness that have never been surpassed',[29] is never mentioned by Yeats.

On one point, however, I am fairly confident: Yeats had not read Theophilus O'Flanagan's translation of *Loinges Mac n-Uisnigh,* published in *Transactions of the Gaelic Society of Dublin,* vol. i (1808).[30] If he had, he would never have written, in the preface already quoted, about 'Deirdre who might be some mild modern housewife but for her prophetic wisdom.' Even before she was born, this 'mild' creature made her mark by screaming in her mother's womb: it is this that inspires Cathbad's prophecy of evil to come, familiar from other versions. King Conor nevertheless had her brought up in seclusion to be his wife. Here is O'Flanagan's account of the formative event that shaped her choice of a love-object:

On a time [w]hen her tutor was slaying a veal calf in the snow, outside in the winter, to prepare food for her, she saw a raven drinking the blood in the snow: Then she says to Levarcam—Lovely truly would the man be who were marked with those three colours; that is, the hair like the raven, and the cheek like the blood, and the body like the snow.[31]

This is Levarcam's cue to reveal the existence of Naisi, who possessed all these attributes.

When Deirdre meets Naisi, she woos him; when he refuses her, she puts him to shame. Their conversation is not so literally bucolic as in the

---

[29] James F. Kenney, *Sources for the Early History of Ireland: An Introduction and Guide* (New York: Columbia Univ. Press, 1929) (all vols. published), i. 60.

[30] *Transactions of the Gaelic Society of Dublin, Established for the Investigation and Revival of Ancient Irish Literature* . . . (Dublin: printed by John Barlow, printer to the Society, 1808), (all vols. published), i. This volume consists of four fasciculi, each with separate title page and pagination, though the first title page is ostensibly that of the complete volume. The last and longest of the fasciculi is entitled *Deirdri, or, The Lamentable Fate of the Sons of Usnach . . . Literally Translated into English, from an Original Gaelic Manuscript . . . to Which Is Annexed, The Old Historic Account of the Facts on Which the Story Is Founded.* By Theophilus O'Flanagan . . . now Secretary to the Gaelic Society. Place, printer, and date are exactly as before. (Hereinafter referred to as O'Flanagan.)

[31] O'Flanagan, *Deirdri,* 155.

version chosen by Thomas Kinsella for *The Tain*, where Naisi is called 'a game young bull', Deirdre 'a fine heifer', and Conor 'the bull of this province'.[32] O'Flanagan's equivalent of Deirdre's pert answer to Naisi's opening gambit, 'The heifers grow big where there are no bulls', is 'It is natural for damsels to be mild where there are no youths'; she then says she 'would prefer a young man such as you' to the elderly Conor. Her way of shaming Naisi is not, as in Kinsella, to grab him by the ears, but to throw a ball at him, hitting him on the head.[33] By this means, she puts him under *geis* and *geasa* to run off with her. The story continues in similar unromantic vein until the treacherous killing of Naisi: Deirdre is handed over to Conor with her hands ignominiously tied behind her back. After the fighting was over, 'Deirdri was for a year indeed in the bed of Conor, and during that year she neither smiled nor laughed, nor took sufficiency of food, drink, or sleep, nor raised her head from her knee.'[34] At this point O'Flanagan translates from his text, apparently related to that in the Book of Leinster, two laments closely resembling those translated by Kinsella; both versions then conclude with almost identical accounts of Deirdre's suicide; here is O'Flanagan's:

What is it you hate most that you see?' says Conor. 'Thou thyself, and Eogan, son of Duthrecht [the slayer of Naisi],' says she. 'Thou shalt be a year in Eogan's bed then,' says Conor. Conor then gave her over to Eogan. They drove the next day to the assembly of Murthemny. She was behind Eogan in a chariot. She looked, that she might not see both her gallants, towards the earth. 'Well, Deirdri,' says Conor. 'it is the glance of a ewe between two rams, you cast between me and Eogan.' There was a large rock near; she hurled her head at the stone, so that she broke her skull, and killed herself.[35]

Like Kinsella's ending, this is strong stuff, even though O'Flanagan appears to omit the seemingly cynical explanation for Deirdre's suicide given by Kinsella: 'She had sworn that two men alive in the world together would never have her.'[36] This vow of hers has not been mentioned earlier in the tale and seems to me both artistically and psychologically wrong. She has already made clear by her behaviour and her poems that she longs for death: Conor's brutal jeer and the opportune rock make her choose a sudden death rather than a lingering one. These earlier, briefer, starker versions of the Deirdre story, in Middle Irish but clearly of Old Irish origin, do tell, however unromantically, of a woman's love that is stronger than the fear of death.

---

[32] *The Táin*, transl. Thomas Kinsella (Oxford: Oxford Univ. Press, 1970), 12.
[33] O'Flanagan, *Deirdri*, 157.   [34] Ibid. 167.   [35] Ibid. 177.
[36] *Táin*, 19. O'Flanagan's corresponding sentence, 'She looked . . . earth', may be a misreading and/or mistranslation of the *same* passage.

It is the versions in Classical Modern Irish, however, that present the romantic Deirdre who has become so familiar to us from Lady Gregory's narrative and the plays of A. E. (George Russell), Yeats and Synge. O'Flanagan himself published one of these under the title, 'The Death of the Children of Usnach', describing it as 'a poetic composition, founded upon historic truth',[37] whereas he called the older version 'The Ancient Historic Tale of the Death of the Children of Usnach'. He also quotes part of what Geoffrey Keating had to say about Deirdre in his seventeenth-century history of Ireland, *Foras Feasa ar Eirinn*, which gave the story of the three colours its widest literary currency.[38] Note that O'Flanagan prints his own editions—good or bad—of all the texts he translates on the facing pages. The Deirdre of his Romantic version, like the heroine of A. E.'s play, does not commit suicide but dies spontaneously: she 'flung herself upon Naisi in the grave, and died forthwith'.[39] When the story begins, she and Naisi are already in exile in Scotland, so that the question of who suggested the elopement does not arise.

This is perhaps all that need be said about the earliest tradition concerning Deirdre: let me add, however, that Douglas Hyde translated the 'oldest' version of the suicide, from the Book of Leinster, in *A Literary History of Ireland* (1899).[40] Yeats knew this work, of course, but he was so impatient with its predecessor, Hyde's *The Story of Early Gaelic Literature* (1895) (see the review in *Uncollected Prose*, i, 358–9) that he probably did not study it with any care.[41] Hyde's translation (p. 317) is almost identical with O'Flanagan's, though he had said earlier (p. 304n.) that O'Flanagan's text 'agrees closely with' BM manuscript Egerton 1782. It is amusing to read Yeats's review lamenting that Hyde is too much the scholar, now that the verdict of history maintains that he was not scholarly enough, though unmatched as a collector of folklore.

How many of our four authors were familiar with the earliest traditions about Deirdre will eventually become clear, but it can be said at once that Lady Gregory was. She includes Hyde and O'Flanagan in her notes on sources at the end of *Cuchulain of Muirthemne*,[42] and also Eugene O'Curry, who had published a similar text from the Yellow Book of Lecan, with translation, in *Atlantis* III (1862), the learned journal of Newman's Catholic University in Dublin.

---

[37] O'Flanagan, *Deirdri*, 12; for 'The Death of the Children of Usnach' see O'Flanagan, *Deirdri*, 16–135; for the 'Historic Tale' (*Longes Mac n-Uisnigh*) see O'Flanagan, *Deirdri*, 146–77.

[38] Ibid. 7.

[39] Ibid. 127.

[40] Douglas Hyde, *A Literary History of Ireland from the Earliest Times to the Present Day* (London: T. Fisher Unwin, 1899).

[41] Yeats nevertheless recommended the 1895 work as *History* [sic] *of Early Gaelic Literature*: *Letters of W. B. Yeats*, ed. Allan Wade (New York: Macmillan, 1955), 247.

[42] Gregory, *Cuchulain*, 359–60.

II

The most important thing to note about A. E.'s *Deirdre: A Legend in Three Acts*, first performed by the Irish National Dramatic Society on 2 April 1902, is that it was written before the publication of *Cuchulain of Muirthemne*. Herbert V. Fackler, in his extremely useful edition of the play, reminds us that the three acts were first published by Standish James O'Grady in his *All-Ireland Review* at irregular intervals between 6 July 1901 and 15 February 1902. (Lady Gregory's and Yeats's prefaces, already quoted, bear the date '*March* 1902'.) Fackler says of its sources, 'In its general tone, *Deirdre* is a curious blend of A. E.'s own mysticism and impressionism and the Nineteenth Century Deirdre materials of Samuel Ferguson (*Deirdre*, 1880), Aubrey de Vere (*The Sons of Usnach*, 1884) and R. D. Joyce (*Deirdre*, 1876).'[43] Without having studied and compared these sources as carefully as Fackler has, I have only the right to say that one would indeed expect A. E. to prefer poetic versions, rather than the more literal translations of scholars like O'Flanagan and O'Curry; both Ferguson and Joyce in fact knew Modern Irish, while Ferguson had more than a smattering of Old Irish. Not that A. E. really cared: if need be, his intuition, he thought, could supply him with the oldest, truest version of any myth. In *The Candle of Vision* (1918) he was to reveal the primal language of man: 'Aum! Hek! Wal! Ak! Lub! Mor! Ma!' as James Joyce remembered it in *Ulysses*. ('Hek' should be 'Hel'.)[44]

Whatever A. E.'s sources, his characterization of Deirdre would not be out of place in a parish magazine. If she woos Naisi, it is only in a dream: 'Then in my dream I came nigh him and whispered in his ear, and pointed the way through the valley to our dun.' When Naisi finds his way there during her waking hours, she is obedient and not coy: 'I will go with thee where thou goest,' she says to Naisi, as soon as he asks her. (A. E.'s phrasing seems limp beside the King James's 'Whither thou goest, I will go.')[45] Deirdre obeys the rather stupid Naisi always; when he gets angry with her for insisting on Concobar's treachery, she cries out:

Have pity on me, Naisi! Your words, like hot lightnings, sear my heart. Never again will I seek to stay thee. But speak to me with love once more, Naisi. Do not bend your brows on me with anger; for, Oh! but a little time remains for us to love![46]

[43] Herbert V. Fackler, 'Introduction', in George W. Russell (A. E.), *Deirdre: A Legend in Three Acts*, Irish Drama Series 4 (Chicago: De Paul Univ., 1970), 2–3.

[44] James Joyce, *Ulysses* (Harmondsworth, Middlesex: Penguin Books in association with The Bodley Head, rpt. with corrections, 1971), 475.

[45] Russell, *Deirdre*, 12–13, 14. Ruth i.16.

[46] Ibid. 22.

We are not surprised when Naisi admits she is a better chess-player than he. Throughout Act III, thanks to her firm grip on reality, she is very frightened and keeps begging Naisi to save their lives by doing something sensible, but when he rebukes her for this, all she says is, 'I am only a woman, who has given her life into your hands, and you chide me for my love.'[47] At this point one wishes that Deirdre would turn into a Shavian heroine and denounce the idiocies of the manly man and the womanly woman. All A. E.'s heroine can think of is to lay her head on Naisi's dead body and expire with indecent haste.

Note that A. E. called his play a 'legend', as if Deirdre was to supply a paradigm of womanly behaviour somewhat akin to that found in the lives of the more depressing female saints. Like Standish James O'Grady, whom he greatly admired, A. E. thought the purpose of heroic literature was to prompt similar heroism in later ages. O'Grady's treatment of Deirdre in *History of Ireland*, vol. i (1878)[48] focuses on her importance as a cause of the enmity between Ulster and Connacht. Following Keating, I think, he stresses Cathvah's prophecy: 'It is the destruction of the wide territories of Ulla that thou bearest in thy womb, O lady— wasting wars and conflagration and blood.'[49] O'Grady mentions not one scream but three, yet he avoids saying that it was the foetus who screamed. The adolescent and adult Deirdre is completely without personality: the story of the three colours is omitted; Naisi is the wooer, but there are no details of the wooing; Deirdre is against returning from Alba, but nobody pays any attention; finally, we are told that she was 'seized' by Concobar when the sons of Usna were killed, but we hear nothing of her death by suicide or any other means.[50] Having played her part in causing 'the wars of the Tân-bo-Cooalney', she is cast aside, apparently without a glimmer of pity for her tragic fate. I think it is time we admitted that Standish O'Grady was a fine writer for boys, who just happened to be first in the field with a more or less complete English version of the *Táin Bó Cuailnge*. Fools rush in where angels fear to tread.

Yeats's *Deirdre* as we now have it is a marvel of tight construction, a one-act play full of tension and surprise. Although he mentions Lady Gregory's version as 'the best', his own characterization of Deirdre shows a mature, scheming woman, faithful to Naoise but willing to flirt with Conchubar in order to buy time and arouse Naoise's jealousy while escape is still possible. After Naoise's death, I find it hard not to

---

[47] Ibid. 28.
[48] Standish O'Grady, *History of Ireland: The Heroic Period*, (London: Sampson Low; Dublin: E. Ponsonby, 1878), i. 113–19.
[49] Ibid. 115.
[50] Ibid. 119.

make comparisons between Yeats's Deirdre and Shakespeare's Cleopatra after the death of Antony. Deirdre here is more an antique Roman than a Celt; like Cleopatra, her death makes her heroic, but actually *her* life is blameless: she does not have to atone by her courageous death for sins like those of the priggish Egyptian. Her own fault, if fault it be, was to make the first move when she met Naoise: 'It was my fault. I only should be punished. / The very moment these eyes fell on him, / I told him; I held out my hands to him; / How could he refuse?' As this quotation suggests, *Deirdre* contains some of the blankest blank verse Yeats ever wrote, the kind a West End actress like Mrs Patrick Campbell could speak as prose. I have an uneasy feeling that Deirdre's emphasis on her sexuality—'my veins being hot'—is as spurious as Mrs Pat's; anything I know of the actress suggests that she was born a comedy star, and that on or off the stage she could hint at passion without ever having experienced it. Think of the genuinely tragic play Yeats could have written in old age, basing it on the Middle Irish versions. Deirdre would have had no need to boast of her sexiness, for her actions would speak louder than words, and her end need be no more sordid than Cuchulain's in *The Death of Cuchulain*.

For me, Synge's *Deirdre of the Sorrows* is ultimately the greatest disappointment among these three plays. He knew, with a certainty that Yeats lacked, just how much Lady Gregory had left out; in fact, his review of *Cuchulain of Muirthemne* ends with this warning:

For readers who take more than literary interest in these stories a word of warning may be needed. Lady Gregory has omitted certain barbarous features, such as the descriptions of the fury of Cuchulain, and in consequence, some of her versions have a much less archaic aspect than the original texts. Students of mythology will read this book with interest, yet for their severer studies they must still turn to the works of German scholars, and others, who translated without hesitation all that has come down to us in the MSS.[51]

This of course was written in 1902, before Synge had perpetrated the two most unconventional—and perhaps amoral—comedies in English, *The Well of the Saints* and *The Playboy of the Western World*. The suggestion that the literary man or woman can be content with a bowdlerized text falls strangely on our ears today, though perhaps fashions will change again.

It is a little surprising, then, that the mature Synge should himself omit 'certain barbarous features' from his Deirdre at the risk of creating a tragedy less full of pity and terror than his two supposedly 'comic' masterpieces. Act I of *Deirdre of the Sorrows* shows Deirdre as the

---

[51] J. M. Synge, *Collected Works, Prose*, ed. Alan Price (Oxford: Oxford Univ. Press, 1966) ii. 370.

wooer of Naisi, but Synge is careful to make her behaviour acceptable by first presenting Conchubor as an ageing, egotistical man who loses dignity in his eagerness to ignore her indifference to him. All through the play, Synge seems anxious lest his heroine should lose the sympathy of an Edwardian audience: he goes to extraordinary lengths to convince us that her suicide is a virtuous act rather than a sin, an entering into communion with the dead sons of Usnach rather than an offence against the community.

The second act is the strangest, a howling anachronism from beginning to end. Consider this typical speech of Deirdre's:

It's lonesome this place, having happiness like ours, till I'm asking each day will this day match yesterday, and will tomorrow take a good place beside the same day in the year that's gone, and wondering all times is it a game worth playing, living on until you're dried and old, and our joy is gone for ever.[52]

This evokes nothing earlier or more primitive than, say, Anna Karenin's disillusioning idyll with Vronsky. The neurotic fear of age and ugliness which fills Deirdre's mind from this point onwards is equally modern, and totally anachronistic for an era in which life expectancy was briefer than the soul of wit. Compare her eagerness to return to Ulster with the reluctance of A. E.'s Deirdre; surely for once A. E. has the right end of the stick? I feel that this anti-life theme may form part of Synge's elaborate attempt to justify her suicide, or at least to prepare the audience for it. It also of course suggests that he himself is trying to view his own possibly imminent death with a like fortitude and even contempt.

What, then, is the cause of all this tampering with or ignoring of the most tragic version of the most sorrowful tale in Irish literature? Is it art or morality? In a neo-classical period, one could blame the ideal of decorum: it is the only viable excuse for Macpherson's massacre of the Deirdre story, referred to already, which he called *Dar-thula*. Although Macpherson virtually invented Romanticism for others, he himself was a neo-classicist, and followed *Ossian* with a prose translation of the *Iliad*. O'Flanagan's splendid prose versions of Deirdre's laments in the Romantic tale were at times plagiarized by Hyde and Lady Gregory, yet he apologetically inserted in his notes 'The English Versification, from the literal Translation, by Mr WILLIAM LEAHY'. This Leahy's anachronistic verses resemble Tate and Brady's translations of the Psalms—without their talent. He had clearly never set eyes on Wordsworth and Coleridge's *Lyrical Ballads*.

[52] J. M. Synge, *Collected Works, Plays* 11, ed. Ann Saddlemyer (Oxford: Oxford Univ. Press, 1968), iv. 219.

There is no doubt in my mind that morality, not art, is the culprit: these children and grandchildren of Church of Ireland Evangelicals experienced the greatest difficulty in freeing themselves, not from dogma but from puritanical habits of behaviour. Much has been said of Irish Catholic puritanism, but in truth it was a skin-deep reaction to Evangelical Protestantism dating from about 1850. As one had every right to expect, literary prudery in English was demolished by an Irish Catholic, James Joyce, a worthy successor to Chaucer and Rabelais.

The Tinker's Wedding

I

PEACHUM [to POLLY]. Married! . . . Do you think your mother and I should have
    lived comfortably so long together if ever we had been married? Baggage!
MRS PEACHUM. I knew she was always a proud slut, and now the wench hath
    played the fool and married, because, forsooth, she would do like the gentry!
                                            John Gay, *The Beggar's Opera*, I, 8.

We need not speculate about whether Synge knew *The Beggar's Opera* or not—he died long before its famous revival in the 1920s—for we know that he found the essentials of *The Tinker's Wedding* in County Wicklow. In his brief essay or reportage, 'At a Wicklow Fair', the following passage occurs:

Then a woman came up and spoke to the tinker, and they went down the road together into the village. 'That man is a great villain,' said the herd [shepherd], when he was out of hearing. 'One time he and his woman went up to a priest in the hills and asked him would he wed them for half a sovereign, I think it was. The priest said it was a poor price, but he'd wed them surely if they'd make him a tin can along with it. "I will, faith," said the tinker, "and I'll come back when it's done." They went off then and in three weeks they came back, and they asked the priest a second time would he wed them. "Have you the tin can?" said the priest. "We have not," said the tinker; "we had it made at the fall of night, but the ass gave it a kick this morning the way it isn't fit for you at all." "Go on now," says the priest. "It's a pair of rogues and schemers you are, and I won't wed you at all." They went off then, and they were never married to this day.'[53]

As a clue to Synge's characterization of the Priest in *The Tinker's Wedding*, it is worth asking who first told the story of the priest and the tinker—assuming it is a true story and not a piece of folklore. As told by the herd to Synge, it seems to illustrate the incorrigibility of tinkers rather than the avarice of priests. Very likely the priest himself would

---

[53] Synge, CW, ii, 228–9.

tell the story in just this way, laughing half-contemptuously at the effrontery of the tinkers. A similar construction can be put on the behaviour of the priest in the final version of *The Tinker's Wedding*: he is a generous enough man according to his lights, although by no means a saint, but he resents being 'played for a sucker', as most of us do.

Although Synge worked on *The Tinker's Wedding* again after he had perfected his special mode of comedy in *The Well of the Saints* and *The Playboy of the Western World*, it was first written, as he notes at the end of his preface to the published play, 'about the time I was working at "Riders to the Sea", and "In the Shadow of the Glen."'[54] One might be tempted to think that the weakness of the finished play stems mainly from the minimal nature of the anecdote on which it was based, but Synge had no more to work with initially in *The Well of the Saints* or *The Playboy*. Ann Saddlemyer allows us to watch Synge extracting, step by step, most of the possibilities from the fundamental situation in the latter play. The various outlines for *The Playboy* as a whole and for the individual acts[55] show us Synge's constructive genius in a nutshell. It is a pity that Professor Saddlemyer does not allow us to watch the growth of *The Well of the Saints* in similar detail. About the growth of *The Tinker's Wedding*, Professor Saddlemyer reveals to us rather more and rather less than we really need to know. Was it necessary to print *both* the first manuscript draft and the first typescript,[56] when they are basically so similar, being the only two extant one-act versions of the play? Both correspond roughly to Act II of the final version. The tinker couple are getting ready for the wedding when a woman from a neighbouring cottage goes to the well and, as she returns, finds that her can is leaking. On the spur of the moment, the male tinker sells her the new can he has just made for the priest; when the latter appears impatiently at the door of the church, the tinkers tell him that they have already left the can with his housekeeper. The priest, knowing that his housekeeper is away, becomes indignant at their ruse and refuses to marry them. He sees the police approaching along the road and threatens to denounce the tinkers to them, alleging their thefts of an ass and hay as in the final version. The tinkers flee without tying the priest up or suffering his Latin malediction. The typescript is somewhat longer and richer in detail than the manuscript, but neither of these brief one-acts allows any scope for the development of character. The priest is a conventional authority-figure, fat and very short-tempered. The young tinker woman (here called Nora, rather than Sarah, Casey) has none of the capriciousness that she shows in the finished play. All she wants is not

54 Synge, CW, iv. 4.   55 Ibid. 294–304.   56 Ibid. 272–84.

to be called bad names any more when selling cans at the fair. Her intended husband does not show the reluctance to marry of his counterpart in the finished play and need not be spurred on by jealousy. Mary Byrne is already a little more firmly drawn than the other tinkers, but she is neither bawdy nor alcoholic. Part of one speech of hers, however, survives almost unchanged from the first typescript to the final version; indeed, it is present in the original manuscript, though very differently worded there:

> MARY [*to the priest*] It's a long time we are now going round on the roads, father and son and his son after him or maybe mother and daughter and her daughter again, and what is it we wanted any time with going up into the church, and swearing—I'm told there's swearing in it—a word no man would believe? Or what is it we wanted with putting dirty rings on our fingers would be cutting our skin maybe in the cold nights when we'ld be taking the ass from the shafts, and pulling the straps the time they'ld be slippy with going round under the heavens in the rain falling?[57]

It is no accident that Synge retained this speech so tenaciously, for in a sense it is the 'moral' of the whole play. The tinkers and 'the establishment' are too much at odds for any compromise to be possible. If they move one step from their pagan—possibly even prelapsarian—world, they might as well travel the whole way and give up their nomadic life altogether. This Synge would not want them to do, for reasons that may be guessed, but that I shall try to make explicit later. The priest is not tied up in a sack when Mary delivers this speech in the two earliest drafts. In the typescript version he answers her sharply: 'What is it I care if the like of you are married or not? It's herself is after talking me round with the long tongue she has.'[58] This gives Mary the opportunity for a reply that occurs later and in truncated form in the final version:

> MARY. Herself is young, God help her, and the young don't be knowing any time the thing they want. But I've had one man and another man, and a power of children, and it's little need we had of your swearing, or your rings with it, to get us our bit to eat, and our bit to drink, and our time of love when we were young men or women, and were fine to look at.[59]

In these speeches Mary is saying very much what Peachum says in the quotation from The Beggar's Opera given above. Professor Saddlemyer dates the original manuscript draft from summer 1902 and the first typescript from autumn 1903. In spring 1904 comes the first two-act version, typescript 'B'. I wish that Professor Saddlemyer had printed more of this version than merely the passages, afterwards omitted,

---

[57] Ibid. 284.   [58] Ibid.   [59] Ibid.

showing the tinker children and the village children. Obviously, once Synge had decided to write the play in two acts, the interview in which Sarah persuades the Priest to marry her and Michael became an indispensable part of Act I. I believe that the weakest point of the play as we have it lies in the ambiguous treatment of the priest. Mary Byrne's character is already implicit in the speeches quoted from typescript 'A', and she only needs to be expanded into a sort of female Falstaff. Sarah's and Michael's characters, as developed, largely embody archetypal male and female attitudes toward marriage. But the Priest of Act I is viewed more sympathetically by the author and the tinkers than the Priest of Act II and his counterpart in the one-act drafts. Did Synge mean us to understand that the Priest is drunk in Act I and sober in Act II? If so, he might have dared to be more explicit in drafts than in the published version. The latter, indeed, is explicit enough up to a point:

MICHAEL. Whisht. I hear some one coming the road.
SARAH [*looking out right*]. It's some one coming forward from the doctor's door.
MICHAEL. It's often his reverence does be in there playing cards or drinking a sup, or singing songs, until the dawn of day.
SARAH. It's a big boast of a man with a long step on him and a trumpeting voice. It's his reverence surely; and if you have the ring done, it's a great bargain we'll make now and he after drinking his glass.[60]

The references to drinking, together with the Priest's willingness to sit and drink some of Mary's porter, suggest that he 'has a sup taken', but Synge drops no hint of it in the stage directions of the published version. The Priest is at first rather brusque with Sarah in Act I and finds it hard to grasp the idea that she wants to get married. Then he is astonished at her suggestion that he marry her without payment. But eventually he agrees to marry her 'for a pound only, and that's making it a sight cheaper than I'd make it for one of my own pairs is living here in the place'.[61] When she pretends to weep, insisting that the price is still too high, he tries to comfort her and reduces his fee to fifteen shillings and the gallon can.

When Mary Byrne comes in and presses him to drink, he finally consents '*with resignation*'. Then he relaxes completely and becomes very human:

PRIEST. If it's starving you are itself, I'm thinking it's well for the like of you that do be drinking when there's drouth on you, and lying down to sleep when your legs are stiff. [*He sighs gloomily.*] What would you do if it was the like of myself you were, saying Mass with your mouth dry, and running

---

[60] Ibid. 11, 13.   [61] Ibid. 15.

east and west for a sick call maybe, and hearing the rural people again and they saying their sins?

MARY [*with compassion*]. It's destroyed you must be hearing the sins of the rural people on a fine spring.

PRIEST [*with despondency*]. It's a hard life I'm telling you, a hard life, Mary Byrne; and there's the bishop coming in the morning, and he an old man, would have you destroyed if he seen a thing at all.[62]

The Priest may sound rather foolish and indiscreet, but he has won some of our sympathy, and he wins more when, appalled by Mary Byrne's ignorance of and irreverence toward prayer, he reduces his fee by a further five shillings; as he says to Sarah, 'I wouldn't be easy in my soul if I left you growing into an old, wicked heathen the like of her.'[63] Admittedly, from the point of view of the average Irish Catholic sixty-five years ago, to treat a priest as a comic character at all was in the worst of taste. Yet the basic kindliness of Synge's Priest in Act I could lessen the sense of shock at his presentation as a figure of fun. At his first appearance in Act II the Priest is somewhat impatient but still entirely human:

PRIEST [*crying out*]. Come along now. Is it the whole day you'd keep me here saying my prayers, and I getting my death with not a bit in my stomach, and my breakfast in ruins, and the Lord Bishop maybe driving on the road to-day?[64]

When he finds the empty bottles in the bundle where the can should be, he is deeply hurt:

PRIEST. Did ever any man see the like of that? To think you'd be putting deceit on me, and telling lies to me, and I going to marry you for a little sum wouldn't marry a child.[65]

When Sarah threatens to kill Mary for the trick she has played in stealing and selling the can, the Priest is still more sorry than angry: 'wasn't I a big fool to have to do with you when it's nothing but distraction and torment I get from the kindness of my heart?'[66] It is not until Sarah begins to threaten him with personal violence that he in return threatens the tinkers with the police. Sarah then promises that the tinkers will smash all his windows and steal all his hens in revenge. Not till then does Synge insert the stage direction '*losing his temper finally*'. The tinkers' response to the Priest's rage is instant and violent: they bind and gag him and make him swear not to tell the police if they free him. He keeps his word, for, as he says in his last speech, 'I've sworn not to

62 Ibid. 19.   63 Ibid. 23.   64 Ibid. 39.
65 Ibid. 41.   66 Ibid. 43.

call the hand of man upon your crimes to-day; but I haven't sworn I wouldn't call the fire of heaven from the hand of the Almighty God.'[67]

As we review the Priest's behaviour in Act II, it perhaps does not seem very inconsistent with that in Act I. What really shocks us is the rough treatment he receives from the tinkers. We have come to sympathize with him, and he simply does not deserve either the brutality actually practised upon him or the threat to drown him. Even more than Pegeen's burning of the Playboy's shin with a lighted sod, this violence seems forced, melodramatic, and aesthetically out of place in a comedy. Aesthetic considerations aside, it was bound to offend pious members of the audience. Furthermore, it lacks credibility. No tinker not out of his mind with drink would have dared to assault a priest in Synge's lifetime. And if Michael refuses to believe that 'the Lord would blight [his] members'[68] for laying hands on a priest, why should he be afraid a few moments later of the Priest's Latin malediction? Synge first used the ending with the Priest tied in sacking in typescript 'D', which Professor Saddlemyer dates from spring 1906. If her dating is correct, this twist of the plot was not added defiantly by Synge after the hostile reception of *The Playboy* in 1907. He may have felt that he had not established a strong enough contrast between the attitudes of the priest and the tinkers earlier in the play; when the Priest laments the hardness of his lot in Act I, he seems to be coming round to the view of life held by the tinkers, and this is precisely where the subtlest humour of the play is to be found. Suddenly, at the end of Act II, Synge changes key and brings the whole situation to the verge of tragedy. There is no element of slapstick about the tying up of the Priest—it is done in deadly earnest. *The Tinker's Wedding* would have been a better play if the Priest and the tinkers had preserved their wary mutual respect and envy, a sort of sportsmanlike antagonism, throughout both acts.

Certainly violence is an essential part of the Irish folk stereotype of the tinker, along with lying, wheedling, thieving, drunkenness, and lechery. But the violence is usually thought of as directed against fellow tinkers, male and female, rather than against established society. Stealing, begging, and fortune-telling are far safer ways of overcoming that enemy than outright violence, which is always countered by the violence of the police. Sarah threatens Mary with violence for stealing the can, but never puts her threat into practice. It would have been better if the violence against the Priest had been left as a mere threat also. By putting it into execution, the tinkers forfeit our sympathy, and at the same time we are temporarily forced to view the Priest as a martyr, a role quite out of keeping with our idea of his character.

[67] Ibid. 49.   [68] Ibid. 45.

II

I have more than once put forward the view elsewhere that Syngean comedy is essentially 'mock-pastoral' in form, to use William Empson's term for describing works like *The Beggar's Opera*. (As a matter of fact, John Gay himself described an earlier work of his, *The Shepherd's Week* (1714), as a mock-pastoral.) *The Tinker's Wedding* is a fair sample of the genre, but all Synge's four comedies fit into it, and none better than *The Well of the Saints*. Synge himself described *The Shadow of the Glen* and *The Well of the Saints* each as 'a play' in the published versions, whereas *The Tinker's Wedding* and *The Playboy of the Western World* each went forth as 'a comedy', but no definition of comedy that will fit the second pair can exclude the former two. In all these four plays, the values of an 'anti-society' of tramps, blind beggars, tinkers, and criminals are contrasted with those of established society—and shown to be equally valid. Peachum, the informer and receiver of stolen goods in *The Beggar's Opera* (I, 1), sets forth the equation as follows:

A lawyer is an honest employment, so is mine. Like me too, he acts in a double capacity, both against rogues, and for 'em; for 'tis but fitting that we should protect and encourage cheats, since we live by them.

In each of Synge's mock-pastoral plays the comic hero (or heroine) is an anti-hero, owing no allegiance to any but the anti-society. He and/or she is banished from the stage before the final curtain, and established society in effect says 'Good riddance', but our hearts go with the Tramp and Nora, with Martin and Mary Doul, with Christy Mahon, and we have nothing but mocking laughter for the solid folk who remain behind. Pegeen's last wild cry tells us that her heart too has gone with 'the only playboy of the western world'.[69] Do our hearts go with the tinkers at the end of *The Tinker's Wedding*, when, as the stage direction tells us, '*They rush out, leaving the* PRIEST *master of the situation*'?[70] That is precisely the question I have been trying to answer in the first part of this essay. For the reasons stated, my own subjective answer is negative. The tinkers have forfeited my sympathy, yet I am not sure that Synge intended them to do so. It would be illogical to claim, however, that the end of this comedy *must* repeat the 'formula' of the other three, since the formula is only arrived at by induction from those three plays and was never given conscious shape by Synge himself. What we can say with certainty is that *The Tinker's Wedding* defines the anti-society and claims for it an equality with established society. Mary's last speech to the Priest, which has already been quoted in draft form, affirms the

---

[69] Ibid. 173.   [70] Ibid. 49.

validity of the tinker way of life: 'it's little need we ever had of the like of you to get us our bit to eat, and our bit to drink, and our time of love when we were young men and women, and were fine to look at'.[71] She says nothing about the satisfying of other than material needs, but then the Priest as presented by Synge has little to say about spiritual satisfactions. Perhaps this is where the real weakness in his characterization lies. He envies the tinkers because they can eat and drink and sleep whenever they want to. His spiritual duties are presented merely as physical burdens: 'saying Mass with your mouth dry, and running east and west for a sick call maybe, and hearing the rural people again and they saying their sins'.[72] Finally, he envies the tinkers their freedom from obedience to authority, while he lives constantly in fear of his bishop.

It is true that the Priest is horrified by Mary Byrne's heathenism and asks God to have mercy on her soul, but he offers no positive spiritual values, only the possibility of escape from damnation. As the tinkers do not believe in an after-life, they are not impressed. They run in fear from the priest at the end of the play only because he is threatening to bring down immediate fire from heaven and end their lives at once. Sarah's one clearly stated motive for wanting to be married is worldly: from this day there will no one have a right to call me a dirty name'.[73]

Mary Byrne points out that a wedding ring will not keep Sarah from growing old and losing her beauty, and goes on to suggest that it may increase the pains of childbirth: 'it's the grand ladies do be married in silk dresses, with rings of gold, that do pass any woman with their share of torment in the hour of birth'.[74] This possibility almost puts Sarah off marriage altogether until she decides that Mary doesn't know anything about 'the fine ladies'.

I have said earlier that the tinkers' world possibly antedates the Fall of Man. As we know from God's curse on Eve, the pains of childbirth did not exist before the Fall, and in this respect at least the tinker women are closer to the Garden of Eden than their bourgeois counterparts. On the other hand, the tinkers are not exempt from the curses of death and work. But they seem never to have eaten of the Tree of Knowledge, for they have no sense of sin. A wholly paradisal anti-society is to be found only in *The Well of the Saints*. In Act I of that play we do not realize that the blind beggars Martin and Mary Doul are Adam and Eve in Eden, for they seem old and ugly and weak and poor. But in Act II, after they have regained their sight, we may suddenly realize that the curse of Adam has belatedly fallen upon Martin. In the first place, now that he can see, he must work: 'In the sweat of thy face shalt thou eat

---

[71] Ibid.   [72] Ibid. 19.
[73] Ibid. 35.   [74] Ibid. 37.

bread.' In the second place, his newly opened eyes lead him to sin through his desire for Molly Byrne. In the third place, though he has always been subject to death, he never became aware of it until he could see 'the old women rotting for the grave'.[75] No wonder he is happy to lose his sight again in Act III and resents it when the Saint tries to drag him from his private Eden by curing his blindness once more. The other comedies cannot offer quite such an Edenic life in the anti-society, but the Tramp's last two speeches in *The Shadow of the Glen* suggest that the world of nature will at least be kinder to Nora than the world of men. Here is the second of these speeches:

Tramp [*at the door*]. Come along with me now, lady of the house, and it's not my blather you'll be hearing only, but you'll be hearing the herons crying out over the black lakes, and you'll be hearing the grouse, and the owls with them, and the larks and the big thrushes when the days are warm, and it's not from the like of them you'll be hearing a talk of getting old like Peggy Cavanagh, and losing the hair off you, and the light of your eyes, but it's fine songs you'll be hearing when the sun goes up, and there'll be no old fellow wheezing the like of a sick sheep close to your ear.[76]

More paradisal still are Christy's visions of his married life with Pegeen in Act III of *The Playboy*:

Let you wait to hear me talking till we're astray in Erris when Good Friday's by, drinking a sup from a well, and making mighty kisses with our wetted mouths, or gaming in a gap of sunshine with yourself stretched back unto your necklace in the flowers of the earth.[77]

Christy even thinks he'd 'feel a kind of pity for the Lord God is all ages sitting lonesome in his golden chair'.[78]

But unless one is happily blind like Martin and Mary Doul, such harmony with nature is only for the young. Mary Byrne's final speech in Act I of *The Tinker's Wedding* foreshadows the terror of old age and the slow, certain approach of death that haunts every page of *Deirdre of the Sorrows* and makes Deirdre eager to die while she is still young and unwithered:

Maybe the two of them [Michael and Sarah] have a good right to be walking out the little short while they'd be young; but if they have itself, they'll not keep Mary Byrne from her full pint when the night's fine, and there's a dry moon in the sky . . . Jemmy Neill's a decent lad; and he'll give me a good drop for the can; and maybe if I keep near the peelers to-morrow for the first bit of the fair, herself won't strike me at all; and if she does itself, what's a little stroke on your head

75 Synge, CW, iii. 117.
76 Ibid. 57.
77 Ibid. iv. 149.
78 Ibid. 147.

beside sitting lonesome on a fine night, hearing the dogs barking, and the bats squeaking, and you saying over, it's a short while only till you die.[79]

If Synge had presented Sarah as believing that marriage in church would guarantee her eternal life, thus freeing her from Mary's anguish, the struggle between established society and the anti-society in *The Tinker's Wedding* would be far more intense than it is, more on a level with that in *The Well of the Saints*. As it is, neither the world of the tinkers nor the world of the Priest seems to have much to offer an old woman like Mary Byrne.

III

It is natural to think of the works produced by the Irish Literary Revival as what Empson would call 'versions of pastoral'. Idealization of the Irish peasant was widespread during the early stages of the movement, while most of the writers were still much higher than the peasant in the social scale and thus neither saw him clearly nor felt him as a personal threat—except, of course, when he began a rent strike.

Perhaps the most interesting Irish pastoral manifestation was linguistic. As Empson writes, 'The essential trick of the old pastoral, which was felt to imply a beautiful relation between rich and poor, was to make simple people express strong feelings . . . in learned and fashionable language.'[80]

But the new Irish pastoral, written by members of the middle and upper classes, sought 'to make simple people express strong feelings' in a stylized version of the language of the simple people themselves. In Synge's *Deirdre of the Sorrows*, for instance, high and low speak the same language—a dialect almost identical with that spoken by the tinkers in *The Tinker's Wedding* or the fisherfolk in *Riders to the Sea*. Similarly, Lady Gregory retells the Old Irish sagas in 'Kiltartanese', a stylization of the dialect spoken by her own tenants. The Gaelic League sought to revive Modern Irish, native speakers of which were among the poorest of the poor. Many of the most enthusiastic Leaguers were members of the middle and upper classes, yet they chose as their linguistic norm not the Classical Modern Irish of the bardic poets but current colloquial Irish, *cainnt na ndaoine* ('the speech of the people'). In the end, though, an astonishing amount of the pastoral writing turned out to be mock-pastoral. Not only Synge's plays but Yeats's are full of mock-pastoral figures. Consider the following list of characters from Yeats (the plays are listed in the order of *Collected Plays*):

[79] Ibid. 27.
[80] William Empson, *Some Versions of Pastoral* (London, Chatto and Windus, 1935), 11.

The Old Woman in *Cathleen Ni Houlihan*;
The Tramp in *The Pot of Broth*;
The Blind Man and the Fool in *On Baile's Strand*;
The Fool in *The Hour-Glass*;
The Beggars in *The Unicorn from the Stars*;
The Players in *The Player Queen*;
The Lame Man and the Blind Man in *The Cat and the Moon*;
The Stroller in *The King of the Great Clock Tower*;
The Fool in *The Herne's Egg*;
The Old Man and the Boy in *Purgatory*;
The Blind Man in *The Death of Cuchulain*.

All of these are members of the anti-society and almost all must make their way by begging and/or stealing; the Players and the Stroller may earn their living, but established society regards them as pariahs: perhaps all the musicians in the plays should be included along with them. *The Pot of Broth*, first performed in October 1902, antedates all of Synge's plays: it was the first comedy of the Literary Revival in which a mock-pastoral character outwitted settled folk—in this case a small farmer and his wife—and got off scot-free. In at least two other early plays by Yeats, *The Land of Heart's Desire* and *Cathleen Ni Houlihan*, the values of Irish peasant life had been implicitly rejected. In other words, the mock-pastoral figure, be he tramp or tinker, stands opposed to peasant society in the same way that the artist was believed to stand opposed to bourgeois society. Synge makes this equation of tramp with artist absolutely explicit in 'The Vagrants of Wicklow.':

In the middle classes the gifted son of a family is always the poorest—usually a writer or artist with no sense for speculation—and in a family of peasants, where the average comfort is just over penury, the gifted son sinks also, and is soon a tramp on the roadside.[81]

It is unimportant to our examination of *The Tinker's Wedding* whether this observation of Synge's be sociologically sound or a piece of arrant mythmaking: Synge believed it and based his sympathy for the tinker way of life upon it. But the professional and land-owning classes were not destined to control the Irish theatre for ever. Protestant (Yeats, Synge, Lady Gregory, Lennox Robinson, Lord Dunsany) or Catholic (George Moore, Edward Martyn), they eventually gave way to the lower-middle and working classes. It happened that O'Casey, the first working-class Irish dramatist, showed great sympathy for mock-pastoral characters like 'Captain' Boyle and 'Joxer' Daly in *Juno and the Paycock*, though

---

[81] Synge, *CW*, ii. 202.

in his Communist Party days he ought to have condemned them as members of the *Lumpenproletariat*. But if we turn to George Shiels, who, as Robert Hogan so rightly says, 'wrote the typical Abbey play of the 1930's and 1940's',[82] we find the true antidote to mock-pastoral comedy. Shiels mainly writes about and presumably came from the small shopkeeper class in a small town—Ballymoney, County Antrim. In his two most successful plays, *The Rugged Path* and *The Summit*, however, he focuses on a law-abiding family of farmers, the Tanseys, and their struggle against the lawless Dolis family. Peter Dolis murders an old man for a small sum of money; although Michael Tansey does not want to earn the hated title of informer, he finally decides to give evidence against Peter, who is acquitted, however, and returns from his trial to terrorize the Tanseys. Here *The Rugged Path* ends. It was the first Abbey play ever to achieve fifty consecutive performances, and there is no doubt that the audience sided with the Tanseys. In the sequel, *The Summit*, the Tanseys' neighbours, who had at first supported the Dolis family, undergo a change of heart; this 'ensures the banishment of Peter Dolis and a speedy end to the reign of his lawless tribe'.[83] In spite of the use of the word 'tribe' here, the Dolis family were not tinkers but mountain farmers; still, if they had been tinkers, Shiels might have dealt even more sternly with them. A whole body of legislation designed to encourage the 'itinerants' to settle down and become law-abiding citizens is now on the statute books of the Republic of Ireland.

Priests on the Irish stage were few in number after Synge until Paul Vincent Carroll introduced a whole spectrum of them in *Shadow and Substance* (1937) and *The White Steed* (1938). He showed that priests could be fastidious or philistine, tolerant or bigoted. In *The Wayward Saint* (1955), Carroll put on the stage a priest who is unequivocally comic, a sort of holy fool with a measure of unholy slyness.[84] One feels that Carroll knows the Catholic clergy from the inside, whereas Synge could only know them from the outside. The last paragraph of Synge's preface to *The Tinker's Wedding* offers a generalization that no Irishman could quarrel with:

In the great part of Ireland, however, the whole people, from the tinkers to the clergy, have still a life, and view of life, that are rich and genial and humorous.

---

[82] Robert Hogan, *After the Irish Renaissance* (Minneapolis: Univ. of Minneapolis Press, 1967), 33.

[83] Mathew O'Mahony, *Progress Guide to Anglo-Irish Plays* (Dublin: Progress House, 1960), 83. See also Hogan, 33–9. I saw both plays in 1940–1.

[84] See Hogan, 52–63, for an account of Carroll that focuses on his changing treatment of the Catholic Church and her clergy.

But he continues thus:

I do not think that these country people, who have so much humour them-selves, will mind being laughed at without malice, as the people in every country have been laughed at in their own comedies.[85]

Here lies the crux: in what sense were the early Abbey Theatre plays 'their own' for the Irish country people? Lady Gregory arranged a performance or two in Loughrea and Foynes in 1903, but otherwise all professional performances took place in Dublin, or London. Yeats admits that 'In some country village an audience of farmers once received [*The Pot of Broth*] in stony silence.'[86] He thought it was because they had never seen a play, but the real reason was surely that the farmers saw a tramp getting the better of one of themselves and didn't think it a laughing matter. Furthermore, Synge might believe that he laughed at the country people 'without malice', but they would naturally feel that Protestant playwrights of English stock and high social position could hardly be free from malice or, at best, condescension. To see the Irish people laughing at themselves without any sense that alien eyes are watching, one has to learn Gaelic. As I have shown in *The Irish Comic Tradition*, the Gaelic upper classes often laughed maliciously at their social inferiors. A close analogue to *The Tinker's Wedding* in Gaelic must have been known to Synge, however, for Douglas Hyde published a Gaelic text and English translation of *An Siota 's a Mháthair* ('The Lout and His Mother') in 1906.[87] Hyde first came across the poem in oral tradition, then obtained two manuscript versions, and also used a printed version published in the *Gaelic Journal* 'six years ago'; Synge could therefore have come across the poem independently, or Hyde might have shown it to him before publication or he might have seen it during the prior serial publication of *The Religious Songs of Connacht* in *The New Ireland Review*. In any case, by the end of 1906, Synge could hardly not have known 'The Lout and His Mother'. This anony-mous poem, dated 1815 in one MS, mainly consists of an argument between an old beggarwoman and her illegitimate son. He reproaches her for her poverty and says that her piety has done her more harm than good. When she promises him better things in a future life, he makes fun of both heaven and hell. He also attacks the Roman Catholic clergy for their love of money:

---

[85] Synge, *CW*, iv. 3.
[86] W. B. Yeats, *Plays in Prose and Verse* (New York: Macmillan, 1930), 429.
[87] Published in *Amhráin Diadha Chúige Connacht* or *The Religious Songs of Connacht*, (Dublin and London, M. H. Gill & Son, and T. Fisher Unwin, n.d. [1906]), ii. 294–315.

> As for marriage it is too dear a business,
> Three gold guineas and a crown to the clerk . . .
> And sure what everyone says after all the business
> Is, that it is the mamram pego [88] which makes the
>   marriage.[89]

A little farther along in the poem the lout says to his mother:

> Silly, you hag, and foolish are your sayings;
> Sure if you were dead to-morrow morning
> And I were to bring you to a priest tied up in a bag
> He would not read a Mass for you without hand-money,
> And as for charity, the name of it is bitter to
>   him.[90]

I have often wondered whether the notion of the old hag's being brought to the priest tied up in a bag did not suggest to Synge that he should have his priest tied up similarly: indeed, Hyde's phrasing, 'to a priest tied up in a bag', is ambiguous at best. Professor Saddlemyer's date of spring 1906 for the addition of this detail to the play makes my speculation all the more tempting.

After all his blasphemy and anti-clerical satire, the lout ends the squabble very piously with a prayer that the Christ-Child will not allow anyone to be damned; then he announces that he is going to be married the next day. The poet himself concludes his poem with the wish:

> If there is folly in it—Christ make it right!
> Mercy from God on us, and let each one ask it.[91]

This is entirely in the spirit of a medieval 'retraction'.

Synge himself offered something very close to a retraction in the typescript draft of his preface to *The Tinker's Wedding* dated 20 November 1907:

I do not think these country clergy, who have so much humour—and so much heroism that everyone who has seen them facing typhus or dangerous seas for the comfort of their people on the coasts of the west must acknowledge—will mind being laughed at for half an hour without malice, as the clergy in every Roman Catholic country were laughed at through the ages that had real religion.[92]

The ending to the preface as it now stands is less apologetic, but it looks the more sincere because of that. I don't suppose any Irishman today would accuse Synge of malice. At most he can be blamed for lack of empathy or lack of tact.

---

[88] Hyde is puzzled by *mamram pego* in the Gaelic, but 'pego' is English slang for 'penis'; mamram or meanram (Latin *membrana*) usually means 'parchment'; could it stand for *membrum* here?
[89] 'The Lout and his mother', *The Religious Songs of Connacht*, 309.
[90] Ibid. 311.   [91] Ibid. 315.   [92] Synge, *CW*, iv. 3–4, note.

Ultimately, Synge can be shown to be truer to Irish tradition, and particularly to Gaelic tradition, in all four comedies, than the critics who denounced him as unIrish. But the fact remains that *The Shadow of the Glen* and *The Tinker's Wedding* are far less satisfying than the other two comedies. *The Shadow of the Glen* ends sentimentally, unlike the folktale on which it is based.[93] *The Tinker's Wedding*, on the other hand, ends too savagely. Christy Mahon's savagery is pardonable because wreaked on a bully (his father) and a coward (Shawn Keogh), but the tinkers' savagery is inexcusable because wreaked on one who is essentially kindly and muddleheaded, for all the awesome power that stands behind his priestly power.

93 For this, see Synge, CW, ii. 70–2.

8   *James Joyce: Creating Ulysses*

Origins

Ulysses was first intended as a short story for *Dubliners*: 'P.P.S. I have a new story for Dubliners in my head. It deals with Mr Hunter.' Richard Ellmann adds the information in a note to this letter that Alfred H. Hunter was a Dubliner, rumoured to be Jewish and to have an unfaithful wife. Stanislaus Joyce must have known all this, so that his brother did not need to gloss the name. The formal 'Mr' suggests that Hunter was a family friend, or at least an acquaintance of their father. When James later asked Stanislaus how he liked the title 'Ulysses' for the story about Hunter, he presumably expected his brother to recognize that the Penelope of the unwritten tale would not remain faithful. Someone familiar with the *Ulysses* Joyce eventually wrote might well be able to imagine a *Dubliners* story that hinged on a husband's reluctance to go home until after midnight for fear of an embarrassing encounter with one of his wife's 'suitors'. In the course of the day, he might parry innuendoes about his Jewishness or his cuckoldry with the guile of a Ulysses; he might also seek a kind of revenge by visiting the red-light district, only to find, perhaps, his own son there.

Bloom/Hunter's befriending of Stephen, not his own son but the son of an acquaintance, who is an exile from home like himself, supplies the indispensable anecdote upon which a short story could pivot—but not, one would have thought, the plot of a novel several hundred thousand words long. Joyce at 24 was probably still too severe to imagine a comic ending to his tale, but it is implicit in the novel: nerved to go home by the plight of Telemachus, whom he brings with him, Ulysses suddenly realizes the strength of his position. Penelope understands his unaccustomed late return to mean that he is aware of her infidelity, especially as he breaks a long habit by ordering breakfast in bed for the morning of 17 June. In the power politics of marriage it is generally the wife who silently uses her husband's infidelity as a lever, but what's sauce for the goose is sauce for the gander, as Molly Bloom is quick to recognize. The

---

*The edition of *Ulysses* used for references in this book is the Random House Vintage Books edition: New York, 1961.

very first words of her monologue are: 'Yes because he never did a thing like that before as ask to get his breakfast in bed with a couple of eggs since the *City Arms* hotel when he used to be pretending to be laid up.' (*U* 738) Furthermore, Bloom is going to have his wish, if only because his wife needs money for clothes: 'Ill just give him one more chance Ill get up early in the morning . . . Ill throw him up his eggs and tea in the moustachecup' (*U* 780). There has been a palace revolution in Ithaca (otherwise known as No. 7 Eccles Street).

Telemachus in Search of a Father

To a reader familiar with *A Portrait of the Artist As a Young Man* the most striking aspect of the opening pages of *Ulysses* must be their continuity with the earlier novel. Stephen Dedalus is still with us, and it is through his brooding consciousness that we observe what happens. His interlocutor is now the extrovert Buck Mulligan rather than the introvert Cranly, but this does not alter the tone of the dialogue as much as one might expect. The techniques and atmosphere are the same as in most of the fifth and final chapter of *A Portrait*, though we soon learn that Stephen's mother is dead and that he feels guilty about having refused to kneel by her deathbed and pray. He has made an Icarian flight to which he was so eagerly looking forward at the end of *A Portrait*: '27 *April*: Old father, old artificer, stand me now and ever in good stead.' Later in *Ulysses* we learn just how disillusioning this flight became and how, symbolically at least, he suffered the fate of Icarus: 'Fabulous artificer, the hawklike man. You flew. Whereto? Newhaven-Dieppe, steerage passenger. Paris and back. Lapwing. Icarus. *Pater, ait.* Seabedabbled, fallen, weltering. Lapwing you are. Lapwing he.' (*U* 210) His father's telegram summoning him to his mother's deathbed (*U* 42) offered him, in a sense, a new escape from another impossible situation.

Almost every reader today knows, before he opens *Ulysses*, that he is about to embark upon a modernization of Homer's *Odyssey*, a work with which he is possibly unfamiliar, despite the many good translations that are available. If he happens to mistake Stephen for the Ulysses/Odysseus of the title, should we blame him? Ought we not rather blame Joyce for his Symboliste affectation in not supplying names of persons and places from the *Odyssey* as chapter headings for the episodes? He himself had used these names constantly while working on the novel and had made no secret of them to his close friends. What's more, in order to pacify his puzzled readers all over the world and create a solid reputation out of the early notoriety of *Ulysses*, he found himself obliged to reveal the names—and much about his intentions for its structure—

to a French novelist and critic, Valéry Larbaud; to an Italian translator, Carlo Linati; to the English explicator of the entire work, and finally to his first American biographer, Herbert Gorman. Joyce's name for the first episode was in fact 'Telemachus'. The practised Joycean is so familiar with the identification of Stephen with Telemachus, son and heir of Ulysses, that it may never occur to him how odd it was of Joyce to retain a fully established character from an earlier novel as one of the three archetypal figures in *Ulysses*, which is not just a sequel to *A Portrait* but a radically new experiment that has enlarged or transgressed the boundaries of the genre. Even on the plane of myth, the persistence of Stephen is hard to justify. Telemachus represents an ideal combination of filial loyalty with manly independence, whereas Icarus is still childishly dependent on his father, Daedalus. The shift from Icarus to Telemachus could be intended to symbolize a new maturity in Stephen, but this is hard to detect in the opening episodes of *Ulysses*. He certainly shows no improvement as a poet (*U* 48; *U* 132). In the ninth episode, 'Scylla and Charybdis', however, he delivers an ingenious impromptu lecture on *Hamlet* to a small audience of his intellectual equals, who find it impressive though far-fetched. Finally, between one and two o'clock the next morning, he 'inexplicably' declines Bloom's offer of a bed for the rest of the night; are we to think that he is refusing to form a new dependence on the Blooms, now that his mother's death and his departure from his father's house have set him free from an old one? His maturity seems at best problematical, for he has informed 'Lord' John Corley that he intends to give up his teaching job 'tomorrow or the next day', following this up with the remark 'I have no place to sleep myself' (*U* 617). He seems determined to start his adult life over again from scratch.

The projected short story of 'Ulysses' may have been based on hospitality actually shown to Joyce by Mr Hunter or some other of his father's friends and acquaintances, who did not like to see the son wasting his talents exactly as his parent had done. At any rate, in March 1914 'Joyce began work on *Ulysses* by "setting down . . . preliminary sketches for the final sections" '.[1] It is natural to assume that this refers to the last three episodes, which Joyce collectively named the 'Nostos' (Vootoѕ, return) and described to Carlo Linati in 1920 as the 'Fusions of Bloom and Stephen'.[2] Also in 1920, while writing the first draft of 'Circe' in Paris, Joyce 'found relief in reworking the first episode of the 'Nostos' (Eumaeus) which already existed in some form.[3]

---

[1] Herbert Gorman, *James Joyce* (New York: Rinehart, 1939). Stuart Gilbert, *James Joyce's Ulysses: A Study* (London: 1930).

[2] See Richard Ellmann, *Ulysses on the Liffey* (London: Oxford University Press, 1972), 149–50.

[3] Michael Groden, *Ulysses in Progress* (New Jersey: Princeton University Press, 1977), 182 ff.

This episode, then, one of the least attractive in the book, may have been the most complete among the preliminary sketches of 1914. Since my concern as a critical historian is with the finished work of 1922, I shall not give any further account of the pre-history of *Ulysses*: fine textual critics like A. Walton Litz, his pupil Michael Groden and Phillip F. Herring have devoted at least four authoritative books and numerous articles to this fascinating subject.[4] I should like to recall, however, that drafts of the first fourteen episodes appeared serially in *The Little Review*, an avant-garde New York monthly, from March 1918 to the issue ominously dated September–December 1920, after which the writ of an American court forbade all further instalments.[5] Also, 'Nestor', 'Proteus', 'Hades', and part of 'Wandering Rocks' were published during the year 1919 in *The Egoist*, a similar London magazine which had already serialised *A Portrait* in 1914–15. Bernard Shaw seems to have formed his essentially favourable opinion of *Ulysses* on the basis of one or both of these serialisations.[6]

One of the received ideas about *Ulysses*, held by many who have read the book as well as many who have not, is that it is written throughout in stream-of-consciousness style; in France and French-influenced countries the preferred term is *monologue intérieur* or a translation thereof. In fact, however, the first sentence of *Ulysses* reads thus, 'Stately, plump Buck Mulligan came from the stairhead, bearing a bowl of lather on which a mirror and a razor lay crossed.' Similar omniscient narration, punctuated by occasional lines of dialogue, continues for most of the episode. Not until the middle of page 6, 'Young shouts of moneyed voices in Clive Kempthorpe's rooms', are we taken fully into Stephen's mind, only to recoil baffled by a literary allusion (if it is one) that has eluded the viligance of even Weldon Thornton.[7] Two pages later we at last feel that we are privileged to dip, however briefly, into the mind of a poet. While the voice of Mulligan, who is descending the stairs, booms out from the interior of the Martello tower, the words of the omniscient narrator merge with those of Stephen's interior monologue as he mentally completes Mulligan's quotation from Yeats:

Woodshadows floated silently by through the morning peace / from the stairhead seaward where he gazed. Inshore and / farther out the mirror of water whitened, spurned by / lightshod hurrying feet. White breast of the dim sea.

⁴ e.g. A. Walton Litz, *The Art of James Joyce* (Oxford: Oxford University Press, 1961). Phillip F. Herring, *Joyce's Uncertainty Principle* (New Jersey: Princeton University Press, 1987). Michael Groden, *Ulysses*.

⁵ Richard Ellmann, *James Joyce* (London: Oxford University Press, 1959), 434 ff.

⁶ Ibid. 457 ff.

⁷ Weldon Thornton, *Allusions in Ulysses: An Annotated List* (Chapel Hill: University of North Carolina Press, 1968).

The / twining stresses, two by two. A hand plucking the / harpstrings merging their twining chords. Wavewhite wedded / words shimmering on the dim tide.

There were no 'woodshadows' near the stark squat tower by the sea's edge in 1904, any more than there are today; they come from Yeats's poem, via Stephen's consciousness. In the 1904 edition of *Poems* the second stanza of the then untitled lyric from *The Countess Cathleen* reads thus;

> And no more turn aside and brood
> Upon Love's bitter mystery;
> For Fergus rules the brazen cars,
> And rules the shadows of the wood,
> And the white breast of the dim sea
> And all dishevelled wandering stars.[8]

Perhaps a neutral observer might have noted white-caps forming on the sea at the touch of a gust of wind, but the image of 'lightshod hurrying feet' is surely meant to be Stephen's. The rest of the brief paragraph quotes the fifth line of the stanza, plays variations on it, comments on its characteristic Yeatsian rhythm, 'The twining [twinning?] stresses, two by two'. Joyce / Stephen reads the line, as one must:

> And the white breast of the dim sea.

Such glimpses into the workings of Stephen's mind are rare in the first episodes, 'Telemachus' and 'Nestor', but this passage and the memories of his mother which follow (*U* 9–10) provide sufficient evidence of the validity of the method. We quickly become aware of how Stephen's idiosyncratic vocabulary, his poetic imagery, his awareness of sound (as in the last sentence of the quotation, full of alliteration and assonance), his mental syntax of incomplete sentences, all differ not merely from the impersonal narrator's but from those of any other character we have yet encountered in literature—except to some extent the Stephen of *A Portrait*. In his second schema for *Ulysses*, the one published by Gilbert in 1930, Joyce described his 'technics' [techniques] in the first three episodes as 'Narrative (young)', 'Catechism (personal)', and 'Monologue (male)', emphasizing the predominance of narrative in 'Telemachus' and of dialogue in 'Nestor'. Only in 'Proteus' does he begin to imitate more fully the interior monologue invented by his model, Eduard Dujardin, for his brief novel *Les lauriers sont coupés* (serialised 1887; first published in book form 1888).

---

[8] W. B. Yeats, 'The Countess Cathleen', *Poems* (London: T. Fisher Unwin, 1904).

Dujardin and 'The Initial Style'

Dujardin's narrative technique is clumsier than Joyce's but it remains more faithful to sense impressions from the outer world and is therefore perhaps more truly phenomenological than his. I translate a passage from Dujardin's third paragraph:

Here is the house I must enter, where I'll find someone; the house; the vestibule; in we go. Night is falling; the air is good; there's gaiety in the air. The staircase; the first steps up. What if he's left early? He sometimes does that; but I want to tell him about my day today. The first-floor landing; the wide, bright staircase; the windows. Such a decent fellow, I've confided to him the story of my love life. I'm going to have another pleasant evening! Anyway, he won't make fun of me any more. What a delightful evening this is going to be! Why is the stair carpet turned back at that corner? It makes a grey stain on the mounting red, the red that mounts from stair to stair. The second floor; the door on the left; 'Office'. Let's hope he's not gone. Where could I go in search of him? Oh well, I'd go to the boulevard. Quick, let's go in. The main office. Where's Lucien Chavainne? The huge room and the circle of chairs. There he is, near the table, bent over it; he has his coat and hat on; he's arranging papers, hurriedly, with another clerk.[9]

Here is a passage from 'Proteus' expressing similar uncertainty:

His pace slackened. Here. Am I going to Aunt Sara's or not? My consubstantial father's voice. Did you see anything of your artist brother Stephen lately? No? Sure he's not down in Strasburg terrace with his aunt Sally? Couldn't he fly a bit higher than that, eh? And and and and tell us Stephen, how is uncle Si? O weeping God, the things I married into. De boys in de hayloft. The drunken little cost-drawer and his brother, the cornet player . . . Jesus wept; and no wonder, by Christ.   (*U* 38)

Joyce saves himself a lot of awkwardness by slipping into third-person, past-tense narration when absolutely necessary, but he could just as well have written 'My pace slackens': the effect, however, would have been to make Stephen the self-conscious narrator on his own doings, instead of a totally self-absorbed consciousness on whom the narrator seems to be eavesdropping. Note the number of voices Joyce commands: Stephen, like his creator, is a mimic and the son of a mimic; besides expressing his own thoughts and mimicking his father, he imitates his father imitating Walter, the 'skeweyed' son of Richie Goulding, husband to Aunt Sara and brother of Stephen's mother. Mr Dedalus's fund of Cork sayings makes Joyce's style here more varied and amusing than Dujardin could ever hope or wish his to be.

---

9 Eduard Dujardin, *Les lauriers sont coupés* (Paris: Messein, 1887).

In a letter to Harriet Shaw Weaver (6 August 1919) à propos of 'Sirens', Joyce explained that he 'did not know in what other way to describe the seductions of music', while admitting that she 'may begin to regard the various styles with dismay and prefer the initial style much as the wanderer did who longed for the rock of Ithaca'. Michael Groden defines this 'initial style' and lists the episodes where it is used, with invisible conciseness and precision:

Joyce wrote the first nine episodes—through 'Scylla and Charybdis'—in the initial style (third person, past-tense narration; first-person, present-tense monologue). Then in 'Wandering Rocks' he used this initial technique to depict the minds of [six] other characters besides Bloom and Stephen, and in 'Sirens' he distorted the style practically beyond recognition. Finally he abandoned it as the book's exclusive narrative device in 'Cyclops', using it again only in the second half of 'Nausicaa'. (In 'Penelope', he closed *Ulysses* with another monologue, this time a pure one lacking the third-person narrator.)[10]

It follows from this summary, with which I almost entirely agree, that Joyce used Dujardin's method fully only in 'Penelope': that he knew exactly what he was doing is confirmed by his own words, as transmitted by Larbaud:

'In *Les Lauriers sont coupés*' said Joyce to me, 'the reader, from the very first lines, finds himself installed in the thought of the principal character, and it is the uninterrupted development of this thought, completely replacing the usual narrative style, that tells us what this character is doing and what is happening to him.'[11]

In the preface to the 1925 edition of *Les Lauriers sont coupés* just quoted, Larbaud has a striking passage on the aspects of the interior monologue that inspired as well as delighted the young writers of his generation:

One of these styles employed in *Ulysses* had particularly struck them by its novelty, its daring, and the possibilities it offered for expressing with strength and speed the most intimate thoughts, the most spontaneous ones, those that appear to take shape without the knowledge of the consciousness and that seem exterior to organised discourse. It was to this style that the name was given, in France and shortly after the publication of Ulysses, of *monologue intérieur*.[12]

Dujardin's emphasis on the power of the interior monologue to reveal, or at least hint at, the unconscious and the preconscious deserves close attention. Other critics have recognized the same tendency, though not all have offered an explanation of it. I would suggest that this mysterious power is conferred by Joyce's use of the free association of

[10] Groden, *Ulysses*.
[11] Valéry Larbaud, preface to special edition of *Les Lauriers sont coupés* (Paris: Messein, 1925).
[12] Ibid.

ideas. A novice reader of *Ulysses* may sometimes pause to ask himself: Now, why did Bloom change his train of thought so abruptly at this point? He or she may even be able, after a minute or two, to answer the self-posed question. One of Bloom's keywords has occurred in his monologue a few lines before, and Bloom is now pursuing the train of thought habitually associated with that word, even though it popped up in another context. What's more, the keyword or key phrase may not have risen to the surface by mere accident: his mind is haunted all day by certain passing hopes and fears, as well as by permanent regrets. So too, of course, is Stephen's.

But there are less obvious examples of the strange workings of these associative processes of the mind discovered by John Locke and exploited by Laurence Sterne (one of Joyce's most important literary predecessors) from the very first pages of *Tristram Shandy*. For instance, Bloom at one point asks himself, 'What was the name of that priestylooking chap was always squinting in when he passed? Weak eyes, woman. Stopped in Citron's saint Kevin's parade. Pen something. Pendennis? My memory is getting. Pen . . .?' Of course it's years ago.' (*U* 155–6) Later in the same Lestrygonians episode he suddenly remembers: 'Penrose! That was the chap's name.' (*U* 181) Why was Bloom able to remember the name at just that point? A less subtle mind than Joyce's might have been content with a reference to a pen or a rose, but none appears in the context. Bloom has been helping the 'blind stripling' who reappears in 'Sirens' as the piano tuner; watching him, Bloom thinks: 'Could he walk in a beeline if he didn't have that cane? Bloodless pious face like a fellow going in to be a priest.' (*U* 181) It is in the very next line that he remembers Penrose's name, because Penrose was 'priestylooking' too. When Bloom is not specifically trying to remember the name, he remembers the whole configuration of *Gestalt*: name, priestly appearance, and doubtless (in his creator's imagination) many other things besides the details given on pages 155–6.

Epiphany of the Unconscious

After abandoning his initial style, Joyce discovered a totally different way of handling the Unconscious in the 'Circe' episode, whose technique is described as 'Hallucination' in the Gilbert schema. Some of the mental images and associations stored in the unconscious minds of both Stephen and Bloom take on a life of their own, elude the repression of the internal censor, and seem to attain objective existence in the visible world. In fact, they are private hallucinations, invisible to Bella Cohen, Lynch, and the three whores; at moments, Stephen and Bloom seem to catch glimpses of each other's visions, or at least to 'remember' each other's keywords, but in general each observes his own private guilts, fears and fantasies (usually sexual); these are often embodied in memories of the day, 16 June 1904, that has now reached its last hour before midnight. The apparition of Stephen's mother, calling on him to repent and causing him to choke '*with fright, remorse and horror*', is the climax of the episode. That his unconscious should summon up his mother in a brothel indicates Stephen's sexual guilt and Oedipal feelings, but it is his awareness of having defied God that prompts his fright and horror, which soon turn into anger at this treacherous assault on his moral independence: as in *A Portrait*, he quotes Lucifer's '*Non serviam!*' (*U* 579–82). The passages devoted to Bloom's fantasies are much longer and richer than those illustrating Stephen's, the most extraordinary being, without question, that on pages 527–54. It begins with the entrance of '*Bella Cohen, a massive whoremistress*' with '*a sprouting moustache*', who is fanning herself with a large black fan. Her first words are, 'My word! I'm all of a mucksweat.' For the next twenty-seven pages we wallow in Bloom's fantasies: masochistic ones at first, prompted by Bella's evident strength and cruelty, which take on a homosexual colouring as the moustached Bella becomes her masculine counterpart, 'Bello'; finally, 'he' is replaced by the nymph from the framed print in the Blooms' conjugal bedroom. The nymph's reproaches confirm our impression that Bloom, in the secret erotic correspondence with 'Marthe' revealed in 'Lotus-Eaters' (*U* 72, 73; 77–9), takes a somewhat sadistic pleasure in shocking innocent women; we may also see the nymph as a surrogate for his daughter Milly, relieving him of guilt for his incestuous feelings about her. Finally he drives the nymph away with an outburst of disgust against his own—and all—sexuality. A stage direction follows: '(*The figure of Bella Cohen stands before him.*)'; then Bella makes her second remark, 'You'll know me the next time'—a pert colloquial reproach addressed to starers. Bloom's mesmerized gaze has been fixed on her for perhaps no more than two or three minutes of clock time, but the corresponding Bergsonian *durée* is crammed with the memories and fantasies of a lifetime. Using a theatrical technique borrowed from German Expressionism, Joyce in 'Circe' has given us a vivid object-lesson in Freudian psychology. Although Bloom also fantasizes about political power, his dreams, like Parnell's, are shattered by a court case involving a woman, so the theme of sexual guilt persists. The dream-like Alice-in-Wonderland logic of the episode causes the trial and condemnation (*U* 456–71) to precede Bloom's political beginnings and triumph (*U* 478–92), but he is destroyed again, this time by the mob instead of a court of law:

THE MOB
Lynch him! Roast him! He's as bad as Parnell was. Mr Fox!
(*U* 492)

'Mr Fox' was a pseudonym used by Charles Stewart Parnell in his adulterous affair with Mrs Katherine O'Shea, just as 'Henry Flower' is Bloom's in his epistolary affair with Martha.

Although Joyce was a reluctant patient of Jung's for a short period during the writing of *Ulysses*, it seems to me beyond question that his chief guide through the Unconscious was Freud. Richard Ellmann, in four pregnant pages of *The Consciousness of Joyce*, notes that Joyce bought, before leaving Trieste in 1915, the German originals of Jung's *The Significance of the Father in the Destiny of the Individual* (1909) and Freud's *A Childhood Memory of Leonardo da Vinci* (1910) as well as the German translation of the first edition of Ernest Jones's *The Problem of Hamlet and the Oedipus Complex* (1911); he later acquired in Zurich the German version of Freud's *Psychopathology of Everyday Life* (1917 edn.).[13] Bloom is particularly prone to the slips of the tongue analysed in this last work: as Ellmann writes, 'When Bloom speaks of "the wife's admirers" and means "the wife's advisers" . . . we are in the age of Freud.'[14] Although Joyce was sceptical about the Oedipus Complex, preferring Jung's early views on the importance of the father (later modified by Jung himself), one has to agree that Freud's influence predominates in *Ulysses*. It confirmed Joyce's own early intuitions of a universal though oft-denied preoccupation. Ellmann aptly cites a letter of November 1906:

if I put down a bucket into my own soul's well, sexual department, I draw up Griffith's and Ibsen's and Skeffington's and Bernard Vaughan's and St. Aloysius' and Shelley's and Renan's water along with my own. And I am going to do that in my novel (inter alia) and plank the bucket down before the shades and substances above mentioned to see how they like it . . . I am nauseated by their lying drivel about pure men and pure women and spiritual love and love for ever: blatant lying in the face of the truth . . . I presume there are very few mortals in Europe who are not in danger of waking some morning and finding themselves syphilitic.[15]

The novel referred to here is *A Portrait of the Artist*, but *Ulysses* may well be regarded as the true fulfilment of this youthful (*aet.* 24) threat, and the 'Circe' episode as its culmination. Joyce argued in a letter that the true derivation of the word 'syphilis' was 'swine-love':[16] Bella is Circe, her way of turning men into swine is to have them contract syphilis,

13 Richard Ellmann, *The Consciousness of James Joyce* (London: Faber & Faber, 1977).
14 Ibid.   15 Ibid.
16 *Letters of James Joyce*, ed. Stuart Gilbert (York: Viking, 1957), i, 147.

and the organ of the body assigned to this episode is the 'locomotor apparatus' attacked by the tertiary stage of the disease. Of course 'they' didn't like either *A Portrait* or *Ulysses*, but the 1906 letter offers a powerful advance justification of Joyce's most notorious work.

Creating Odysseus

Having failed to write the short story based on Mr Hunter as Ulysses, and having from the first thought of Stephen Dedalus as Telemachus, Joyce must have realized that Hunter would not do as the Ulysses of even a short modern Odyssey, now imagined as a novel; in the first place, he knew hardly anything about Hunter. The logical next step might have been to consider the possibility of putting Stephen's 'real' father into the role. Simon Dedalus's experience had certainly been various, and when it was a matter of where the next drink was coming from or how the latest landlord was to be pacified for another month, he deserved the epithet *polymetis* ('of many wiles'). But Odysseus was a byword for wisdom and common sense; furthermore, no matter how many misfortunes he may undergo, the epic hero must be crowned with success at last. The thumbnail biography of Mr Dedalus given in *A Portrait* ruled him out completely:

A medical student, an oarsman, a tenor, an amateur actor, a shouting politician, a small landlord, a small investor, a drinker, a good fellow, a storyteller, somebody's secretary, something in a distillery, a taxgatherer, a bankrupt and at present a praiser of his own past

(*U* 241)

Homer's hero could reasonably be described as, for instance, a small landlord or, in the *Iliad*, almost a shouting politician, but the economic and social failure implied by bankruptcy *c.*1900 disqualified Simon forever; besides, he was a widower.

What sort of hero, then, *was* required? First of all, a man in his prime, married and a father, to whom Joyce could transfer much of his later experience without disturbing the reader's sense of verisimilitude; Bloom is 38, the age Joyce attained in 1920, the year he hoped to finish *Ulysses*. Each by then had a daughter, Lucia Joyce being 13, Milly Bloom 15. Joyce's son, Giorgio, was 15, whereas Bloom's Rudy had only lived 11 days; his place as a son could be filled by a surrogate, Stephen Dedalus. Secondly, Joyce wanted his Odysseus to seem to be as different from his creator as was humanly possible—though he then dropped numerous hints about their similarities. Thirdly, since so much of the mature Joyce's life had already been passed in Europe, including all of his experience as (common-law) husband and father, the hero must, although dwelling continuously in Dublin, have a great many ties in Europe and be in fact a clearly recognizable exotic, though not an alien, in the city of his birth.

As an Irish interpreter of Joyce in the United States for almost forty years, I have found that the commonest question about Joyce has always been the same: 'Why did he make the hero of Ulysses a Jew?' In view of the requirements above stated, my answer is 'How could he make him anything else?' Before the Holocaust, in the early twentieth century, the Jew was regarded as the model cosmopolitan city-dweller: today, New York and London are still more deeply marked by Jewish culture. Furthermore, an astonishing percentage of significant twentieth-century French writers are wholly or partly Jewish; remembering Joyce's encouragement of Italo Svevo, we may recognize the phenomenon on a smaller scale in Italy. Isaac Bashevis Singer and other writers of Yiddish have since reminded us of the little Jewish townships scattered through-out Poland and Western Russia. If Joyce wished to write a novel about the modern city and felt obliged to base it upon the atypical capital that he knew best, then he *must* ignore Dublin statistics and give a leading role to a Jew. The Medieval legend of the Wandering Jew, together with the wanderings of the Hebrews in the Sinai Desert and those of the Jews after the Diaspora, provided striking parallels with the wanderings of Ulysses after the fall of Troy. Hence a Jew—or someone who was mistaken for a Jew—could be an appropriate hero for a modern Odyssey. Joyce makes it abundantly clear that, whatever his ancestry, Bloom is not and has never been a Jew by religion.[17] In the 'Nausicaa' episode we learn with surprise that his foreskin is intact (*U* 373). Since Jewishness descends through the mother, not the father, a comparable surprise is the revelation (*U* 438) that Bloom's mother is a Roman Catholic. In this her only appearance ('Circe' episode), she behaves as follows, crying out '*in shrill alarm*':

O blessed Redeemer, what have they done to him? My smelling salts! (*She hauls up a reef of skirt and ransacks the pouch of her striped blay petticoat. A phial, an Agnus Dei, a shrivelled potato and a celluloid doll fall out.*) Sacred Heart of Mary, where were you at all, at all?

The invocation of the 'Sacred Heart' of what Anglicans call 'the BVM' and her possession of that now-obsolete religious article, an Agnus Dei, prove that even though her husband is a Jewish convert to the Church

---

[17] Erwin R. Steinberg, 'James Joyce and the Critics Notwithstanding, Leopold Bloom is not Jewish', *Journal of Modern Literature*, 9 (1981/2), 27–49. This article seems definitive to me, a gentile, on every point except the statement that Bloom's 'mother was born a Protestant'.

of Ireland Ellen Bloom remains true to her childhood faith. Later (*U* 682) we learn that her maiden name was Ellen Higgins, 'second daughter of Julius Higgins (born Karoly) and Fanny Higgins (born Hegarty)'. The name Julius Karoly suggests a Hungarian Jew, but it seems more likely that he was conceived by Joyce as a Roman Catholic. As for Rudolf, Bloom's father, he became a Protestant in 1865. His son Leopold Bloom was first baptized 'by the reverend Mr Gilmer Johnston M.A. alone in the protestant [Anglican] church of Saint Nic[h]olas Without, Coombe' (*U* 682). He was subsequently baptized a Roman Catholic by laymen, his schoolfellows, 'James O'Connor, Philip Gilligan and James Fitzpatrick, together, under a pump in the village of Swords'. If the ceremony was carried out by Bloom's wish—though the participation of all three 'laymen' suggests coercion—it would constitute valid Catholic baptism. Both the native Irish surnames and the apostolic first names of his schoolmates suggest that they were all Catholics. Bloom seems never to have been confirmed in either Church, but he was baptized a Catholic once again, for good measure, 'by the reverend Charles Malone C.C., in the church of the Three Patrons, Rathgar' (*U* 682). An explanation of this third baptism is supplied by the following passage:

Prove that he had loved rectitude from his earliest youth. To master Percy Apjohn at High School in 1880 he had divulged his disbelief in the tenets of the Irish (protestant) church (to which his father Rudolf Virag, later Rudolf Bloom, had been converted from the Israelite faith and communion in 1865 by the Society for promoting Christianity among the Jews) subsequently abjured by him in favour of Roman catholicism at the epoch of and with a view to his matrimony in 1880.

(*U* 716)

For statistical purposes, then, Bloom is a Catholic, though originally baptised a Protestant; his father's conversion must have been superficial, for there were Jewish elements in Bloom's home life (*U* 122; *U* 723–4). Bloom is definitely not a practising Catholic; he seems never to have known much about his adopted faith, and some of what he once knew has been forgotten, as he reveals while watching Mass at the church in Westland Row (*U* 80–3). In short, Bloom is a subscriber to all three religions as well as to agnosticism: idiosyncratic from one point of view, he is symbolic of all his fellow-citizens from another. Finally, of course, as both Jew and Catholic Irishman, Bloom represents two oppressed peoples, victims respectively of Roman and British Imperialism, with a perhaps otherwise unparalleled demographic feature in common, namely that the descendants of their respective diasporas far outnumber the populations of their homelands.

Ulysses *and the* Odyssey: *'Proteus', 'Scylla and Charybdis'*

When one compares the three divisions of *Ulysses*, indicated by Roman numerals, with the corresponding passages of the *Odyssey*, Joyce's sense of their relative importance at once reveals itself as strikingly different from Homer's. Joyce supplies no equivalent of the council of the gods in Book I, but his version of the 'Telemachia' ('Telemachus', 'Nestor', 'Proteus'), while not forming one-sixth of the work, is not too far out of proportion with Books I–IV in Homer. The next twelve episodes of *Ulysses* correspond to the *Odyssey* proper (i.e Odysseus's wanderings on his way home from Troy), while the last three episodes, prefixed by the numeral III, form the 'Nostos', as already mentioned. The fourth and thirteenth episodes, 'Calypso' and 'Nausicaa', correspond to Homer's Books V–VIII, while no fewer than ten episodes ('Lotus-eaters', 'Hades', 'Aeolus', 'Lestrygonians', 'Scylla and Charybdis', 'Wandering Rocks', 'Sirens', 'Cyclops', 'Oxen of the Sun', 'Circe' are derived from Books IX–XII, the folklore part of the *Odyssey* that everyone delights to remember. Finally, the three episodes of the 'Nostos' ('Eumaeus', 'Ithaca', 'Penelope'), admittedly quite lengthy, are left to cover the entire second half of the *Odyssey*, Books XIII–XXIV. These disproportions, far from being a blemish on *Ulysses*, do Joyce great credit. He has produced no stilted neo-classical pastiche of the *Odyssey* but a free artistic reworking in a modern genre and a modern idiom. The vitality of the liveliest passages in *Ulysses* often springs from the folklore in Books IX–XII; the oldest, and at the same time the most universal in its human appeal, of the substrata underlying the Greek oral epic.[18]

'Hades', 'Sirens', 'Cyclops' and 'Circe' are probably the episodes most easily recognizable as based on Homer (without reference to the Gilbert schema): these, along with 'Nausicaa' and 'Penelope,' are also the most entertaining. 'Telemachus' and 'Nestor' resemble the last chapter of *A Portrait* too closely to be Homeric, while missing its fierce iconoclasm. As for 'Proteus', many a reader without training in philosophy has given up in despair when confronted with its fragmentary opening sentence: 'INELUCTABLE MODALITY OF THE VISIBLE; AT LEAST THAT IF NO more thought through my eyes.' (*U* 37) Anyone who feels ashamed at finding this incomprehensible can comfort himself with the inescapable inference that Joyce was striving to establish once and for all Stephen's right to be thought a superintellectual. The ineluctable modality of the visible, if the reader will only persevere, soon turns out to be space, and

---

[18] On 'oral epic', see Walter Ong S. J., *Orality and Literacy: The Technology* (London: Methuen, 1982), especially chs. 1 and 2.

'the ineluctable modality of the audible' is of course time. The *nacheinander* ('one after the other') and the *nebeneinander* ('one beside the other') are again, respectively, time and space. The use of German here suggests that Lessing's famous essay on the difference between painting and poetry—the first being an art of space, the second, like music, an art of time—is being alluded to. Joyce's library in Trieste included an English translation of *The Laocoon and Other Prose Writings*, and no doubt he looked into *Lakoon*, the German original, as well.[19] Lessing's name is not mentioned in 'Proteus'; neither is that of Aristotle, whose *De Anima* underlies the baffling opening paragraph; he is referred to, in Dante's famous phrase, as *maestro di color che sanno* ('the master of those who know'). On the same page 37 there is a reference to yet a third philosopher important to Stephen's meditations on time and space and especially on the nature and existence of matter— a question raised in the first paragraph by Aristotle's mention of 'bodies'. In one of the rare interventions of the narrator we read that 'Stephen closed his eyes to hear his boots crush crackling wrack and shells.' Later his own interior monologue makes us aware that he has opened his eyes again: 'See now. There all the time without you: and ever shall be, world without end.' This idea undoubtedly comes from George Berkeley, the great Irish philosopher: Joyce owned A. C. Fraser's standard biography of him and may well have also picked up the Everyman edition of *A New Theory of Vision and Other Selected Philosophical Writings*, first published in 1910. Berkeley is more clearly identified later in the episode by his episcopal title:

The good bishop of Cloyne took the veil of the temple out of his shovel hat: veil of space with coloured emblems hatched on its field . . . Flat I see, then think distance, near, far, flat I see, east, back. Ah, see now. Falls back suddenly, frozen in stereoscope.

(U 48)

Behind the casual phrase 'think distance' lie sections I–LI of Berkeley's *A New Theory of Vision*: whether Joyce fully understood their argument or not must be left to the judgement of professional philosophers. At any rate, Berkeley's concern with the relation between appearance and reality is symbolized in the *Odyssey* by Proteus, 'that ancient one of the sea, whose speech is sooth', but who, to avoid telling the truths he knows, can 'take all manner of shapes of things that creep upon the

---

[19] Lessing's actual words in the second paragraph of his crucial sixteenth chapter are *neben einander* and *auf einander*, but a note to my edition says 'In the language of German philosophy *Space* is called "das Nebeinander der Dinge", the coexistence of things, and *Time* is called "das Nacheinander der Dinge", the succession of things'. Note that Lessing speaks of 'bodies' (Körper) and 'signs' (Zeichen), which are also keywords in the first paragraph of 'Proteus', where Aristotle's *De Anima* is the main reference.

earth, of water likewise, and of fierce fire burning'. It is he who tells Menelaus, who in his turn tells Telemachus, that Odysseus is still alive. But the art of the 'Proteus' episode is philology, according to Joyce. Why? Is it because language is deceptive and forever changing? That is one good reason, certainly, but another brings us back to Berkeley, whose philosophy predominates over even Aristotle's in this episode. At one point we read: 'These heavy sands are language tide and wind have silted here.' (*U* 44) This idea is not original: if Joyce read to the end of *A New Theory of Vision*, he cannot have passed lightly over the astonishing idea of section CXLVII:

Upon the whole I think we may fairly conclude, that the proper objects of vision constitute a universal language of the Author of nature, whereby we are instructed how to regulate our actions . . . And the manner wherein they signify, and mark unto us the objects which are at a distance, is the same with that of languages of human appointment, which do not suggest the things signified, by any likeness or identity of nature, but only by an habitual connexion, that experience has made us to observe between them.[20]

Joyce could never wholly accept the fact that the signifier bears no relation to the things signified: on the other hand, the notion that the visible world constituted the language of an author would validate the god-like privilege of creating his own world from language.

No matter how much one explains and attempts to justify its title, the 'Proteus' episode, full of introspection and indecision, seems a far cry from the hand-to-hand struggle of Menelaus and Proteus on the noonday sands. Stephen is struggling with himself, trying to decide not only where he will sleep that night but what goal to choose in life, now it is clear that he has neither the money nor the inclination to go back to medical school. Yet Joyce had good precedent for intellectualising the myth of Proteus. Bacon had written of it thus in chapter XIII of *The Wisdom of the Ancients*: 'This fable may seem to unfold the secrets of Nature, and the properties of *Matter*. For under the person of *Proteus*, the first Matter (which next to God is the ancientist Thing) may be represented.'[21] In the Gilbert schema Joyce also identifies Proteus with Primal Matter.

One further reason for the difficulty of the episode arises from its position in Joyce's structural plan, at the end of the first triad of episodes. The styles of these are described by Joyce as respectively 'Narrative (young)', 'Catechism (personal)', and 'Monologue (male)'. The corresponding styles of the last three episodes are 'Narrative (old)', 'Catechism

20 George Berkeley, *A New Theory of Vision* (London: J. M. Dent, 1910), 81.
21 Francis Bacon, *The Wisdom of the Ancients* (London: Bell & Daldy, 1857), 291.

(impersonal)', and 'Monologue (female)'. Stephen's monologue, for artistic reasons if no others, must differ as much as possible from the musings in very simple, concrete language of Penelope (Mrs Bloom). His language and thought are therefore made as abstract and complex as possible. Stephen's male monologue is at the same time sharply differentiated from Bloom's, which is more complex than Molly's and more concrete than Stephen's. Bloom's longest monologue, shorter than those of the other two, and more often interrupted by the narrator, occurs in the second half of 'Nausicaa' (U 367–82), almost midway between theirs.

Other episodes which may not seem to live up to their titles, once we have learned these from the Gilbert schema or elsewhere, are Bloom's first two, 'Calypso' and 'Lotus-Eaters'. It is a surprise to be asked to identify the enchanting nymph Calypso with the chocolate-box picture of a nymph over the Blooms' bed: Mrs Bloom seems far more enthralling. I find it much more satisfying to accept the paradox that Penelope the wife and Calypso the mistress are one and the same. 'Lotus-Eaters' contains many references to flowers and plants, and its final word is 'flower' as Bloom looks forward to his bath at the Turkish baths. (7 Eccles Street, his home, does not contain a bathroom.) Nevertheless, it would be hard to guess its title from its content. Hades, on the other hand, seems an appropriate name for a cemetery, especially as we see the mighty dead there—Daniel O'Connell and Charles Stewart Parnell—in effigy at least. A newspaper office, especially a draughty one, seems an appropriate equivalent for Aeolus' cave of the winds. Lestrygonians, however, while full of references to food and eating, does not quite suggest cannibalism.

'Scylla and Charybdis', which promises so much excitement to those familiar with *Odyssey* XII, is perhaps the most descriptive title of all, more so even than 'Proteus'. The confused and perhaps bitterly disappointed reader gradually discovers that this is a Platonic dialogue in which Stephen plays the part of a brash young sophist—or perhaps that of Aristophanes in the *Symposium*. The late-arriving Mulligan may be cast as Alcibiades from the same dialogue. At any rate, John Eglinton plays Socrates. The chief subject of discussion is the relationship between life and art, exemplified by that between 'Saxon Shakespeare's Hamlet' and his creator. Stephen insists that the mature Shakespeare is not to be identified with 'young' Hamlet but with 'old' Hamlet, the Ghost. It follows, I think, that the mature Joyce who is writing *Ulysses* (at about the same age as Shakespeare wrote *Hamlet*) is to be identified with Bloom rather than with his previous alter ego, Stephen Dedalus. Also, the fusion between Bloom and Stephen mentioned in the Linati schema is foreshadowed by a quotation from Maeterlinck: 'If Socrates leaves his house today he will find the sage seated on his doorstep. If Judas go forth tonight, it is to Judas his steps will tend'. A little later Stephen supplies a gloss: 'We walk through ourselves, meeting robbers, ghosts, giants, old men, young men, wives, widows, brothers-in-love. But always meeting ourselves.' (*U* 213) As Stephen and Mulligan leave the National Library, just before the end of the episode, there is a reprise of the same idea:

Part. The moment is now. Where then? If Socrates leave his house today, if Judas go forth tonight. Why? That lies in space which I in time must come to, ineluctably.

My will, his will that fronts me. Seas between.

A man passed out between them, bowing, greeting.

(*U* 217)

The man is Bloom, who thus passes between the Scylla and Charybdis of two opposed temperaments, to which his own temperament supplies a middle term. This correspondence with the *Odyssey*, at least, is clear enough to the patient reader, but he will not find it in Joyce's own plan, which instead offers, for example, Aristotle as the Rock ('Scylla') and Plato as the Whirlpool ('Charybdis'). To understand these correspondences we must turn again to Bacon's *Wisdom of the Ancients*: chapter XXVII there is entitled 'Scylla and Icarus, or the Middle Way'. Its final paragraph contains an unmistakable reference to the opposition between Aristotle's love of definitions or distinctions and the Platonic Ideas or universals:

The Moral of this Parable (which we will but briefly touch, although it contain Matter of infinite Contemplation) seems to be this: That in every Art and Science, and so in their Rules and Axioms, there must be a mean observed between the Rocks of Distinction and the Gulfs of Universalities; which two are famous for the Wrack both of Wits and Arts.[22]

Wandering Rocks: A Dublin Panorama

In the tenth episode, 'Wandering Rocks', as Groden points out, the initial style is being used almost for the last time—and with a difference. Joyce professed to be especially pleased with this episode because Bloom navigates among the Symplegades ('the Rocks Wandering' in Butcher and Lang's translation) whereas Odysseus avoided them. Much of the episode consists of omniscient narrative, but we are privileged to eavesdrop on the interior monologues of several diverse new characters as well as the more familiar ones of Stephen and Bloom. The first of these new characters is the Very Reverend John Conmee, S. J., familiar to readers of *A Portrait* as the benevolent Rector of Clongowes Wood College, appearing once again under his name in real life. By 1904 he

[22] Ibid. 339–40.

has become the Superior of the Jesuit Order in Ireland and lives in the presbytery of St Francis Xavier's Church, Upper Gardiner Street, whence he sets out for the village of Artane, outside the northern boundary of Dublin, walking most of the way. In the Hades episode, Bloom, Mr Dedalus, and others attended the funeral of Patrick Dignam; Father Conmee hopes to get Patrick Dignam, Jr., accepted as a free pupil at the Artane Industrial School. Joyce tries to provide him with an interior monologue that will sound authentically priestly: for example, his mnemonic for the name 'Dignam' comes from the Tridentine Mass, '*Vere dignum et justum est*' (U 219), a very Joycean pun.

After Father Conmee's fairly long introduction, the second section (much briefer) reveals the structural principle of the episode as a whole. Corny Kelleher, an undertaker who will later come to the aid of Bloom and Stephen in 'Circe', is talking to a police constable at his mortuary; Father Conmee has recently passed by them in his northward progress, so that a sort of *liaison de vue* has been established between the two scenes: 'Corny Kelleher sped a silent jet of hayjuice arching from his mouth *while* a generous white arm from a window in Eccles street flung forth a coin.' (U 225; italics mine) Here, no *liaison de vue* is possible, for Eccles Street is a mile or more west of North Strand Street. The clue 'while' is never given again, but similar brief interruptions in the remaining sections indicate two events are taking place simultaneously in widely separated parts of Dublin.

The next piece of interior monologue in the episode consists of only three words. Blazes Boylan, Mrs Bloom's lover, is buying fruit and wine at Thornton's and ordering it to be sent to her as a gift to herald his arrival at their rendezvous. As the girl makes up the parcel, 'Blazes Boylan looked into the cut of her blouse. *A young pullet.*' Moments later her thoughts respond: 'The blond girl glanced sideways at him, *got up regardless, with his tie a bit crooked,* blushing.' (U 228); italics mine). This is the only glimpse we are vouchsafed into the mind of Hugh E. Boylan; it sums him up pretty accurately: though he prefers older game, he is not averse to pullets. Miss Dunne, Boylan's secretary, whom he telephones from Thornton's, is granted a longer monologue than her employer: for example, we learn her opinion of Wilkie Collins's *The Woman in White*: 'Too much mystery business in it' (U 229). She also thinks of clothes, dancing, and how to attract men. Inserting 'gaudy notepaper' in her typewriter, obviously for a private letter, she reveals the complete date of Bloomsday for the first time by typing '16 June 1904.' Is she perhaps the 'Martha' of Bloom's clandestine correspondence?

We are twice (U 227, 233) shown a glimpse of Bloom scanning books on a hawker's cart at Merchant's Arch, but the little episode entirely devoted to him takes place in an unnamed shop, probably on the neighbouring Merchant's Quay; references to the shopman and the counter show that Bloom is no longer outdoors. He is looking for the kind of erotic literature his wife likes to read and eventually borrows rather than buys a book entitled *Sweets of Sin*, having first read some excerpts to himself.[23] (U 233–5) Phrases from these recur to his mind during the rest of the day. After a little scene between Simon Dedalus and his daughter Dilly (Delia), the interior monologue of one 'Mr Kernan' is presented, immediately followed by a scene, mostly consisting of Stephen's interior monologue, in which he also meets Dilly. The last minor character shown through interior monologue is Master Patrick Aloysius Dignam, the boy Father Conmee wants to get into Artane. Many characters from *A Portrait* reappear in *Ulysses*, but Joyce was sufficiently Balzacian to draw on *Dubliners* as well. Tom Kernan is the protagonist of 'Grace' in that work, an alcoholic and a reluctant convert from the Church of Ireland. He has already reminded us of this earlier by his comment to Bloom at Dignam's funeral service: 'The service of the Irish church, used in Mount Jerome [Cemetery], is simpler, more impressive, I must say.' (U 105) He is the only person in *Ulysses* to address Bloom as a fellow-Protestant, though both are technically Catholics to oblige their wives. No wonder Bloom 'gave prudent assent' to Kernan's opinion. Joyce's attempt at a Protestant middle-class interior monologue is fairly trite, not at all the *tour de force* that Father Conmee inspires. Snobbery and loyalty to the British Crown motivate Kernan almost exclusively: while admiring Robert Emmet and Lord Edward Fitzgerald because 'They were gentlemen'—and, in fact, Protestants— he quickly remembers that 'they were on the wrong side'. The section ends with his chagrin at missing a chance to give a loyal salute to 'His Excellency' as the Viceregal cavalcade passes 'in easy trot along Pembroke quay . . . Damn it! What a pity!' (U 241)

   Master Dignam, sent from distant Sandymount to buy pork-steaks among the fashionable shopping streets, is returning as slowly as possible to the boredom of his grief-filled home. His monologue is laced with Dublin slang, some of it perennial, as when he calls Marie Kendall, the actress whose posters are all over the city, 'One of them mots'. Other slang is more ephemeral, as when he sees Boylan: 'In Grafton street Master Dignam saw a red flower in a toff's mouth and a swell pair of kicks on him' (U 251). The section ends with the young Dignam's memories of his father, in life and in death. 'Poor pa. That

---

[23] 'Borrows' because Bloom has already two books which appeal to his masochism, *Tales of the Ghetto* by Leopold von Sacher Masoch and *Fair Tyrants* by James Lovebirch. Joyce owned an Italian translation of the former.

was Mr Dignam, my father. I hope he is in purgatory now because he went to confession to father Conroy on Saturday night.' (*U* 251–2)

The nineteenth and last section of the episode narrates omnisciently the progress of the then Viceroy or Lord Lieutenant of Ireland, the Right Honourable William Humble, Earl of Dudley, GCVO, and the viceregal party, in two open carriages, through the streets of Dublin. His mission is to inaugurate the Mirus bazaar [in Sandymount] in aid of funds for Mercer's hospital' (*U* 254). His route runs diagonally across the city from northwest to southwest, crossing the River Liffey from north to south at Grattan Bridge. On the way, he is saluted, admired, smiled at 'with unseen coldness', or ignored by most of those who figure in the episode, themselves a majority of the significant secondary characters in the novel. The only conspicuous absentees are the major characters— Bloom, his wife, and Stephen—who do not see the Viceroy, and of course, Father Conmee who has made his own priestly progress in the opposite direction, receiving the salutes considered due to his office. Dublin is circumscribed by the Roman Church on the one hand and the British Empire on the other.

'Wandering Rocks' thus constitutes—to borrow a term from heraldry— a sort of *mise en abîme* (or epitome) of *Ulysses* as a whole. It also offers a panorama of Dublin, spread out in time as well as space. The episode makes us realize our need for a map of the city: once we have one, we can roughly measure the passage of time between the hours of three and four by the movements of the citizens. Dublin becomes a vast clock rendering time in term of space and *vice versa*: they seem like large misshapen clock-hands; draw a circle around Central Dublin with the centre at, say, Grattan Bridge and it will form an appropriate clock-face. It is hard to believe that this episode did not provide the inspiration for the mobile panorama of the Borough of Westminster presented at the beginning of *Mrs Dalloway* (1925). Virginia Woolf uses the sight and sound of Big Ben and the sky-writing aeroplane to unify her scene, as Joyce had used the Viceroy's and Father Conmee's respective progresses to unify his. Irish readers, especially Dubliners, should respond with pride and delight to Joyce's *tour de force*, as Londoners no doubt did to Mrs Woolf's. And as I have said earlier, it is virtually certain that Claude Mauriac modelled an entire novel, *La Marquise sortit à cinq heures* (1961), upon this one episode of *Ulysses*.

'Sirens': A Change of Tune

As we have seen, Joyce embarked on *Ulysses* with the intention of writing a relatively short work that would not stretch unduly the materials intended for a short story. Gradually, however, he seems to have become fascinated with the character of Bloom on the one hand and the vast symbolic implications of the *Odyssey* on the other. The pagination of the finished work in the edition used here provides a crude but striking measure of the consequences: the first nine episodes, theoretically half of the book, conclude on page 218; the second 'half' ends on page 783 and is therefore more than two-and-a-half times as long as its predecessor. This does not only mean that Joyce had padded out his basic anecdote with irrelevancies, though indeed certain episodes, especially 'Ithaca' are crammed with them. Consider, for example, Bloom's turning on of a water-tap in that episode (*U* 671): the flow of the water, in spite of the current drought, is traced all the way from the reservoir in a passage of twenty-four lines. In answer to the question 'What in water did Bloom, waterlover, drawer of water, watercarrier returning to the range [with a kettle] admire?' we are given more than a page on the symbolic, physical, chemical, and aesthetic qualities of water—beginning with 'Its universality' and ending with 'its ubiquity as constituting 90% of the human body: the noxiousness of the effluvia in lacustrine marshes, pestilential fens, faded flowerwater, stagnant pools in the waning moon.' (*U* 671–2).

On the last page of the fair copy of the ninth episode, 'Scylla and Charybdis', Joyce wrote 'End of First Part of "Ulysses"' and the date, 'New Year's Eve 1918'. From this point onwards *Ulysses* departs farther and farther from the accepted tradition of the novel as a work 'portraying characters & actions representative of real life in continuous plot'. Only the later passages that return to the initial style—notably the second half of 'Nausicaa' and all of 'Penelope'—continue to fall within this definition. Michael Groden says truly that 'a book that in some aspects began as a sequel to *A Portrait of the Artist as a Young Man* ended as a prelude to *Finnegans Wake*'. 'Wandering Rocks', for all its intricate motion, really forms a pause in the narrative: we receive some background information about major and minor characters, but the plot hardly advances one iota. In 'Sirens', the eleventh episode, we find ourselves at moments not just on the brink of *Finnegans Wake* but within its linguistic world of 'portmanteau' words like 'Siopold' (*U* 276) and onomatopoeic puns like 'Krandkrankran' (*U* 291) to describe the sound of the electric tram, which contains a suggestion of 'crank'—not to mention German *Kran* (crane, hoist) and *krank* (ill, sick). The page-and-a-half of syntactic fragments with which 'Sirens' begins are at least as disorienting as the first page of the *Wake*. They all appear again—usually in a slightly different form—at appropriate points in the episode, where the reader can make sense of them because of the context, and they are generally described by critics as musical motifs interwoven in the verbal fugue that is alleged to follow; unfortunately, there are far too many of them to be incorporated in even the most complex fugue. I see them as the *Leitmotiven* of a Wagnerian overture, intermezzo or prelude for full orchestra—closely resembling a Straussian tone-poem. Their presentation before the piece suggests the orchestra warming-up: each instrumentalist plays snatches of his part until the conductor summons them with the word 'Begin!'

'Sirens', therefore, is from one point of view an exercise in imitative form: the whole thrust of the episode is directed to producing in English prose an effect equivalent to the irresistible power of the Sirens' song whose music was so beguiling that Ulysses, though fully aware of the disastrous consequences, begged his comrades to untie him from the mast; fortunately their ears were full of wax, so that they could hear neither the song nor his entreaties. In Joyce's novel, the Sirens are Miss Douce and Miss Kennedy, barmaids at the Ormond Hotel; although they do not sin they are well trained to entice men by other means and make them dally and drink instead of going about their business; even Boylan delays for their sake his departure to meet his own siren, Molly Bloom, which is observed by Bloom from the adjoining dining-room.

On the other hand, from this turning-point in *Ulysses* to the very last of the seventeen episodes in *Finnegans Wake*, one finds in every episode, carefully interwoven with the imitative form and other experimental techniques, a body of tougher, more resistant threads: calculated to baffle the international reader with no special knowledge of Ireland, their patterning would be self-evident to a relatively unsophisticated Dubliner of Joyce's own generation. In 'Sirens', this material appropriately consists of four songs and an operatic aria. Two of the songs have strong Irish associations, while a third, 'Sweetheart, Goodbye' (U 264-7), seems to have been popular in Ireland during the decade before the First World War. It may have formed part of the tenor repertoire of Joyce's father, for Simon Dedalus plays the melody on the piano in the 'saloon' of the Ormond:

> —*The bright stars fade . . .*
> A voiceless song sang from within, singing:
> —*. . . the morn is breaking.*
>
> (U 264)

Who, one wonders, supplies the italicized words from this 'voiceless' song? If we read the text literally, the song sings itself, itself becoming the narrator: or Joyce may be the narrator; or the song may be so familiar that everybody present knows the words. One thing is certain, though: they are not part of Bloom's interior monologue, for he is still outside the hotel, buying notepaper in Daly's. In breaking away from his initial style, Joyce has begun to realize the almost infinite number of ways in which a story can be told: my own opinion here is that the song is the narrator, as it might be in the *Wake*.

Ben Dollard then sings and plays snatches of a song popular for bass voices like his own, 'Love and War' (*U* 267–70). Finally Dollard and Father Cowley persuade the reluctant Mr Dedalus, who feels his 'dancing days are done', to sing one of his and their old favourites, the aria *M'appari* from Flotow's *Marta*, recorded since 1904 by some of the greatest tenors of the century. Cowley sings the opening lines in Italian (*U* 271) and Dedalus then sits down to accompany himself, but we do not read the opening line of the English version sung by him, 'When first I saw that form endearing', until two pages later. During the pause, Cowley insists on accompanying Dedalus and makes the latter get up from the piano-stool; meanwhile, Bloom and Richie Goulding are discussing an entirely different tenor aria, 'All is lost now', from *La Sonnambula*.

The singing of the aria from *Marta*, rendered by a generous selection of its words, by an omniscient description of the reactions of the audience, and above all by the response to it of Bloom's interior monologue, is one of the most moving passages in the entire novel (*U* 273–6). Joyce has woven it of many strands, some of which must be autobiographical: memories of one or many times when he heard his father sing the same aria with the artistry that they both shared, other memories of his father—including his genuine, deep love for his wife—and memories too of his own experience of love at first sight with Nora Barnacle. The opera *Marta*, which is set in England, has a plot somewhat like that of Goldsmith's *She Stoops to Conquer*: Lionel, having fallen in love at a fair with a lady of his own class disguised as a servant named Martha, naturally runs into difficulties when he tries to find again a woman who never existed. In the great aria by which the opera survives, he recalls their only meeting and passionately cries out to his lost love, '*Martha! Ah, Martha! . . . Co-ome, thou lost one! Co-ome thou dear one! . . . Come! . . . To me!*' (*U* 275–6) Not only has the character Lionel lost his beloved, but Simon, the singer who portrays him, has recently lost his wife; Bloom, his most attentive listener, seems about to 'lose' his wife too, to the seductive Blazes Boylan. Although Bloom recognizes the coincidence between the name of the opera heroine and that of his pseudonymous correspondent, to whom he is soon going to write and answer, it is his first meeting with Molly that fills his reverie: 'First night when first I saw her at Mat Dillon's in Terenure, Yellow, black lace she wore. Musical chairs. We two the last. Fate. After her. Fate.' (*U* 275)

The technique used here of mingling interior monologue with the words and even the melody of vocal music was not invented by Joyce—perhaps not even by Dujardin—but I think that Joyce, as so often before, is borrowing a trick of his master's and improving it almost beyond recognition. There is a passage in *Les lauriers sont coupés* where Daniel Princ listens to a barrel-organ playing a popular tune of which he knows the rather silly words, 'I love you more than my geese', etc. These mingle with his reverie about his deceitful beloved, the actress Léa.

The impromptu concert continues with Cowley playing 'a light bright tinkling measure for tripping ladies'; Bloom says to himself: 'Minuet of *Don Giovanni* he's playing now.' (U 282) Finally Dollard is persuaded to sing a pathetic Irish ballad, 'The Croppy Boy', about the aftermath of the 1798 Rising. Note that it is not the original folk ballad, supposed to be sung by an Irish guerrilla fighter, which begins with the brave lines, 'It was early, early all in the spring; / The birds did whistle and sweetly sing; / Changing their notes from tree to tree, / And the song they sang was "Old Ireland Free"'. Instead, it is the Victorian adaptation of that ballad by 'Carroll Malone', an unrelievedly pathetic narrative of betrayal and defeat, in which a British officer disguised as a priest hears the croppy boy's confession and then condemns him to death. No wonder Bloom becomes more and more depressed about his wife's infidelity, though his mood throughout the whole episode has been one of acceptance rather than desire for vengeance, of self-pity rather than jealousy. He seems to have followed Boylan into the Ormond in a spirit of masochism, and this feeling is reinforced by Simon's aria and Dollard's ballad. The words of the latter are mostly paraphrased, by the way, and there is only one explicit italicized quotation (U 282–7). Although Thomas Moore's song 'The Last Rose of Summer' (inserted in *Marta* as a typical English folk-song!) is not actually sung in the Ormond, it keeps being referred to in the last pages of the episode (U 288–91): Bloom's apparent self-identification with the rose is explained by the pun revealed when the second line is known: 'Tis the last rose of summer / Left blooming alone.' From one point of view, the episode may be heard as ending with a rousing crescendo based on the famous peroration of Robert Emmet's speech from the dock after the failure of his Rising in 1803: the last note of the tone-poem is a single thud on the bass drum, '*Done.*' Unfortunately, Emmet's noble words, read by Bloom beneath 'a gallant picture hero in Lionel Marks's window' (U 290), are accompanied by what I might call a piccolo *obbligato* from his own digestive tract which began more than two pages earlier with 'Pwee! A wee little wind pipes eeee. In Bloom's little wee.' (U 288) This combined with Bloom's silent criticisms of 'The Croppy Boy', might deeply offend many sincere if sentimental patriots. I regard it as a blemish on one of Joyce's supreme achievements, although it bears out Bloom's theory: 'Sea, wind, leaves, thunder, waters . . . There's music everywhere.' (U 282)

'Cyclops': The Nightmare of History

If 'Sirens' is offensive to patriots, then 'Cyclops', in which most of Irish history, tradition, and politics is held up to ridicule, must be anathema. (Joyce assigned politics as the 'art' of this episode.) The Irish equivalent of Polyphemus is a real-life character, Michael Cusack, a former Fenian and one of the founders of the Gaelic Athletic Association, whose 'cave' is the bar of Barney Kiernan's public-house near the Four Courts. Known familiarly as 'the Citizen', he is presented as rude and coarse of speech, fanatical in his politics, hostile to any 'stranger' who is not one hundred per cent Irish and nationalist. Like his prototype, he has only one eye and is fond of strong drink.

We see him in the first instance through the words of the anonymous first-person, past-tense narrator of the episode, identified in Joyce's scheme as 'Noman'—a translation of the pseudonym 'Outis' chosen by Odysseus to deceive the Cyclops. This narrative voice is the quintessence of lower-class Dublin speech in both idiom and vocabulary, with the rapid speech-rhythm of a cocky urban know-all. Noman has picked up a knowledge of the seamy side of everything and everybody—and especially of the Blooms' marital life. He views the ideals of his neighbours, the citizen included, with a blighting irony that is compounded of envy, philistinism, and sheer native incredulity. Presented, like Cusack, as an anti-Semite, he mistakenly believes that Bloom has backed Throwaway, the outsider that has just won the Ascot Gold Cup: his boozer's code is outraged by the lucky man's neglect of his clear duty to buy drinks all round. He, Cusack, and others build up such an atmosphere of xenophobia that Bloom is forced to escape from the bar. Like Ulysses on his retreating ship, Bloom cannot resist provoking the citizen / Cyclops when he thinks he is safe on a jaunting car: Cusack furiously hurls a missile at him—a large tin biscuit-box instead of Polyphemus's rock—which fortunately misses its mark.

After he has entered the bar, the narrator is often merely the recorder of the quarrelsome conversations that go on there, punctuated by the citizen's endless diatribes against the British Government and its Empire. Even before this, however, the flat realistic style of a 'scrupulous meanness' far exceeding that of *Dubliners*, begins to be interrupted by paragraphs of lofty, pedantic and sentimental prose which an Irish reader ought to recognize as parody or pastiche. The first of these (U 292–3) imitates legal language pretty accurately; the second (*U* 293–5) reminds us of early Irish romance and saga from its very first words: 'In Inisfail the fair there lies a land, the land of holy Michan.' The gruesome corpses preserved more or less intact in the vaults of St Michan's Church are fulsomely described as 'the mighty dead as in life they slept, warriors and princes of high renown'. The passage goes on to describe the Dublin Corporation markets nearby, one for fish, the other for fruit and vegetables; after these we hear of the flocks and herds making their way to the cattle market farther west; the gusto and lavish detail with which all these comestibles are described reminds me irresistibly of Kuno Meyer's translation of *The Vision of Mac Conglinne*. The narrator resumes, anti-climactically; 'So we turned into Barney Kiernan's and there sure enough was the citizen up in the corner . . . and he waiting for what the sky would drop in the way of drink.' (*U* 295)

Joyce appropriately named the technique of Cyclops 'Gigantism': the next inflated description (*U* 296–7) portrays the citizen as a giant figure straight out of the cycle of tales of Finn and the Fianna, who in the decadence of the tradition are almost always shown as giants—and comic ones at that. Joyce knew exactly what he was doing when he compared the old Fenian with the legendary Fenians after whom the revolutionary organization was so poetically named. (Take note that Joyce does not at all exaggerate the multiplicity of compound adjectives to be found in medieval Irish narrative prose):

The figure seated on a large boulder at the foot of a round tower was that of a broadshouldered deepchested stronglimbed frankeyed redhaired freely freckled shaggybearded widemouthed largenosed longheaded deepvoiced barekneed brawnyhanded hairylegged ruddyfaced sinewyarmed hero. . . . The eyes in which a tear and a smile strove for the mastery were of the dimensions of a goodsized cauliflower.

(*U* 296)

In the description of his clothing which follows we read this:

From his girdle hung a row of seastones . . . and on these were graven with rude yet striking art the tribal images of many Irish heroes and heroines of antiquity, Cuchulin, Conn of hundred battles, Niall of nine hostages, Brian of Kincora.

(*U* 296)

All very well and good, but some of those in the long list that follows are neither heroes nor heroines, and sometimes not even Irish: Francy Higgins, better known as 'The Sham Squire', was an informer against those who rebelled against British rule in 1798. Farther on, we find 'The Man that Broke the Bank at Monte Carlo', from a song still current in 1904, and 'Sidney Parade', the name of a Dublin suburban street.

I have no space to analyse further examples of gigantism: this one shows the strength and weakness common to all. The parody/pastiche element is at first skilfully handled, and there is always a rapier-point of satire directed at a political pose or a literary affectation—and sometimes at both. But Joyce, like Swift in *A Tale of a Tub*, draws out these 'digressions' at too great length, and makes feebler and feebler puns as he does so. Still, there is much left to enjoy: the operation of Guinness's brewery, property of the Lords Iveagh and Ardilaun, is recounted in the style of the Irish Mythological Cycle (*U* 299); a séance calls up the spirit of Paddy Dignam, with anti-climactic results (*U* 301–2); Bloom gives a brief scientific lecture on a grisly physiological phenomenon (*U* 304–5); the execution of an Irish hero takes place before a 'distinguished' foreign audience whose childishly punning names would disgrace even the pages of *The Magnet* or some similar English schoolboy magazine of the time (*U* 306–10). A little more sophistication appears when the citizen's mongrel dog, Garryowen, to which he talks, as Polyphemus does to his favourite ram in the original, supposedly breaks into Gaelic verse. The 'translation' that follows is both pastiche and parody of Hyde, Synge, and Lady Gregory, though not of Yeats:

> The curse of my curses
> Seven days every day
> And seven dry Thursdays
> On you, Barney Kiernan,
> Has no sup of water
> To cool my courage.
> And my guts red roaring
> After Lowry's lights.
> (*U* 312)

Parodies follow of a House of Commons debate as recorded in Hansard (*U* 315–16) and a newspaper report (presumably from the *Irish Independent*) of a discussion 'on the revival of ancient Gaelic sports', which meticulously lists all the clergy present while dismissing the laity as 'P. Fay, T. Quirke, etc., etc.' (*U* 316–18). The citizen's plea to 'Save the trees of Ireland' inspires a society-page account of a wedding between John Wise Nolan, 'grand chief ranger of the Irish National Foresters' (a politico-charitable organization), and 'Miss Fir Conifer of Pine Valley' (*U* 326–7). The citizen's handkerchief is then described in terms of an Irish illuminated manuscript: unfortunately Joyce, whether from ignorance or out of malice aforethought, compares it to the relatively colourless Book of Ballymote, rather than to some masterpiece of illumination and ornament like the Book of Kells or the Book of Durrow. The amusing list of 'wonderfully beautiful' Irish scenes depicted on the cloth is as full of incongruities as the list of heroes and heroines already analysed (*U* 331–2).

A pause soon follows while the narrator goes 'round to the back of the yard to pumpship' (*U* 335); as he urinates, we are vouchsafed a few present-tense quotations (in parentheses) from his interior monologue, mainly concerned with the state of his bladder. One would be tempted to identify him with 'Andrew (Pisser) Burke' (*U* 731) did he not himself mention that gentleman's nickname on page 338. After Noman's return to the company, only six further set-pieces of gigantism occur, each with its own special interest. A passage of Elizabethan narrative prose and dialogue recalls the improvisation in Shakespearean blank verse that occurs in 'Scylla and Charybdis', and at the same time looks forward to the chronological pastiche-history of English prose in 'Oxen of the Sun' (*U* 336–7). Shortly afterwards, Martin Cunningham, in an attempt to quiet the storm over Bloom, utters the prayer 'God bless all here': at his words, an immense, august procession forms, led by representatives of all the better-known religious orders. 'And after came all the saints and martyrs, virgins and confessors', many of whom are perfectly genuine, including the patron saints of most of those present, though Garryowen's patron, 'S. Owen Caniculus', seems about as authentic as 'S. Anonymous and S. Eponymous', and others whose names immediately follow his. We may also legitimately question the title of 'S. Marion Calpensis [i. e. of Gibraltar]'. The saints' symbols, however incongruous they may seem, are also generally authentic. Chanting and performing miracles, the members of the procession wend their way, doubtless from the Catholic Pro-Cathedral in Marlborough Street, to Barney Kiernan's. 'And last, beneath a canopy of cloth of gold, came the reverend Father O'Flynn [hero of a half-comic, half-sentimental song by the father of the poet Robert Graves] attended by Malachi and Patrick', the great reformer and the great founder respectively, of the Roman Catholic Church in Ireland. The celebrant blesses the public-house and then enters to invoke a blessing on all present in a highly appropriate and authentic Latin prayer. In spite of Father O'Flynn and the other comic touches, Joyce dare not prick the bubble of the giant institution that he sought to confront every day of his life. (*U* 338–40) Bloom has no sooner climbed on the jaunting-car than it becomes a ship in full sail accompanied by nymphs, all being described in euphuistic style as unHomeric as most translations of Homer (*U* 341). A fine old Irish send-off for the departing Hungarian nobleman 'Lipóti Virag' (alias Leopold Bloom) is then giganticized: note that the tin which formerly contained biscuits manufactured by the well-known Dublin firm of W. & R. Jacob is now dignified as 'the gift of a silver casket, tastefully executed in the style of ancient Celtic ornament, a work which reflects every credit on the makers, Messrs Jacob *agus* Jacob' (*U* 342–3). The sound of 'the old tin box clattering along the street' provokes a description of an earthquake and of the comic efforts of the British authorities to cope with its aftermath (*U* 344–5). Finally the ascent of Bloom in a chariot of fire is narrated in the language of the Authorized Version of the Old Testament, except that Noman is given the last word: 'And they beheld Him even Him, ben Bloom Elijah, amid clouds of angels ascend to the glory of the brightness at an angle of forty-five degrees over Donohoe's in Little Green Street like a shot off a shovel.'

'Nausicaa', Virgin and Voyeur

The first half of 'Nausicaa', which focuses on a 21-year-old girl named Gerty MacDowell, achieves a stylistic effect that is in some ways close to that of 'Cyclops'. Once again, an inflated conventional narrative technique is being contrasted with events and dialogue presented in the sordidly realistic way: but the 'gigantism' here represents Gerty's interior monologue, conveyed in the third person. So far, we have assumed that all interior monologue must be in the first person, but suppose the subject is telling herself a story—about herself. This sort of thing might be the result:

Gerty MacDowell who was seated near her companions, lost in thought, gazing far away into the distance, was in very truth as fair a specimen of winsome Irish girlhood as one could wish to see. She was pronounced beautiful by all who knew her though, as folks often said, she was more a Giltrap than a MacDowell. Her figure was slight and graceful, inclining even to fragility but those jelloids she had been taking of late had done her a world of good, much better than the Widow Welch's female pills and she was much better of those discharges she used to get and that tired feeling. The waxen pallor of her face was almost spiritual in its ivorylike purity though her rosebud mouth was a genuine Cupid's bow, Greekly perfect. Her hands were of finely veined alabaster with tapering fingers and as white as lemon juice and queen of ointments could make them though it was not true that she used to wear kid gloves in bed or take a milk footbath either. Bertha Supple told that once to Edy Boardman, a deliberate lie, when she was black out at daggers drawn with Gerty (the girl chums naturally had of course their little tiffs from time to time like the rest of mortals) and she told her not to let on whatever she did that it was her that told or she'd never speak to her again.

(*U* 348)

Clearly, the earlier sentences of this passage form a very successful pastiche of a short story or novelette such as one could find in certain cheap magazines in 1904—and indeed for many years after. In my boyhood, many young Irishwomen were reading a magazine addressed to single girls who had presumably left school at 14, *Peg's Paper*. Like the works mentioned by Joyce himself—'the Princess novelette', 'the *Lady's Pictorial*', 'Pearson's Weekly'—this was published in London and contained advice on health, beauty, and emotional problems, as well as the innocuous fiction Joyce is parodying. Naturally these publications attracted advertising from the manufacturers of patent medicines and cheap beauty preparations. As we see, the advertisements and the fiction have become intermingled by the third sentence: in the 1920s 'iron jelloids' were still being advertised in the most expensive and sophisticated ladies' monthlies. In a few more sentences, the genteel prose begins to falter under the pressure of bitter feelings that require a more colloquial expression. Amusingly, the Dublin expression 'black out with' is set down side by side with the would-be poetical 'at daggers drawn with'; gentility, in desperation, tries to cover up such unladylike anger with the parenthesis about 'the girl chums', only to be swept aside by the barely intelligible flood of colloquialism that ends our quotation. Gerty often manages to restore order among her unladylike feelings in the ensuing pages, but the reader cannot fail to notice undercurrents of bitterness, ill-temper and prurience. In fact, except for the change of tense in Gerty's interior monologue, easily explained by her reading and her habit of dramatizing her own life in its terms, the first half of 'Nausicaa' is just as much a return to the 'initial style' as the second half. Gerty's self-dramatization is all the more justifiable because, as we shall see, like many another heroine of a novelette, she has a secret sorrow.

It is unfair of Joyce thus to emphasize the division between the two 'halves' of 'Nausicaa', the first being seen through the consciousness of Gerty / Nausicaa, the second through that of Bloom / Ulysses. Despite the sharp stylistic contrast between their two interior monologues, there is hardly a more unified episode in all of *Ulysses*. Joyce's model, Book VIII of the *Odyssey*, has been famous for millennia as the perfect, infinitely delicate, presentation of the interest in each other shown by a nubile girl and a man in his prime. The Greek epic first takes us inside the consciousness of the Phaeacian princess Nausicaa, who is prompted by Athena in a dream to ask her father to let her have a waggon in which to bring the family linen down to the shore, where she and her maidens will wash it. Her pretext is that her brothers are running short of dancing clothes, but her father guesses that she is thinking about her own marriage, which must be arranged soon, and for which her trousseau ought to be made ready. After their task is completed, the girls bathe and then play with a ball on the beach. When the ball accidentally goes into the water, the girls scream and awaken Ulysses, who has been sleeping on the sand nearby, naked and exhausted after his escape from storm and shipwreck. He thus becomes aware of Nausicaa, as we do of his consciousness, and she sees him soon afterwards, approaching her with nothing to hide his nakedness but a leafy branch. Like a true princess, she does not lose her head, but gives him some of her brother's clothes to wear. She has already appreciated the compliments of her divine beauty addressed to her by the ever-plausible Ulysses, and when he has bathed and dressed and been given a touch of glory by his patroness Athena, she feels he would be a worthy husband for her. She lets him ride on the waggon as far as the outskirts of the city, but then discreetly leaves him to make the rest of the way to her father's palace on foot. Like the heroine of a novelette, she provides the model of correct deportment for a particular class in a particular society: she does not want to provoke gossip among her father's subjects about this stranger, especially as she has been slow to marry any of the Phaeacians who are courting her. In the end, of course, Ulysses, having triumphed at the Phaeacians' sports meeting and told the story of his life and wanderings, is brought home to Ithaca in a Phaeacian ship, and we hear nothing more of Nausicaa. Nevertheless, the beauty, discretion, and skill in household works of this virgin on the threshold of marriage will never be forgotten by hearers or readers of the *Odyssey*.

Joyce's own view of 'Nausicaa' differed considerably from the traditional one, as he revealed in a letter to Frank Budgen (3 January 1920;[24] he planned to write the episode in 'namby-pamby jammy marmalady drawersy (alto la!) style with the effects of incense, mariolatry, masturbation, stewed cockles, painter's palette, chitchat, circumlocutions, etc etc)'. I can't discover any hint of stewed cockles in the episodes as finally published, but the other effects are certainly present. Jam and marmalade suggest sweet stickiness of the namby-pamby style. 'Drawersy' obviously refers to Joyce's well-known obsession with feminine underwear, which is given free rein when Gerty congratulates herself on being in full panoply this particular evening, including 'finespun hose with high spliced heels and wide garter tops. As for undies they were Gerty's chief care' (*U* 350). Later, she exposes all that she has on, including her garters, to Bloom's voyeur eyes, as she leans farther and farther to watch the Mirus Bazaar firework display. Her own display is a response to the erotic interest shown by the handsome

---

[24] Frank Budgen, *James Joyce and the Making of Ulysses* (Oxford: Oxford University Press, 1972), 210–14.

though aging 'stranger'. The excuse for all this is of course supplied by the waggon-load of linen and under-linen present in the *Odyssey*. Since Gerty's body is virgin, whatever about her mind, the mariolatry and incense are not wholly inappropriate, though no doubt offensive to many Irish readers. In the neighbouring church, dedicated to Our Lady, Star of the Sea (*Stella Maris*), 'the men's temperance retreat conducted by the missioner, the reverend John Hughes S. J.' is taking place: 'rosary, sermon and benediction of the Most Blessed Sacrament.' The liturgy includes 'reciting the litany of Our Lady of Loreto' (*U* 354). The whole service can be heard through the open windows of the church on this summer evening.

The masturbation is chiefly Bloom's, though Gerty has previously heard from Bertha Supple about her family's 'gentleman lodger' who 'used to do something not very nice that you could imagine sometimes in the bed' (*U* 365–6). We do not become aware of Bloom, 'the gentleman in black who was sitting there by himself', until one of the Caffrey twins kicks their ball 'as hard as ever he could down towards the seaweedy rocks' (*U* 355). The parallel to the *Odyssey* is clear, but Bloom, being awake and fully clothed (he will fall sleep later), intercepts the ball and throws it back rather awkwardly, so that it 'stopped right under Gerty's skirt' (*U* 356). From this point until Gerty's departure, Bloom and she rarely take their eyes off each other and remain in constant emotional contact at a distance of about fifteen yards. Bloom masturbates with his hands in his pockets and reaches his climax simultaneously with the bursting of the 'long Roman candle' in the firework display; Joyce seems to imply that Gerty has a spontaneous orgasm at the same moment (*U* 366–7). Shortly afterwards Gerty, who has been sitting on the rock throughout the episode, gets up to go home with her friends Cissy Caffrey and Edy Boardman, the Caffrey twins, and Baby Boardman. The first words of Bloom's interior monologue, which now takes over from Gerty's, show that he has recognized her secret grief: 'Tight boots? No. She's lame! O!' Joyce described the technique of the episode as 'Tumescence, detumescence'; the latter phase begins as we enter Bloom's mind. Although the sexual arousal and release—not to mention the interest shown in him by a younger woman—have made him feel young, he has to admit that he is now exhausted. Nevertheless he thinks about Gerty, his recent experience, his relations with his wife, and the nature of woman in general for a number of pages before falling asleep (*U* 367–82).

It is worth noting that the scene of 'Nausicaa' is laid throughout on Sandymount Strand, or at least on the rocks at one end of it; this beach has already provided the setting for 'Proteus', and a number of themes from Stephen's monologue recur in Bloom's: for instance women's clothing, menstruation, and the influence on the latter of the moon. The coming 'fusion' of Stephen and Bloom is thus foreshadowed, and at the same time, as already suggested, the structure of *Ulysses* is tightened by this presentation of an uninterrupted monologue by Bloom to match Stephen's in 'Proteus'; also Molly's in 'Penelope', which is still to come. Bloom thinks constantly of his wife, yet feels no resentment against Boylan: 'Suppose he gave her money. Why not? All a prejudice. She's worth ten, fifteen, more a pound. All that for nothing.' (*U* 369) Nevertheless he decides not to go home, because Molly might be still up; instead, he will inquire about Mrs Purefoy at the lying-in hospital. Meanwhile he'll have a short snooze. As he falls asleep, his monologue drifts off in a 'night language' similar to that of *Finnegans Wake*; it does so again at the end of 'Ithaca', when he is safe at last in his own bed. The paragraph below recapitulates 'Nausicaa' in fragments which mingle with motifs from earlier episodes:

O sweety all your little girlwhite up I saw dirty bracegirdle made me do love sticky we two naughty Grace darling she him half past the bed met him pike hose frillies for Raoul to perfume your wife black hair heavy under embon *señorita* young eyes Mulvey plump years dream return tail end Agendath swoony lovey showed me your next year in drawers return next in her next her next
(*U* 382)

Apart from Gerty, the major themes are Molly's adultery with Boylan (Bloom's watch stopping at half-past four seems to him an omen); the erotic novel *Sweets of Sin* which Bloom has borrowed for Molly and in which he identified Raoul, the practised seducer, with Boylan; Molly's reminiscences of her adolescence in Gibraltar, where Mulvey was her first lover, mingling with thoughts of Milly, the Blooms' daughter, as she looks now at 15; finally and surprisingly, the word 'Agendath' (an error throughout *Ulysses* for the Hebrew word *Agudath*, whether supposedly misread by Bloom or actually by Joyce), linked with 'return' and 'next year' (in Jerusalem), refers to Bloom's romantic Zionism. Perhaps this last theme is taking on new meaning, as Bloom like Ulysses must return home in the Nostos. Also two hopeful notes have been struck in his recent meditations. On the one hand, in 'Sirens', it occurred to him that the Blooms might well summon up courage to abandon contraception, which they have practised since the death of their son in infancy: 'I too, last my race. Milly young student. Well, my fault perhaps. No son. Rudy. Too late now. Or if not? If not? If still?' (*U* 285) It is possible, of course, that Boylan may oblige him with an heir, but the novel virtually ends with the onset of Molly's period, which proves that she is still fertile, yet despite her self-confessed neglect of precautions during the afternoon, not pregnant. The possibility of a return to natural inter-course and child-bearing implies a return to conjugal love and fidelity. The most hopeful note in 'Nausicaa' occurs in this passage charac-teristically linking Milly with Molly:

> Frightened she [Milly] was when her nature came on her first. Poor child! Strange moment for the mother too. Brings back her girlhood. Gibraltar. Looking from Buena Vista . . . Looking out over the sea she told me. Evening like this, but clear, no clouds. I always thought I'd marry a lord or a gentleman with a private yacht. . . . Why me? Because you were so foreign from the others.
>
> (U 380)

The reason Molly gives here for choosing Bloom is not the whole story, but it prepares us for the final cadence of 'Penelope', in which this passage occurs:

> he said I was a flower of the mountain yes so we are flowers all a womans body yes that was one true thing he said in his life and the sun shines for you today yes that was why I liked him because I saw he understood or felt what a woman is and I knew I could always get round him and I gave him all the pleasure I could leading him on till he asked me to say yes.
>
> (U 782)

It must never be forgotten that 'Penelope'—and therefore *Ulysses* itself—concludes with an orgasm ('yes I said yes I will Yes'), whether male or female or both, which links it indissolubly with 'Nausicaa'. Also, Bloom's sympathy for his daughter proves that 'he understood or felt all that a woman is', though his touching expression 'her nature' is not original but traditional, and indeed still current in Ireland. An earlier passage in 'Nausicaa' where it is used ought long ago to have destroyed all the still parroted stereotypes about Joyce's attitude to the Roman Catholic Church and its clergy; Gerty is thinking of young Father Conroy, the curate of Star of the Sea:

> He looked almost a saint. . . . He told her that time when she told him about that in confession crimsoning up to the roots of her hair for fear he could see, not to be troubled because that was only the voice of nature and we were all subject to nature's laws, he said, in this life and that that was no sin because that came from the nature of woman instituted by God, he said and that our Blessed Lady herself said to the archangel Gabriel be it done unto me according to Thy Word.
>
> (U 358)

'Nausicaa' ends with the 'clock on the mantlepiece in the priest's house' (U 382) crying 'Cuckoo' nine times over the sleeping Bloom to indicate the hour, but a man who can sleep peacefully with the knowledge that he has been cuckolded surely has the best of the joke.

'Oxen of the Sun': the Garden of Parodies

The severest criticism that can be levelled against the next episode, 'Oxen of the Sun', lies implicit in Joyce's own plan for it. His celebrated letter of 13 March 1920 to Frank Budgen sums it up:

Am working hard at *Oxen of the Sun*, the idea being the crime committed against fecundity by sterilizing the act of coition. Scene, lying-in hospital. Technique: a nineparted episode without divisions introduced by a Sallustian-Tacitean prelude (the unfertilized ovum), then by way of earliest English alliterative and monosyllable and Anglo-Saxon . . . then by way of Mandeville . . . then Malory's *Morte d'Arthur* . . . then the Elizabethan chronicle style . . . then a passage solemn, as of Milton, Taylor, Hooker, followed by a choppy Latin-gossipy bit, style of Burton-Browne, then a passage Bunyanesque . . . after a diarystyle bit Pepys-Evelyn . . . and so on through Defoe-Swift and Steele-Addison-Sterne and Landor-Pater-Newman until it ends in a frightful jumble of Pidgin English, nigger English, Cockney, Irish, Bowery slang and broken doggerel. This progression is also linked back at each part subtly with some foregoing episode of the day and, besides this, with the natural stages of development in the embryo and the period of faunal evolution in general. The double-thudding Anglo-Saxon motive recurs from time to time ('Loth to move from Horne's house') to give the sense of the hoofs of oxen. Bloom is a spermatozoon, the hospital the womb, the nurse the ovum, Stephen the embryo. How's that for high?[25]

This seems and is a recipe for pedantry unparalleled in any of the authors Joyce chooses to imitate: not even the Burton of *The Anatomy of Melancholy* could have envisaged such a work. It is true that Swift of *A Tale of a Tub* and Part Three of *Gulliver's Travels* might have imagined such a pedant as Joyce and sketched the outline of a 'treatise' comparable to 'Oxen of the Sun', but he would never have wasted his time writing more than a few sample paragraphs of such a gallimaufry. The philosophical justification for Joyce's undertaking, if any, is implied rather than stated in his letter: literature, like life, evolves from rudimentary beginnings into ever higher and more complex forms (of which presumably the newest, i.e. *Ulysses*, is necessarily the best). The analogy between the two kinds of 'evolution' seems patently false; I don't believe Joyce himself, in his saner moments, ever thought of it as true, and the whole discussion of Shakespeare in 'Scylla and Charybdis' surely refutes it. Besides, Joyce's knowledge of English literary history was far too sketchy for him to make an informed judgement either way. His note-sheets for this episode still exist and have been published by Phillip F. Herring, who has traced most of the sources for the notes. Joyce's

---

[25] Gilbert (ed.), *Letters of James Joyce*, 138–9.

greatest debt is to George Saintsbury's *A History of English Prose Style*, as one might expect, but he also made use of humbler works, including William Peacock's one-volume anthology in the 'World's Classics' series, *English Prose from Mandeville to Ruskin*. Joyce's ear for style was so accurate that he could brilliantly parody the style of an author like Burton or Pepys when he knew only excerpts. When he is imitating an author whom he truly respects—Newman, for example—what we find is no longer parody but true pastiche, where the traits are so delicately reproduced that the original is harder to recognize. A letter of Joyce's complains indignantly that the beautiful Newman imitation which begins 'There are sins or (let us call them as the world calls them) evil memories' (*U* 421) has been assigned to a quite different model by a misguided critic.[26]

At least Joyce could claim that he had studied English literature as an undergraduate and was already recognized, on the strength of *A Portrait*, as a minor master of English prose; but what is one to say about the non-literary aspects of the plan? The 'art' of 'Oxen of the Sun' is medicine, a discipline to which he never seriously applied himself, either in Dublin or in Paris. In Dublin, writes Ellmann, 'he attended a few lectures in biology, chemistry and physics, but his faculty of application to disagreeable subjects, which had sustained him at Belvedere, had diminished during his truant years at University College.'[27] In Paris, like Stephen Dedalus, he was nominally a student of 'Paysayenn P. C. N., you know: *physiques, chimiques et naturelles*' (*U* 41). But in fact he gave up attending lectures there within a week, on the grounds that he would have to pay his fees immediately and was unable to do so.[28] In a curious way, 'Oxen of the Sun' can be read as an attempt at psychic compensation: Joyce seems to be trying to prove that he could have earned a medical degree if he had had enough money and been willing to spare the time. He complained and / or boasted that 'Oxen of the Sun' had cost him a thousand hours from start to finish. I see no reason to question the correctness of this figure: what I am asking is what compulsion drove him to a literary demonstration of the dubious proposition that 'ontogeny recapitulates phylogeny'?

Joyce, being a logician of sorts, if no scientist, can see something of the weakness of his own position; furthermore, his unique narrative method permits him to attack it at one stage of the running debates among the students. A discussion, chiefly on the cause of infant mortality, is here (*U* 418–20) being reported in a highly partisan manner for a learned journal in a style that has been attributed to Thomas Henry

---

[26] Ibid.   [27] Ellmann, *James Joyce* (2nd edn.), 104–5.   [28] Ibid. 113.

Huxley. Stephen is attacked immediately for his 'perverted transcendentalism', which 'runs directly counter to accepted scientific methods. Science, it cannot too often be repeated, deals with tangible phenomena.' Later, he is described with lofty contempt as 'this morbidminded esthete and embryo philosopher who for all his overweening bumptiousness in things scientific can scarcely distinguish an acid from an alkali' (*U* 420). It isn't always justifiable to identify Stephen with Joyce, but here at least the cap fits perfectly, in view of what Ellmann has told us. For those who are interested, analyses of 'Oxen of the Sun' that include the 'scientific' background do exist, although studies of the literary-historical-stylistic aspect are inevitably much more common.[29] The theological doctrine conveyed by Stephen that 'at the end of the second month a soul was infused' (*U* 390) seems the most useful piece of learning to be found in the whole episode.

Here and in the 'Ithaca' episode—whose art is 'Science' *tout court*—Joyce is most clearly paying himself with words: he thinks he has mastered a subject when in fact what he has mastered is its vocabulary only. The tendency can already be seen in *A Portrait* and in the philosophical meditations based on Aristotle, Lessing, and Berkeley which form part of 'Proteus'. A curious example is the outburst of slang (see the letter to Budgen) which concludes 'Oxen of the Sun'. (*U* 424–8). Stephen and the medicals, all drunk, pour out of the hospital/womb like the after-birth, which the jumbled phrases also represent. (Bloom, who is not drunk, follows because he is anxious about Stephen's safety.) The American slang, for instance, is not merely dated but often wrong for its own time. Excellent as Joyce's ear was, he had not heard many Americans speak, in slang or otherwise: his own speech appears on most occasions to have been meticulous standard English.

No one can deny that 'Oxen of the Sun' contains some excellent parodies, especially where the subject-matter and tone closely match the style of the author imitated; but there are clever parodies in 'Cyclops' too, some of which sketch the outline of early Irish literature. These, however, stand apart from the narrative, whereas in 'Oxen of the Sun' they are integrated with it. For indeed there is a narrative, however distorted and interrupted by the constant changes of style, though it does not get under way until two pages of the episode have elapsed: 'Some man that wayfaring was stood by housedoor at night's oncoming. Of Israel's folk was that man that on earth wandering fared. Stark ruth of man his errand that him lone led till that house'. (*U* 385) Before this comes the monumentally dull 'Sallustian-Tacitean' passage about the

[29] See, e.g., J. S. Atherton, 'Oxen of the Sun', *James Joyce's Ulysses: Critical Essays* (London: University of California Press Ltd., 1974), 313–40.

importance of maternity care, which reads like a literal translation from Latin. Joyce has, however, found some authentic information in his notoriously unreliable Irish sources, including the names of some hereditary Irish medical families and that of a disease, the 'loose boy-connell flux', known in Gaelic as *Buidhe Chonaill*. In a modification of Joyce's original plan, the episode now begins with a threefold invocation to the sun as a fertility god, addressed as 'bright one, light one, Horhorn'; the syllable 'horn' is phallic, as in the phrase 'have you the horn?' already met with in 'Sirens'. The first sentence of the invocation and of the episode is the polyglot 'DESHIL HOLLEAMUS' (*U* 383)—meaning 'Let us go sunwise around (or 'to') Holles. The institution now known as the National Maternity Hospital is still in Holles Street, Dublin. *Deiseal* is the Gaelic word for clockwise or sunwise, the correct direction for ritual movement, especially when the sun is being invoked, as opposed to *tuathail* (anticlockwise or 'widdershins'). In 1904 Dr Andrew Horne was Master of the hospital: 'Of that house A. Horne is lord. Seventy beds keeps he there'. (*U* 385)

Bloom is admitted to the hospital by his old acquaintance Nurse Callan, who tells him that Mrs Purefoy has been in labour for three days but will soon give birth now. Another acquaintance, Dixon, a medical student who played a small part in *A Portrait*, then appears in the corridor and invites Bloom to a drinking party in his room; Bloom at first prudently refuses, but finally consents because he is weary after his day's adventures. When he discovers that Stephen is of the party—in fact the host—and very drunk, he stays on until the bitter end. A passage in the style of Malory gives his motive: 'And sir Leopold sat with them for he bore fast friendship to sir Simon and to this his young son Stephen . . . Ruth red him, love led on with will to wander, loth to leave.' (*U* 388) (Note, by the way, the recurrence in this last sentence of the 'double-thudding Anglo-Saxon motive'.) The chivalric style being imitated calls for stronger emotions than Bloom at this point is prepared to feel. He and Simon Dedalus seemed anything but fast friends in the funeral coach during the 'Hades' episode. Furthermore, Bloom hardly knows Stephen at all, though he saw something of him at the newspaper office in the 'Aeolus' episode. A little farther on we have a more accurate picture of Bloom's feelings:

and now sir Leopold that had of his body no manchild for an heir looked upon his friend's son . . . and as sad as he was that him failed a son of such gentle courage (for all accounted him of real parts) so grieved he also in no less measure for young Stephen that he lived riotously with these wastrels and murdered his goods with whores.

(*U* 390–1)

Most of the episode is taken up, however, with wide-ranging arguments about such topics as the possible conflicts between medical ethics and Roman Catholic canon law, the causes of infant mortality, the arguments (statistical and theological) for and against contraception—none of which lends itself to a generally acceptable conclusion. Many of the contributions to the discussion are obscene, but Stephen's are usually blasphemous as well. A sudden peal of thunder, followed by a storm of rain, terrifies him: he feels God is about to punish him for his defiance. Bloom tries to comfort him, and the style shifts to that of Bunyan's *Pilgrim's Progress*: 'But was young Boasthard's fear vanquished by Calmer's words? No.' (U 395) Stephen is too fond of 'scortatory love and its foul pleasures' (U 201), as are his drinking companions; its possible consequences do not discourage them, 'for that foul plague Allpox and the monsters they cared not for them, for Preservative had given them a stout shield of oxengut and . . . that they might take no hurt neither from Offspring . . . by virtue of this same shield which was named Killchild' (U 396). Joyce positively frolics with Bunyan, who had his own grim vein of humour—but Anglo-Saxon rigour now intervenes once more:

Wherein, O wretched company, were ye all deceived for that the peal of thunder was the voice of the god that was in a very grievous rage that he would presently lift his arm and spill their souls for their abuses and their spillings done by them contrariwise to his word which forth to bring brenningly biddeth.

(U 396)

In the corresponding episode of the *Odyssey*, the anger of the sun-god at the sacrilegious killing of the sacred oxen is conveyed first by the hideous lowing of the hides of the slaughtered animals and then by the darkening of the sky.

The oxen motif is occasionally sustained by references to bulls, most notably in a passage strongly reminiscent of Swift's *A Tale of a Tub*, where the Roman Church in Ireland is compared with a prize bull. (U 399–401) Allusion is being made to the alleged Bull of Pope Adrian (Nicholas Breakspear, an Englishman) on which Henry II of England based his claim to the sovereignty of Ireland. When the long-awaited Malachi Mulligan arrives at the hospital 'from Mr Moore's the writer's (that was a papish but is now, folk say, a good Williamite)' (U 397), his latest jape is that he will stand at stud like a prize bull on Lambay Island, ready to fertilize all comers. He is suggesting that the seemingly opposed practices of celibacy and contraception have together reduced the population of Ireland dramatically, while at the same time causing sexual frustration for many Irishwomen.

On his way to the hospital Mulligan has run into one Alec Bannon, whom he has brought along to the party. Bannon proves to be none other than the 'young student' Milly has met several times in Mullingar, where she is working for a photographer. She mentioned him in the letter Bloom received this very morning, in which she thanked her father for the 'tam' or 'Tam O'Shanter' cap he sent her for her 15th birthday, the previous day (U 66). When Mulligan first ran into Bannon in the rainy street, he described Milly in cattle-market terms as 'a skittish heifer, big of her age and beef to the heel'—an allusion to the familiar Irish phrase 'beef to the heels like a Mullingar heifer', which Milly also referred to in her letter (U 397). Later, Bannon, 'overjoyed as he was at a passage that had befallen him, could not forbear to tell it to his nearest neighbour', who fortunately was Crothers, not Bloom (U 403). Bannon tells his story in Sterne's *Sentimental Journey* style, as follows:

Ah, Monsieur, he said, had you but beheld her as I did with these eyes at that affecting instant with her dainty tucker and her new coquette cap (a gift for her feast day as she told me) in such an artless disorder, of so melting a tenderness, 'pon my conscience, even you, Monsieur, had been impelled by generous nature to deliver yourself wholly into the hands of such an enemy or to quit the field for ever. I declare I was never so touched in all my life. God I thank thee as the author of my days! Thrice happy will be he whom so amiable a creature will bless with her favours.

(U 404–5)

The young man's prattle, however, soon takes on a more sinister note—to a father's ear at any rate:

How mingled and imperfect are all our sublunary joys! Maledicity! Would to God that foresight had remembered me to take my cloak along! I could weep to think of it. Then though it had poured seven showers, we were neither of us a penny the worse. But beshrew me, he cried, clapping hand to his forehead, tomorrow will be a new day and, thousand thunders. I know of a *marchand de capotes*, Monsieur Poyntz, from whom I can have for a livre as snug a cloak of the French fashion as ever kept a lady from wetting.

(U 405)

The *sous-entendre*, so characteristic of Sterne, is in fact original with Joyce: the French euphemism for a contraceptive sheath used to be *une capote anglaise* ('an English cloak'), corresponding to the English usage 'a French letter'.

This little narrative, so admirably appropriate to the chosen style, is one of the few significant novelistic developments in the last five episodes of *Ulysses*. Some further brilliant parodies have yet to come, however, before the conclusion of the episode. Bloom is furiously denounced, for his lack of offspring and practice of contraception and masturbation, in the style of the *Letter of Junius* (*U* 409–10). If this is the voice of Bloom's conscience, it has adopted a hectoring tone indeed. A corresponding passage, the last before the slang, praises Mrs Purefoy's husband to the skies: 'By heaven, Theodore Purefoy, thou hast done a doughty deed and no botch! Thou art, I vow, the remarkablest progenitor barring none in this chaffering allincluding most farraginous chronicle.' (*U* 423) Just who is the narrator here, with his casual critical definition of *Ulysses*? Is it the ghost of Thomas Carlyle or at any rate of one of his narrative *personae*? We know, of course that the narrator is Joyce himself, commenting on his work as he loves to do, but are the views expressed his own or what he imagines Carlyle's views would have been? The Dickens passage (*U* 420–1) expresses a similar attitude to 'Doady' Purefoy with nauseating unction. In the felicitous Landor imitation (*U* 414–16) we learn that it was Vincent Lynch, a character already familiar from *A Portrait*, whom Father Conmee observed emerging from a field with his lady friend in 'Wandering Rocks'. I must end consideration of this episode—so frustrating to the novel reader yet so fascinating to the Anglicists—by drawing attention to the moving passage clearly based on Charles Lamb's essay 'Dream Children' (*U* 412–14). Bloom's mood throughout the episode is summed up in these not entirely sentimental words: 'No son of thy loins is by thee. There is none now to be for Leopold, what Leopold was for Rudolph.' (*U* 413–14)

'Circe': 'La tentation de Saint Léopold'

The Freudian aspect of the hallucinations in 'Circe', the next episode, has already been discussed above, but the primary difficulty of this episode for the reader lies in deciding which parts are intended to be hallucinatory and which 'really' happen. Having struggled for many hours over this problem at a first reading, I made an outline in which the hallucinatory passages are summarized in italics. The fact that the whole episode is presented dramatically, with long and detailed stage directions *à la* Shaw, means that the reader now encounters yet another new kind of narration. Shaw invented his first style of stage directions out of sheer necessity: he wanted to bring a banned play, *Mrs Warren's Profession*, before the public, including people who for moral, economic, or literary reasons, had never been to the theatre. His 'stage' directions, which often contained notes on the personality and motives of his characters as well as their physical appearance, enabled such readers to approach a dramatic work in much the same way as they would a novel. Joyce avoids all psychological commentary in his directions, but his descriptions of physical appearance, costume and stage properties (especially where all these are symbolic, in the hallucinations) can be very long and extremely meticulous. Joyce of course knew Shaw's work very well, but he may have used it unconsciously; the model he was consciously using, I assume, was Flaubert's *Tentation de Saint Antoine*, probably in its third and final version.[30]

Unlike readers of Shaw, the reader of 'Circe' cannot afford to skip a single word of the directions: first of all, as in the *Tentation*, they supply all the third-person narration, which for dramatic purposes is given in the present tense, instead of the past tense of novelistic convention. Also, though it has already been suggested that the hallucinations act out—and speak out—the interior monologues of Bloom and Stephen (one or other or both are always on-stage) the stage directions are often influenced or even distorted by their thought. Yet another of these is implicit in the directions at the very beginning of the episode:

The Mabbot street entrance of nighttown . . . rows of flimsy houses with gaping doors. Rare lamps with faint rainbow fans. Round Rabaiotti's halted ice gondola stunted men and women squabble. They grab wafers between which are wedged lumps of coal and copper snow. Sucking they scatter slowly. Children.

(U 429)

This little scene is observed through Stephen's myopic eyes, although his presence (along with Lynch) is not announced until a direction which appears at the bottom of the next page. He first sees the children as stunted men and women, later recognizing his mistake. But it is not entirely a mistake: these are slum children, looking old for their age. In a direction lower down the page, 'A *pigmy woman swings on a rope slung between the rails, counting.*' The adults presented on this page are even less prepossessing: 'A *deafmute idiot*'; 'a *form sprawled against a dustbin*'; 'a *gnome*' and 'a *crone*' collecting rags and bones from 'a *rubbishtip*'; a '*drunken navvy*'; 'a *slut*'. To these add two more children, one bandy-legged and the other scrofulous. It could be argued that some of these distorted figures are victims of hereditary syphilis, the 'swinelove' that links this part of the novel with Homer's 'Circe'; but the rest of the details are irrelevant to such a context. I see them as the only kind of social commentary that Joyce's aesthetic permits him to employ: Stephen insisted in *A Portrait* that true art is static not kinetic; it must never arouse its audience to take action, as do pornography and polemic.

Those who think that Joyce never admitted his socialist beliefs into his work—and those who deny he ever held any such beliefs—have not

---

[30] Ellmann, *The Consciousness of Joyce*, 109. Joyce's edition (in French) was bought in Trieste, 1913–14.

read 'Circe' aright. It is here that he exposes, by a method anthitethical to Shaw's, the ugliest aspects of capitalism: not just prostitution as exploitation of women on the lowest economic level, for that has been endemic in many precapitalist societies, but all the corruption and callousness of slum landlordism. Public health care, sanitation, even garbage collection, which were taken for granted in other parts of 1904 Dublin, are denied to 'Nighttown'. The very existence of this brothel quarter is condoned by the British state—the soldiers of its garrison, such as Private Carr and Private Compton, being among the whores' best customers. Joyce does not suggest that Irish nationalist politicians or the Roman Catholic Church in Ireland condone it in the same way, but a conspiracy of silence kept its existence out of the public press, let alone out of literature. Until *Ulysses* appeared, this blight on the city had been frankly treated only in certain government documents. Partly thanks to *Ulysses*, perhaps, hardly any of the street names mentioned in 'Circe' will be found in modern maps of Dublin. Not only were these streets renamed after the setting-up of the Irish Free State but some of them were rebuilt by Dublin Corporation. The Irish-founded Legion of Mary did some remarkable social work in the area too, evangelizing many of the girls, rehabilitating them and finding them alternative employment.

The technique of 'Circe', then, is the translation of the initial style into dramatic terms: third-person, *present*-tense narration is now sup-plied in the stage directions, while the interior monologues of Stephen and Bloom are exteriorized by the largely grotesque words and actions of the characters ('real' or imagined) who enact their fantasies. Besides the *Walpurgesnachten* of Goethe's *Faust*, Parts I and II, and the *Tentation*, Joyce's models may have included the late plays of Strindberg, fore-runners of Expressionism in the drama: nevertheless we only know for certain that he owned German translations of three earlier plays—*Miss Julie, Creditors*, and *The Father*.[31] We must not forget, though, that much of 'Circe' consists of undistorted realistic dialogue between persons who are 'actually' present according to the normal novelistic convention.

The theme of 'Circe' can be stated, I think, in a single word: Temptation. When we look at Bosch's great painting of the *Temptation of St Anthony* with its myriad grotesque creatures—a mixture of the human with the animal, the vegetable, the mineral, or the artefact—we realize to the full the archaic meaning of the word. The saint is not being incited to sin, he is being tested to breaking point. Our chief anxiety for Flaubert's Saint Antoine is lest his sanity might be destroyed by the strains due to his conflicting visions: his own greatest fear, as the heretics and the false gods of his time parade before him or the infinite

[31] Ellmann, *The Consciousness of Joyce.*

possibilities of matter and energy are revealed to him, is that he will lose his faith. At the end, Christ's face appears to him in the disc of the sun, and he knows that his faith and sanity have been preserved (*U* 440). He is still numbered among the saved.

Stephen seems to begin the episode with the conviction that he too is saved: he '*chants with joy the* introit *for paschal time*' (*U* 431). In English the words of the Latin chant run as follows: 'I saw the water flowing from the right-hand side of the temple. Alleluia / And all to whom that water came, / They were saved.' (*U* 431–2) The passage does not in fact occur as an *introit* during Passion week or Easter Week, but it is significant that Stephen chants with joy on entering the brothel quarter. A little farther on, when Lynch asks him where they are going, he replies with a parody of the *introit* from the order of low mass: 'Lecherous lynx to *la belle dame sans merci*, Georgina Johnson, *ad deam qui laetificat juventutem meam*.' (In English, 'I will go in to the altar of God. / To God who gladdens my youth.') He is trying to make of his visit to the brothel a joyous sacred ritual; instead, he finds that Georgina has married a Mr Lamb 'of London', and his mother's apparition proves his breaking-point. Smashing the chandelier with what seems to him the sword of Wagner's Siegfried, *Nothung*, he flees from the brothel only to find himself among the damned as 'Father Malachi O'Flynn' celebrates a black mass:

FATHER MALACHI O'FLYNN
Introibo ad altare diaboli.
THE REVEREND MR HAINES LOVE
To the devil which hath made glad my young days.

(*U* 599)

Although he has fled from temptation, Stephen's testing time is not yet over. He is knocked unconscious by Private Carr, who thinks his girl, Cissy Caffrey, has been insulted by Stephen; just before this, Lynch has left the scene, identified by Stephen with Judas. (*U* 600) Bloom remains to enact the role of the Good Samaritan—or is it that of Joseph of Arimathea?[32]

Clearly Stephen is identifying himself with Christ, at least monetarily, just as he did at the end of *A Portrait*, where Cranly was John the Baptist; we have become used to this idea in *Ulysses* too, especially since the casuistry about father and son in 'Scylla and Charybdis'. What one is not prepared for in 'Circe' is the predominance of identifications of Bloom with Christ. Let me cite the most astonishing examples, those on page 495. Bloom is imagining his own trial, which becomes first that of

---

[32] Ellmann, *James Joyce*, 161–2.

Christ before Pilate ('Art thou the King of the Jews? . . . Thou sayest it,') and then the Temptation of Christ:

A VOICE
Bloom, are you the Messiah ben Joseph or ben David?
BLOOM
(*Darkly.*) You have said it.
BROTHER BUZZ
Then perform a miracle.

Farther down the same page, the Papal Nuncio to Ireland reads out a mock genealogy of Bloom beginning '*Leopoldi autem generatio*' and ending (*U* 496) with 'and Virag begat Bloom *et vocabitur nomen eius Emmanuel*'. This is a parody of the opening of St Matthew's Gospel: in Latin, the first words are '*Christi autem generatio*'. Whether Joyce knew it or not during the writing of *Ulysses*, these words inspired the 'Chi-Ro' page of the Book of Kells, arguably the masterpiece among the illuminations of that famous Irish manuscript of the Gospels. When he wrote *Finnegans Wake* he had been aware of the most important pages of the Book of Kells at least since 1922; in fact, the *Wake* may have been written in conscious rivalry of that work.[33] Retrospectively, he referred to *Ulysses* as 'his uselessly unreadable Blue Book of Eccles'. (*FW* 179. 25–6)

In the same passage of 'Circe', at page 498, Bloom '*In a seamless garment marked I.H.S.*'[34] says 'Weep not for me, O daughters of Erin.' This corresponds to the passage in the twenty-third chapter of St Luke's Gospel where Jesus says, in part, 'Daughters of Jerusalem weep not for me, but weep for yourselves, and for your children.' The episode has become the eighth among the traditional fourteen Stations of the Cross. I suspect that 'Circe' contains allusions to all fourteen, though not necessarily in chronological order; they seem to be divided between Bloom and Stephen. If my hypothesis is correct, at least one of the Stations, the fourth, 'Jesus meets his afflicted Mother', is duplicated. It has already been noted that both Bloom and Stephen meet their mothers, though Ellen Bloom's reason for feeling afflicted is less serious than May Dedalus's. Jesus traditionally fell three times under the weight of His cross; because of the association of locomotor ataxia with syphilis, there is much falling, near-falling, staggering, and tripping in 'Circe'. For example, Bloom trips awkwardly as he crosses the threshold of Bella Cohen's brothel. In answer to Zoe's 'Hoopsa! Don't fall upstairs,' he says, 'The just man falls seven times.' (*U* 501) Because Joyce's mind often equates the heroic or the divine with the base and the all-too-human,

33 James S. Atherton, *The Books at the Wake* (New York: Viking, 1960), 61–7.
34 See *Ulysses*, 544 for Bloom's misinterpretation of 'IHS'.

one soon begins to see the *Via Crucis* in the most unlikely places: and one remembers that Joyce wrote of the poet Mangan in an early essay, 'his nights were so many stations of the cross in the low dives of the Liberties'.[35] When '*His Eminence, Simon Stephen Cardinal Dedalus, primate of all Ireland, appears in the doorway*' in response to Lynch's description of Stephen as 'A Cardinal's son', he wears round his neck '*a rosary of corks ending on his breast in a corkscrew cross*' (U 523–4). Is this an allusion to the fifth Station, in which Simon the Cyrenian helps Jesus to carry His cross? Suffice it to say that when Stephen lies unconscious in the street there are overtones of the fourteenth and final Station, 'Jesus is Laid in the Tomb'. Stephen's blessed mother is not there to arrange his body in the sepulchre with her own hands, but Bloom is ready to perform any necessary offices. In the final hallucination of the episode, his dead son Rudy, with whom he identified Stephen in 'Oxen of the Sun', '*appears slowly, a fairy boy of eleven, a changeling . . . holding a book in his hand*'. His Jewish heritage is proved as '*He reads from right to left inaudibly, smiling, kissing the page.*' (U 609) Despite the incongruity of some of the details, this is one of the most pathetic moments in *Ulysses*.

Because Homer's Circe was a sorceress, it is highly appropriate that the 'art' of the episode is Magic, though Joyce originally chose Dance in the Linati schema. More than medicine or science, magic liberates his artistic impulses, despite a certain amount of the pedantry I have deplored in other later episodes: for example, the introduction of Masonic signs and ritual—material that Joyce had to swot up for the occasion—on the specious pretext that Bloom is a Freemason. (Once again, Bloom's equivocal position in Irish society is reinforced, because Roman Catholics in general are forbidden to join secret societies, while Irish Catholics in particular resented the fact that the Irish lodges were centres of British influence and focuses for Protestant loyalty to the English Crown.)

'Wandering Rocks' has already been described as a *mise-en-abîme* of events and themes in all the episodes that preceded it—'in a kind of retrospective arrangement', to borrow from Mr Kernan (U 241). Joyce himself, as we have seen, described 'Oxen of the Sun' as 'linked back at each part subtly with some foregoing episode of the day'. One of the reasons why 'Circe' is easily the longest episode of the book—though it seems even longer because of the extra space needed for its presentation as a playscript—is that once again Joyce presents a *mise-en-abîme* of the entire work up to this point. Furthermore, there are smaller *mises* within the greater one. For instance, Bloom's entire day is recapitulated, episode by episode, in what one may call the Litany of the Daughters of Erin:

---

[35] Ellmann, *Ulysses on the Liffey*, 184.

[Calypso]	Kidney of Bloom, pray for us.
[Lotus-Eaters]	Flower of the Bath, pray for us.
[Hades]	Mentor of Menton, pray for us.
[Aeolus]	Canvasser for the Freeman, pray for us.
[Lestrigonians]	Charitable Mason, pray for us.
[Scylla and Charybdis]	Wandering Soap, pray for us.
[Wandering Rocks]	Sweets of Sin, pray for us.
[Sirens]	Music without Words, pray for us.
[Cyclops]	Reprover of the Citizen, pray for us.
[Nausicaa]	Friend of all Frillies, pray for us.
[Oxen of the Sun]	Midwife Most Merciful, pray for us.
[Circe]	Potato Preservative against Plague and Pestilence, pray for us.

(U 498–9)

In the words of Arnold Goldman, 'By its fifteenth chapter, *Ulysses* has begun to provide its author enough in the way of material to become self-perpetuating.' Michael Golden comments on the same phenomena from a slightly different viewpoint: 'By the time he finished "Circe" he had included so much previous material that, in addition to the characters' psyches, *Ulysses* itself was turned inside out.'

The association of the potato with the 'Circe' episode may surprise or confuse even those who have read the entire episode. It is, however, so characteristic of Joyce at his most genial—in both the most current sense of that word and the older sense which makes it the adjective derived from 'genius'—that it may serve as a final *aperçu* on the infinite overtones of 'Circe'. We have seen how Stephen broke down under Temptation, but Bloom's ability to resist it has not been explored at all. Yet he, like his prototype Odysseus, seems to possess a charm against the very real temptations of the flesh offered him by Bella and by the young prostitutes Zoe, Kitty, and Florrie. Odysseus's charm was the herb *moly* (μῶλυ); Bloom's is the potato that he carries about in his left trousers' pocket—a folk remedy against rheumatism well-known in Ireland. His mother carried one (see above) and encouraged him to do so. When Zoe takes the *'hard black shrivelled'* tuber from his pocket, he truthfully describes it as 'A talisman. Heirloom.' (U 476) While the potato is in her possession, he undergoes his most searching temptation, with Bella. Soon after his return to himself, he asks Zoe to give back the potato, adding '(*With feeling.*) It is nothing, but still a relic of poor mamma.' (U 555) She reluctantly returns it to him and thereafter he is proof against temptation.

Interestingly, Liddell and Scott, in their famous dictionary *Greek-English Lexicon*, describe *moly* as having 'a black root and white blossom'; the potato blossom is white, but Joyce has taken the trouble to make the fruit black, if not the root.

A letter from Joyce to Frank Budgen dated Michaelmas 1920 indicates that Bloom's immunity had other roots besides the potato:

I am sorry you do not think your ideas on Circe worth sending. As I told you a catchword is enough to send me off. *Moly* is a nut to crack. My latest is this. Moly is the gift of Hermes, god of public ways, and is an invisible influence (prayer, chance, agility, *presence of mind*, (power of recuperation) which saves in case of accident. This would cover immunity from syphilis. . . . (οὐ φιλος = swine-love?) In this special case his plant may be said to have many leaves, indifference due to masturbation, pessimism congenital, a sense of the ridiculous, sudden fastidiousness in some detail. It is the only occasion on which Ulysses is not helped by Minerva but by her male counterpart or inferior.[36]

A book-length analysis of 'Circe' would show that all of the factors here listed by Joyce do contribute to Bloom's successful endurance of his Temptation in the completed episode. A single example of 'sudden fastidiousness' will have to suffice here: when Bloom has recovered from his temporary infatuation with Bella Cohen, he can see that she is 'Passée. Mutton dressed as lamb. Long in the tooth and superfluous hairs.' (*U* 554) And Bloom is vouchsafed, in parody and at the beginning of his trials, the vision that concludes the ordeal of Flaubert's St Anthony:

> ([*Bloom*] *points to the south, then to the east. A cake of new clean lemon soap arises, diffusing light and perfume.*)
> THE SOAP
> We're a capital couple are Bloom and I;
> He brightens the earth, I polish the sky.
> (*The freckled face of Sweny, the druggist, appears in the disk of the soapsun.*)
> SWENY
> Three and a penny, please.

(*U* 440)

'Eumaeus': Narrative Grown Senile

Although 'Eumaeus' is heralded by the Roman numeral III as the beginning of the third and last part of *Ulysses*, there is no break in time between it and 'Circe'. We are told on page 613 that 'Mr Bloom brushed off the greater bulk of the [wood] shavings' from Stephen's clothes: he had already been brushing them off before the end of 'Circe' (*U* 608).

---

[36] *Selected Letters of James Joyce*, 272.

There has been a break, however short, in the continuity of time and place between each two episodes up to and including 'Circe', but the Return can be read as a continuous narrative. Bloom and Stephen move from place to place, together and separately, yet the unity of time is preserved.

'Narrative (old)', the technique of 'Eumaeus', is as tired and hung-over as Stephen and Bloom are. Not only is it bathetic and cluttered with clichés, but its syntactic errors often create ambiguities which, contrary to Joyce's usual practice, impede understanding without hinting at subtleties. A typical passage, 'evidently there was nothing for it but put a good face on the matter and foot it' (*U* 613), is unredeemed by the absurdity of the juxtaposing of 'foot' and 'face'. The entire episode consists of third-person narrative, but who, we wonder, is the foot-in-mouth narrator. Although Bloom is a character in the story told, we could almost imagine that he is also the author of it. Except for snatches of his letter to Martha in 'Sirens', we know nothing of his *written* style: despite his racy interior monologue and ingratiating though not eloquent conversation, his lack of self-confidence and his doubts about the quality of his education might inhibit free expression when he 'takes pen in hand'—one cliché *not* used by the narrator. Alternatively, the episode might have been written by a hack journalist like Joe Hynes, author of the misleading report of Dignam's funeral in the *Evening Telegraph* (*U* 647). Bloom's name appears as L. Boom (*sic*): he is 'Nettled not a little' by the error, 'but tickled to death simultaneously by C. P. M'Coy and Stephen Dedalus, B.A., who were conspicuous, needless to say, by their total absence (To say nothing of M'Intosh)' (*U* 647–8).[37]

The reader of 'Eumaeus' is expected to suffer through fifty pages of atrocities against English prose for precious little reward. Bloom tries very hard to ingratiate himself with Stephen, who behaves politely but hardly says anything at all: what he does say usually leads to total misunderstanding. For example, Stephen, remembering what he has been taught about the soul, says, 'They tell me on the best authority it is a simple substance and therefore incorruptible.' Bloom, totally ignorant of the philosophical and theological meaning of 'simple', replies thus: 'Simple, I shouldn't think that is the proper word. Of course, I grant you, to concede a point, you do knock across a simple soul once in a blue moon.'

And yet this, the first written of all the eighteen episodes, may therefore be the most autobiographical. Bloom at one point makes the common-sense suggestion that Stephen should return to his father's

37 For identification of the mysterious 'man in the macintosh' as 'M'Intosh' see the passage in *Studies* (*U* 112–14).

house. 'Walking to Sandycove is out of the question and, even suppose you did, you won't get in after what occurred at Westland Row station. Simply fag out there for nothing.' (*U* 619) Bloom goes on to praise Mr Dedalus, 'A gifted man . . . in more respects than one and a born *raconteur* if ever there was one. He takes great pride, quite legitimately, out of you. You could go back perhaps.' (*U* 620)

Stephen's mind's eye being too busily engaged in repicturing his family hearth the last time he saw it, with his sister Dilly, sitting by the ingle, her hair hanging down, waiting for some weak Trinidad shell cocoa that was in the sootcoated kettle to be done so that she could drink it with the oatmeal water for milk after the Friday herrings they had eaten at two a penny.

(*U* 620)

Although Stephen has three other sisters, 'Maggy, Boody and Katey' (*U* 626), it is the waste of Dilly's quick intelligence and humour that stirs his conscience. We have seen her in action in the section of 'Wandering Rocks' devoted to her and her father: of the two pennies Simon gave her for herself, she spends one on a coverless copy of Chardenal's French primer (*U* 237–9; 243). Soon afterwards she meets her brother:

—What have you there? Stephen asked.
—I bought it from the other cart for a penny, Dilly said, laughing nervously. Is it any good?
   My eyes they say she has. Do others see me so? Quick, far and daring. Shadow of my mind . . .
—What did you buy that for? he asked. To learn French?
She nodded, reddening and closing tight her lips.
Show no surprise. Quite natural.
—Here, Stephen said. It's all right. Mind Maggy doesn't pawn it on you. I suppose all my books are gone.
—Some, Dilly said. We had to.
   She is drowning. Agenbite. Save her. Agenbite. All against us. She will drown me with her, eyes and hair. Lank coils of seaweed hair around me, my heart, my soul. Salt green death.
   We.
   Agenbite of inwit. Inwit's agenbite.
   Misery! Misery!

(*U* 243)

The last three lines rather overdo Stephen's remorse of conscience ('Agenbite of inwit', a Middle-English phrase), but the passage as a whole is, I believe, truer to Joyce's own feelings than Stephen's remorse at having refused to pray by his mother's death-bed—something that Joyce in fact was not guilty of.[38]

---

[38] On the truth of this matter see Ellmann, *James Joyce*, 141.

In his anxiety to continue the relationship, however tenuous, that he has finally established with Stephen, Bloom goes so far as to tempt him with Molly. He begins by mentioning her Spanish blood and temperament (*U* 637): later, he produces a photograph of her, 'Mrs Bloom, my wife the *prima donna*, Madam Marion Tweedy.' (*U* 652) Later still, he invites Stephen to stay the night at 7 Eccles Street: 'My wife, he intimated, plunging *in medias res*, would have the greatest pleasure in making your acquaintance as she is passionately attached to music of any kind.' (*U* 662–3) Bloom's motives are complex, as we learn from this episode and its successor: the overriding motive, no doubt, is a desire to help Stephen and establish a claim akin to paternity: but he also sees him as 'a successful rival agent of intimacy'(*U* 733) to replace Boylan in Molly's affections. When, in Ithaca, he formally invites Stephen to spend the rest of the night at his house (*U* 695), the following passage occurs:

What various advantages would or might have resulted from a prolongation of such extemporisation?

For the guest: security of domicile and seclusion of study. For the host: rejuvenation of intelligence, vicarious satisfaction. For the hostess: disintegration of obsession, acquisition of correct Italian pronunciation.

Already in 'Eumaeus' 'All kinds of Utopian plans were flashing through his (Bloom's) busy brain.' (*U* 658) If Stephen has in fact inherited his father's tenor voice, as Bloom 'more than suspected', then 'duets in Italian with the accent perfectly true to nature and a quantity of other things' begin to seem possible; Bloom has a great capacity for combining the practical with the sentimental. At the end of 'Ithaca', when he relates the events of the day to Molly, 'Stephen Dedalus, professor and author,' emerges as 'the salient point of his narration' (*U* 735). Molly takes the bait with an alacrity inconceivable in Bloom's wildest dreams: her fantasy about Stephen fills two pages (*U* 744–6) of 'Penelope', culminating thus:

Im sure itll be grand if I can only get in with a handsome young poet at my age . . . Ill read and study all I can find or learn a bit off by heart if I knew who he likes so he wont think Im stupid . . . Ill make him feel all over him till he half faints under me then hell write about me lover and mistress publicly too with our 2 photographs in the papers when he becomes famous O but then what am I going to do about him though

Although the reference of pronouns is almost always problematical in the 'Penelope' episode, I am fairly confident that this last 'him' refers to Boylan rather than Bloom, on whose discretion she can always rely. Her thoughts revert to Stephen on pages 778–80, and it occurs to her that if she is to have a young poet staying in the house, 'Id have to get a nice pair of red slippers . . . or yellow and a nice semitransparent morning gown that I badly want or a peachblossom dressing jacket'. To get the money for these, she will give Bloom just one more chance. She plans his seduction next morning: 'Ill tell him I want £1 or perhaps 30/—Ill tell him I want to buy underclothes then if he gives me that well he wont be too bad.' (*U* 780) Just a few lines later, the coda of the final episode begins: her awareness of Bloom's essential generosity to her leads on to her memories of the first consummation of their love. Thus Stephen plays an important part in restoring equilibrium between the Blooms. Joyce can hardly have failed to read or see Shaw's *Candida*, though he is not known to have had it in his library. If Stephen had in fact accepted Bloom's offer, a *Candida* situation would have existed at Eccles Street. Another possible model for Joyce is Jules Renard's little masterpiece, *L'Encornifleur* (*The Sponger*), first published in 1904. Here, a poet of sorts actually lives with a bourgeois family, as Marchbanks does not in Shaw's play. He has the worst of intentions towards his hostess, but she contents herself with flirtation; he then perpetrates *un demi-viol* (a semi-rape) on her innocent niece and leaves the family in great haste, never to see them again.

The remaining themes introduced in 'Eumaeus' appear sterile by comparison with the splendid flowering of the Stephen-Molly one. They seem to be dictated by an anxiety to conform to the patterns of the *Odyssey*, but again there may be an autobiographical element. Perhaps Mr Hunter did in fact bring the injured Joyce to the cabmen's shelter near Butt Bridge, of which the proprietor was reputed to be 'the once famous Skin-the-Goat, Fitzharris, the Invincible', though Bloom 'wouldn't vouch for the actual facts, which quite possibly there was not one vestige of truth in' (*U* 621). Stephen has in fact heard some of these alleged facts in the *Evening Telegraph* office (*U* 136–7), during the 'Aeolus' episode. Skin-the-Goat was the nickname of the jaunting-car driver who aided the escape of the Phoenix Park murderers, members of a terrorist group called the Invincibles, on 6 May 1882, the year of Joyce's birth. Their victims were Lord Frederick Cavendish, Gladstone's new Chief Secretary of State for Ireland, who had just arrived in Dublin that very day, and his under-secretary, T. H. Burke. Parnell was accused of complicity in the crime on the basis of forged letters, but was later vindicated by a Royal Commission. We hear much more of this matter in *Finnegans Wake*.

Skin-the-Goat, unprepossessing but totally loyal to his fellow-conspirators, corresponds quite neatly to Eumaeus, the loyal swineherd in whose hut Odysseus takes refuge and reveals his true identity to

Telemachus. At first Odysseus is understandably reluctant to say who he really is, and in fact tells a pack of lies about himself: in 'Eumaeus' this understandable piece of dishonesty is not attributed to Bloom; instead we have the yarn-spinning sailor W. B. Murphy, who is identified in Joyce's final schema as 'Ulysses Pseudangelos ['The false Messenger']'. I find him the most boring character in all Joyce—because of, rather than despite, his total verisimilitude. Odysseus poses as a Cretan in the original, both when he meets the goddess Athene disguised as a young man and when he first meets Eumaeus: nevertheless, he makes one true statement to the latter: 'I tell thee not lightly but with an oath, that Odysseus shall return.'[39] The corresponding passage in 'Eumaeus' contains perhaps the most blatant untruth in an episode crammed with half-truth, folklore and misinformation of every kind. Ironically, it is spoken by Skin-the-Goat rather than the lying sailor: 'One morning you would open the paper, the cabman affirmed, and read, *Return of Parnell.*' (*U* 648) Before *Ulysses* appeared in book form, Lennox Robinson had already written a full-length play, *The Lost Leader*, on the return of Parnell, first performed at the Abbey Theatre, 19 February 1918. Bloom's thoughts about Parnell as a myth-attracting figure occur on pages 649–50: as usual, humour breaks in: he reflects that 'Still, as regards return, you were a lucky dog if they didn't set the terrier on you directly you got back.' Odysseus was attacked by Eumaeus's dogs until the swineherd drove them off by pelting them with stones. Mindful of his own situation, Bloom has already thought of the dangers of the sailor's return to Mrs Murphy after a long absence: 'Quite a number of stories there were on that particular Alice Ben Bolt topic, Enoch Arden and Rip Van Winkle and does anybody hereabouts remember Caoch O'Leary . . .?' (*U* 624) Does anybody hereabouts remember Odysseus? Not Bloom, certainly, but Joyce is plainly offering all these characters from popular literature as analogues of Homer's returning hero. Finally Bloom pays the bill, takes Stephen by the arm, and guides him towards Eccles Street. They fall 'to chatting about music' (*U* 661), a subject on which they can have a real conversation at last, though even here they do not achieve perfect harmony. Bloom finds 'Wagnerian music . . . a bit too heavy . . . and hard to follow at the first go-off' (*U* 661); he inexplicably identifies Mendelssohn with 'the severe classical school' as well as making other blunders. When Stephen in turn speaks of his love for Elizabethan music and his intention of buying a lute from Arnold Dolmetsch, Bloom does not recognize the name of the great musical antiquarian, though he will not

---

[39] Samuel H. Butcher and Andrew Lang, *The Odyssey of Homer done into English Prose*, 3rd edn. (New York: Macmillan, 1893), 227.

admit it. He keeps urging Stephen to exploit his tenor voice, insisting that 'he would have heaps of time to practise literature in his spare moments when desirous of so doing without its clashing with his vocal career' (*U* 664). Stephen does not answer this, but the defecation of a passing horse, rather elegantly described on the last page of the episode, may have seemed to him a sufficient reply (*U* 665).

Throughout 'Eumaeus' we look in vain for any equivalent of the recognition scene that is one of the finest moments of the second half of the *Odyssey*: when Odysseus has at last revealed to Telemachus who he is, 'he kissed his son, and from his cheeks let a tear fall to earth: before, he had stayed the tears continually.' Telemachus cannot believe the truth at first, and Odysseus has to explain that Athene is responsible for his change from a beggar to a god-like figure.

With this word then he sat down again: but Telemachus, flinging himself upon his noble father's neck, mourned and shed tears, and in both their hearts arose the desire of lamentation. And they wailed aloud, more ceaselessly than birds, sea-eagles or vultures of crooked claws, whose younglings the country folk have taken from the nest, ere yet they are fledged. Even so pitifully fell the tears beneath their brows.[40]

Joyce seems to offer an ironic equivalent of this scene, not in 'Eumaeus' but in 'Ithaca': no tears but a more plentiful and perhaps more intimate moisture falls as Bloom and Stephen urinate side by side in the garden of 7 Eccles Street under the stars, just prior to Stephen's final exit through the garden door into the laneway (*U* 702–4).

'Ithaca': Bad Science and Worse Irish

Where 'Circe' recapitulated the events of the day in terms of magic and hallucination, with all the verve and illogicality of a Dublin or Cockney Christmas pantomime (akin to American vaudeville or burlesque), 'Ithaca' is supposed to view those events and the contents of Bloom's house with the cold eye of science, the 'art' of the episode. The technique is 'Catechism (impersonal)': at one point it is used to convey the following information about Bloom and Stephen respectively: 'What two temperaments did they individually represent? The scientific. The artistic.' (*U* 683) Such is the prestige of the written word that this completely unverifiable pseudo-statement leads an exceptionally wary critic, Michael Groden, to use the expression 'Bloom's scientific mind'.[41]

[40] Butcher and Lang, 265–6.
[41] Arnold Goldman, *The Joyce Paradox* (London: Routledge & Kegan Paul, 1966), 162. Groden, 61.

Joyce, not Bloom, is the author of 'Ithaca', but since Bloom and Stephen are both aspects of himself, the passage quoted may represent his claim to possess the 'scientific temperament' as well as the 'artistic' one. The claim is indisputable because it is unverifiable. What we *can* verify is the accuracy of Joyce's knowledge of various sciences in terms of the state of the art in 1904, not 1922. No doubt he relied heavily on the *Encyclopaedia Britannica* or some similar work published in one of the continental languages he knew well. But would the results of such research be worth the effort put into it? The characteristic reaction to 'Ithaca' of the cranky J. F. Byrne (original of 'Cranly' in *A Portrait*) was to take pencil and paper and make a few calculations, the effect of which was to reinforce his estimate of the poor quality of Joyce's scientific bent.[42]

Joyce's own intentions in writing the episode were clearly set forth in a letter to Frank Budgen at the end of February 1921:

I am writing *Ithaca* in the form of a mathematical catechism. All events are resolved into their cosmic, physical, psychical etc. equivalents, e.g. Bloom jumping down the area, drawing water from the tap, the micturating in the garden, the cone of incense, lighted candle and statue so that the reader will know everything and know it in the baldest and coldest way, but Bloom and Stephen thereby become heavenly bodies, wanderers like the stars at which they gaze.

Clearly, Joyce did carry out these intentions in part, but fortunately his imperfect knowledge of science and his irrepressible sense of humour make the episode more human than he intended. There is a special warmth in the passage where, out of the depth of their respective ignorances, Bloom and Stephen endeavour to compare the Irish and Hebrew languages. Stephen 'wrote the characters for gee, eh, dee, em, simple and modified', presumably as follows: ᵹ, ϵ, ꝺ, m ; ᵹ̇, é, ꝺ̇, ṁ. The letters in the second group are modified by a mark indicating length when added to the vowel and aspiration when placed above the consonant. Bloom 'in turn wrote the Hebrew characters ghimel, aleph, daleth and (in the absence of mem) substitute goph, explaining their arithmetical values as ordinal and cardinal numbers, videlicet 3, 1, 4, and 100.' (*U* 688) The answer to the next question concedes that their knowledge of both languages was 'Theoretical . . . practically excluding vocabulary.' It is astonishing that Joyce, a master of English, meticulous in Latin, and fluent in several continental European languages, should know only a few phrases of spoken Irish and be unable to write even these correctly.[43] He has already demonstrated his illiteracy on this same page

42 J. F. Byrne, *Silent Years: An Autobiography with Memoirs of James Joyce and Our Ireland* (New York: Farrar Straus & Young, 1953), 161.

43 James Joyce, *Ulysses: A Facsimile of the Manuscript* (New York: Farrar Straus & Giroux, 1975), ii, 'Ithaca' ii, opening 6.

688 where Stephen quotes two lines from one of the most familiar Irish songs, known to English speakers as 'Shule Aroon'. We cannot blame the original French printers for garbling the text, because the words appear in Joyce's own hand as follows: *suil, suil, suil arun, suil go siocair agus suil go cuin*. This should read: *siúl, siúl, siúl a rún, siúl go socair agus siúl go ciúin*. Joyce does not seem to know that *si* or *se* in Irish give a sound equivalent to English 'sh'. One could go on. As for Stephen's 'translation' of the lines, 'walk, walk, walk your way, walk in safety, walk with care', it is almost as bizarre as his Irish: it should read, 'walk, walk, walk my dear, walk quietly and walk silently.' I think this is the only occasion in either 'Ithaca' or 'Eumaeus' where Stephen is shown as equal in ignorance with Bloom. The latter may know more than Stephen about mathematics and general science, but this superiority is displayed only once, in the passage where he points out 'various constellations' (*U* 698).

Joyce's humour at the expense of science is shown in a number of contexts: the insistence on quantification is mocked in, for example, 'a man regulating a gasflame of 14 C P [candle power], . . . a man leaving the kitchen holding a candle of 1 C P', but Joyce's instinct is usually right when his object is to ridicule pedantry rather than to practise it. Sometimes the humour lies in pseudoscientific language that contains a sly pun like 'the . . . uncondensed milky way' (*U* 698). But in fact, precisely because of Joyce's ignorance of science, the majority of the pedantic material derives as usual from scholasticism in logic, theology and metaphysics. *A Portrait* is crammed with such allusions.

When Stephen has left, Bloom makes a survey of his house, observing with a detective's if not a scientist's eye the traces of Boylan's presence, including 'the music in the key of G natural for voice and piano of *Love's Old Sweet Song* . . . open at the last page with the final indications *ad libitum*, *forte*, pedal, *animato*, sustained, pedal, *ritirando*, close.' (*U* 706) This is one of the songs Molly is to sing on her forthcoming concert tour under Boylan's management. No doubt he accompanied her in a run-through, but the 'final indications' are suggestive when read in a proper (or improper) spirit. Flushed with musical excitement, the pair certainly obeyed these 'indications' sooner or later, as 'Penelope' reveals.

Passing over the description of Bloom's rudimentary library (*U* 708–10)—except to note the presence in it of *Thom's Dublin Post Office Directory* for 1886, a publication of which the 1904 edition was an indispensable source for *Ulysses*—and Bloom's 'budget' or balance-sheet for 16 June 1904 (*U* 711), we may pause for a moment to note his 'ultimate ambition', which is to own outright a modest suburban house in Dundrum or Sutton, 'standing in 5 or 6 acres of its own ground, . . . not more than 5 minutes from tram or train line'. The lists of contents of the house and grounds read like excerpts from furniture catalogues and estate agents' advertisements, as in fact they must have been. Bloom then characteristically rehearses mentally various far-fetched schemes that might help him to achieve this ambition: 'similar meditations . . . when practised habitually before resting for the night alleviated fatigue' and ensured a good night's sleep. (*U* 720) We are then offered an exhaustive list of the contents of two drawers in an unspecified piece of furniture: presumably Bloom keeps these locked and possesses the only key, since they contain not only all his valuables and memorabilia, but his secrets as well: condoms, erotic photographs, and the three letters from Martha Clifford to 'Henry Flower': he unlocks the first drawer to add a fourth letter to this correspondence. The second drawer, which he has no present need to unlock, contains, among other documents, an insurance policy of reasonable size for a man of his circumstances in 1904, a bank balance with a modest credit balance, and, surprisingly, a 'certificate of possession of £900 Canadian 4% (inscribed) government stock' (*U* 723).

Among the contents of this second drawer is his father's suicide note, which naturally evokes some depressing memories and a 'sentiment of remorse' in Bloom, 'because in immature impatience he had treated with disrespect certain beliefs and practices', which, by the way, Rudolph Bloom was supposed to have renounced before his son Leopold was born (*U* 724:7). From these memories arise a vision of Bloom's suffering even greater destitution than his father and coming to resemble one of Samuel Beckett's anti-heroes, subjected to 'the simulated ignorance of casual acquaintances, the latration of illegitimate unlicenced vagabond dogs, the infantile discharge of decomposed vegetable missiles' (*U* 726). He might escape this fate by departure 'to the extreme limit of his cometary orbit' and return, like Odysseus or the Count of Monte Cristo, as 'an estranged avenger, a wreaker of justice on malefactors, . . . a sleeper awakened' (*U* 728). At this point the supposedly impersonal catechism, which in fact runs a gamut of styles, takes on a Homeric note *à la* Butcher and Lang:

> What tributes his?
> Honour and gifts of strangers, the friends of Everyman.
> A nymph immortal, beauty, the bride of Noman.
>
> (*U* 727)

Natural inertia and other factors prevent his departure on this hypo-thetical new voyage. He sits a moment longer in his chair, meditating on the causes of his accumulated fatigue: the events of his day present themselves to his memory in terms of Jewish 'beliefs and practices'.

Breakfast is a burnt offering, the earth closet in the garden is the holy of holies, and so on. Most significantly, 'nocturnal perambulations to and from the cabman's shelter, Butt Bridge' is identified with 'atonement'— not I think in the Old Testament sense, but in the New Testament one, atonement of the Father with the Son.

On his way up to bed, Bloom enumerates to himself the four 'imperfections in a perfect day', hardly those that the reader would have expected him to list. Once he enters the conjugal bedroom on page 730, a series of questions is raised by the interrogator in regard to the number of Molly/Penelope's suitors and their annihilation by Bloom/Ulysses which cannot be answered to the reader's full satisfaction until Mrs Bloom has given her evidence in the final episode, 'Penelope'. I will therefore postpone discussion of pages 730–7 for the moment and conclude my commentary on the scientific aspects of 'Ithaca' by noting Joyce's biggest 'howler'. After the Blooms have fallen asleep, the question is asked, 'In what state of rest or motion?' to which this answer is given: 'At rest relatively to themselves and to each other. In motion being each and both carried westward, forward and rereward respectively, by the proper perpetual motion of the earth through everchanging tracks of never changing space.' (*U* 737) I think that Joyce was genuinely interested in astronomy: certainly he takes a cosmic viewpoint in *Finnegans Wake* which is derived from science as well as theology. Nevertheless, he may have acquired all his knowledge of astronomy from Sir Robert Ball's best-seller, *The Story of the Heavens*, which figures in Bloom's 'library'. Ball was a member of a distinguished Dublin family, and his book was as successful in his own day as any later work of 'popular science' has been. We need not question the expression 'perpetual motion' here, but we can be sure that no professional geographer or astronomer would ever think of the Blooms as moving westward with the rotation of the earth. If Joyce's statement were correct, the Blooms would awake on the morning of 17 June 1904 to learn that the sun had risen in the west, a revolution in the history of Earth more startling even than that which Joyce was achieving in the history of the novel.

'Penelope': The Last Word

'Penelope' consists entirely of Mrs Bloom's virtually continuous interior monologue. Even when a train whistle penetrates her consciousness from the outside world, there is no need of a third-person narrator. We become aware of it through Molly's mental imitation: 'Frseeeeeeeeeeeeeeeeeeeeeeeefrong that train again.' (*U* 762) Divided into eight very long 'sentences' or rather paragraphs—there is no punctuation nor are there initial capitals to indicate where sentences begin— 'Penelope' starts and finishes with the word 'yes'. It commences on a note of astonishment at Bloom's daring to ask for breakfast in bed, 'Yes because he never did a thing like it before as ask to get his breakfast with a couple of eggs since the City Arms hotel'.

Molly naturally then goes on to speculate about the reasons for Bloom's unusual self-assurance, and it becomes clear very quickly that she has seen through many of his lies and suppressions of the truth. Bloom's narrative in 'Ithaca' of his day's adventures contained certain 'modifications', both negative and positive: 'he omitted to mention the clandestine correspondence between Martha Clifford and Henry Flower, . . . the erotic provocation and response thereto caused by the exhibition of Gertrude (Gerty), surname unknown. Positive: he included mention of an invitation to supper at Wynn's (Murphy's) Hotel.' (*U* 735)

In the first two pages of 'Penelope' his wife demolishes all three of these evasions thus:

yes he came somewhere Im sure / by his appetite / anyway love its not / or hed be off his feed thinking of her / so either it was one of those night women / if it was down there he was really / and the hotel story he made up a pack of lies to hide it . . . / or else if its not that its some little bitch or other he got in with somewhere / or picked up on the sly / if they only knew him as well as I do / yes / because the day before yesterday he was scribbling something / a letter / when I came into the front room . . . as if something told me / and he covered it up with blottingpaper / pretending to be thinking about business / so very prob- ably that was it to somebody who thinks she has a softy in him . . . / and then the usual kissing my bottom was to hide it / not that I care two straws who he does it with/ or knew before that way / though Id like to find out . . . /

(*U* 738–9)

Bloom's 'response' to Gerty, his presence in the brothel quarter and absence from Wynn's, and his secret correspondence with Martha are all guessed at shrewdly by Molly: she only fails to gauge the full extent of his duplicity by assuming that Gerty and 'Martha' are one and the same.

The passage just quoted is virtually an epitome of the whole episode in both style and content. The first thing one notices, perhaps, is that it is presented without punctuation and capitalization, even to the omis- sion of the apostrophe. Yet there *are* capitals, notably for the first person pronoun: Joyce writes 'Id' not 'id'. (Elsewhere proper names are correctly capitalized.) It is possible, on the other hand, that many readers will first be struck, and indeed scandalized, not by the seeming illiteracy of this text but by its tone, its 'vulgarity'—to use no stronger word. To them, phrases like 'he came somewhere Im sure' and 'the usual kissing my bottom' are too coarse to be employed by a woman with any pretensions at all to gentility: furthermore, they indicate a degree of cynicism and sexual experience appropriate only to the night women of whom Molly seems to disapprove. In describing 'Penelope' as 'the clou of the book' to Frank Budgen, Joyce himself must have been expecting *a succès de scandale* for the episode and the book—though he may have greatly underestimated the dimensions both of the success and of the scandal.

One could justly argue that Molly does not appear nearly so coarse-grained in daily life as she does in this nocturnal reverie. Joyce is intruding on her privacy and inviting us to do the same. Like anyone, male or female, she has the right to freedom of speech when talking to herself. During the course of *Ulysses*, especially in 'Circe', we have already encountered women of the oldest profession, as well as men of every occupation or none, who speak aloud in language more obscene than any to be found in the passage here examined. Mrs Bloom, however, will later find occasion to use 'the soldier's word' in a moment of silent fury against Bloom and his shortcomings:

Ill let him know if that's what he wanted that his wife is fucked yes and damn well fucked too up to my neck nearly not by him 5 or 6 times handrunning theres the mark of his spunk on the clean sheet . . . serve him right its all his own fault if Im an adulteress . . . O much about it if thats all the harm ever we did in this vale of tears God knows its not much doesnt everybody only they hide it.

(*U* 780)

In fact, once we are aware of Joyce's codewords, the passage quoted from page 735 may appear more obscene than this one. Mrs Bloom never uses the familiar four-letter Anglo-Saxon word for the female sex-organ: her equivalent is what Joyce called 'the female word *Yes*'. In the letter to Frank Budgen, dated 16 August 1921, from which this phrase is taken we find the four keywords of 'Penelope': 'It turns like the huge earthball slowly surely and evenly round and round spinning. Its four cardinal points being [*sic*] the female breasts, arse, womb and cunt expressed by the words *because, bottom . . . woman, yes*.[44]

As we read on through the episode, we become convinced that Molly's knowledge of Bloom's life history and psychology exceed his of hers. While he may know all about her affair with Boylan, including the fact that it has just been consummated, he does not even know the name of his most dangerous rival before Blazes. When Bloom entered, 'reverently the bed of conception and of birth, of consummation of marriage and of breach of marriage, of sleep and of death' (*U* 731), his limbs encountered among other things 'the imprint of a human form,

[44] *Selected Letters of James Joyce*, 16 August 1921.

male, not his, some crumbs, some flakes of potted meat'. This prompted him to recall the series of Boylan's predecessors: 'Assuming Mulvey to be the first of his series, Penrose, Bartell d'Arcy', and twenty-one other men, some anonymous, including the twenty-first, 'a bootblack at the General Post Office'. Not only is this a modest list compared with Penelope's 108 suitors in the *Odyssey*, but Molly's monologue shows that, with the exception of the first three, these admirers were not attractive to her and in any case had no opportunity to make advances to her.

One crucial name, however, is missing from this roll-call in 'Ithaca', suggesting that Bloom and not the omniscient interrogator/narrator is the compiler of the list. Molly recounts the tragicomic little story in the following passage:

I hate the mention of politics after the [Boer] war that Pretoria and Ladysmith and Bloemfontein where Gardner Lieutenant Stanley G 8th Bn 2nd East Lancs Rgt of enteric fever he was a lovely fellow in khaki and just the right height over me Im sure he was brave too he said I was lovely the evening we kissed good-bye at the canal lock my Irish beauty he was pale with excitement about going away or wed be seen from the road he couldn't stand properly and I so hot as I never felt they could have made their peace in the beginning . . . instead of dragging it on for years killing any finelooking men there were with their fever if he was even decently shot it wouldn't have been so bad.

(U 748–9)

We cannot of course be sure whether Joyce intended us to think that this potentially adulterous relationship had already been consummated on some earlier night beside the canal: it seems likely, though, that he would have had Molly inform us if it had been. At any rate, on their evening together only Gardner's temporary impotence ('he couldn't stand properly') prevented her from eagerly breaking her marriage vow. Her imperial patriotism, very understandable in one who grew up in the British garrison at Gibraltar as the daughter of a sergeant-major, may be partly blamed for her feelings about the young lieutenant. The stark, abbreviated words in a newspaper casualty list could have been the first she had ever heard of him since he left Dublin: certainly they are imprinted on her memory for ever.

Having mentioned the slang meaning of 'to stand' as the equivalent of 'to have an erection', I had better take the opportunity to clear up the various misconceptions offered by otherwise intelligent critics and commentators concerning Bloom's potency and his marital relations generally. I do this, however reluctantly, because these misconceptions can lead to absurd misreadings of a masterpiece. 'Nausicaa' has shown us that Bloom is not impotent in the absolute sense of the word, though of course he might for a number of reasons, the most compelling being the death of his only son, have become incapable of normal relations with Molly. In fact, however, he is not impotent with her: in order to wheedle money for new clothes to make herself attractive to Stephen, she plans to seduce Bloom next morning:

> I know what Ill do Ill go about rather gay not too much singing a bit now and then mi fa pietà Masetto then Ill start dressing myself to go out presto non son più forte Ill put on my best shift and drawers let him have a good eyeful of that to make his micky stand for him.
>
> (U 780)

If she understands the words, Molly's brief quotations from the famous duet she is to sing in Belfast are appropriate but ambiguous: as Zerlına she feels a little guilty about Masetto/Bloom, yet she lacks the strength to resist Don Giovanni/Boylan. Or does *presto non son più forte* now suggest her readiness to yield herself to Bloom?

My task requires me to turn back just once more to the final pages of 'Ithaca', which include the most misunderstood passage in all of *Ulysses*:

> What limitations of activity and inhibitions of conjugal rights were perceived by listener and narrator concerning themselves during the course of this intermittent and increasingly more laconic narration?
>
> By the listener a limitation of fertility inasmuch as marriage had been celebrated 1 calendar month after the eighteenth anniversary of her birth (8 September 1870), viz. 8 October, and consummated on the same date with female issue born 15 June 1889, having been anticipatorily consummated on the 10 September of the same year and complete carnal intercourse, with ejaculation of semen within the natural female organ, having last taken place 5 weeks previous, viz. 27 November 1893, to the birth on 29 December 1893, of second (and only male) issue, deceased 9 January 1894, aged 11 days, there remained a period of 10 years, 5 months and 18 days during which carnal intercourse had been incomplete, without ejaculation of semen within the natural female organ.
>
> (U 735–6)

This account in legal-sounding prose of the marital life of the Blooms seems explicit enough in all conscience not to be misunderstood. Some might even consider it too explicit, except for the ambiguous phrase 'on the 10 September of the same year' (1888 or 1889?). Yet the number of critics, scholars, and men in the street who have understood it to mean that the Blooms have had *no* sexual intercourse whatever for over ten years passes belief. I do not propose to cause embarrassment by citing a number of famous names: apparently scholastic precision is even less valued than one had thought. 'Ejaculation of semen within the natural female organ' is the translation of a Latin phrase which occurs in the interior monologue of Father Conmee (Wandering Rocks):

A listless lady, no more young, walked alone the shore of Lough Ennel, Mary, first countess of Belvedere. . . . Who could know the truth? Not the jealous lord Belvedere and not her confessor if she had not committed adultery fully, *ejaculatio seminis inter vas naturale mulieris* with her husband's brother? . . . Only God knew and she and he, her husband's brother.

(U 223)

Since Rudy's death the Blooms have resorted to *coitus interruptus* and various other expedients: the reader who is sufficiently interested can confirm this by a careful reading of 'Penelope'. Molly was ripe for adultery because none of these expedients satisfies her: 'pretending to like it until he comes and then finish it off myself anyway and it makes your lips pale.' (*U* 740) Bloom has some contraceptive shields (*U* 721), known to his wife by the slang term 'French letters', which would also prevent complete intercourse in the theological sense, but these are apparently not for conjugal use. (By the way, any doubt that may have arisen in the reader's mind about whether Mrs Bloom has 'committed adultery fully' may be resolved by the words 'the last time I let him finish it in me' on page 742.)

These observations do not exhaust the subject of the Blooms' conjugal relations or lack of them, for it seems of absorbing interest to Joyce, partly no doubt for autobiographical reasons. Every marriage or other lasting sexual relationship has its peaks and chasms: furthermore, on at least one occasion in his life Joyce—to his own amazement, I assume—felt all the rage, humiliation, jealousy, and self-contempt traditionally associated with the cuckold. The circumstances are too well known to need recapitulation here: it will be sufficient to quote Joyce's letter from Dublin to Nora Barnacle in Trieste, 6 August 1909:

I have been frank in what I have told you of myself.
You have not been so with me.
    At the time when I used to meet you at the corner of Merrion Square and walk out with you and feel your hand touch me in the dark and hear your voice (O, Nora! I will never hear that music again because I can never believe again) at the time I used to meet you, *every second night* you kept an appointment with a friend of mine . . . you stood with him: he put his arm round you and you lifted your face and kissed him. What else did you do together? And the next night you met *me*!
    I have heard this only an hour ago from his [Vincent Cosgrave's] lips . . . O, Nora, pity me for what I suffer now. I shall cry for days . . .
    O Nora is all to be over between us?
    Write to me, Nora, for the sake of my dead love. I am tortured by memories.
    Write to me, Nora, I loved you only: and you have broken my faith in you
    O, Nora, I am unhappy. I am crying for my poor unhappy love.
    Write to me, Nora.   Jim[45]

45 *Letters of James Joyce*, ed. R. Ellmann (New York: 1966), ii. 231–2.

J. F. Byrne—the original of Cranly—soon convinced Joyce that Cosgrave was lying, but the shock of his imagined cuckolding, which reduced a lord of language to a stammering schoolboy (an epiphany indeed!) provided inspiration not only for the play *Exiles*, his last attempt to imitate Ibsen, but for *Ulysses*. The idea of an unfaithful Penelope was not original with Joyce: he would have known this passage from the sixth chapter, 'Pan, or Nature', in Bacon's *Wisdom of the Ancients*:

The Ancients have exquisitely described *Nature* under the person of *Pan*, whose original they leave doubtful: for some say that he was the son of *Mercury*: others attribute unto him a far different beginning, affirming him to be the common Offspring of *Penelope's* Suitors, upon a Suspicion that everyone of them had to do with her.[46]

Another connection between the Blooms' marital difficulties and the *Odyssey* is so obvious that it only recently occurred to me: their partial estrangement for a period of over ten years is the equivalent of Odysseus's twenty-year absence from Ithaca. Butcher and Lang renders Book XXIII, lines 210–12, with a poignancy verging on bitterness. Penelope says, 'It is the gods that gave us sorrow, the gods who were jealous that we should abide together and have joy of our youth, and come to the threshold of old age.'

The rapid, elusive, allusive free-associating style of 'Penelope' permits the inclusion of an astonishing number of persons and themes. Many of the persons mentioned were previously unknown to the reader because they were unknown to Mr Bloom: Mr and Mrs Stanhope, Captain Groves, Mrs Rubio the Spanish servant, and others from the Gibraltar period, including of course her first lover, Lieutenant Harry Mulvey, R. N. Molly, then 16, did not lose her virginity with him, but it was a near thing. Unlike many previous episodes in which much familiar material is so to speak recycled, 'Penelope' has a freshness rare in the concluding phases of long novels. This is due not only to the introduction of new characters but even more to the presentation of Bloomsday from a fresh and novel point of view. We have heard so very much of Molly in Bloom's uxorious reverie and in the conversation of other characters: now here she is at last, ready and willing to speak for herself. Education she may lack but not intelligence: her harum-scarum upbringing, with Mrs Rubio as a mother-substitute and Hester Stanhope as a combination mother-sister figure, has made her world-view a muddle of superstitions, street-wisdom, opportunism, and unexpected gentilities—along with some real virtues, supreme self-confidence, and a highly idiosyncratic version of what must be called integrity. Above all, she possesses the gift

---

[46] Bacon, *Wisdom of the Ancients*, 262.

of language. Especially after the self-conscious, pseudo-scientific tone and diction of 'Ithaca', the colloquial, even slangy flavour of 'Penelope' gives the reader an astonishing sense of liberation, as if in the rest of the book he had struggled up the slope of Purgatory and arrived at last in some sort of earthly paradise. There is no room here for careful analysis of dialects and speech-rhythms, but I will hazard a few generalizations. The basic rhythm (as well as the punctuation!) derives from Nora Barnacle's Galway upbringing, though Joyce, knowing virtually no Irish, could rarely capture her exact turn of phrase. Molly's idiom is largely Dublin but spiced with Cork phrases that Joyce picked up from his father. She also uses Spanish words, supplied by her creator to remind us of her Gibraltar life. Nevertheless I hear the authentic voice of a Galway girl, however poorly educated, in this rhapsodic passage:

I love flowers / Id love to have the whole place swimming in roses / God of heaven there's nothing like nature/ the wild mountains / then the sea and the waves rushing / then the beautiful country / with fields of oats and wheat and all kinds of things / and all the fine cattle going about that would do your heart good to see / rivers and lakes and flowers / all sorts of shapes and smells and colours / springing up even out of the ditches / primroses and violets / nature it is / as for them saying there's no God / I wouldn't give a snap of my fingers for all their learning / why don't they go and create something I often asked him [Bloom} / atheists or whatever they call them.

(U 781–2)

Not only does 'Penelope' give us a new perspective on familiar characters like Bloom, Boylan, Stephen, Molly's daughter Milly, Simon Dedalus, Ben Dollard, and many more: there was also, for the early readers of *Ulysses* at least, the astonishing novelty that, for the first time in the history of literature, as it seemed, it was a totally uninhibited woman's perspective. A moment's reflection, of course, will remind us that it was not a *woman's* but James Joyce's. The monologue may however owe something to the frankness of Nora's answers to his questions: such an intimate catechism is fictionally rendered in the first act of *Exiles*, after the departure of Robert Hand.

Arnold Bennett, for one, accepted Joyce's insights as authentic in an early review of *Ulysses*:[47]

The long unspoken monologue of Mrs Bloom which closes the book (forty difficult pages, some twenty-five thousand words without any punctuation at all) might in its utterly convincing realism be an actual document, the magical record of inmost thought by a woman that existed. Talk about understanding 'feminine psychology'! . . . I have never read anything to surpass it, and I doubt if I have ever read anything to equal it.

47 Arnold Bennett, 'Concerning James Joyce's *Ulysses*', *Bookman* LV, August 1922, 567.

Joyce himself would have agreed heartily with Bennett: in the letter to Budgen already quoted he concludes the paragraph on 'Penelope' as follows: 'Though probably more obscene than any preceding episode it seems to me to be perfectly sane full amoral fertilisable untrustworthy engaging shrewd limited prudent indifferent *Weib. Ich bin das Fleisch das stets bejaht.*' If we apply Joyce's smug list of adjectives solely to his own creation, Molly Bloom, we can admit their exactness. If, on the other hand, encouraged by the parody of Goethe and the use of the foreign (and therefore seemingly more generalized) word *Weib*, we treat the whole passage as a philosophical statement about women in general, I cannot accept it as valid. Beatrice Justice in *Exiles* is Joyce's only attempt at the intellectual woman: he obviously dislikes her, but no audience could possibly be either for or against such a lifeless stereotype. Yeats's letters reveal an attitude towards women of intelligence and culture standing at the opposite pole to that shown in Joyce's. Where Goethe writes of 'The Spirit that always denies', Joyce prefers 'The Flesh that always says yes'. The 'organ' of the body assigned to Penelope is Flesh, whereas the first three episodes of *Ulysses* correspond to no organ whatever because, according to the Linati Schema, 'Telemachus [and, by extension, the intellectual Stephen] does not yet bear a body'. Penelope is assigned no hour and no art, suggesting that Molly (perhaps other women too) is timeless and artless.

The two most notorious novels in English during the first half of the twentieth century, *Ulysses* and *Lady Chatterley's Lover*, both owe their notoriety to their authors' attempts to convey in words the sensations preceding, accompanying, and following not male but female orgasm. Joyce met with some success in this difficult endeavour through his use of the bursting rocket as a metaphor in 'Nausicaa'. In 'Penelope' he relied on an accelerating speech rhythm beginning with

the sun shines for you he said / the day we were lying among the rhododendrons on Howth head / in the grey tweed suit and his straw hat / the day I got him to propose to me / yes first gave him the bit of seedcake out of my mouth and it was leapyear like now / yes 16 years ago / my God after that long kiss I nearly lost my breath / yes he said I was a flower of the mountain / yes so we are flowers all a woman's body / yes that was one true thing he said in his life and the sun shines for you today / yes.

(U 782)

The word 'yes' recurs at shorter and shorter intervals above, indicating Molly's growing excitement. Then there is a short pause while she considers the reasons for choosing him as her mate: 'that was why I liked him because he understood or felt what a woman is / and I knew

I could always get round him / and I gave him all the pleasure I could / leading him on till he asked me to say yes.'

At last she has reached the point where both her marriage and her pleasure are assured. Having climbed to a plateau she artfully post-pones the downhill rush: 'and I wouldn't answer first only looked out over the sea and the sky I was thinking of so many things he didn't know of Mulvey and Mr Stanhope and Hester and father and old captain Groves and the sailors.' For over half a page 'yes' disappears, a rapid series of repetitions of 'and' taking its place and linking all the memories of Gibraltar that suddenly overwhelm her. Then, as in Beethoven or Wagner a single note recalls an entire mood, the word 'yes' reappears three lines from the top of the last page and again four lines farther on, and yet again in the next line after that, until the acceleration can no longer be checked:

and I thought well as well him as another / and then I asked him with my eyes to ask again / yes / and then he asked me would I / yes / to say / yes / my moun-tain flower / and first I put my arms around him / yes / and drew him down to me so he could feel my breasts all perfume / yes / and his heart was going like mad and / yes I said / yes / I will / Yes.

(U 783)

The love scene that Molly is remembering may have occurred on 10 September 1888, when the Blooms 'anticipatorily consummated' (*U* 736) their marriage, or on a somewhat earlier date. The point to be kept in mind is that her climax is not the result of 'complete carnal intercourse', though that may have taken place only minutes later: similarly, her present orgasm in the small hours of 17 June 1904 occurs in the presence but not with the assistance of Leopold Bloom (now fast asleep). The same is true of the climax experienced by Gerty MacDowell.

Mellors, the game-keeper, on the other hand, is indispensable to the pleasure of Connie Chatterley, thus satisfying Lawrence's male vanity even as he strives to identify himself with his female character. To the extent that Lawrence tries to describe her sexual appeasement directly instead of finding a visual or rhythmic equivalent (T. S. Eliot's 'objective correlative'), he fails where Joyce succeeds. Joyce's sense of humour prevents him from fully identifying himself with Molly: the subtly ironic tone of Penelope creates a distance between author and character and at the same time contributes to her credibility. Lady Chatterley, on the other hand—the humourless creation of a humourless author—is no more credible than Joyce's Beatrice Justice.

Despite the apparent male chauvinism of Joyce's letter to Budgen, he was in awe of women, their worshipper rather than their would-be god.

He identifies himself not with Blazes Boylan, the conquering male, but with the sly Bloom who worms his way into the affections of women and is content to be a cuckold so long as his wife keeps the bed warm for him. Whereas Mellors is an efficient little British earth-god who supposedly liberates the sexuality of Connie Chatterley, it is Molly whom Joyce identifies with the earth itself, 'left hand under head, right leg extended in a straight line and resting on left leg, flexed, in the attitude of Gea-Tellus, fulfilled, recumbent, big with seed' (*U* 737). She is not in fact 'big' in the sense of 'pregnant', for she begins to menstruate in the 'Penelope' episode. Nevertheless, Bloom lies beside her with his head pointing towards her feet, 'the childman weary, the manchild in the womb'. Meanwhile she paradoxically thinks of his son-figure Stephen as a truly adult male, ripe to become her next lover. And so the Father and the Son meet in the Mother, whose birthday, by the way, is the same as that of the Blessed Virgin, and her baptismal name, Marion, but a variant of Mary.

Some Conclusions

Ulysses ends as ambiguously as any good short story—as the short story it was originally intended to be might have ended. Despite Molly's mental enactment, we have no idea what will actually happen when the Blooms awake the following morning. On the assumption that the book was even more autobiographical than it actually is, William Empson suggested that Stephen and Mrs Bloom would become lovers, as Joyce became the lover of her prototype. Soon afterwards, Ellmann's biography revealed that there was no such prototype—except of course Mrs Joyce in her maturity—and that 16 June 1904 was memorable as the day on which Nora Barnacle, still in her teens, and James Joyce first went walking out together. My own feeling is that Joyce's conception of the Blooms' future ran something like this: Molly, because of her menstruation, does not have intercourse with her husband next morning but gives him breakfast in bed: with his usual generosity, he hands over the money she needs for clothes. Stephen, however, will never return to 7 Eccles Street, and Molly's affair with Boylan will continue until it reaches its natural end. After this, her first fully consummated adulterous affair, others will occur more easily: Bloom meanwhile will pursue pleasure in his own devious ways. Ultimately, though, there will be a reconciliation prompted by the birth of their first grandchild, analogous to the reconciliation between Shakespeare and his wife which Stephen imagines as the inspiration of the last plays: '— Marina, Stephen said, a child of storm, Miranda, a wonder, Perdita, that which was lost. What was lost is given back to him: his daughter's child. *My dearest wife,* Pericles says, *was like this maid.*' (*U* 195) If this seems a lame and impotent conclusion, totally sentimental and petty bourgeois, I would ask the reader to remember that the Blooms do in fact belong to the lower middle class. Also, though we have received so much more information about them than about any similar couple in the history of literature, I think Joyce saw them as quite ordinary people, no better and no worse than their neighbours would seem if equally thoroughly documented. Their apparent preoccupation with sex would be regarded as commonplace by Freud. Furthermore, *Ulysses* deals with a unique day in their lives: after a long period of unresolved sexual tension, the wife has finally broken her marriage vow and experienced a physical release far surpassing her expectations. Is it any wonder that she goes over every detail of her experience with what St Thomas Aquinas called 'morose delectation'? (*U* 47) Or that her husband, aware of and consenting to his cuckolding, cannot keep his mind off 'the swelling act'?

Looking into the future from the end of a fiction is at best a flight of fantasy or an intellectual game. Far more important is what we see when we look back at the work, after one reading or a hundred. Roughly two-thirds of a century of interpretation and criticism offer us a temporary or historical perspective: this peak on the literary horizon seems neither so high nor so vast as it once did, its faces are not so abrupt nor its chasms so deep. *Ulysses* has become more accessible; also less awe-inspiring when seen alongside the Zauberberg and the Proust range. Other contours are beginning to fill in the middle distance: Woolf, Faulkner, Solzhenitsyn.

It is notorious that we cannot speak of time except in terms of space, as in the paragraph above. Stephen may be alluding to Bergson when he thinks of himself walking on Sandymount Strand as 'A very short space of time through very short times of space.' (*U* 37) By 9 May 1914 Joyce had bought Bergson's *L'Evolution créatrice*.

So this seemingly pessimistic novel has a happy ending. It does not end with the Protestant stoicism of Beckett's *Unnamable*, 'I can't go on', nor entropically like *The Lost Ones*, in which a small community or system finally comes to a full stop. Instead we have a Catholic world oriented to eternity, in which, despite the supposed puritanism of the Irish Church, everybody is thinking about what we call in Ireland 'the one thing'. One could safely say that this unifying symbol is none other than the carnal Rose, represented in Joyce's symbolic system by Molly's last word, 'Yes'.

9 'All That Fall': Samuel Beckett and the Bible

I do not propose to engage in a minute analysis of Beckett's radio play, *All That Fall* (BBC, January 1957), which might be described as Ireland's sardonic answer to Dylan Thomas's *Under Milk Wood* (BBC, January 1954). The phrase is quoted in my title to remind us of a passage where Beckett, for once, makes it clear to his audience that he is quoting from the Bible. His work, as we shall see, is full of hidden biblical quotations, but this most emphatically is not one of them. Just to make conversation, Mr Rooney of *All That Fall* asks his wife:

> Who is the preacher to-morrow? The incumbent?
> MRS ROONEY: No.
> MR ROONEY: Thank God for that. Who?
> MRS ROONEY: Hardy. . . .
> MR ROONEY: Has he announced the text?
> MRS ROONEY: 'The Lord upholdeth all that fall and raiseth up all those that be bowed down'. *(Silence. They join in wild laughter . . .)*[1]

Except for the omission of a comma after 'fall', this is an exact quotation from the 145th Psalm, verse 14, according to the King James version. (In the Douay version, the fourteenth verse of Psalm 144 is translated more succinctly and a little more intelligibly as 'The Lord lifteth up all that fall; and setteth up all that are cast down'). It is very likely that Beckett quoted this verse from memory, as he often does quote the Bible. We know that he was in the habit of quoting from memory, paradoxically, because his memory was sometimes at fault. In *How It Is* he mentions 'the sky whence cometh our help', a misquotation from the first verse of Psalm 121 in the King James Bible, which reads, 'I will lift up my eyes unto the hills from whence cometh my help'.

To return to the passage in *All That Fall*, let us assume that Beckett is quoting from memory and ask ourselves what inferences we can draw from that assumption. On the one hand, we might argue that Beckett

[1] The following works by Beckett are cited in the following editions: *All That Fall*, in *Krapp's Last Tape and other Dramatic Pieces* (New York: Grove Press, 1960); *How It Is* (Grove, 1964); *Endgame* (Grove, 1958); *Murphy* (London: Routledge & Kegan Paul, 1938); *More Pricks Than Kicks*, Collected Works (Grove, 1970); *Waiting For Godot* (Grove, 1954); *Happy Days* (Grove, 1961); *Molloy* and *The Unnamable*, in *Three Novels* (Grove, 1959); *Lessness*, Signature Series (London: Calder & Boyars, 1970); *That Time* (London: Faber & Faber, 1976).

was required to learn some or all of the Psalm by heart while at school. Verses 15 and 16 of Psalm 145 are in fact more familiar to me than verse 14:

> The eyes of all wait upon thee, and thou givest them their
>   meat in due season.
> Thou openest thine hand, and satisfiest the desire of every
>   living thing.

Though Beckett may not have known it, the Vulgate Latin of these two verses is incorporated almost word for word into one of the graces recited every day in the dining hall of Trinity College, Dublin:

> Oculi omnium in te sperant, Domine;
>   tu das eis escam eorum in tempore opportuno.
> Aperis tu manum tuam,
>   et imples omne animal benedictione tua.

After he moved into College rooms in 1926, Beckett must often have heard these words. The fact that he was entitled to free Commons every night as a Foundation Scholar may even have convinced him of their literal truth. On the other hand, if nobody had compelled him to learn the passage by heart, then the fact that verse 14 implanted itself spontaneously in Beckett's memory encourages profounder speculation. After all, these are among the most comforting and reassuring words in the whole English Bible. We can hardly deny the thought that this sentence once held deep meaning for Samuel Beckett. At the very least, its rhythm must have enchanted his ear. The first clause contains four iambic feet with an internal rhyme—'The Lord upholdeth all that fall'; the second clause is a complete line of Miltonic blank verse, 'and raiseth up all those that be bowed down'. The last two syllables, with their assonance 'bowed down', may be read as a spondee, and 'those' assonates with 'hold' in the first line.

It was by no accident, in any case, that Beckett chose it as the title of what is surely his most deeply pessimistic play: almost everything that happens in *All That Fall* directly contradicts the psalmist's blessed assurance. Maddy and Dan Rooney's life experience seems to deny at every turn the existence of a merciful God. Yet they are not unbelievers: as far as we know, they attend their church every Sunday, no matter how boring the incumbent's sermons may be. The use of this very word 'incumbent' proves that they are members of the Church of Ireland, although the word is more familiar to English Anglicans than to Irish ones; in Ireland, we would be more apt to say 'the rector' or, if there were no rector, 'the curate'. In writing 'the incumbent', Beckett may be having his little joke, since the imagery of the word suggests a clergyman

lying in or on his parish. The point is that the Rooneys are definitely
not Presbyterians, their theology is not Calvinist. It is true that there are
Calvinist elements in the Thirty-nine Articles, but Anglican theology
envisages a far more merciful God than Calvin's. Even dotty old Miss
Fitt seems aware of this when she helps Mrs Rooney up the steps at
Boghill (i.e. Foxrock) railway station: 'Well', she says, 'I suppose it is
the Protestant thing to do.' It would be more natural, of course, to say
it is the Christian thing to do, but Beckett is having his joke again. Miss
Fitt, although she worships in the same church as Mrs Rooney, is an
ultra-Protestant. When Mrs Rooney reminds her that 'Last Sunday we
worshipped together. We knelt side by side at the same altar. We drank
from the same chalice,' she emphasizes the ritual, High Church side of
Anglicanism. Miss Fitt, on the other hand, being so Low Church as to
resemble a Quaker, is shocked by this reminder: 'Oh but in church, Mrs
Rooney, in church I am alone with my Maker. Are not you?' This attitude of Miss Fitt's is a logical outcome of the history of Protestantism,
which began with secessions of minority groups from the universal
Catholic Church. Once the process of splitting off has begun, there is no
logical end short of One Man One Church or, in Miss Fitt's case, One
Woman One Church. The next step after that is One Man No Church.
As Professor Augustine Martin has pointed out, this step has been taken
very easily by several Irish Protestant writers—Synge for example—without much soul-searching, whereas an Irish Catholic author's parting from
his faith may well provide material for one or more autobiographical
novels in the tradition of *A Portrait of the Artist as a Young Man*.[2] Brian
Moore seems to need constant reassurance that his hard-won unbelief
remains unshaken: see, for example, that remarkable novel *Cold Heaven*.

Beckett, on his own admission, felt no symptoms of withdrawal. As
he told Tom Driver: 'The family was Protestant, but for me it was only
irksome and I let it go.'[3] The only hint of anguish about breaking with
the faith learned quite literally at his mother's knee is to be found in the
'wild laughter' attributed to the Rooneys. There is surely no more blasphemous moment in any Beckett work, except Hamm's cry in *Endgame*,
after a moment of silent prayer: 'The bastard! He doesn't exist!' That is
black humour, if you like, but Beckett would have expected that an
Irish audience, Catholic or Protestant, would react to it first of all as
blasphemy: any subsequent laughter, however loud, would sound uneasy.
Every blasphemer, obviously, must once have been a true believer: there

[2] Augustine Martin, 'Anglo-Irish Literature', in *Irish Anglicanism 1869–1969*, ed. Michael
Hurley (Dublin: Allen Figgis, 1970), 120–1.

[3] Tom Driver, 'Tom Driver in "Columbia University Forum"', in *Samuel Beckett: The Critical
Heritage*, ed. Lawrence Graver and Raymond Federman (London: Routledge & Kegan Paul,
1979), 220.

is no thrill—at least for an intelligent person—in breaking a prohibition by which one has never felt threatened. The harshness of the blasphemy is perhaps a measure of one's sense of loss or of having been deceived by what one trusted most.

Before leaving *All That Fall*, let us look for a moment at the *hidden* biblical allusions in the play. Mr Tyler, one of those who overtake Mrs Rooney on her weary way to the railway station, finds that the back tyre of his bicycle has got flat again. Mrs Rooney hears him muttering, and with her usual politeness says, 'I beg your pardon?' 'Nothing, Mrs Rooney, nothing, I was merely cursing, under my breath, God and man, under my breath, and the wet Saturday afternoon of my conception.' The reference here is to the Book of Job, chapter 3, verse 3: 'Let the day perish wherein I was born, and the night in which it was said, There is a man child conceived.' Tyler's response to his flat tyre seems a little excessive: Job's bitter cry was torn from him not only because he had lost all his children and all his wealth but because he had been smitten with 'sore boils from the sole of his foot unto his crown'. Furthermore, despite the urging of his wife, Job did not curse God at any time. By the way, this was not Beckett's first allusion to a text beloved by pessimists. In the fourth chapter of Murphy, Neary is in dire need of a drink; the following dialogue occurs:

'But by Mooney's clock', said Wylie, 'the sad news is two-thirty-three'.

Neary leaned against the Pillar railings and cursed, first the day in which he was born, then—in a bold flash-back—the night in which he was conceived. 'There, there,' said Wylie. 'Needle knows no holy hour'.

'Needle' Wiley then brings Neary to 'an underground café close by', where they circumvent the licensing laws by drinking two large coffees ordered by Wylie, who specifies 'Three star'. Was this subterfuge the origin of Irish coffee?

There is yet another type of biblical allusion to be found in *All That Fall*, perhaps not quite so carefully concealed as the quotation from Job. Here, Mrs Rooney surprisingly ventures into the arena of textual scholarship. 'It wasn't an ass's colt at all, you know', she says to her husband, apparently apropos of nothing. 'I asked the Regius Professor.' After a pause, Mr Rooney gives a safe answer: 'He should know.' Mrs Rooney goes on, 'Yes, it was a hinny, he rode into Jerusalem or wherever it was on a hinny. (*Pause.*) That must mean something. (*Pause.*) It's like the sparrows, than many of which we are of more value, they weren't sparrows at all'. Mr Rooney accuses her of exaggerating the number of sparrows, but Maddy is quoting accurately from St Matthew, 10:31: 'Fear ye not therefore, ye are of more value than many sparrows.'

Christ's entry into Jerusalem 'sitting on an ass's colt' is described in these exact words in St John's Gospel; in St Matthew the King James has 'a colt the foal of an ass'; in the other two gospels the animal is described simply as a 'colt'. The Regius Professor mentioned is presumably the Regius Professor of Divinity at Trinity College, Dublin, but whether Beckett had any particular holder of that office in mind is a question which might lead us into a morass of pedantry.

We have had perhaps enough for the moment about Beckett's accuracy and ingenuity in the quoting of Scripture. Let us ask: What sort of education made this possible? *A Portrait of the Artist* has made millions of readers aware of the thoroughness of James Joyce's Catholic education under the Jesuits, but Beckett's Anglican training was, in its own way, almost as thorough. I say 'in its own way' because there was one extraordinary gap in it—an almost total absence of theology. This was certainly true of my own education, which I believe to have resembled Beckett's very closely. Nobody ever told us who Luther and Calvin were, let alone discussed how their teachings differed from each other. More surprisingly, perhaps, we learned very little about the points of dogma that separated our Church from Roman Catholicism. I heard rumours of a book called *Roman Claims* that was sometimes set for examinations in Religious Knowledge, but to this day I have never seen a copy. I can find nothing to disagree with in the following passage from a review by George Steiner:

The very anti-intellectuality, the abstentions from philosophical rigour and abstraction which have, since the end of the seventeenth century, afforded the life of the Churches in England their enviable civility, mutual tolerance and low-key presence, may, under today's exactions, prove a fatal virtue. So very little in contemporary Anglican thought or practice seems equipped to face, on comparable terms, either the summons of atheism and agnosticism or the temptations of dogma.[4]

This may be the true explanation of the Irish Anglican's readiness to abandon his faith, already mentioned.

What did we learn, then? First of all, the habit of involuntary public worship. At Portora Royal School, Enniskillen, where Beckett spent three-and-a-half years as a boarder (1920–3) and I spent eight (1928–36), we were subjected to a thoroughly Evangelical regime. Until recently, the Headmaster was always a Church of Ireland clergyman: throughout Beckett's and my time there, he was the Revd E. G. Seale. Every weekday morning, Seale read prayers and a passage from the Bible at Assembly. He or some other master read prayers and Scripture again at

---

[4] This reference has eluded me but I presume I found it in *TLS c.* Nov.–Dec. 1986.

the end of homework preparation for bedtime. The roll-call of boarders before breakfast was performed with care by the master on duty, but the prayer that followed was usually brief and hasty. On Sunday mornings the Church of Ireland boarders paraded to St Macartan's Cathedral, wearing Harrow-style straw boaters if the weather was clement. On Sunday evenings in summer, we walked to church again in the nearby country parish of Rossory; during the rest of the year, Sunday evening service was in the dining hall, usually conducted by the Headmaster. Occasionally there would be a missionary sermon by an ordained 'old boy', who was already labouring in the vineyard, whether with the Church Missionary Society in the British Empire, or in the slums of Belfast. We used the *Public Schools Hymnal*, bound in the school colours—the British Royal Arms in yellow on a black ground. The biographical notes told us that Henry Francis Lyte, author of 'Abide with me' and other fine hymns, was educated at Portora and Trinity. We liked the many hymns at these evening services, and naturally we sang Lyte's *fortissimo*.

All this 'gentility and church-going'—to quote yet again from *All That Fall*—was less important for Beckett's development as a writer than the almost daily teaching of Holy Scripture as a regular school subject up to the fourth or fifth form. In a Protestant School, the Old Testament of course received at least as much attention as the New. We learned some of the Psalms and some of the prophecies of Isaiah by heart, as well as passages from the Gospels and from the Epistles of St Paul. The Acts of the Apostles made a particularly strong impression because of the thrilling adventures by land and sea, and especially the conversion of St Paul. When I heard of the publication of Beckett's first volume of fiction, *More Pricks Than Kicks*, later banned by the Irish Censorship Board, I recognized the allusion in the title at once. When a light from heaven shines round about the future Apostle on the road to Damascus, he hears a voice saying, 'Saul, Saul, why persecutest thou me?' Saul, not yet christened Paul, answers the question with another, 'Who art thou, Lord?' In the King James version, the Lord replies, 'I am Jesus whom thou persecutest: it is hard for thee to kick against the pricks.' The Douay version, more readily intelligible, has 'It is hard for thee to kick against the goad.' In a Scripture class at Portora, normally taught by a layman, the image of the ox kicking against the goad would have been explained, like other archaic allusions or words, but, as I have said, theological explanations were rare. Of course there were other Protestants in these classes besides members of the Church of Ireland—Presbyterians, Methodists, perhaps an occasional Quaker or Baptist—whose doctrine might disagree on this or that point. I have a feeling, however, that the basic principle underlying this practice was the widely accepted Protestant Evangelical doctrine of the 'sufficiency' of Holy Scripture. If one already possessed the necessary faith, the Bible contained all the teaching necessary to attain salvation. The Hibernian Bible Society prided itself on distributing Bibles, whether in Irish or English, that were printed 'without note or comment'. The assumption was that if Catholics read these Bibles, or had someone read them aloud, in their own language, they would almost automatically be converted to Protestantism.

Since Beckett did not enter Portora until he was almost 14, he must have picked up much of his familiarity with the Bible earlier: in church, in Sunday school, and in Scripture classes at the other Protestant schools he attended. All I am suggesting is that his biblical knowledge when he left Portora at 17 was roughly the same as mine at that age. One of the peculiarities of Bible teaching at Portora was that we took examinations set by our teachers rather than those approved by the Church of Ireland Diocese of Clogher. I assume this was another ecumenical gesture to the boys of other Protestant denominations attending the school. Beckett, however, must have taken examinations in the Diocese of Dublin at some stage before he went to Portora. Otherwise, he would hardly have been inspired to write the following humorously incongruous passage in *More Pricks Than Kicks*: 'He had underlined, as quite a callow boy, a phrase in Hardy's *Tess*, won by dint of cogging in the Synod: *When grief ceases to be speculative, sleep sees her opportunity.*'

'Cogging' is a word used all over Ireland for copying or cheating, but what is 'the Synod'? I recognize it as shorthand for an annual examination in Religious Knowledge inaugurated by the Board of Education of the General Synod of the Church of Ireland over a century ago, which I often heard mentioned as 'the Synod exam'. Indeed, I took it once in the Diocese of Ossory while I was briefly at school in Abbeyleix. My prize was a Prayer Book. No doubt there were different prizes as well as different examinations according to age, but I'm prepared to bet that no amount of cogging would ever have won Thomas Hardy's notorious *Tess of the D'Urbervilles* as a prize in any diocese of the Church of Ireland, however enlightened, to this very day!

Many Bibles, especially nowadays, do of course include much more than the text 'without note or comment'. Estragon, in *Waiting for Godot*, does not seem to remember the Gospels, but he does remember 'the maps of the Holy Land. Coloured they were. Very pretty. The Dead Sea was pale blue. The very look of it made me thirsty. That's where we'll go, I used to say, that's where we'll go for our honeymoon. We'll swim. We'll be happy.' Besides maps, one may find a concordance, a subject-index, and other 'helps'. A widely circulated Oxford edition of the King James includes a 'Dictionary of Scripture Proper Names'. In it, the meaning of the name Shuah is given as 'depression'. This may help to explain why Beckett named the central character of *More Pricks Than Kicks* Belacqua Shuah: Belacqua, from Dante's *Purgatorio*, was famous for indolence and procrastination; the name Shuah emphasizes another characteristic of the unhappy anti-hero.

The passage just quoted from *Waiting for Godot* forms part of the longest and best-known biblical allusion in Beckett's work: that concerning the fate of the two thieves crucified with Jesus. Vladimir says, 'One of the thieves was saved. . . . It's a reasonable percentage.' Later it occurs to him that 'of the four Evangelists only one speaks of a thief being saved. . . . One out of four. Of the other three two mention no thieves at all and the third says that both of them abused him.' It is odd that so many of the commentators on what some believe to be a crux in the play accept Vladimir's statement as gospel truth. St Luke is indeed the only Evangelist to mention the penitent thief, but St Matthew and St Mark state that both the thieves abused Jesus. St John alone does not identify the two men crucified with the Saviour as thieves. Curiously, the King James translation of St Luke used the word 'malefactors' rather than 'thieves', but this does nothing to validate the account given by Vladimir, who goes on to say that 'Everybody' believes St Luke. 'It's the only version they know.' On which Estragon's comment is, 'People are bloody ignorant apes.' I would not dream of calling Mr Beckett a bloody ignorant ape; some of his commentators, however—myself included—might pay heed to Estragon now and again.

One thing at least is certain: the presence of the discussion of the two thieves so early in the play has encouraged many people to read *Waiting for Godot* as some sort of Christian parable. Vladimir and Estragon (or Didi and Gogo, as they call each other) may be waiting for God, or at any rate for some kind of salvation. I myself have argued that Godot does arrive, in both acts, disguised as Pozzo: Didi and Gogo fail to recognize him, just as, Christians believe, the Jews failed to recognize the Messiah. The cruelty and uncharitableness of Pozzo, however, make this theory hard to defend. A more plausible hypothesis might be that Lucky is the Messiah; he is a man of sorrows and acquainted with grief, a true Suffering Servant. Pozzo, his cruel or indifferent master, reminds one at times of Herod and at other times of Pontius Pilate. The 'country road' on which the play is set might be the road to Calvary, though the rope around Lucky's neck suggests hanging rather than crucifixion. If this is so, Didi and Gogo are the two thieves. They think seriously of hanging themselves in both acts. Vladimir, who once says, 'suppose we repented', is thus obviously the penitent thief.

I do not expect this interpretation to be accepted; frankly, I do not quite believe in it myself. I am just putting it forward as an example of how the simple yet universal elements and relationships in *Waiting for Godot* can be interpreted as symbols of so many truths, both human and divine. Beckett told Colin Duckworth, who edited the French text of *Waiting for Godot* for use in English schools and universities, that 'Christianity is a mythology with which I am perfectly familiar, so I naturally use it.'⁵ Be that as it may, he never again used it with quite the subtlety and ingenuity displayed in *Waiting for Godot*. In *Happy Days*, I see—and hear—Beckett making a different, though still subtle, use of his Protestant heritage.

It seems to me significant that this play, like *All That Fall* and *Krapp's Last Tape*—but unlike most of his other dramatic works—was written first in English. Winnie and Willie of *Happy Days* are just as clearly a Foxrock couple as the Rooneys in *All That Fall*: the difference is that they are more normal—or at any rate they manage to conform better outwardly to a rather Anglicized suburban stereotype. Far from being grotesque like the Rooneys, they are well-preserved for their respective ages, and try to keep well-groomed under most trying conditions. Because of some tremendous catastrophe, the world has ceased to turn and time can no longer be measured by the alternation of day and night, yet just before the final curtain Willie manages to appear '*dressed to kill—top hat, morning coat, striped trousers, etc, white gloves in hand*', much as he must have looked on his wedding day. In the heat of perpetual noon, such punctilio reminds us of the legendary Englishmen who used always to dress for dinner, even in the Tropics.

Winnie's fortitude is less concerned with externals, though she is anxious that her hat should be at a becoming angle even when she has lost her hand-mirror. Her religious training has already been Anglican: she concludes her brief prayers with the formulas 'For Jesus Christ sake Amen' and 'World without end Amen'. She remembers sitting on the knees of 'Charlie Hunter', who afterwards became a bishop. She proclaims 'another heavenly day' and constantly speaks of 'Many mercies'. If we have read Newman's *Idea of a University*, however, we may begin to feel that her relentless optimism—so unlike Mrs Rooney's encircling gloom—is more appropriate to a pagan Stoic than to a Christian. Nevertheless, one cannot help admiring what Belacqua Shuah calls 'The grand old family Huguenot guts'. Although Beckett's mother, unlike my own, did not attend Alexandra School and College in Dublin, I cannot help feeling that Winnie did. Despite her ladylike speech, she is not

---

⁵ Samuel Beckett, *En Attendant Godot*, ed. Colin Duckworth (London: Harrap, 1966), lvii.

above dropping into the slang of her generation occasionally. 'Come on, dear', she says to Winnie, 'put a bit of jizz into it.'

If it were not for one recurrent biblical allusion, we might lose patience ultimately with Winnie's apparent shallowness. It is very important to her that Willie should be there within earshot, even though he does not always hear and often does not answer her, perhaps for days on end. As long as this is true, she can say to herself, 'Something of this is being heard, I am not merely talking to myself, that is in the wilderness, a thing I could never bear to do—for any length of time.' Over and over again the word 'wilderness' recurs in a similar context, in phrases like 'such wilderness'. The reference is primarily to the description of John the Baptist, in the third chapter of St Matthew's Gospel, as 'The voice of one crying in the wilderness'; this in turn echoes a passage in the fortieth chapter of Isaiah; 'The voice of him that crieth in the wilderness.' *Vox clamantis in deserto* is the Latin version of both passages, but the King James often prefers the resounding Anglo-Saxon word 'wilderness' to the Latin word 'desert'. If Willie has died or gone away, Winnie will be left alone, buried in a heap of sand, with nothing but sand around her; all the vegetation has burned up long ago.

The audible conclusions of Winnie's otherwise silent prayers remind us that Beckett was of course familiar with the Book of Common Prayer, though in quoting from the Psalms, for instance, he always prefers the wording of the King James rather than the somewhat different translations in the Prayer Book. As for the *Irish Church Hymnal*, there is an extraordinary passage in, of all places, *The Unnamable*, where the reader is suddenly confronted with the opening lines of four well-known Anglican hymns. The Unnamable in this novel constantly denies that he has ever existed, maintaining that what appears to be his own interior monologue or stream of consciousness is actually spoken by other people: 'That's one of Mahood's favourite tricks,' he says, 'to produce ostensibly independent testimony in support of my historical existence.' His alleged parents relate instalments of the Unnamable's alleged life-story: 'The instalment over, all joined in a hymn, Safe in the arms of Jesus, for example, or Jesus lover of my soul, let me to thy bosom fly, for example.'

I first read this passage in French, before it was translated by the author, and I vividly remember how incongruous it seemed to read *Jésus amant de mon âme* instead of the words familiar since childhood. Yes, I suppose *amant* is the absolutely correct translation of 'lover', but one is used to reading the word in a quite different context in French. The two other hymns referred to were 'Gentle Jesus, meek and mild', a children's hymn by Charles Wesley—also the author of 'Jesu, lover of my soul'—and another that Beckett seriously misquotes. He remembers the first two lines as 'Jesus, my one, my all, hear me when I call'; actually they run thus:

> Jesu, my Lord, my God, my All,
> Hear me, blest Saviour, when I call.[6]

Yet again such errors may be taken as evidence that the other hymns were quoted, almost correctly, from memory. Once we know the kind of upbringing and the kind of education Beckett received, his knowledge of the Bible and other religious texts ceases to be surprising; it would be pointless to continue adding further examples. The questions we need to ask now are twofold. First of all, why did Beckett make so much use of Christianity rather than of some other 'mythology' with which he was perfectly familiar? Secondly what effect, in the widest possible sense, has Christianity had on his development as a writer?

As might be expected, all Beckett's most significant references to Christianity focus upon the Passion of Christ, the pivotal scene of the Christian drama, where God sacrifices Himself as Man, for Man. There is one scene yet more dramatic, namely the Resurrection; to that, however, Beckett pays no heed at all: one assumes that he does not believe in it. The Crucifixion he accepts as an historical fact: it is in keeping with his sense of man's inhumanity to man. But whenever the Crucifixion is mentioned, Beckett is making an implied or explicit comparison between the suffering of Christ and the suffering of man. A classic example of explicit comparison is this passage from *Waiting for Godot*:

VLADIMIR: But you can't go barefoot!
ESTRAGON: Christ did.
VLADIMIR: Christ! What has Christ got to do with it? You're not going to compare yourself to Christ!
ESTRAGON: All my life I've compared myself to him.
VLADIMIR: But where he lived it was warm, it was dry!
ESTRAGON: Yes. And they crucified quick.
Silence.

God's suffering in human form can never equal man's, according to Beckett, because it has a self-imposed limit: three days after the Crucifixion, it will all be over. But consider the case of Molloy: 'my progress . . . from the slow and painful progress it had always been . . .

---

[6] *Church Hymnal*, new edn., rev. and enlarged, by permission of the General Synod of the Church of Ireland (Dublin: Association for the Promotion of Christian Knowledge, 1922). The hymns but not the pages are numbered: no. 710, 'Safe in the arms of Jesus'; no. 587, 'Jesu, lover of my soul'; no. 611, 'Gentle Jesus, meek and mild'; no. 557, 'Jesu, my Lord, my God, my All'. The full name of the publisher, used only on the title-page, is the Association for Discountenancing Vice and Promoting the Knowledge and Practice of the Christian Religion.

was changed, saving your presence, to a veritable calvary, with no limit to its stations and no hope of crucifixion, though I say it myself, and no Simon.' Although he speaks on the same page of 'the immemorial expiation', it is likely that Molloy does not believe in life after death: the idea of suicide attracts him momentarily from time to time. 'But I never succumbed', he says. An eternity of torment would almost necessarily guarantee that man's sufferings were greater than Christ's; Molloy, however, suggests that his prolonged suffering on earth is at least equal to that of the Saviour; note his deprecatory 'saving your presence': Molloy, though alone in his room, knows that Christ is always with us.

I must leave any further discussion of comparative suffering to the theologians. The subject is, however, fundamental to Beckett's thinking about the human condition. As an artist, his first premise is that life on earth consists chiefly of suffering, a view which, as we all know, has been held by many Christians, both Catholic and Protestant. Beckett's most concise statement of this belief will be found in *Endgame*. Hamm, after being told that his mother is dead, asks whether his father is dead too. Clov, his servant, answers: 'Doesn't look like it.' Hamm next asks: 'What's he doing?' 'He's crying,' comes the answer. 'Then he's living,' says Hamm. Beckett has never quite accepted Descartes' axiom, 'I think, therefore I am.' Here he offers an alternative: 'I cry, therefore I am.' To drive home the point, Hamm asks Clov one more question: 'Did you ever have an instant of happiness?' 'Not to my knowledge,' answers Clov.

To my mind, however, the aspect of Beckett's works that has been most powerfully affected by his religious training is his style. A century from now he may well be regarded as the last—or nearly the last—great writer in English to model his style on the King James Bible. There is always the possibility, of course, that literary people will continue to deplore the aesthetic quality, or lack of it, shown by such well-intentioned translations as *The New English Bible*, *The New American Bible*, and *The Jerusalem Bible*. It is interesting to compare the versions of the 'all that fall' passage in these three Bibles, only the first-named of which is Protestant. An ecumenical touch is provided by the fact that all three now locate it in the 145th Psalm. First, *The New English*:

The LORD holds up those who stumble and straightens backs which are bent.

Next, the *New American*:

The LORD lifts up all those who are falling and raises up all who are bowed down.

I must preface the quotation from the *Jerusalem* with a reminder that this is the most determinedly scholarly of the translations; also, its ecumenism, in the Old Testament, is naturally first directed to Judaism:

Only stumble, and Yahweh at once supports you, if others bow you down, he will raise you up.[7]

Far be it from me to comment on these three 'modern' translations, but it is not inconceivable that they may eventually provoke cries of 'Back to King James', 'Back to Douay'. In fact, to some degree they already have done so. My present task, however, is not to convince anyone that Beckett is the last in a great English prose tradition, but to show that he belongs in that tradition at all. James Knowlson remarks in his brilliant foreword to *The Beckett Country*,

I have heard some Beckett scholars speak of a marked vein of lyricism in his writing about nature, while others have disputed whether one can speak of lyricism in the case of a writer who so drastically and so self-consciously deflates his own descriptive effects.

I have never had the pleasure of discussing the matter with Professor Knowlson, but he may count me among those who recognize this lyricism, and not merely in descriptive passages; what is more, this lyricism can often be compared with the poetry of the Old Testament. Before offering some examples, let me quote Professor Knowlson once more:

although Beckett self-consciously manipulates fiction within the tradition of Sterne and Diderot and is also acutely conscious of and struggles with the unreliability of language . . . , none the less a form of stark yet moving lyricism remains, as his prose strives above all to 'sing'—a term that Beckett has used to me several times, half apologetically, as being the only term that he could find appropriate to what he was trying to achieve in his prose.[8]

Armed with the magic word 'sing', I began to turn the pages of Beckett's trilogy in search of inspiration. He that seeketh findeth, as the Bible says. There, in the middle of the famous sucking-stones passage in *Molloy*, I found this:

one day suddenly it dawned on me . . . that I might perhaps achieve my purpose without increasing the number of my pockets, or reducing the number of my stones, but simply by sacrificing the principle of trim. The meaning of this illumination, which suddenly began to sing within me, like a verse of Isaiah, or of Jeremiah, I did not penetrate at once.

Why did the illumination *sing like a verse of Isaiah, or of Jeremiah?* One's first thought might be that the illumination or revelation was in some sense a prophecy, whose meaning, especially the word 'trim', did not

---

[7] *The Jerusalem Bible* (Garden City, NY: Doubleday, 1966); *The New American Bible* (New York: Nelson, 1971); *The New English Bible with the Apocrypha* (Oxford: Oxford University Press; Cambridge: Cambridge University Press, 1970).

[8] James Knowlson, 'Foreword', in Eoin O'Brien, *The Beckett Country: Samuel Beckett's Ireland* (Dublin: Black Cat Press; London: Faber & Faber, 1986), xvii (both quotations).

reveal itself without some interpretation. But then, why use the word 'sing' in referring to a verse from either of these Old Testament prophets? Because, of course, these prophets' words are poetry in the original Hebrew, and are printed as such in most contemporary translations of the Bible. Furthermore, they are so printed in my 1947 edition of the Latin Vulgate. The hallmark of ancient Hebrew poetry is its paired parallel structure, often so well imitated by the King James translators, even though they may not have consciously recognized it. Robert Lowth, Anglican Bishop of London in the late eighteenth century, seems to have been the first English-speaking scholar to perceive this underlying principle, which naturally also characterizes the Psalms and certain songs that occur in the historical books. Of these last, the most powerful is surely David's lamentation over Saul and Jonathan:

> The beauty of Israel is slain upon thy high places: how are the
>   mighty fallen!;
>
> Tell it not in Gath,
> publish it not in the streets of Askelon;
> lest the daughters of the Philistines rejoice,
> lest the daughters of the uncircumcised triumph . . .
>
> How are the mighty fallen,
> and the weapons of war perished.

One can hardly fail to notice the same parallelism in the 'all that fall' verse, though the *New English Bible* pretty well destroys it. When one starts looking for this parallel structure in Beckett's work, one soon finds that it was there almost from the beginning, and that it gives a lyrical quality to narrative passages at least as often as to descriptive ones. Listen to the conclusion of the first chapter of *Murphy*, published in 1938:

> The rock got faster and faster,
> shorter and shorter,
> the iridescence was gone,
> the cry in the mew was gone,
> soon his body would be quiet.
> Most things under the moon got slower and slower and
>   then stopped,
> a rock got faster and faster and then stopped.
> Soon his body would be quiet,
> soon he would be free.

I have written out this last passage as verse so as to emphasize the parallelism, but sometimes the subject-matter and the language are enough to supply the biblical ring without much parallelism. Take this sentence from *Lessness*, a work I do not particularly admire, published in 1970: 'He will curse God again as in the blessed days face to the open sky the passing deluge.' Take it and roll it on your tongue while you consider its implications: God and man together again, believing in each other, blaming each other, afflicting each other. Not happy days exactly, but blessed days, and certainly happier than those after the recent greatly exaggerated death of God, when man suddenly found it hard to believe in his own existence, as Bishop Berkeley said he would.

It is in ending a chapter or a work that Beckett uses this biblical lyricism most freely. *That Time*, a short play from 1976, is lyrical—or perhaps I should say elegiac—almost throughout, and particularly the final speech:

not a sound / only the old breath / and the leaves turning / and then suddenly this dust / whole place suddenly full of dust / when you opened your eyes / from floor to ceiling / nothing only dust / and not a sound only what was it it said / come and gone / was that it something like that / come and gone / come and gone no one / come and gone in no time / gone in no time

Though Listener, the protagonist, is still alive on stage—'*Breath audible*' is the stage direction—this is his own recorded voice describing perhaps the first moments in the grave; his life, viewed from the perspective of eternity, has 'come and gone in no time'. Reassured by this prophetic voice that his few times of happiness and his many times of suffering will soon be over, Listener manages a smile—'*toothless for preference*' says the stage direction—as the curtain falls. It may be objected that some of the passages I have quoted don't sound like the Bible, but that is a matter of the choice of vocabulary: the point is to keep listening for the underlying rhythms and the parallel structure. Beckett's latest works—*Company*, for example,—can be better understood and appreciated in this light. I have only one quotation, the conclusion of *The Unnamable*, perhaps the most often quoted passage in all Beckett's works. Some readers hear it as a description of Beckett's literary method; others as a rambling, almost meaningless example of so-called automatic writing. What I hear is a skilfully ordered rhythmic sequence that comes to a natural close, even though the words deny the possibility of an ending:

you must go on, I can't go on, you must go on, I'll go on, you must say words, as long as there are any, until they find me, until they say me, strange pain, strange sin, you must go on, perhaps it's done already, perhaps they have said me already, perhaps they have carried me to the threshold of my story, before the door that opens on my story, that would surprise me, if it opens, it will be I, it will be the silence, where I am, I don't know, I'll never know, in the silence you don't know, you must go on, I can't go on, I'll go on.

10 *European-Irish Literary Connections in the Twentieth Century*

Irish writers of international reputation never cut much ice at home until they become as localized as our saints. Yeats will never be forgotten in Sligo and Drumcliff and Lissadell, but it took a man of his genius to understand that the best place of pilgrimage for saint or sinner in Ireland is an imposing ruin. The Irish Tourist Board has restored Thoor Ballylee; Yeats himself, on the other hand, with his sound instinct about the country people, looked forward to the day 'When all is ruin once again'. No folklore can accumulate around his tower in its present state: it must wait until the ivy gets in among the stones once more. The so-called 'Joyce's Tower', which the writer never owned or lived in except for a couple of nights, is a potent symbol, but it might mean more to Ireland if it were allowed to fall into decay. The only hope for a Beckett legend lies in the preservation of the ruins of Foxrock Railway Station. If the Abbey Theatre had been abandoned for good after the fire of 1953, it would have done wonders for the local reputations of O'Casey and Synge. Dean Swift is the only great Irish writer associated with an intact building whose local standing has not suffered thereby. I am sure there are people still alive in the Liberties of Dublin who believe that Swift founded St Patrick's Cathedral in the same sense that St Kevin founded Glendaloch.

Recent writers whose fame is something less than world-wide have wisely cultivated their local reputations, helped by enthusiastic supporters: the annual Kavanagh rites at Inniskeen, and those at Listowel, are cases in point. We assemble every year for the annual celebration of Brian Merriman, the eighteenth-century Clare poet who wrote his best-remembered work in Irish. In all of these festivals there is a link with the past, with the Irish 'pattern' in honour of local saints' days, which were famous for both intensity of devotion and alcoholic excess—not to mention faction fighting.

I believe the Irish writer is slowly but surely replacing the saint as an object of local veneration. Thus does the whirligig of time bring in its revenges, for many a saint put the local bard out of a job by introducing the Roman alphabet and the study of Latin. Besides, if the saint had no skill in Irish verse, there were always converts eager to become his ghost-writers. Kenney lists seventy-nine Irish poems attributed to

St Colmcille, who died about AD 597: the earliest of these date from the ninth century. He goes on to say that 'at the time of production they were no more forgeries than were, say, the monologues which Robert Browning put into the mouths of historical characters'. However, there must have been a painful sacrifice of authorial vanity involved in prefixing a good or even an indifferent poem with the word 'Colmcille *cecinit*' instead of one's own.

Against the historical and sociological background I have just sketched, Patrick Kavanagh's profound though self-serving aphorism takes on new meaning. He said in effect that all great poetry is parochial, all mediocre poetry provincial; by 'provincial' he meant 'aping the manners of the capital', whether the capital be thought of as London or Paris or New York. It does not seem to have occurred to him that a writer can be simultaneously provincial and parochial. Kavanagh admired Joyce and hailed him as a parochial writer because he never wrote about anywhere but Dublin; on the other hand, I think we have proof that Joyce was even more strongly influenced by French writers than is usually supposed, and could therefore also be defined as a provincial. It can be shown, too, that he had a very strong influence in his turn on French writers younger than himself. However parochial they may be, the inhabitants of Paris are by definition not provincial; nevertheless their passion for novelty and their anxiety to circumvent their professional rivals make them very sensitive to new trends from the provinces. For this reason, inter-cultural traffic has very seldom been a one-way street for long. The parochials may resist influence, but the metropolitans very rarely do, once they sense its availability. Celtic literature in Irish and Welsh remained impenetrable until James Macpherson produced his pseudo-translations from Ossian in the 1760s. Thereafter, the sensibility of Europe and North America underwent, if not a revolution, then an astonishingly rapid evolution. Romanticism in due course became the dominant fashion, giving rise to countless translations and adaptations 'from the original Irish'.

Patrick Rafroidi, in *L'Irlande et le Romanticisme*, has shown the strength of the Anglo-Irish influence upon French *Romantisme*. Among the writers he mentions are Thomas Moore and Maria Edgeworth; C. R. Maturin's *Melmoth the Wanderer*, which inspired Balzac's *Melmoth reconcilié*; Lady Morgan and Mrs Roche; the Banim brothers. James Clarence Mangan, however, who might have shared in the French vogue for Edgar Allan Poe as 'L'Edgar Poe irlandais', have been translated by Baudelaire and have been mourned by Mallarmé, was published in New York and Dublin but never in London, where his work might have caught the eye of a French translator, publisher or magazine editor.

Rafroidi's epoch-making book has been translated as *Irish Literature in English: The Romantic Period*. It is a brilliant study, and is followed by a monumental bibliography.

Although Rafroidi may have been reluctant to admit it, the reciprocal French influence on Anglo-Irish literature in the first half of the nineteenth century comes second to that of Germany: John Anster published *Poems with Some Translations from the German* as early as 1819; his complete version of the first part of *Faust* appeared in 1835, to be followed by the second part in 1864, three years before his death. The only book by Mangan published in his lifetime was the *German Anthology* in two volumes, in 1845. By her admission, Lady Morgan modelled her first novel, *St Clair*, published in 1803, on *Werther*. These facts are all contained in Rafroidi's book.

It is not until the last quarter of the century that we find an Irish writer who is totally saturated in the French literature and painting of his own day. George Moore (1852–1933). When he came into his patrimony in 1873, he made straight for Paris to study painting—or at any rate to enjoy the *vie d'artiste*—at the expense of his tenants in County Mayo. After a couple of years he gave up painting because he had no talent for it, and took up reading French literature, first poetry and then prose. Of English writing he knew almost nothing except Shelley, Dickens, and George Eliot, but in *Confessions of a Young man* (1888) he lists the four 'visions of life' that have been given to him so far: those of Shelley, Théophile Gautier, Balzac, and Walter Pater's *Marius the Epicurean*. Gautier's sacred book for Moore was the semi-pornographic *Mademoiselle de Maupin*. He acknowledges 'minor awakenings' caused by the novels of Zola (especially *L'Assommoir*, 1877), Flaubert, and the Goncourt brothers. He had also read Huysmans' *À Rebours* by 1888. At the first impact of Zola in 1877, Moore conceived the wild idea of writing a book of *Naturaliste* poetry, to be entitled *Poems of Flesh and Blood*. It would surely have been better than the volumes he actually published, *Flowers of Passion* (1878) and *Pagan Poems* (1881). Like these titles, the poems contain faint echoes of Baudelaire and Leconte de l'Isle and other less famous *Parnassiens*. About the only thing one can say in their favour is that few English speakers besides Swinburne knew even the names of such relatively up-to-date French poets. Moore loved Verlaine's early work: 'Never shall I forget the first enchantment of "Les Fêtes Galantes", Here all is twilight.' Later he quotes in full the famous *Parsifal* sonnet, whose last line, 'Et O ces voix d'enfants, chantant dans la coupole!' has become so familiar thanks to Eliot's *The Waste Land*. This poem was suggested and first published in the *Revue Wagnérienne* (1885) by Moore's friend, Éduard Dujardin, of whom more later. More surprising still, Moore himself translates three prose poems by Mallarmé, 'Plainte d'automne', 'Frisson d'hiver', and 'Le phénomène futur', in the *Confessions*.

But it was of course the great nineteenth-century French novelists who most powerfully influenced Moore's work. When he received the 'Odious epistle', as he called it, from his land-agent, announcing that his Irish tenants were refusing to pay rent because of the Land League, he must have realized that writing was the only way in which he could earn a living. After some false starts, he published his first novel, *A Modern Lover*, in 1883. The scandal Zola was beginning to cause in England made useful publicity for his rather tame imitator, especially as Zola's English publisher, Henry Vizetelly, had taken on Moore and made his book the first of a series of 'Realistic Novels', to which the Irishman eventually contributed several titles. *A Modern Lover*, later rewritten as *Lewis Seymour and Some Women*, was at least partly modelled on Zola's *Pot-Bouille*, published the year before: Zola's hero lives in an apartment building in Paris, and fornicates his way up the social scale from floor to floor of the building until he becomes the top executive of the suitably named department store Aux Bonheur des Dames, which supplied the title for Zola's next novel. Lewis Seymour gets his start towards being a Royal Academician and a knight by persuading a working girl rather like Shaw's Eliza Doolittle to pose for him in the nude, but, unlike Zola's hero, who ends by marrying his salesgirl mistress, Lewis lacks the guts either to wed her or to bed her. Instead, by means of a couple of unconvincing adulteries with wealthy or titled women, he reaches the summit of his profession.

A Mummer's Wife, in its first version (1885), is far more original, challenging comparison with Zola and even Flaubert for two-thirds of its length: then it collapses as Moore tries to imitate *L'Assommoir* directly. The title character, a small-town landlady who deserts her ailing husband for a touring actor, takes to alcohol, and dies.

A Drama in Muslin (1886) is made of tougher, more durable cloth than its rewritten version, *Muslin* (1915). It views the Land League through the landlord's eyes, satirizes the hunt for husbands at the Viceregal 'court' in Dublin, and portrays a frustrated lesbian with sympathy, tinged a little by 'decadent' prurience. Now that the original has been reprinted by Colin Smythe, I hope it will oust *Muslin* from the Moore canon. *A Drama in Muslin* and *Esther Waters* (1894) are the only novels in which Moore comes within hailing distance of Balzac. After *Esther Waters*, Moore became more or less immune to French influence, though the stories in *The Untilled Field* (1903) owe something to Turgenev, whom he met in Paris and presumably read in

French translation. Moore's involvement with the Anglo-Irish and Gaelic Revival movements made him obsessed with folklore, especially the technique of oral narrative. Every young Irish novelist and short-story writer should steep himself in the best of *The Untilled Field* and *A Story-Teller's Holiday*; as for *Hail and Farewell*, he should shun it like the plague: its petty malice comes all too easily to Irish writers, young and old, and they need no George Moore to give them lessons.

As a journalist, Moore made England aware of the new trends in French art and literature well before Arthur Symons and Roger Fry, writing the first articles in English on Huysmans, Rimbaud, Laforgue, and Verlaine. As for Impressionism, 'The first eulogies written in English, I might almost say in any language, of Manet, Degas, Whistler, Monet, Pissarro, are in this book of Confessions,' he claimed in his 1916 preface, 'and whosoever reads will find himself unable to deny that time has splendidly vindicated all of them.' It is fortunate that Moore revelled in his own praise, for France remained unaware of her debt to him: so far was he from being admitted to the Légion d'honneur that one will look vainly for his name even in the *Petit Larousse*. His spirit must content itself with Manet's portrait and a monumental *thèse* of 700 pages, published about fifteen years ago in Paris.

Oscar Wilde, on the other hand, has received more than his due in France: so far as I know, he is the only Irish writer before Samuel Beckett to write a play directly in French and have it performed in Paris. Wilde seems to have known nothing about contemporary French painting that he did not learn from Whistler, who also gave him a taste 'for all one sees that's Japanese', to quote the Gilbert and Sullivan operetta *Patience*. During his first long visit to Paris, three months in 1883, he modelled himself on two incompatible French writers, struggling to combine the industry of Balzac with the decadence of Baudelaire. Swinburne had written far better English poetry in imitation of Baudelaire in the 1860s than Wilde could produce in the 1880s; as for Balzac, Wilde was too lazy to imitate anything of his except the monk's cowl and habit that he wore while writing.

One French novel, *À rebours* by Joris-Karl Huysmans, had a decisive influence on Wilde, however. His first (and last) novel, *The Picture of Dorian Gray* (1891), is not only modelled on *À rebours* in some respects, but its hero is represented as having been 'poisoned by a book'—none other than *À rebours*, as Wilde admitted at his first trial.

It was the strangest book that he had ever read. It seemed to him that in exquisite raiment and to the delicate sound of flutes, the sins of the world were passing in dumb show before him. Things he had dimly dreamed of were suddenly made real to him. Things of which he had never dreamed were gradually revealed.

À rebours is in fact a healthier, earthier, and more humorous book than this description suggests: its parade of erudition and 'fine writing' must have attracted Wilde most, since they are what he most strives to imitate. Nevertheless, Huysmans' coy description of Des Esseintes' one homosexual love affair doubtless made Wilde think it feasible to hint at the homosexuality of Dorian Gray. When Joyce came to read Wilde's book in 1906, he was disappointed that its author had lacked the courage to reveal *more* about his own sexual nature. A single sentence in a letter to his brother Stanislaus shows that he too, like Moore and Wilde, had read *À rebours*: 'Some chapters are like Huysmans, catalogued atrocities, lists of perfumes and instruments.' I might add that all three Irishmen had an excellent knowledge of French, acquired wholly or partly in Paris. Otherwise they could not have attempted to read *À rebours* in the original; its vast, exotic vocabulary must cause many of its less literate French readers to give up in despair or *ennui*. Luckily, we now have the late Robert Baldick's excellent version, *Against Nature*, in the Penguin Classics.

The death of Wilde occurred in 1900. For the first time since about 1850, an Irish influence was making itself felt in France, mainly that of Wilde on André Gide. It was first of all a personal influence, dating from Gide's 1895 encounter with Wilde and Lord Alfred Douglas in Algiers. As Gide recounted in *Si le grain ne meurt* (1926), Oscar asked him quite casually, 'Do you like boys?' whereupon Gide 'came out of the closet' for the first time by shyly answering 'Yes'. Wilde broke into a roar of laughter, and continued to laugh uproariously in the open carriage which took them in search of Arab boys. Lord Alfred wasn't present on this particular night, but Wilde pointed out one handsome lad as Bosie's. It may have been his Algiers experience which inspired Gide to publish, two years later, his prose poem *Les Nourritures terrestres* (*Fruits of the Earth*), a hymn to the physical side of life, which his earlier hyperintellectual works had denied. Unlike the poems of Wilde's heterosexual disciple Pierre Louÿs, *Fruits of the Earth* is not erotic: a drink of cold water in hot weather seems thrill enough. *L'Immoraliste* (1902) is more frank about heterosexuality and leaves its hero, Michel, poised on the brink of homosexual love—a boundary that he has already skirted several times. Michel has fallen under the spell of a somewhat older man named Ménalque, who gives conscious expression to many of his latent thoughts and feelings. To a non-French ear, Ménalque's teachings sound like a mélange of Nietzsche and Walter Pater, but Gide may only have known Pater as mediated by Wilde, Pater's ardent pupil. Despite his 'enormous drooping mustache', Ménalque reminds us of Wilde by his insolence and by the fact that 'Recently an absurd, shameful trial that caused a scandal gave the newspapers a convenient opportunity to throw filth at him.' A change in the moral climate after the First World War enabled Gide to become much more frank about his sexual bent, but Wilde's frankness in life though not in literature had an incalculable effect on Gide's whole career as both man and writer.

I mentioned earlier Moore's lifelong friend, Édouard Dujardin: shortly after giving up the *Revue Wagnérienne*, he became in 1886 the editor of the equally remarkable *Revue indépendante*. Both periodicals fostered the crystallization of the *Symboliste* movement: Mallarmé was a leading contributor, followed by a number of his young disciples—René Ghil, Stuart Merrill, Gustave Kahn, and others—most of whom appear in Moore's *Confessions*, a translation of which was incestuously serialised in the *Indépendante*. Other serials to appear there before Dujardin gave up the editorship in 1889 were Huysmans' novel *En rade* and Dujardin's own short novel, *Les Lauriers sont coupés*, which ran from May to August in 1887, a year saddened by the untimely death of a contributor, the poet Jules Laforgue, just four days after his 27th birthday. Twenty years were to pass before Laforgue became the dominant literary influence on T. S. Eliot, and fifty or sixty before he became better known in English-speaking countries than in France. A similar fate befell Dujardin's novella: from the 1940s to 1968 it was out of print in French but available in English translation as *We'll to the Woods No More*. ('Nous n'irons plus au bois, / Les lauriers sont coupés' come from an old French song.) It survived in English because James Joyce told Valéry Larbaud and anybody else who would listen that *Les Lauriers sont coupés*, slight as it seems beside *Ulysses*, was the unique source of the stream-of-consciousness or interior- monologue technique in Joyce's novel, published in 1922. The 1925 reissue of *Les lauriers* with a preface by Larbaud proved that, as Joyce insisted,

the reader finds himself established from the opening lines in the thought of the principal character, and it is the uninterrupted development of this thought, completely replacing the usual narrative style, which tells us what this character is doing and what happens to him.

Dujardin himself published an excellent critical book, *Le Monologue intérieur*, in 1931, where he explained for the first time that his novella 'was undertaken in the mad hope of adapting Wagner's techniques to literature'.

Joyce employed the Wagnerian device of the *Leitmotiv* throughout *Ulysses*—not to mention *Finnegans Wake*—achieving effects of great complexity, especially in those sequences that pass in review and/or reinterpret the day's events. Dujardin points out passages in his own work where he did the same under the inspiration of Wagner:

A particularly striking example will be found at the beginning of the eighth chapter, in the reprise of the motifs of the prelude; or in the account that the hero gives to Lea, in the middle of the last chapter, of how he has passed the day; this account is systematically built up out of the motifs of the novel, some unchanged, others deliberately distorted.

Like that of Daniel Prince, Leopold Bloom's account to his wife Molly of the events of *his* day also involves suppressions and distortions of the facts.

At first sight, *Les lauriers* seems too ethereal to be compared with *Ulysses*, notorious for its sexual and excremental detail. Nevertheless, Dujardin too accepted the logical consequences of his narrative method: if a writer wishes to record the stream of consciousness of a character without interruption, a time must come when that character has to answer a call of nature. Joyce, *sans peur* but not *sans reproche*, follows Mr Bloom to the 'necessary house' in the first episode in which he appears. Dujardin more discreetly, waits until his story is nearly over— until the final chapter, to be precise. Daniel Prince suddenly realizes that he hasn't urinated for almost six hours—since before the novel began, in fact. Alone in Lea's *salon* for a few minutes, he slips out to the *cabinet* of the hall: 'allons . . . gare aussi à ne pas me salir . . . ouf! la précaution n'était pas inutile'. The main event of Bloomsday is that Bloom is cuckolded by his wife, perhaps for the first time. As for Daniel Prince, he is a born cuckold. Lea, though she plays small parts in the theatre, is little better than a whore; perhaps worse than one, indeed, since she constantly accepts money from Daniel yet has only allowed him to possess her once. Daniel hopes to spend the night of what we might call (by analogy with Bloomsday) 'Princesday' in her bed, yet feels that he ought to be content with a platonic friendship, since he knows she does not love him. In the event, he asks her to let him stay and she replies that it's impossible. 'The next time, I promise you . . . I can't.' Doubtless she is expecting a client. They say *au revoir*, promising to meet again on Wednesday at three. Daniel says to himself that he will never see her again. The reader does not believe him.

Dujardin's little novel illuminates *Ulysses* in a very special way: we see that both books are fundamentally concerned with a man wandering through a modern city, thinking about a woman whom he rejoins before the end of the story; the reader is thus enabled to form a judgement about the woman that may be strikingly different from the man's. Very little happens outwardly, but within the man's mind there is a constant shifting of attitude toward the woman, a constant vacillation among possible courses of action that he may take in regard to her. Valéry Larbaud, even before he had obeyed Joyce's admonition to read Dujardin, published a novella whose theme is amorous vacillation;

although he modelled his *monologue intérieur* on that of *Ulysses*, the story reads more like Dujardin's. *Mon plus secret conseil . . .* concerns a man wavering mentally between two women during a train journey which he takes alone. Even before this, Larbaud had written what amounts to a short story in stream-of-consciousness style, *Amants, heureux amants . . .* He must be counted as Joyce's first French imitator as well as his most important French publicity man. In 1920 he read all the instalments of *Ulysses* that had appeared in the *Little Review*, published in New York, and soon afterwards he had several long discussions of *Ulysses* with Joyce, who revealed to him many of the correspondences between it and the *Odyssey*. In November 1921 Larbaud finished *Amants, heureux amants . . .* , and on 7 December he delivered his famous lecture on *Ulysses*, later published in the *Nouvelle Revue Française*. It was almost an anti-climax when *Ulysses* was published in Paris (in English) on Joyce's 40th birthday, 2 February 1922. One wonders if George Moore in his later years, as he watched the reputation of *Ulysses* grow to surpass that of any of his own works, regretted that he had failed to see the tremendous possibilities of the technique invented by Dujardin, who himself never used it again.

Before going on to note Joyce's influence on other French writers besides Larbaud, it is only fair to acknowledge his debt to writers other than Dujardin. Flaubert has been the name most often mentioned, ever since Ezra Pound's article, '*James Joyce et Pécuchet*', praised the newly published *Ulysses* and compared it to Flaubert's last, not quite finished novel, *Bouvard et Pécuchet* (1881). Although their surnames—and their three Christian names apiece—suggest that the two were meant to be foils, each has a great deal in common with Bloom: François Denys Bartholomée Bouvard is fat, Rabelaisian, a lover of the pleasures of the flesh, a true Gaul, whereas Pécuchet is thin, abstemious, fond of the pleasures of the mind, a true representative of France's Roman, classical heritage. Pécuchet's names are Juste Romain Cyrille, suggestive of Bloom's passion for justice and his respect for civic virtue; although abstemious as regards drink, Bloom shares Bouvard's love for food and women and, like him, prefers Romanticism to classicism in the arts. Bloom's naive faith in science parallels that of Pécuchet, and he shares the inadequate secondary education, *petit bourgeois* status, and reverence for learning of both Flaubert's *bonshommes*.

Bouvard and Pécuchet are copying clerks from the French Civil Service who retire to the country and pursue there a series of crazes, beginning with agriculture and ending with education; along the way, they also seek salvation in love, religion, and politics. Thanks partly to their own incompetence and partly to the nature of the human condition, they always end in disillusion. Typically, each chapter begins with wild hopes of success in the new pursuit, followed by a long, slow process of disillusionment; each chapter also tends to become a sort of encyclopaedia article on the branch of human endeavour that the two old boys are currently making a shambles of. Most chapters of *Ulysses* have this same encyclopaedic quality, being dedicated in Joyce's master-plan to some branch of art or science: for instance, the chapter set in the National Library of Ireland has literature for its art, centres on a discussion of Shakespeare, and mentions almost every Irish writer of English who was practising his trade in 1904.

It seems entirely possible, however, that *A Portrait of the Artist As a Young Man* also owes a debt to *Bouvard et Pécuchet*. The first four chapters of the five that make up Joyce's first novel all follow the same pattern: the lowly, defeated hero, Stephen Dedalus, by virtue of his unswerving integrity in pursuit of his chosen end, achieves a moment of triumph and falls into his besetting sin, pride. It is pride in his name and family in chapter I, followed by swift disillusion at the beginning of chapter II; then the pursuit of love ends in his first encounter with a prostitute, which provokes pride of the flesh; this in turn is destroyed by the famous retreat sermons in chapter III. For all his humility at the end of that chapter, the beginning of the next finds him full of spiritual pride, but when he realizes that he lacks a vocation for the priesthood, he quickly rises to a new peak of pride in his calling as an artist. Except that Joyce prefers a crescendo to a diminuendo, these chapters seem to be constructed on Flaubert's principle.

The character of Stephen Dedalus, on the other hand, shares certain traits with Duc Jean des Esseintes, the hero of *À rebours*. As Robert Baldick remarks, 'almost every unhappy, solitary hero of a twentieth-century novel could probably trace his descent back to Huysmans' great creation': nevertheless, the poverty-striken young Irishman is a collector and connoisseur of poems and prose styles, though he cannot afford the paintings, prints and rare books owned by Des Esseintes.

His morning walk across the city had begun, and he foreknew that as he passed the sloblands of Fairview he would think of the cloistral silver-veined prose of Newman; that as he walked along the North Strand Road, glancing idly at the windows of the provision shops, he would recall the dark humour of Guido Cavalcanti and smile; that as he went past Baird's stonecutting works in Talbot Place the spirit of Ibsen would blow through him like a keen wind, a spirit of wayward boyish beauty; and that passing a grimy marine dealer's shop beyond the Liffey he would repeat the song by Ben Jonson which begins:

I was not wearier where I lay.

Both heroes are Jesuit-educated, and the religious pedantry of Stephen in both *A Portrait* and *Ulysses* is vividly anticipated in chapter VII of *À rebours*. There too we read the following: 'This idea, that he was possibly living in a state of sin, filled Des Esseintes with a certain pride and satisfaction'. Compare this passage from chapter III of *A Portrait*:

A certain pride, a certain awe, withheld him from offering to God even one prayer at night, though he knew it was in God's power to take away his life while he slept and hurl his soul hellward ere he could beg for mercy. His pride in his own sin, his loveless awe of God, told him that his offence was too grievous to be atoned for in whole or in part by a false homage to the All-seeing and All-knowing.

It must have been from Huysmans as well as from Flaubert that Joyce learned the technique of turning a chapter into a treatise. Note, too, that the repetition of motifs and key-words in *A Portrait* may have been suggested by Joyce's reading of Dujardin. What seems to be Joyce's first reference to Wagner occurs near the end of *A Portrait* as Stephen and Cranly leave the National Library: 'The bird call from *Siegfried* whistled softly followed them from the steps of the porch.'

How well Joyce knew the work of the Symboliste poets has not yet been satisfactorily established. Almost all the knowledge of Mallarmé's work shown in the published and unpublished writings of Joyce can be found in a single second-hand source, Arthur Symons's *The Symbolist Movement in Literature*, which Joyce indisputably read. The only clear reference to Mallarmé in Joyce's creative work occurs in the library episode in *Ulysses*: first A. E. and then R. I. Best mentions his name, A. E. being very censorious, 'France produces the finest flower of corruption in Mallarmé'. Best is more tolerant:

Mallarmé, don't you know, he said, has written those wonderful prose poems Stephen MacKenna used to read to me in Paris. The one about *Hamlet*. He says: *il se promène, lisant au livre de lui-même*, don't you know, *reading the book of himself*. He describes *Hamlet* given in a French town, don't you know, a provincial town. They advertised it.

His free hand graciously wrote tiny signs in air.

HAMLET

ou

LE DISTRAIT

Pièce de Shakespeare

He repeated to John Eglinton's newgathered frown:
—*Pièce de Shakespeare*, don't you know. It's so French, the French point of view. *Hamlet ou* . . .

—The absentminded beggar, Stephen ended.
John Eglinton laughed.
—Yes, I suppose it would be, he said. Excellent people,
no doubt, but distressingly shortsighted in some matters.

A nice piece of Anglo-Irish chauvinism, that last remark!

The *Hamlet* passage, not really a prose poem, appeared in the bibliography of *Divagations*: it must have been pointed out to Joyce by someone like MacKenna or Best who really knew his Mallarmé. Joyce was perhaps influenced by the Mallarméan aesthetic as expounded by Symons, but it seems clear that he imbibed little of it from the fountainhead. His favourite French poet was Verlaine, some of whose early poems he knew by heart, including the famous 'Chanson Automne'—of which he made a disappointing translation. From *Chamber Music* to *Finnegans Wake* I believe Joyce spent his life trying to imitate the vowel music and onomatopoeia of the young Verlaine. Of Rimbaud he knew nothing but the sonnet of the vowels, mentioned in *Stephen Hero* (the first draft of *A Portrait*); Symons had quoted it complete in French. In my opinion, the Symboliste who influenced Joyce most was Édouard Dujardin. I also suspect that Joyce never finished *À rebours* and thus never read chapter XIV, in which Huysmans, through Des Esseintes, expresses his admiration for several *poètes maudits*, including the mature Verlaine, Corbière, Villiers de l'Isle-Adam, and above all Stéphane Mallarmé. If Joyce had read that chapter, he might have been persuaded to deepen his knowledge of contemporary French poetry, a subject of which he was really surprisingly ignorant. Yet it is just possible than A. E.'s sour remark derives from the paragraph where Huysmans writes: 'The truth of the matter was that the decadence of French literature . . . had been embodied by Mallarmé in the most consummate and exquisite fashion.'

It is high time to return to the history of Joyce's influence on French literature, with which he repaid the immense debt incurred by his free use of Dujardin, Flaubert, and Huysmans. Since few French writers possessed the command of English shown by Valéry Larbaud, the essential next step was a French version of *Ulysses*: it appeared in 1929, 'Translated from the English by M. Auguste Morel assisted by M. Stuart Gilbert. Translation completely revised by M. Valéry Larbaud with the author's collaboration.' On this occasion too many cooks did *not* spoil the broth: the translation is extremely reliable and now available cheaply in the *Livre de Poche* series. Raymond Queneau began reading Joyce in 1929, and we may presume that Henri-Louis Destouches, not yet notorious as Louis-Ferdinand Céline, did the same. Queneau eventually plucked up enough courage to imitate Joyce, publishing his first novel, *Le Chiendent*, in 1944. (*Chiendent*, incidentally, is the French for what we call 'scutch-grass' in Ireland; 'crab grass' in America.) One of Queneau's hopes was that his novel would be the first work to employ spoken French, instead of the more formal written language, for a serious literary purpose; unluckily for him, he was forestalled by Céline's *Voyage au bout de la nuit* in 1932. This was a fictional auto-biography told in the first person by a certain Bardamu, who uses a highly colloquial French, full of *argot* and sprinkled with obscenities. It could hardly have been published at all, if Joyce's *Ulysse* had not pre-pared the French reader for it. Though never using the interior mono-logue, Céline's narrative style closely resembles that of the foul-mouthed anonymous Dubliner who describes the events in Barney Kiernan's pub.

Le Chiendent does not in fact make very much use of the spoken language for narration, though there is a very funny passage of advanced philosophical disquisition put in the mouth of a concierge, Saturnin, who is an untutored genius: he uses and abuses the French language in just the way one would expect a Paris concierge of the 1930s to do. It is by its very elaborate structure that *Le Chiendent* most closely resembles *Ulysses*. The book consists of seven chapters, each containing thirteen sections; each of these ninety-one sections is a self-contained unit, written in a predetermined style, and playing its part in the unity of the work as a whole. Like *Finnegans Wake*, which was not completed until 1939, this novel is circular: its last two sentences are the same as the first two, suggesting that we immediately start to read the book over again and continue reading indefinitely. Some of these aspects of *Le Chiendent* can be seen by any reader, but others have been revealed by the author himself in one of his essays on the theory of fiction. The influence of Joyce on Queneau in this and later novels has so many ramifications that it becomes necessary to refer the reader to a book of mine which has never been published outside the US: *The New Novel from Queneau to Pinget* (New York: Farrar, Straus & Giroux, 1971). Queneau translated some paragraphs of his own second novel into a French equivalent of the language of *Finnegans Wake*, but this is neither the most ingenious nor the most amusing of his tributes to Joyce. In 1947, under the pseudonym 'Sally Mara', he published a blackly humorous, semi-pornographic novel entitled *On est toujours trop bon avec les femmes*. An English translation of this book has been published, *One Is Always Too Good to Women*. It deals with an imaginary episode of the Easter Rising in Dublin, and several of the Irish revolutionaries—Mat Dillon, Cissy Caffrey, Larry O'Rourke, and Corny Kelleher—bear names borrowed from *Ulysses*; their leader is named John MacCormack. At one point the eagerly violated heroine,

Gertie Girdle, claims to be an agnostic, whereupon Cissy remarks, 'Well, we're learning new words today. You can see we're in the native land of James Joyce.' The author points out in a footnote, 'There is a slight anachronism here, but Caffrey, being illiterate, could not have known in 1916 that *Ulysses* had not yet been published.'

As some readers may remember, the 1950s and 1960s in France saw the growth of a literary movement known as *le nouveau roman*, the New Novel, which rejected the political commitment of Sartre and Camus in favour of a preoccupation with form and narrative technique. Philosophically, the movement was very sceptical about the 'old' novel's presentation of human experience, questioning the very existence of such a phenomenon. The phrase 'human experience' implies on the one hand a *subject*—a human being who experiences—and on the other hand an *object*, something that is being experienced. The New Novelist often found himself unable or unwilling to make the distinction between subject and object, and therefore tried to find a technique which would force or coax his reader into a similar incapacity. Joyce had already done this on an enormous scale in *Finnegans Wake*, as some of the New Novelists realized. All those arguments about who the dreamer is in the *Wake* seem a waste of time: the dream dreams itself, subject and object becoming one, as form and content do, in the new language coined by Joyce. Without distorting language radically, novels like Beckett's *The Unnamable* and Alain Robbe-Grillet's *Jealousy* also manage to dissolve the boundary-line between subject and object. For this and other reasons I decided to beat the French at their own game of cultural chauvinism by claiming Joyce as 'the greatest precursor' of the *nouveau roman*. I lost of course. The authors I had discussed wrote me polite letters, however; some of them had so often been ignored by the French literary establishment that they may have been sincerely grateful. The events ('Les Événements') of 1968 made commitment fashionable again and set a gulf between the New Novelists and the youth of France that has not been bridged since, I believe.

Nevertheless, the New Novelists and their fellow-travellers have written some excellent novels and may still write more. Most of them admit familiarity with Joyce even when, like Robbe-Grillet and Nathalie Sarraute, they clearly do not imitate him. Michel Butor, who wrote an appreciative and penetrating article on Joyce in 1948, before he himself had written any novels, has shown his affinity for Joyce in several ways. Although he does not use interior monologue as a rule, Butor developed what seemed at the time an interesting variation of it for *La Modification*;[1]

---

[1] Published in Paris (Les Editions de Minuit, 1957): Titled *Second Thoughts* in England (London: Faber & Faber, 1958) and *A Change of Heart* in the US (New York: Simon & Schuster, 1959) Translated by Jean Stewart.

a man travelling overnight from Paris to Rome recounts his journey, thoughts, and dreams in the present tense and second person (*vous* not *tu*) throughout. The device has been imitated too often lately, however. The opening sentence is, 'Standing with your left foot on the grooved brass sill, you try in vain with your right shoulder to push the sliding door a little wider open.' In that one sentence Butor has caught the sympathy of all his readers who have ever travelled on a European or Irish train; we identify all the more easily with the narrator/hero because we don't learn his full name until we have read nearly a hundred pages: he might just as well be ourselves. Like Joyce too, Butor is fascinated with the unities of time and place: while teaching in Egypt, he wrote his nostalgic first novel, *Passage de Milan* (1954), about twelve hours in the life of a Paris apartment house, one chapter to an hour, as in *Ulysses*. *Degrees*, his fourth novel, focuses on a single classroom hour in a Paris *lycée* and proves up to the hilt that to tell everything about even so restricted a subject is beyond human power: the monomaniac narrator dies in the attempt.

Claude Simon is another self-confessed admirer of Joyce, acknowledging in an interview that he had read Proust and Joyce a lot and was a Faulkner enthusiast. 'But what I prefer in Faulkner is his Joycean and Proustian side.' This confirmation from an impartial French source of Joyce's evident share in the development of Faulkner's art is most reassuring to an Irish critic. In *The Flanders Road*, which may well be Simon's masterpiece, his affinities with the three novels he has named are well displayed. The novel consists of a series of events and impressions—including scenes of battle and imprisonment—from the years 1936–45, recalled by Georges Thomas on a single night in 1946. As he spends this night in the bed of Corinne, his former cavalry captain's widow, for whom he had developed an obsession among the privations of prisoner-of-war camp, he has difficulty remembering whether he is making love or war. The rigid time limitation of a night reminds us of Joyce, while the preoccupation with the past is both Proustian and Joycean. The style, mixing stream of consciousness with direct narration, recalls Faulkner. On the other hand, the shifts from past to present and vice versa, or from one flashback to another, are sometimes prompted by sexual puns, a device frequently used in *Finnegans Wake*. In at least one case, Richard Howard found the pun impossible to translate: it hinges on the French word *gland*, meaning both 'acorn' and '*glans penis*'. The botanical association whisks Georges from the task in hand to a memory of collecting acorns for food as a prisoner of war. No critic can adequately describe the experience of reading this remarkable book; I urge readers to try it for themselves.

Claude Mauriac, eldest son of François, the Nobel Prize winner, has carried the method of *Ulysses* to lengths undreamed of even by Joyce, whom he first read when he was 23 or 24. In *The Dinner Party*, titled in England *Dinner in Town*, we are given the conversation and unspoken thoughts of eight characters seated round a dinner-table for three hours. We have to guess for ourselves which character is thinking or speaking, though some editions make the game easier by including the hostess's seating plan. In his next novel, *The Marquise Went Out at Five*, the time is restricted to a single hour at the Carrefour de Buci, between the Seine and the Boulevard Saint-Germain, where five streets of old Paris intersect. We are confronted with the conversations and/or interior monologue of more than seventy characters, major and minor, again without any indication of who is speaking. It resembles the 'Wandering Rocks' episode of *Ulysses*, in which the citizens of Dublin go about their business between three and four o'clock, while the Lord Lieutenant rides in his carriage across the city. I regret to say that Mauriac's next novel, the conclusion of the series, did not find an English translator. *L'Agrandissement* (The Enlargement) is yet another *tour de force*, an enlargement to almost novel-length of just two minutes from *The Marquise Went Out at Five*. Much of it consists of a meditation by the leading character of the series, the novelist Bertrand Carnéjoux, on the novel he is about to write to complete a tetralogy. Mauriac intervenes in his own person at the end to tell us something we already know. 'This book is the story of a gentleman who is asking himself how he's going to write a novel that I have already written.' There can literally be no end to the influence of such a seminal writer as Joyce: it will stretch into the future as long as the human species remains viable and literate.

I am confining myself almost entirely to prose fiction, on the ground that 'poetry is what gets lost in translation'. Irish influence on the French theatre is difficult to assess but must have some weight, for almost every play of Shaw's except *Back to Methuselah* has been translated into French; so has most of O'Casey, and perhaps the whole of Synge. Behan's *The Quare Fellow* was performed as *Le Client du matin*. And of course Beckett has translated most of his own dramatic work that was not written in French in the first place, including *All That Fall*, *Krapp's Last Tape*, and *Happy Days*. His influence on French literature in general seems likely to equal Joyce's in the distant future, but one can never be sure. Robert Pinget was certainly deeply under Beckett's influence in his early novels and plays: for example, the one-act *Architruc*, a sort of *Waiting for Godot* in which Godot unexpectedly arrives in the shape of Death, complete with his scythe. This play derived from a short novel called *Baga* which also reminds one of Beckett. Another one-act, *The*

Old Tune (*La Manivelle*), about two old men and a barrel-organ, was translated by Beckett into O'Casey-language from Pinget's equally colloquial French: it is as poignant a comment on old age as *Krapp's Last Tape*. Pinget has written several novels in the manner of *Molloy* and *Malone Dies*, where a character sits down to write a long self-exculpatory narrative which rambles all over the place, perhaps never reaching a conclusion. Not until 1962, when he published *L'Inquisitoire*, afterwards translated as *The Inquisitory*, did he emerge fully from Beckett's shadow as a great tragicomic artist in his own right.

Beckett himself, who began as a student and teacher of French literature, necessarily underwent a variety of influences, the strongest being that of Racine. Rudmose-Brown, Beckett's and my Professor of French at Trinity College, made us read every play by the classical French dramatist—not only all eleven tragedies, but also the only comedy, *Les Plaideurs*. Beckett lectured on Racine at Trinity later, pointing out the essentially circular construction of *Andromaque*. He also paid particular attention to *Bérénice*, whose plot might well be described in the words of *Waiting for Godot*: 'Nothing happens, nobody comes, nobody goes, it's awful!' Racine himself felt impelled to defend *Bérénice* in a preface, one sentence of which must have appealed strongly to Beckett: 'Toute l'invention consiste à faire quelque chose de rien.' ('All creativity consists of making something out of nothing'). No other French influence on Beckett seems to me quite so overpowering as Racine's. Proust, on whom Beckett wrote a critical study commissioned by the publishers, was by no means as great an influence on Joyce. Céline, everyone seems to agree, was the primary source of the slangy, embittered first-person narration in the trilogy—*Molloy, Malone Dies, The Unnamable*—though I sometimes think I detect a slight flavour of Queneau too. Beckett's first novel in French, not published until long after the trilogy, was *Mercier et Camier*: French readers may not realize that it is set in Dublin and nearby—one scene taking place on the Old Military Road over the Featherbed Mountain—and that its title unites two Irish Huguenot names. The style of this tale, narrated in the third person, reminds me of Queneau, but much more of a book that Beckett *must* have read, a favourite of Dr Owen Sheehy-Skeffington's and possibly of Rudmose-Brown's too. This was Jules Romains's *Les Copains*, a book full of bicycles, practical jokes, and insults to strangers: Beckett did, or intended to do, some postgraduate research on the Unanimistes, a group of which Romains was one of the leaders; in fact *Les Copains*, for all its humour, taught and exemplified Unanimist doctrine.

Mention of bicycles inevitably makes one think of Flann O'Brien, also known as 'Myles'. I suppose the notion of a character who steps out of a book and participates in the real world was one whose time had come in 1939, when *At Swim-Two-Birds* was first published. Already in 1933 we come across something similar to the early pages of *Le Chiendent*. Pierre le Grand, the intelligent observer through whose eyes we watch much of the early action in the novel, tells Narcense, 'I am observing a man.' 'You don't say! Are you a novelist?' 'No. A character.' Those familiar with Flann O'Brien's first novel will remember how Mr Furriskey and others escape from a novel which Dermot Trellis is writing and proceed to drug him so that they can get on with their own lives. Robert Pinget almost certainly had not read *At Swim-Two-Birds* when in *Mahu* (1952) he invented a trio of novelists whose characters come to life as soon as they created them: one of the comic results is that when M. Latirail decides to change a character's name from Fion to Bouchèze, he soon reads in the local newspaper that Bouchèze has been arrested for murdering Fion. What *is* certain is that Queneau knew of 'Myles', for it was his firm, Gallimard, which in 1964 published the French translation of *At Swim-Two-Birds* under the title *Kermesse irlandaise*. It may have inspired his own fantasy *Les Fleurs bleues* (1965), in which two characters dream each other's lives, but is more likely to have influenced *Le Vol d'Icare* (1968). In *The Flight of Icarus*, Icarus escapes from the early pages of a novel by the (fictitious) novelist Hubert Lubert into the Paris of 1895. Other novelists try to steal him for their own books, while Lubert himself employs a stupid detective to track him down. Evading them all, Icarus becomes an aviation pioneer like his classical namesake and falls to his death. Meanwhile, other characters escape from novels, including one 'born' at the age of 40 with an unfaithful wife. One is irresistibly reminded of Mr Furriskey, who was thus described at his birth in *At Swim-Two-Birds*:

Stated to be doing 'very nicely', the new arrival is about five feet eight inches in height, well-built, dark, and clean-shaven. The eyes are blue and the teeth well-formed and good, though stained somewhat by tobacco; there are two fillings in the molars of the left upperside. . . . He is apparently not a virgin, although it is admittedly difficult to establish this attribute with certainty in a male.

pp. 54–5

I like to think of Flann O'Brien, two years after his death, inspiring a new novel in the Mylesian tradition. Possibly, however, remembering his *Dalkey Archive*—in which James Joyce has survived his own death and is writing away as usual—we may prefer to think of him as still alive, endowed with perfect French, and with the kind help of his colleague Queneau, trying to beat Beckett at his own game.

Appendix: Published Works of Vivian Mercier

YEAR	TITLE	JOURNAL/BOOK	CATEGORY
1943	'Tristram Shandy and Locke's Essay Concerning Human Understanding'	The Dublin Magazine	Article
1944	'The Verse Plays of Austin Clarke'	The Dublin Magazine	Article
1942–5	9 reviews	The Dublin Magazine	Reviews
1946	'Letters from Ireland, II'	Horizon	Article
1946	'The Satires of Eimar O'Duffy'	The Bell	Article
1946	'Kate O'Brien'	Irish Writing	Article
1945–6	2 articles 1 review	The Bell	Article Review
1947	'The Real Oliver Goldsmith'	Literary Digest	Article
1947	'Austin Clarke: The Poet in the Theatre'	Life and Letters and The London Mercury	Article
1947	'Austin Clarke—The Poet in the Theatre'	Chimera	Article
1947	'The Arts in Ireland'	Commonweal	Article
1947	'Seamus Murphy'	Commonweal	Article
1947	'The Poet as Sociologist— George Crabbe'	The Dublin Magazine	Article
1947	'A Note on Irish Regionalism'	Albion	Article
1948	'Who Killed the Drama?'	Commonweal	Review Article
1948	'We Irish'	Commonweal	Review Article
1948	'Progressive Higher Education'	Commonweal	Article
1948	'Speech After Long Silence'	Irish Writing	Article
1948	4 reviews	Saturday Review of Literature	Reviews
1948	'Dublin Under the Joyces'	James Joyce: Two Decades of Criticism	Contribution to Scholarly Book
1949	'I Never Liked England Before'	Commonweal	Article
1950	'Daniel Corkery'	Commonweal	Review Article
1950	'Alphabet of Abominations'	House Beautiful	Article
1950	'The Inside View'	Commonweal	Review Article
1951	'James Stephens: His Version of Pastoral'	Irish Writing	Article

YEAR	TITLE	JOURNAL/BOOK	CATEGORY
1952	'Traduttore-Traditore'	*Hudson Review*	Article
1952		*1000 Years of Irish Prose Part 1: The Literary Revival* (New York: Devin-Adair, 1952)	Book (Co-editor) with David H. Greene
1953	'Teachers vs Learners'	*As a man thinks*	Contribution to Scholarly Book
1953	'Perfection of the Life or of the Work?'	*Hudson Review*	Review Article
1954	'Ars Poetica'	*Commonweal*	Article
1954	'Another Look at the Sitwells'	*Hudson Review*	Article
1955	'The Fate of Oscar Wilde'	*Commonweal*	Review Article
1955	'Yeats' Lifelong Immersion in the Spirit of Ireland'	*Commonweal*	Article
1955	'When is a Literature National?'	*Commentary*	Review Article
1955	'Albert Schweitzer, Wagner and Nietzsche: A Desideratum'	*History of Ideas News Letter*	Article
1955	'Beckett and the Search for Self'	*New Republic*	Review
1955	'Godot, Molloy et Cie'	*New Statesman and Nation*	Review Article
1955	'A Pyrrhonian Eclogue'	*Hudson Review*	Review
1956	'The Uneventful Event'	*The Irish Times*	Review
1956	'An Irish School of Criticism?'	*Studies*	Article
1956	'Irish Comedy: The Probable and the Wonderful'	*University Review*	Article
1956	'Riddle of Sean O'Casey'	*Commonweal*	Article
1956	'Toronto's Joyce'	*Irish Writing*	Review Article
1956	'Parody: James Joyce and an Irish Tradition'	*Studies*	Article
1956	'The Dublin Tradition'	*New Republic*	Article
1956	'Paradox of an Englishman'	*Commonweal*	Review
1945–56	7 reviews	*The Irish Times*	Reviews
1956	'Introduction'	*The Stories of Liam O'Flaherty*	Article
1956	'James Joyce and an Irish Tradition'	*Society and Self in the Novel: English Institute Essays 1955*	Contribution to Scholarly Book
1957	'Delightful Dickensian Detective'	*Commonweal*	Review
1957	'Difference Between Novelists as an Index to Cultures'	*Commonweal*	Review

YEAR	TITLE	JOURNAL/BOOK	CATEGORY
1957	'Laforgue's Despairing Humor'	*Commonweal*	Review Article
1957	'Savage Humor'	*Commonweal*	Review
1957	'The Limitations of Flaubert'	*Kenyon Review*	Article
1957	'We Choose The Finest Stories of Sean O'Faolain'	*Catholic Book Club Newsletter*	Review Article
1958	'Rediscovery'	*Commonweal*	Review
1958	'When the Artist was a Young Man'	*New York Times Book Review*	Review
1958	'Baudelaire Revisited'	*Kenyon Review*	Article
1958	'Biography of the Britannica'	*Commonweal*	Review
1958	Review of T. G. E. Powell, *The Celts*	*Commonweal*	Review
1958	'Oliver St. John Gogarty'	*Poetry*	Article
1958	'Proust, Rivière and Mauriac'	*Hudson Review*	Review Article
1958	'Briscoe of Dublin'	*Commonweal*	Review
1958	'Standish James O'Grady'	*Colby Library Quarterly*	Article
1947–8 1957–8	7 reviews	*New York Times Book Review*	Reviews
1958	3 reviews	*Nation*	Reviews
1958	A review	*History of Ideas Newsletter*	Review
1957–8	'Letters Wrote by Shem and Shaun'	*Hudson Review*	Review
1959	Review of Kunitz, *Selected Poems 1928–1958*, and Nemerov, *Mirrors and Windows: Poems*	*Commonweal*	Review
1959	'The Mathematical Limit'	*The Nation*	Review
1959	'Houseman's Life'	*Commonweal*	Review
1959	'Art of Exclusion'	*Nation*	Review
1959	'Arrival of the Anti-Novel'	*Commonweal*	Article
1959	'How to Read *Endgame*'	*The Griffin*	Article
1959	'Stories, Songs and People'	*Nation*	Review
1959	'Ovid and Sappho in Translation'	*Poetry*	Review Article
1960	'Everyman and the Coterie'	*The Griffin*	Article
1960	'Sins of Biography'	*Nation*	Review
1960	'Truth and Laughter'	*Nation*	Article
1960	'Priestley on Literature; Readers' Guide'	*Commonweal*	Review
1960	'Experience Came Naked'	*Nation*	Review
1960	'Sex, Success and Salvation'	*Hudson Review*	Review Article
1960	'To Pierce the Dark Mind'	*Nation*	Review
1960	'O'Casey Alive'	*Hudson Review*	Review Article

YEAR	TITLE	JOURNAL/BOOK	CATEGORY
1961	'Parody and the Zeitgeist'	*The Griffin*	Article
1961	'Many Irelands'	*Commonweal*	Article
1961	'Samuel Beckett and the Sheela-na-gig'	*Kenyon Review*	Article
1961	'Plays of Johnston'	*Nation*	Review
1959–61	5 reviews	*Commonweal*	Reviews
1961	'Irish Underground'	*Nation*	Review
1959–61	3 reviews	*Nation*	Reviews
1961	'In Joyce's Wake, a Booming Industry'	*New York Times Book Review*	Review Article
1959–61	7 reviews	*New York Times Book Review*	Reviews
1961		*1000 Years of Irish Prose I*	Book reissued in paperback
1962	'The Spirit of the Original'	*Nation*	Review
1962	'Novels as Tracts'	*Commonweal*	Review
1962	'Triumph of Francis Parkman'	*Nation*	Review
1962	'Swift and the Gaelic Tradition'	*A Review of English Literature*	Article
1962	'Critic vs. The Scholar'	*Nation*	Article
1962		*The Irish Comic Tradition* (Oxford: Clarendon Press 1962; reissued in paperback, New York, 1969; London: Souvenir Press, 1991)	Book
1962	'A Review of *An Only Child* by Frank O'Connor'	*Experience and Expression*	Contribution to Scholarly Book
1962	'In the Wake of the Fianna'	*A James Joyce Miscellany*, 3rd. series	Contribution to Scholarly Book
1962–3	Review of 2 books	*Hudson Review*	Review
1962–3	'Misprints on the Sands of Time'	*Hudson Review*	Review Article
1962	Review of 2 vols. of *Oxford History of English Literature*	*The Griffin*	Review
1963	Review of Auden's *The Dyer's Hand and Other Essays*	*The Griffin*	Review
1963	'A Note on Finnegan's Wake'	*A Wake Newsletter*	Note
1963	'My Neighbor's Garden, and What I Saw There'	*Hudson Review*	Review Article
1963	'How Sincere is Art?'	*Nation*	Review

YEAR	TITLE	JOURNAL/BOOK	CATEGORY
1964	'Salon Saboteur'	*Nation*	Review
1964	Review of Bieler's *Ireland: Harbinger of the Middle Ages*	*Hudson Review*	Review
1964	'Paperbacks: Ireland's "Big Four"'	*New York Times Book Review*	Review Article
1964	'Bloomsday in Gotham'	New York: *Sunday Tribune*	Article
1964	Review of Farrell's *Thy Tears Might Cease*	*Book Week*	Review
1964	'Defective Detectives'	*Nation*	Review
1964	Review of David Clark's *W. B. Yeats and the Theatre of Desolate Reality*	*Modern Drama*	Review
1964	2 reviews of Irving Howe, Leslie Fiedler, and J. I. M. Stewart	*The Griffin*	Review
1964		*Great Irish Short Stories* (New York: Dell Laurel Edition, 1964; London: Souvenir Press, 1990, 1992)	Book (Editor)
1964	'From Myth to Ideas— and Back'	*Ideas in the Drama: Selected Papers from the English Institute*	Contribution to Scholarly Book
1964	'The Irish Short Story and Oral Tradition'	*The Celtic Cross: Studies in Irish Culture and Literature*	Contribution to Scholarly Book
1965	'Immobilization of Time'	*Nation*	Review
1965	'Douglas Hyde's "Share" in *The Unicorn from the Stars*'	*Modern Drama*	Article
1965	'In Defense of Yeats As a Dramatist'	*Modern Drama*	Article
1965	'Bibliographical Note: Some French Joyceana'	*James Joyce Quarterly*	Note
1965	'James Joyce et la tradition irlandaise de la parodie'	*Configuration critique de James Joyce*	Contribution to Scholarly Book
1966	Review	*New York Times Book Review*	Review
1966	Review of McGahern's *The Dark*	*New York Times Book Review*	Review
1966	'My Life in the New Novel'	*Nation*	Article
1966	'Claude Simon: Order and Disorder'	*Shenandoah*	Article

YEAR	TITLE	JOURNAL/BOOK	CATEGORY
1966	Review of J. C. Beckett *The Making of Modern Ireland 1603–1923*	*Commonweal*	Review
1966	'Man Against Nature: The Novels of Liam O'Flaherty'	*Wascana Review*	Article
1966	'The Future of Landor Criticism'	*Some British Romantics: A Collection of Essays*	Contribution to Scholarly Book
1966	'James Joyce and the Macaronic Tradition'	*Twelve and a Tilly: Essays on the Occasion of the 25th Anniversary of Finnegan's Wake*	Contribution to Scholarly Book
1967	Review of Pinget's *The Inquisitory*	*New York Times Book Review*	Review
1967	'Justice for Edouard Dujardin'	*James Joyce Quarterly*	Article
1967	'Swift Conviviality'	*Nation*	Article
1967	'James Joyce and the French New Novel'	*TriQuarterly*	Article
1967	'More French Joyceana'	*James Joyce Quarterly*	Note
1967	'Swift and the Gaelic Tradition'	*Fair Liberty Was All His Cry: a Tercentenary Tribute to Jonathan Swift 1667–1745*	Contribution To Scholarly Book
1967	'Swift's Humour'	*Jonathan Swift 1667–1967: a Dublin Tercentenary Tribute*	Contribution to Scholarly Book
1968	'Irish Literature and a Cross Fertilized Culture'	*Commonweal*	Review
1969		*The Irish Comic Tradition*	Reissued in Galaxy Books (paperback)
1970	'Master Percy and/or Lady Chatterley'	*Perspectives on Pornography*	Contribution to Scholarly Book
1971	Review of Lidderdale, *Dear Miss Weaver*	*New York Times Book Review*	Review
1971	Review of Castelain, *Sentimental Talks*; Ollier, *Law and Order*	*Nation*	Review
1971	Review of Sturrock, *The French New Novel*	*Contemporary Literature*	Review
1971	Review of Lavin, *Collected Stories*; Farrell, *Troubles*	*Nation*	Review
1971	Review of Forster, *Maurice*	*Nation*	Review
1971	'Critic, Review Thyself'	*Nation*	Review

YEAR	TITLE	JOURNAL/BOOK	CATEGORY
1971	Review of Sheed, *The Morning After*	*Nation*	Review
1971	'Beckett's Anglo-Irish Stage Dialects'	*James Joyce Quarterly*	Article
1971		*The New Novel: From Queneau to Pinget* (New York: Farrar, Straus & Giroux, 1971)	Book
1972	Review of Stuart, *Black List Section H*	*Book World*	Review
1972	Review of Auchincloss, *Edith Wharton*	*Nation*	Review
1972	Review of Richardson, *Verlaine*	*Nation*	Review
1972	'More Stories and Literary Portraits, Please'	*Nation*	Review
1972	Review of Roudiez, *French Fiction Today*	*Nation*	Review
1972		*A Reader's Guide to the New Novel*	Book (paperback)
1972	'The Tinker's Wedding'	*Sunshine and the Moon's Delight: a Centenary Tribute to J. M. Synge*	Contribution to Scholarly Book
1973	Review of Cruise O'Brien, *States of Ireland*	*Nation*	Review
1973	Review of O'Flaherty, *The Novel in France 1945–65*	*Irish Press*	Review
1973	Review of Sheed, *People Will Always Be Kind*	*Commonweal*	Review
1973	*Common Ground*	*Journal of Irish Literature*	One Act Play
1974	'James Joyce and French Literature'	*France–Ireland Literary Relations*, 215–227	Essay
1974	'Unity of Inaction: Beckett and Racine'	*Nation*, 31 August 1974, 149–151	Essay
1974	'Mortal Anguish, Mortal Pride. Austin Clarke's Religious Lyrics'	*Irish University Review*, 4, Spring, 91–9	Review
1975	'Victorian Anti-Victorian' Review of S. Bedford, *Aldous Huxley*	*Nation*, 1 February 1975, 118–120	Review
1975	'The Sense of Being Alive' Review of R. T. Finneran, *Letters of James Stephens*	*Nation*, 12 April 1975, 438–440	Review

YEAR	TITLE	JOURNAL/BOOK	CATEGORY
1975	'Shaw and the Anglo-Irish Comedy of Manners'	*New Edinburgh Review*, no. 28, 22–4	Essay
1975	Review of *Oscar Wilde* by Martin Fido	*English Language Notes*, 12, No. 3 (March 1975), 222–5	Review
1976	'The Professionalism of Sean O'Faolain'	*Irish University Review* Spring, vol. 6, no. 1, p. 45–53	Article
1976	'Missing Myles', review of Anne Clissmann's *Flann O'Brien*	*Irish Press*, 3 January 1976	Review
1976	Excerpts of an article on Aldous Huxley reprinted	*Contemporary Literary Criticism*, vol. 5, ed. Carolyn Riley & Phyllis Carmel Mendelson (Gale Research Co.), pp. 193–4	Article
1976	Excerpts from a chapter on Raymond Queneau reprinted	*Contemporary Literary Criticism*, vol. 5, ed. Carolyn Riley & Phyllis Carmel Mendelson (Gale Research Co.), pp. 360–2	Article
1976	'Der Mathematische Limes'	*Materialen zu Becketts Romanen*, pp. 253–7	Contribution to a Book
1976	'Ireland/The World: Beckett's Irishness'	*Yeats, Joyce and Beckett*, pp. 147–52	Contribution to a Book
1976	'An Unnecessary Provincialism?' Review of *Two Decades of Irish Writing*	*Cyphers*, No. 4 (Winter 1976), pp. 48–52	Review Article
1976	'Dramatis Personae', review of Bernard Benstock, *Paycocks and Others: Sean O'Casey's World*	*Times Literary Supplement* (August 13), p. 1006	Review
1977		*Beckett/Beckett* (New York & Oxford: Oxford University Press, 1977, 1979; London: Souvenir Press, 1990)	Book
1977	'Minute Particulars: Blake Echoes in Victorian Dublin'	*Blake: An Illustrated Quarterly*, 11 (Summer), pp. 32–4	Article
1977	Review of four Irish Plays	*American Committee for Irish Studies Newsletter* (Feb. 7), pp. 4–5	Review Article

YEAR	TITLE	JOURNAL/BOOK	CATEGORY
1977	'In love with the unobtainable' a review of three books by/ about Liam O'Flaherty	*Times Literary Supplement* (May 13), p. 593	Review Article
1977	'Evidence of identity', on James Joyce's *Finnegans Wake*	*Times Literary Supplement* (June 17), p. 735	Review Article
1977	'At One With a That', on Augustine Martin, *James Stephens*	*Times Literary Supplement* (Dec. 23) p. 1509	Review
1978	'The Greek, the Latin, and the Irish', review of Brendan O'Hehir and John Dillon, *A Classical Lexicon for Finnegans Wake*	*Times Literary Supplement* (April 7), p. 399	Review
1978	'Samuel Beckett, Bible Reader'	*Commonweal*, (April 28), pp. 266–8	Article
1978	'James Joyce as Medieval Artist'	*The Crane Bag*, 2 (1978) pp. 11–17	Article
1978	Review of *Paddy No More: Modern Irish Short Stories* and of *Selected Stories of Sean O'Faolain*	*New York Times Book Review* 26 Nov. 1978, pp. 22, 24, 28, 32	Review
1979	Autobiography in *Contemporary Authors*	Vols. 81–4, ed. Francis Carol Locher. Detroit: Gale Research Co., 382–3	Contribution to Reference Work
1979	'Vivian Mercier in "New Statesman."'	*Samuel Beckett: The Critical Heritage*, ed. Lawrence Graver and Raymond Federman. London: Routledge & Kegan Paul, 70–3	Contribution to Book
1979	'Eine pyrrhonische Ekloge. *Waiting for Godot*, von Samuel Beckett.'	*Materialien zu Samuel Becketts 'Warten auf Godot'*, 82–8, 387–8	Reprint & Translation of 'A Pyrrhonian Eclogue' (see p. 346)
1979	'Joyce: Before, During, After'	*Modern Philology*, 77 August, 59–65	Review Article
1979	'Anglo Irish Literary Figures'	*Irish Times*, 11 Dec. 1979	Letter
1979		*Beckett/Beckett* Oxford University Press (issued for world-wide distribution)	Book
1980	'1837–1870: The Literary Scene'	*Victorian Dublin*, ed. Tom Kennedy. Dublin:	Article

YEAR	TITLE	JOURNAL/BOOK	CATEGORY
		Albertine Kennedy Publishing with the Dublin Arts Festival, 30–7	
1980	'Victorian Ireland'	*Times Literary Supplement*, 13 June 1980	Letter
1981	'A Sufficient Nationalism', review of *Irish Literature in English: The Romantic Period (1789–1850)*, by Patrick Rafroidi	*TLS*, 17 April 1981, 444	Review
1981	'Perfection of the Life, or of the Work?'	*Denis Johnston: A Retrospective*, ed. Joseph Ronsley. Gerrards Cross: Colin Smythe; Totowa, N.J.: Barnes and Noble Books, 228–44	Article in Scholarly Book
1982	'Victorian Evangelicalism and the Anglo-Irish Literary Revival'	*Literature and the Changing Ireland*, ed. Peter Connolly. Gerrards Cross: Colin Smythe; Totowa, N.J.: Barnes and Noble Books, pp. 59–101	Monograph in Scholarly Book

Select Bibliography

Primary texts are dealt with in the footnotes.

ADAMS, J. R. R., 'Simms and M'Intyre: Creators of the Parlour Library', *Linen Hall Review*, 4:2 (Summer 1987).

AKENSON, DONALD HARMAN, *The Church of Ireland: Ecclesiastical Reform and Revolution, 1800–1885* (New Haven: Yale University Press, 1971).

ALSPACH, R. and C. (eds.), *The Variorum Edition of the Plays of W. B. Yeats* (New York: Macmillan, 1966).

ANNAN, NOEL GILROY, *Leslie Stephen: His Thought and Character in Relation to his Time* (London: MacGibbon & Kee, 1951).

AUDEN, W. H., *Collected Shorter Poems 1927–1952* (New York: Random House, 1967).

ATHERTON, J. S., *The Books at the Wake* (New York: Viking, 1960).

——'Oxen of the Sun', *James Joyce's Ulysses: Critical Essays* (London: University of California Press, 1974), 313–40.

BACON, FRANCIS, *The Wisdom of the Ancients* (London: Bell & Daldy, 1857).

BAKHTIN, MIKHAIL, *Rabelais and His World* (Cambridge, Mass. and London: M.I.T. Press, 1968).

BALDERSTON, KATHERINE C. (ed.), *The Collected Letters of Oliver Goldsmith* (Cambridge: Cambridge University Press, 1928).

BALL, J. T., *The Reformed Church of Ireland (1537–1886)* (London: Longmans Green & Co., 1886).

BENNETT, ARNOLD. 'Concerning James Joyce's *Ulysses*', *Bookman*, LV (August 1922).

BERKELEY, GEORGE, *A New Theory of Vision* (London: J. M. Dent 1910).

BIBLES: *The Jerusalem Bible* (New York: Doubleday, 1966); *The New English Bible with the Apocrypha* (Oxford: Oxford University Press; Cambridge: Cambridge University Press, 1970); *The New American Bible* (New York: Nelson, 1971).

BOWEN, DESMOND, *Souperism: Myth or Reality?* (Cork: Mercier Press, 1970).

——*The Protestant Crusade in Ireland, 1800–70* (Dublin: Gill & Macmillan, 1978).

BOYD, ERNEST, *Ireland's Literary Renaissance* (Dublin: The Talbot Press, 1916; New York: Alfred Knopf, 1916).

BROOKE, RICHARD SINCLAIR, *Poems* (Dublin: James McGlashan, 1852).

——*Recollections of the Irish Church* (London: Macmillan, 1877).

——Second Series (Dublin: Hodges, Foster & Figgis, 1878).

BROWN, MALCOLM, *The Politics of Irish Literature: From Thomas Davis to W. B. Yeats* (London: George Allen & Unwin, 1971).

BUDGEN, FRANK, *James Joyce and the Making of Ulysses* (Oxford: Oxford University Press, 1972).

BUTCHER, SAMUEL H. and LANG, ANDREW, *The Odyssey of Homer done into English Prose*, 3rd edn. (New York: Macmillan, 1893).

BUTLER, MARILYN, *Maria Edgeworth: A Literary Biography* (Oxford: Clarendon Press, 1972).

BUTLER, SAMUEL, *Erewhon* (London: Trüber, 1872).

——*Life and Habit* (London: Trüber, 1878).

——*Luck or Cunning?* (London: Trüber, 1887).

BYRNE, J. F., *Silent Years: An Autobiography with Memoirs of James Joyce and Our Ireland* (New York: Farrar, Straus & Young, 1953).

CORKERY, DANIEL, *Synge and Anglo-Irish Literature: A Study* (Cork: Cork University Press; London: Longmans, Green 1931).

COXHEAD, ELIZABETH, *Daughters of Erin* (Gerrards Cross: Colin Smythe, 1979).

CROSS, T. P. and SLOVER, CLARK H., *Ancient Irish Tales* (London: Harrap, 1937).

DALY, DOMINIC, *The Young Douglas Hyde* (Dublin: Irish University Press, 1974).

DILLON, MYLES, *The Cycles of the Kings* (London, New York: Oxford University Press, 1946).

DOHENY, MICHAEL, *The Felon's Track* (New York: W. H. Holbrooke, 1849; Dublin, M. H. Gill, 1914).

DUFFY, SIR CHARLES GAVAN, HYDE, DR DOUGLAS, and SIGERSON, DR GEORGE, *The Revival of Irish Literature* (London: Fisher Unwin, 1894).

DUJARDIN, EDUARD, *Les Lauriers sont coupés* (Paris: Messein, 1887).

EDGEWORTH, RICHARD LOVELL, *Memoirs*, 2 vols. (London: R. Hunter, 1820).

ELIOT, GEORGE, *Middlemarch* (Edinburgh: Blackwoods, 1871).

ELLMANN, RICHARD, *James Joyce* (London: Oxford University Press, 1959).

——*Ulysses on the Liffey* (London: Oxford University Press, 1972).

——*The Consciousness of James Joyce* (London: Faber & Faber, 1977).

ELRINGTON, CHARLES RICHARD (ed.), *The Whole Works of the Most Rev. James Ussher*, 17 vols. (Dublin: Hodges & Smith, 1847–64). Vols. xiv and xvii were edited by James Henthorn Todd.

FARRELL, WILLIAM, ed. Roger MacHugh, *Carlow in '98* (Dublin: Browne & Nolan, 1949).

FERGUSON, Lady, *Sir Samuel Ferguson in the Ireland of his Day*, 2 vols. (Edinburgh and London: William Blackwood & Sons, 1896).

FIEROBE, CLAUDE, *Charles Robert Maturin (1780–1824): L'homme et l'oeuvre* (Paris: Editions Universitaires, 1974).

FRAYNE, JOHN P. (ed.), *Uncollected Prose by W. B. Yeats* (New York: Columbia University Press, 1970).

GIBBON, MONK, *The Masterpiece and the Man: Yeats as I knew him* (London: Hart-Davis, 1959).

GIDE, ANDRÉ *L'Immoraliste* (Paris: Mercure de France, 1902).

GILBERT, STUART, *James Joyce's Ulysses: A Study* (New York: Alfred A. Knopf, 1930).

——(ed.) *Letters of James Joyce*, vol. 1 (New York: Viking, 1957).

GODKIN, JAMES, *Ireland and her Churches* (London: Chapman & Hall, 1867).

GOLDMAN, ARNOLD, *The Joyce Paradox* (London: Routledge & Kegan Paul, 1966).

GORMAN, HERBERT, *James Joyce* (New York: Rinehart, 1939).

GRAVER, LAWRENCE and FEDERMAN, RAYMOND (eds.), *Samuel Beckett: The Critical Heritage* (London: Routledge & Kegan Paul, 1979).

GREENE, DAVID H. and STEPHENS, EDWARD M., *J. M. Synge 1871–1909* (New York: Macmillan, 1959).

GREGORY, AUGUSTA, *Gods and Fighting Men* (London: John Murray, 1904).

——Lady, *Seventy Years* (Gerrard's Cross: Colin Smythe, 1974).

GRENE, NICHOLAS (ed.), *The Synge Manuscripts in the Library of Trinity College, Dublin.*

GRODEN, MICHAEL, *Ulysses in Progress* (New Jersey: Princeton University Press, 1977).

HERRING, PHILLIP F., *Joyce's Uncertainty Principle* (New Jersey: Princeton University Press, 1987).

HOGAN, ROBERT, *After the Irish Renaissance* (Minneapolis: University of Minneapolis Press, 1967).

HONE, JOSEPH, *W. B. Yeats 1865–1939* (New York: Macmillan, 1943).

——ed. Yeats, John Butler, *Letters to his Son W. B. Yeats and others* (New York: Dutton, 1946).

HULL, ELEANOR, *The Cuchullin Saga in Irish Literature* (London: Grimm Library No. 8, 1898).

HYDE, DOUGLAS, *Amhráin Diadha Chúige Connacht* or *The Religious Songs of Connacht* (Dublin and London: M. H. Gill & Son, and T. Fisher Unwin. n.d.).

——*Love Songs of Connacht* (Dublin: Gill, 1893; Facsimile edition, Shannon: Irish University Press, 1969).

——*A Literary History of Ireland from the Earliest Times to the Present Day* (London: Unwin, 1899; revised and edited by Brian O' Cuiv (London: Ernest Benn; New York: Barnes and Noble, 1967).

JAMES, LIONEL, *A Forgotten Genius: Sewell of St. Columba's and Radley* (London: Faber & Faber, 1945).

JOYCE, JAMES, *A Portrait of the Artist as a Young Man* (New York: W. B. Huebsch, 1916).

——*Finnegans Wake* (London: Faber & Faber, 1939).

——ed. Richard Ellmann, *Letters of James Joyce*, 2 vols. (New York: Viking, 1966).

——*Ulysses: A Facsimile of the Manuscript* (New York and London: Faber & Faber, 1975).

——ed. Richard Ellmann, *Selected Letters of James Joyce* (New York: Viking, 1976).

KEATING, GEOFFREY, transl. P. S. Dineen, *History of Ireland* (Dublin: Irish Texts Society, 1908).

KENNELLY, BRENDAN (ed.), *Penguin Book of Irish Verse* (London: Penguin Books, 1970).

LACLOS, PIERRE CHODERLOS DE, *Les Liaisons Dangereuses* (Paris: 1782).

LARBAUD, VALÉRY, Preface to special edition of *Les Lauriers sont coupés* (Paris: Messein, 1925).

LAURENCE, DAN H. (ed.), *Selected Non-Dramatic Writings of Bernard Shaw* (Boston: Houghton Mifflin, 1965).

LAWRENCE, D. H., *Lady Chatterley's Lover* (London, Penguin Books, 1960).

LESLIE, JAMES B., *Clogher Clergy and Parishes* (Enniskillen: Printed for the Author, 1929).

LITZ, WALTON A., *The Art of James Joyce* (London: Oxford University Press, 1961).

MACDONAGH, THOMAS, *Literature in Ireland* (Dublin: The Talbot Press, 1916).

MAHAFFY, J. P., 'The Drifting of Doctrine', *Hibbert Journal*, 1 (1902–3).

MARCUS, PHILIP L., *Standish O'Grady* (Lewisburg: Bucknell University Press, 1970).

MARTIN, AUGUSTINE, 'Anglo-Irish Literature', in *Irish Anglicanism 1869–1969*, ed. Michael Hurley (Dublin: Allen Figgis, 1970).

MATHIAS, Revd B. W., *Brief Memorials of the Rev B. W. Mathias Late Chaplain of Bethesda Chapel* (Dublin: William Curry, Jun. 1842).

MATURIN, CHARLES ROBERT, *The Wild Irish Boy*, 3 vols. (London: Longmans, 1808).

——*The Milesian Chief*, 4 vols. (London: Henry Colburn, 1812).

——*Sermons* (Edinburgh: Constable; London: Hurst, Robinson, 1819).

——*Melmoth the Wanderer*, 4 vols. (Edinburgh: Constable, 1820; Oxford: Oxford University Press, 1968).

——*Five Sermons on the Errors of the Roman Catholic Church* (Dublin: William Folds, 1824).

MEYER, KUNO, *The Voyage of Bran Son of Febal* (Dublin: Royal Irish Academy, 1895), i, Appendix II and III.

MILL, JOHN STUART, 'On Liberty' (first published London: 1859; New York: in *On Liberty and Other Essays*, Oxford and Oxford University Press, 1991).

MONCK MASON, HENRY J., *Primitive Christianity in Ireland: A Letter to Thomas Moore, Esq.* (Dublin: William Curry, Jun., 1836).

MONTGOMERY-MASSINGBERD, H. J. (ed.), *Burke's Irish Family Records*, (London: Burke's Peerage, 1976).

MOORE, GEORGE, *Flowers of Passion*: Poems (London: Provost, 1878).

——*Pagan Poems* (London: Newman, 1881).

——*A Modern Lover* (London: Tinsley Brother, 1883).

——*A Mummer's Wife* (London: Vizetelly & Co., 1885).

——*A Drama in Muslin* (London: Vizetelly & Co., 1886).

——*Confessions of a Young Man* (London: Swan & Sonnenschein, 1888).

——*Esther Waters* (London: Walter Scott, 1894).

——*The Untilled Field* (London: T. Fisher Unwin, 1903).

——*Hail and Farewell: Ave* (New York: Appleton, 1911).

MURPHY, WILLIAM MICHAEL, Prodigal Father: *The Life of John Butler Yeats* (Ithaca, NY: Cornell University Press, 1978).

NEWMAN, JOHN HENRY, *The Idea of a University* (London: Longmans, 1873).

O'BRIEN, EOIN, *The Beckett Country: Samuel Beckett's Ireland* (Dublin: Black Cat Press; London: Faber & Faber, 1986).

O'BRIEN, FLANN, *At Swim-Two-Birds* (London: Longmans Green, 1939).

O'CONNOR, FRANK, *The Midnight Court* (transl.) (Dublin: Fridburg, 1946).

——*The Backward Look* (London: Macmillan, 1967; Published in the United States as *A Short History of Irish Literature*, Putnam, 1967).

O'DONOVAN, JOHN, *Annals of Ireland: Three Fragments* (Dublin: Irish Archaeological and Celtic Society, 1860).

O'DONOVAN, JOHN, *G. B. Shaw* (Dublin: Gill & Macmillan, 1983).

O'GRADY, HUGH ART, *Standish James O'Grady: The Man and the Writer* (Dublin: Talbot Press, 1929).

O'GRADY, STANDISH, *History of Ireland*, vol. ii. (Sampson, Low, Searle, Marston & Rivington, 1880).

——*History of Ireland: Critical and Philosophical* (London: Sampson Low, 1881).

——*The Story of Ireland* (London: Methuen & Co., 1894).

O'MAHONY, MATHEW, *Progress Guide to Anglo-Irish Plays* (Dublin: Progress House, 1960).

ONG, WALTER, S. J., *Orality and Literacy: The Technology of the Word* (London: Methuen, 1982).

PETRE, MAUD DOMINICA MARY, *Autobiography and Life of George Tyrell* (London: Arnold, 1912).

PORTER, RAYMOND J. and BROPHY JAMES D. (eds.), *Modern Irish Literature: Essays in Honor of William York Tindall* (New York: Iona College Press, 1972).

RAFROIDI, PATRICK, *Irish Literature in English, The Romantic Period*, 2 vols. (Gerrard's Cross: Colin Smythe, 1980).

REYNOLDS, HORACE (ed.), *Letters to the New Island* (Harvard University Press, 1934).

RYAN, W. P., *The Irish Literary Revival* (London: Privately printed for the Author, 1894).

SEDDALL, HENRY, *Edward Nangle: The Apostle of Achill* (London: Hatchards, 1884).

SHAW, CHARLES MACMAHON, *Bernard's Brethren* (New York: Henry Holt, n.d.)

SHAW, GEORGE BERNARD, *Prefaces* (London: Odhams, 1938).

——*Sixteen Self Sketches* (New York: Dodd, Mead, 1949).

——*Complete Prefaces* (London: Hamlyn, 1965).

STANFORD, WILLIAM BEDELL and MCDOWELL, ROBERT BRENDAN, *Mahaffy: A Biography of an Anglo-Irishman* (London: Routledge & Kegan Paul, 1971).

STEINBERG, ERWIN R., 'James Joyce and the Critics Notwithstanding, Leopold Bloom is not Jewish', *Journal of Modern Literature*, 9, 1981/2.

STEPHENS, JAMES, *Irish Fairy Tales* (London and New York: Macmillan, 1920).

——*In the Land of Youth* (London: Macmillan, 1924).

STERNE, LAURENCE, *A Sentimental Journey* (1766).

STOKES, WHITLEY, *Lives of Saints from the Book of Lismore* (London: Oxford University Press, 1890).

SULLIVAN, KEVIN, *Joyce Among the Jesuits* (New York: Columbia University Press, 1958).

SUMMERFIELD, HENRY, *That Myriad-Minded Man: A Biography of George William Russell. 'A. E.'* (Gerrard's Cross, Bucks.: Colin Smythe, 1975).

SWIFT, JONATHAN, *Gulliver's Travels* (Various printings, 1726; Printed with an introduction by Harold Williams, Oxford: Oxford University Press, 1941).

——*A Tale of a Tub* (Oxford: Oxford University Press, 1973).

SYMONS, ARTHUR, *The Symbolist Movement in Literature* (London: Heineman, 1899).

SYNGE, J. M., 'La vieille littérature irlandaise', in *L'Européen* (Paris, 15 March 1902).

——*Letters to Molly*, ed. Ann Saddlemyer (Cambridge, Mass: Belknap-Harvard University Press, 1971).

——ed. Ann Saddlemyer, *Collected Letters of John Millington Synge* (Oxford: Clarendon Press, 1983), i.

SYNGE, Revd SAMUEL, *Letters to my Daughter* (Dublin: Talbot Press, n.d. [1931]).

THORNTON, WELDON, *Allusions in Ulysses: An Annotated List* (Chapel Hill: University of North Carolina, 1968).

Trinity College Record Volume (Dublin: Hodges, Figgis, 1951).

WADE, ALLAN (ed.), *Letters of W. B. Yeats* (New York: Macmillan, 1955).

WILDE, OSCAR, *The Picture of Dorian Gray* (London: Ward Lock, 1891).

YEATS, WILLIAM BUTLER, *Fairy and Folk Tales of the Irish Peasantry* (London: Walter Scott; New York: Thomas Whittaker, 1888).

——*Representative Irish Tales*, 2 vols. (London: G. P. Putnam's Sons; New York: The Knickerbocker Press, 1891).

——*A Book of Irish Verse* (London: Methuen, 1895).

——'The Countess Cathleen': *Poems* (London: T. Fisher Unwin, 1904).

——*Collected Letters*, vol. I, ed. John Kelly and Edward Domville (Oxford: Clarendon Press, 1986).

YOUNG, GEORGE MALCOLM, *Victorian England: Portrait of an Age* (London: Oxford University Press, 1936).

Index

Note: Titles of works under the names of various authors are alphabetized without reference to the definite or indefinite article. Relatives of authors are indicated in brackets only where there is similarity in forenames.

Index compiled by Frank Pert